The Play of Time

The Play of Time

Kodi Perspectives on Calendars, History, and Exchange

JANET HOSKINS

University of California Press

BERKELEY   LOS ANGELES   LONDON

University of California Press
Berkeley and Los Angeles, California

University of California Press, Ltd.
London, England

First Paperback Printing 1997

Portions of chapter 10 were published in an earlier form in "Entering
the Bitter House: Spirit Worship and Conversion in Sumba," in
Indonesian Religions in Transition, ed. Rita Kipp and Susan Rogers
(University of Arizona Press, 1987). Reprinted by permission of the
University of Arizona Press.
Portions of chapter 11 were published in an earlier form in "The
Headhunter as Hero: Local Traditions and Their Reinterpretation in
National History," *American Ethnologist* 14, no. 4 (Nov. 1987), 605–
22. Reprinted by permission of the American Anthropological
Association. Not for sale or further reproduction.

Library of Congress Cataloging-in-Publication Data

Hoskins, Janet.
    The play of time : Kodi perspectives on calendars, history, and
exchange / Janet Hoskins.
        p.   cm.
    Includes bibliographical references (p.   ) and index.
    ISBN 0-520-20892-7
    1. Calendar, Kodi.   2. Time—Social aspects—Indonesia—Kodi.
3. Kodi (Indonesian people)—Rites and ceremonies.   4. Kodi
(Indonesian people)—History.   5. Ceremonial exchange—Indonesia—
Kodi.   I. Title.
DS632.K6H68   1993
959.8—dc20   92-31669
                                                              CIP

Printed in the United States of America

9 8 7 6 5 4 3 2

Contents

Illustrations

Tables

Preface

Our time on this earth. . . .	Ghica pimoka la panu tana
Resting for a moment as we stand	Li hengahu ndende mema
Catching our breath as we sit	Li lyondo eringo mema
Before the tide goes down at dusk	La lena ndiki myara
Before the river sinks to meet the sea	La nggaba kindiki lyoko
The stick cannot be extended any more	Kaco njapa dughuni kiyo
The rope cannot be made any longer	Kaloro njapa lamenda kiyo

Excerpt from a
Kodi death song

The shortness of human lives is a fact of time and of each person's experience. The measurement of time derives its poignance from the inevitable end to each biographical cycle. The cultural value placed on time begins with the shared significance of our own mortality.

This book is an ethnography of the cultural perception and organization of time in an Eastern Indonesian society. I begin with the collective construction of the past through the model of the calendar. The yearly cycle, apprehended in days, months, and seasons, is synchronized by a calendrical priest, the Rato Nale or "Lord of the Year," who coordinates agricultural activities and their ritual stages. His task, together with the implements associated with its performance, is seen as partially imported from a distant island to the west. But it is given a local meaning that makes the naming of the months and the "New Year" festival of the sea worms into the mark of a distinctly Kodi identity.

The collective, encompassing structure of the calendar provides a form of repeated, reversible time in which human lives can be inscribed. Biographic time, a second form of temporality, moves through these cycles to spotlight unique and irrevocable events, forming chains that leave their mark on houses, villages, and landscapes. This time is not totalizing but particular: it constitutes the value of objects and animals by measuring the investment of human lives in producing and conserving them. Acting subjects distribute their biographies in different directions, striving for a sort of immortality both through acts that will remain in memory and descendants who will repeat their names in invocations. Their movements are restrained by the calendar, but they are not part of the annual cycle. They embody a cumulative, irreversible time that ties the past to the present and extends into an uncertain future.

The time of the calendar relates human lives to the rhythms of the natural world, the movement of celestial bodies, and the order of the cosmos. Biographic time binds persons to things, to localities, and to other groups of persons through the experience of living and remembering the past. More recently, a third sort of time has been added to locally generated temporalities by the intrusions of colonial conquest, the new Indonesian nation-state, and Protestant and Catholic missionization. This new temporality has shifted the relations of power by presenting a modern, secular, and universal measurement of time—in printed calendars, clocks to record the passage of hours and minutes, and books to trace the succession of historical periods and epochs. In this way, a diversity of different temporal systems is made subservient to a single, overarching system, internally consistent but no longer sensitive to local variations in meaning and sense.

Local systems of time reckoning were struggles against mortality, attempts to preserve a sense of a continuing heritage over the generations by giving a vast authority to the past and to the ancestors. Precedents established in the past were used to validate present actions by calling up a complex repository of images. These "images of the past" were not, however, used simply to replicate what had happened earlier. Rather, they were debated and reflected upon in order to select those that provided patterns worthy of repeating, precedents to guide future innovation. The past was not merely the residue of earlier acts, "history turned into nature" as a simple "habitus" (Bourdieu 1977). It was dialectically involved with the present and offered an alternative model of potentialities to be realized.

This book makes three different arguments in each of its three sections. In part one, I argue for the complexity of the past, the many different ways in which it is represented in narratives, objects, and actions. All of these representations contribute to a collective heritage that is invested, as a whole, in the indigenous calendar, but none is determinate or absolute in its authority. A study of the collective construction of the past reveals its flexibility and diversity, its openness to multiple interpretations.

In part two, I make the case that time is constitutive of value through an accumulation of biographical experience invested in objects, places, animals, and events. "Value" here is directly related to the perception of human mortality and efforts to construct a ritual order in which—although people still die—something of what they stood for is allowed to live on after them. This notion of value is used in all forms of traditional exchange but today is being increasingly challenged by external forces that propose other standards of value, measuring these values with money, clocks, and schedules.

Part three examines the confrontation of a local heritage that emphasizes the continuity of tradition with a notion of "history" as a progressive series of unique, irrevocable acts. Temporal directionality is here removed from the local context and placed on a global stage. It comes with an awareness of the loss of autonomy and the danger of a loss of diversity as well, as disparate regional voices are increasingly silenced or displaced by the universalizing discourses of church and state.

The book explores three different approaches to the study of time: the "totalizing" approach, in which time is seen as a dimension of a more encompassing classification system, whose origin is social; "practice" theory, in which time is viewed as a strategic resource, manipulated by particular actors in specific contexts; and the "historicist" approach, which emphasizes how time has changed relative to the different values accorded to past, present, and future.

The first mode, established by Henri Hubert's early essay on temporal representation in religion and magic (1909), was continued in the work of Emile Durkheim ([1912] 1965) and in much of British social anthropology (Evans-Pritchard 1940; P. Bohannan 1967). In Eastern Indonesia, it achieved its most complete synthesis in the seminal comparative study of F.A.E. Van Wouden, who tried to demonstrate the essential "unity of culture" in which myth, rite, and social structure were all exhibited in the "rhythmic character of time" ([1935] 1968, 2). Insights from this tradition formed the basis of structuralist analysis, as well as of a series of essays by Edmund R. Leach (1950, 1954a, 1961) dealing with the relationship of calendars, time reckoning, and various cultural categories. These studies help us to understand how time has been invented and constituted within particular cultural systems, given a logic based on certain principles and their relationship to the whole.

The integrity of the calendar as an intellectual system that provides a sort of unwritten score for social action has been challenged by Pierre Bourdieu as the "synoptic illusion" that separates ideas from practices. Arguing that "time derives its efficacy from the state of the structure of relations within which it comes into play" (Bourdieu 1977, 7), he proposes a "practice" theory focusing on the strategic importance of the tempo of transactions, not their place in an abstracted system of representation.

"Play" is stressed as a critical element because it implies that the flexibility and overt intentionality of people manipulating time can be calculated. An apparently unidimensional, linear time thus becomes a tool that both creates and symbolizes social relationships by the strategic manipulation of intervals. Holding back on an action, putting off a payment, and maintaining suspense and expectation are all analyzed as tactics for temporal gamesmanship. Through a series of loosely choreographed or stylized improvisations, time and its ambiguities are manipulated by individual agents with particular goals. Other versions of practice theory may stress the unintended consequences of action (Ortner 1984, 1989) or the multiple overlapping contexts of relevance for differently constituted temporal orders (Giddens 1984).

To "historicize" is to locate a phenomenon in time and see how this temporal location can relativize our appreciation of its significance. The "historicist" offers one resolution for the conflict between "totalizing" theorists and "practice" theorists, in that each approach is best seen as limited by its own temporal assumptions. Put briefly and rather schematically, the totalizing theorists focus on long-term processes and their outcomes. Classificatory systems produce "order" only by means of a retrospective glance. Things "fall into place" in terms of a wider logic as they are reinterpreted by actors and given meanings that relate to other parts of the system. This does not, in my view, make classifications invalid or mean that classificatory orders have no reality in the minds of acting subjects. But it does give them a particular position within indigenous systems of knowledge. Often the prerogative of some cultural interpreters in privileged positions, the perspective of the guardian of the calendar or a ritual authority charged with ensuring consensus is quite different from that of other members of the society.

Practice theorists, by contrast, focus on the negotiation of meaning in short-term processes, where actors procure symbolic as well as material capital (Bourdieu 1977). Many of the assumptions of practice theory are correct within this limited time span, but when such notions are extended over longer periods they tend to flatten out notions of cultural difference and reduce complex liturgical cycles to "practical maneuvers." Such analysis does an injustice to the complexity and intellectual sophistication of other peoples, who do attempt to "totalize" their social relations in various contexts but do not always agree on a method for doing so.

Practice theorists are right to argue that values are disputed and societies may be organized according to various interacting principles. But the new attention to actors and agency becomes meaningful only in relation to larger structures of temporal sequences and stages defined over the *longue durée*. In a society like Kodi, the strategies of individual persons are worthy of our attention, but so is the process by which these strategies may eventually be encompassed into the larger temporal frame of the social life of the house, the heirloom, the garden site, and the village.

The "person" and his or her life span represent but a single moment in the complex historical development of institutionalized sequences such as the calendar, the ritual cycle, or the narrativized "past." Although each life requires its own accounting and each ritual event can have its own temporal dynamics, they must be juxtaposed to the wider cultural context in which they occur. Despite the technical difficulties of studying historical change in a society with few historical records, time must be seen as a crucial (perhaps *the* crucial) dimension of analysis.

Classification can be historicized, studied not as a final "moment" in which holistic integration is achieved but as a continous process of sorting out events and reordering them according to cultural values. An understanding of temporal configurations requires a movement between "person" and "process," between "events" that are inflected by actors' strategies, on the one hand, and retrospective interpretations that reabsorb them into longer-term sequences, on the other.

The historicist perspective adopted here borrows heavily from Mikhail Bakhtin's "historical poetics" (1981, 1984a, 1984b), Paul Ricoeur's treatment of time and narrative (1988), and a philosophical position that goes back to Wilhelm Dilthey but has recently reemerged in contemporary debates (Biersack 1991; Ohnuki-Tierney 1990; Veeser 1989). It begins with the idea that although there can be a multiplicity of perspectives on the past, these perspectives—constituted through a retrospective glance—are vitally involved in shaping actions and motivations in the present. Cultural perceptions are not based on fixed essences or orders but on understandings that are produced over time. The critical evaluation of the importance of the past, thus, is not a recent development, the product of literacy, capitalism, or the emerging world system. "Historical consciousness" has been with us for centuries but has taken many different forms in different societies, often interacting in dialogue.

Thirty years ago Evans-Pritchard (1961, 178) wondered, "Why among some peoples are historical traditions rich and among others poor?" He has been answered by arguments about hierarchy and political centralization, which assert that there is "more history in the center" (Fox 1971) and that the amount of "the past in the present" is related to the coercive authority structures of domination and inequality (Bloch 1977). But if "historical traditions" are defined broadly, as an omnipresence of the past and its signs, coded not only in narrative but also in objects, places, and actions, then "the past" makes itself felt in complex ways, offering precedents for innovation as well as reproducing earlier states (Valeri 1990). Recent attention to different genres of historical representation has shown that the otherness of earlier experience can include the coexistence of antagonistic pasts that are themselves subject to a shared narrative framework (Appadurai 1981, 202) and provide the wellsprings of social change (Peel 1984, 127).

This case study of a single Eastern Indonesian people examines their complex relations to outside forces and how these have been involved in the construction of a cultural notion of the past. It then turns to the interplay of sequences and strategies in exchange and the transformation of local notions in dialogue with an externally introduced "history." The key questions asked are: Is there a hierarchy of temporal notions, so that one, for instance the calendar, is preeminent over others? Can this hierarchy change over the course of events, and can we chart the changes in other perceptions of time—duration, process, cumulative effects? How are the political consequences of everyday negotiations of time—in exchange transactions, offerings to ancestors, and decisions about the timing of ritual performances—related to wider conceptions that make them meaningful?

The study questions the notion of historical representation and in particular the assumption that narrative representations are always in some way primary over other forms. In Kodi, I argue, the most significant forms for representing the past are often objects (exchange valuables or part of the "inalienable wealth" of a house) or actions (ritual sequences and procedures). Objects and sequences do not necessarily result in a "reification" or "objectification" of the past, but can also be part of a process of creative regeneration. "All relics of the past," as Greg Dening (1991, 359) has noted, "have a double quality. They are marked with the meanings of the occasions of their origins, and they are always translated into something else for the moments they survive." The social life of objects shows them to be deeply enmeshed in historical processes, in which they may move between the categories of "gifts" and "commodities," acquiring new meanings and values in the course of exchange. Local perspectives on the past use objects to mark the relationships between actors and events, giving a visual and tactile form to memories and historical configurations.

Temporal categories provide both ways of thinking and ways of acting. In order to sort out Kodinese perspectives on their own society and its transformations, I distinguish between "time" (as the culturally encoded experience of duration), "the past" (as a retrospectively constructed view of what has happened), and "history" (as a specific technique and interpretation of how past and present are represented). Each of these is investigated and described independently in the pages that follow, and at the end I try to assess how they may be related. I argue that in the past, the indigenous ritual calendar was the key sequence that structured much of social life. In the absence of a centralized polity, the control of time was the main hierarchical function of the "Priest of the Year" and the focus of a sense of cultural unity—however diffuse and contested that unity often was. In the postcolonial period, the calendar has been increasingly displaced by the structures of the Christian church, the Indonesian state, and the wider ideological forces now identified with an ideal of national progress. Kodi has not been so "sheltered" from world events that these forces were not felt in the past, but in the thirty years since independence their influence has become dramatically more powerful.

The earlier classification of time and ritual order remains a "voice" within Kodi society, and it is not entirely a voice of the past because efforts are being made to preserve many of its features in transformed form. This study asks the reader to pay attention to the way past and present can speak to each other in a single cultural context and can inflect a certain "historical consciousness," which, while it may not be our own, is worthy of consideration.

Acknowledgments

I owe a debt of gratitude to the many people who helped me to write this book. Two years of doctoral research in 1979–1981 were supported by the Fulbright Commission, the Social Science Research Council, and the National Science Foundation, under the auspices of the Indonesian Academy of Sciences (LIPI) and Universitas Nusa Cendana, Kupang. Six months of additional fieldwork in 1984 and a three-month trip in 1985 were funded by the Anthropology Department of the Research School of Pacific Studies, Australian National University. In 1986 I returned to Kodi for three months with Laura Whitney to study ritual communication, using film and video, supported by the Faculty Research and Innovation Fund of the University of Southern California. In 1988 we continued this research project for six months with funding from NSF Grant No. BMS 8704498 and the Fulbright Consortium for Collaborative Research Abroad.

My first rethinking of the Kodi material after writing the dissertation took place in 1984–1985 at the Anthropology Department of the Research School of Pacific Studies, headed by Roger Keesing and James J. Fox, where I was fortunate to have been a member of the research group on gender, power, and production, led by Marilyn Strathern. The book was written in 1990–1991, when I was a member of the Institute for Advanced Study, Princeton, and part of an interdisciplinary group focusing on the historical turn in the social sciences. I am particularly grateful to Clifford Geertz for offering me the opportunity to complete the manuscript and live with my family under such pleasant conditions. After I submitted the book, my husband and I were invited by Signe Howell to come as guest researchers in 1992 to the Institute for Social Anthropology at the University of Oslo, where we enjoyed generous hospitality and a chance to discuss our work with many new colleagues. People at each of these institutions provided both intellectual stimulation and friendship which helped me while finishing this work.

The final compilation of the manuscript was done at my home institution, the University of Southern California, with the gracious assistance of Debbie Williams and Mae Horie. The Center for Visual Anthropology, and the film-making example set by Tim and Patsy Asch, encouraged me to use forms of visual documentation as well as the more conventional notebook and tape-recorder, and inspired me to work with Laura Whitney to produce and write two 25-minute films on Sumbanese ritual, *Feast in Dream Village* and *Horses of Life and Death* (distributed by the University of California Extension Media Center, Berkeley). Other faculty and students at USC provided a congenial working environment and generous leaves to return to Indonesia and write up the results.

Many people read portions of this manuscript and offered valuable comments, only some of which I have been able to incorporate. I am especially indebted to Marie Jeanne Adams, Greg Acciaioli, Ann Geissman Canright, Lene Crosby, James Fernandez, Gregory Forth, James J. Fox, Rita Kipp, Joel Kuipers, Signe Howell, J. Stephen Lansing, Sheila Levine, Nancy Lutkehaus, David Maybury-Lewis, Stanley Tambiah, Laura Whitney, and three anonymous readers from the University of California Press. My most exacting critic has always been Valerio Valeri, who has however tempered his intellectual demands with gifts of love, companionship and caring. He accompanied me on return trips to Sumba in 1986 and 1988, and his thinking has influenced my own in countless ways over eight years of shared living and writing.

In Kodi, I enjoyed the hospitality of four different families: Hermanus Rangga Horo in Bondokodi, Gheru Wallu in Kory, Maru Daku (Martinus Mahemba Ana Ote) in Balaghar, and Markos Rangga Ede in Bukambero. My "teachers" in traditional lore are described in the first chapter, but I owe a great debt to all the Kodi people who took me into their homes and spent hours discussing their language and customs with me.

My parents, Herbert and Katharine Hoskins, taught me to love literature and oral narrative in many different cultural guises and have given me great encouragement and practical help. My sisters, Susan Hoskins and Judy Robinson, both visited me in the field, and Susan came a second time to take sound and edit the film project in 1988. I dedicate this book to my family, for all the emotional support they have given over the years, including its newest additions, my daughters Sylvana and Artemisia Valeri.

Note on Transcription

This book presents the first extended series of texts transcribed in the Kodi language of West Sumba. The transcription system used is an adaptation of one already in use on the island and taught by elementary school teachers to their students. When I first arrived on Sumba in 1979, I was told by literate Kodi speakers that, although no Westerner had ever managed to learn to speak their language, they knew quite well how to write it with "Indonesian" letters, but that Kodi, like English, is a language that is not always written the way it is pronounced.

The first transcription system devised for all the Sumbanese languages came from the Dutch linguist Louis Onvlee, who worked with local assistants to translate the New Testament into the Kambera and Weyewa languages and published general descriptions of the linguistic diversity of the island (Onvlee 1929, 1973). As his system was also used by my informants, I follow it for the transcription of most words, as well as for the convention that many sounds are written with combinations of Latin characters. Consistent with modern Indonesian spelling, the sounds that were written in an older Dutch Malay as /tj/ and /j/ are here /c/ and /y/.

Kodi has three nasal consonants: /m/ a bilabial nasal, /n/ an alveolar nasal, and /ng/ a velar nasal. There are nine stops: /mb/ a prenasalized bilabial voiced stop, /b/ a preglottalized, implosive bilabial voiced stop, /p/ a bilabial voiceless stop, /nd/ a prenasalized voiced alveolar stop, /d/ a preglottalized, implosive voiced alveopalatal stop, /t/ a voiceless alveolar stop, /ngg/ a prenasalized voiced velar stop, and /'/ a glottal stop. There is also /gh/ a voiced velar fricative, the semiconsonants /w/ labiodental voiced and /y/ palatal, and the laterals /l/ apico-alveolar and /r/ alveolar, with two affricates: /c/ a voiceless alveopalatal, and /nj/ a prenasalized voiced palatal affricate.

There are five vowels /i,e,u,o,a/ and four diphthongs /au,ai,ou,ei/ pronounced approximately the same as in other Sumbanese languages (Onvlee 1929, 1973, Kuipers 1990, Geirnaert Martin 1992).

Kodi is a highly inflected language, and sounds are often affected by the phonetic environment in which they are found; this is why informants claimed it could not be pronounced as written. But through a special use of certain letters it is possible to reflect the spoken language more closely. I use /y/ to indicate an extra syllable inserted after a consonant which follows the /ei/ sound in a preceding word. The /y/ sound is also inserted after the first consonant of a proper name to indicate that reference is in the third person (somewhat akin to the Indonesian practice of referring to an absent person as "Si Someone"). The insertion of this syllable changes the consonant /t/ to /c/ and the consonant /nd/ to /nj/ and may affect the way other parts of the word are pronounced. Thus, the prominent ancestor called Temba is referred to as Cyemba in Kodi, but if he is called with his title Rato the original form of the name returns, as in Rato Temba. A man who is called by his horse name is addressed as /ndara/ but referred to as /njara/. Kodi speakers do not modify the way they pronounce proper names when discussing absent persons in Indonesian, so I use the modified spelling of inflected names only in Kodi texts. These phonetic traits may explain some apparent inconsistencies in the transcription of proper names.

The book contains texts both in vernacular speech and in the special register of ritual speech which the Kodi call *panggecango* or "speech which is sewn up into couplets" (Hoskins 1988b). To reflect the marked social status of this indigenous verse form—the "words of the ancestors," which are believed to be relatively fixed and unchanging—I have arranged the paired lines to show their form as verse, and wherever possible I have included the precise Kodi text. These are considered words which have been passed down from past generations, and they represent a prized cultural heritage. I hope that these ways of representing the Kodi language on the page will be recognizable to my Kodi informants, who corrected many pages of transcribed texts so that their words could "travel over the oceans and reach people on the other side."

Introduction

The Land and People of Kodi

When I first arrived on Sumba in 1979, strapped onto a wooden bench as the only passenger of a tiny Twin Otter plane, it seemed an island out of time. Leaving behind the crowded, involuted civilizations of Java and Bali and their desperate struggle with the crises of modernization and development, I landed on a strip of asphalt laid out on an otherwise empty, grassy plateau called Tambolaka. With no human being in sight, the plane's arrival was of interest only to a lazy herd of grazing horses and buffalo who looked up from a desolate landscape of rolling hills and sharp gullies, a few thatched, high-towered bamboo houses just visible at the horizon. Two outbound passengers arrived mounted on small lively horses, their heads wrapped in red headcloths and their bodies draped with indigo loincloths and mantles. These were members of an important Kodi family, the people I had come to study for the next two years. They did not speak to me, but silently loaded their baggage, which included a screaming pig and a bundle of fine textiles, into the plane and left a small offering of betel on the runway. Other family members walked up to retrieve the two horses and erected a small post, on which chicken feathers had been tied, to show that sacrifices had been made at home to secure the blessings of the ancestors for this voyage overseas to seek medical treatment. As the plane taxied around and prepared to fly back to Bali, I had the brief sensation that I was about to be marooned in an another era, where horsemen with feathered headdresses herded buffalo and fought tribal wars with little or no awareness of the world beyond them.

Particularly disconcerting was the fact that my presence provoked no surprise or gawking stares—though the arrival of strange white women

1

was hardly routine; instead the others simply turned away, avoiding contact, which made me feel all the more invisible and out of place. Two years later, when I met members of the same family I had seen on the runway that first day, I asked them what they had thought at the time. "Oh, we didn't know then that you come to Kodi to study our language, to live with us and take a Kodi name. All we could see then was a foreign lady who came from a land where the sun set into the tides and the moon rose on shifting sands. We thought our hands would never join, and our feet would never meet."

An anachronism is usually defined as something that remains or appears after its own time. What I felt in these first few minutes most vividly was not that I was confronted with an anachronism, that these people represented some archaic or obsolete way of life, but that I myself had come unstuck from any familiar temporal framework and was quite simply misplaced in time. Sumba seemed not a survivor from the past, but an area that was profoundly out of sync with the modern world, moving to its own rhythms and unbothered by much distant turmoil. What the people on the runway felt, in contrast, was that a Westerner could have little interest in them and would not want to become a part of the very different temporal framework of their lives. The meeting that they thought inconceivable seemed unlikely because of the long historical and geographical isolation of their island.

Retrospectively, it is easy to see that this first impression, like so many others, was an illusion. Nevertheless, it opened the way to an intuition that I did not come to understand for another ten years. It showed me that I was confronting something very different, even alien, not so much in the people as in their temporality—their ideas of their own place in the world and how they moved through time. The idea that some people could exist separated from our own time worlds has long been part of the romantic appeal of isolated islands for travelers, adventurers, and, of course, anthropologists. While anthropologists have recently been criticized for constructing a great temporal distance between other worlds and our own (Fabian 1983; Thomas 1989), these experiences of temporal dissociation can also be heuristic. They can serve to awaken us to some of our own assumptions and unsettle the taken-for-granted relations among past, present, and future. As Fabian noted, "Experience of difference and otherness begins only when received time-space fusions begin to become undone" (1991, 199). That moment of confusion on the runway was to be the beginning of a long apprenticeship in the study of time.

"A Land Apart": Geography and Subsistence

The islands of the outer arc of the Lesser Sundas (map 1) do not have the great volcanoes and fertile tropical soils of Indonesia's main islands of Java, Sumatra, Bali, or Sulawesi. Largely comprising uplifted coral reefs, Sumba has low mountain ranges and a heavily weathered, rugged topography of limestone and other sedimentary rocks. It is a relatively large island of 11,500 km², 200 km long and from 36 to 75 km wide, dominated by wide grasslands. Southeast trade winds blowing off the Australian continent bring a hot dry climate to the eastern part of the island, which has virtually no rainfall for eight months of the year. Low, grass-covered hills appear stark and rather forbidding along the northern coast, broken only occasionally by dry gullies cutting their way toward the sea. As one moves inland and farther south, the rolling hills give way to a more rugged highland region of rocky inclines and forested mountains. None of these peaks reaches a great height, however: Mount Wanggameti in East Sumba is the island's highest point at only 1,225 meters.

Many areas are only sparsely populated; the island's four hundred thousand people are spread unevenly over the eastern and western halves of the island because of differential access to water. In the savanna grasslands of the east, population density averages only 18/km², whereas in the damper western half it rises to 50/km², with annual population growth standing at 2 percent (Helmi 1982). Rainfall differences range from a sparse thirty inches on the dry plains of the northeast, near Waingapu, to over a hundred at the wettest part of the island, Waimangura in the western highlands (Hoekstra 1948, 8). The physical contrast between the wet and dry areas seems greater than the difference in rainfall would indicate because much of the water that flows northward disappears underground, percolating into the porous limestone.

The Kodi district, to which I was headed, lies at the western tip of the island (map 2), perched at the "base of the land" (*kere tana*); this area is seen by the Sumbanese as the lower half of a human body whose head lies in the east. Kodi is lush in the rainy season but dries out to a parched, dusty plain in the months from March to November. The region is not suitable for wet rice cultivation; indeed, it is ecologically closer to the eastern grasslands with their pattern of swidden cultivation of dry rice and extensive livestock grazing.

Rice and corn form the basis of Kodi subsistence. Both are planted in mixed gardens, along with beans, tubers, chilies, and vegetables. Rice is believed to have special life-giving, nutritional qualities, and hence it is the focus of collective life (it is the only proper food to serve to guests)

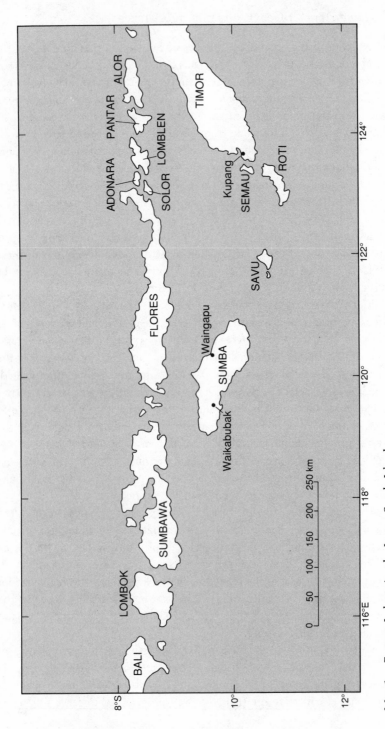

Map 1. Eastern Indonesia: the Lesser Sunda Islands

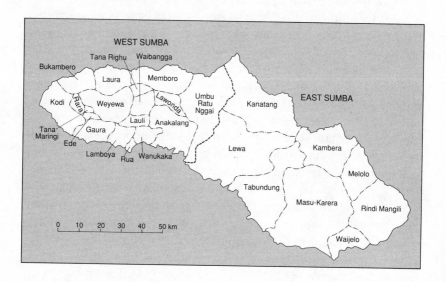

Map 2. Ethnolinguistic map of Sumba. Each area corresponds to a traditional ceremonial domain.

and has primary importance in the ceremonial system; yet because only a single annual wet-season crop can be produced, actual eating patterns depend heavily on other inferior crops. Corn is less appreciated than rice, but it can be harvested twice a year, so it comes closer to being the true staple of most households. The absence of rice is culturally defined as "hunger," and the long period from October to January is called the "hungry season," since it comes after most rice supplies from the previous year have been exhausted. A small share of rice is always set aside for calendrical festivities in late February or early March; this meal may represent the last time rice is eaten before the new harvest in April.

The fifty thousand Kodi people live widely dispersed in garden hamlets scattered through three different river valleys (Kodi Bokol, or "Greater Kodi"; Bangedo; and Balaghar). Despite its many problems, the Kodi coast presents a picture of fertility and abundance during much of the year. The main road that runs the eighty kilometers from the regency capital of Waikabubak is lined with banana and mango trees, and as it approaches the coast the view opens up to take in the sea and plantations of coconut and areca. The low-roofed thatch houses in garden hamlets are in fact only temporary dwellings, for the people's more permanent attachments are to the sixty-five ancestral villages that line the coast (map 3).

Land is used in three different ways in Kodi: as gardens (*mango*), as fallow plots (*rama*), and as pastures for livestock (*marada*). Traditional methods of shifting cultivation have become less effective now that so much land has been brought under cultivation, and the Kodi are well aware of the diminished fertility of their fields. Pastoralism—raising herds of buffalo, horses, and cattle—has long been the center of the Kodi prestige economy, but it is becoming more important to subsistence as well. Grassland farming is still possible, but it requires extensive time and effort. The coarse, tall tufts of swordgrass are burned off in the dry season, to expose new tender green shoots that can be grazed by herds of horses and buffalo. The ground must then be broken up, turned, and allowed to dry for six weeks to remove plant residues. It is worked again, the soil being chopped into smaller chunks and dried for a second burning. Such methods are similar to those used in grassland areas of Sumatra (Sherman 1990) and highland Burma (Leach 1954b), which share the high cultural valuation placed on rice but also suffer from severe ecological constraints.

Because of climatic variation and the uncertainty of agricultural production, relations between the interior and the coastal regions have long been based on a system of internal trade known as *mandara* (literally, to ride on a horse in search of food). Toward the end of the dry season, people from Kodi and other seaside districts travel inland to find vegetables, tubers, and other early-ripening foods to sustain them through the hunger months. These crops are exchanged for salt, dried fish, lime, pigs or livestock, and cloth. Gifts of cloth—a product largely of the coastal regions, where indigo plants grow in profusion—are particularly important, since textiles are required for all traditional exchanges. Although commercial dyes have largely replaced natural ones in textile production in many areas of the interior, making the Kodi monopoly on indigo less important, natural dyes are still required for the finest ritual cloths. In this domain, several older Kodi women maintain their preeminence as specialists in the secret art of dye-making (Hoskins 1989c).

In years of serious drought or famine, the line between the subsistence sphere and the prestige sphere of livestock raising becomes blurred, and then not only textiles but even horses or buffalo are exchanged for food.

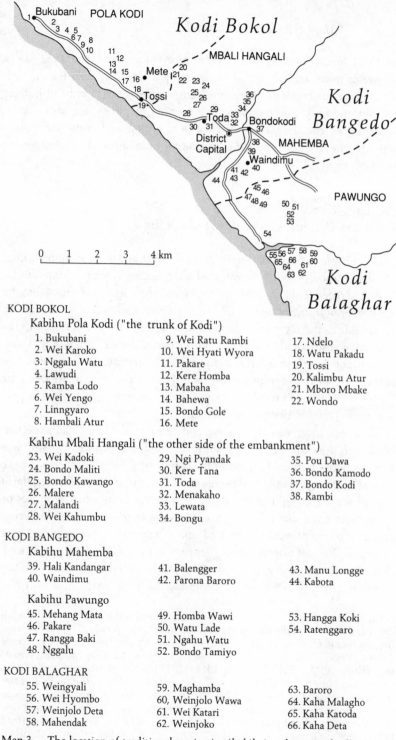

KODI BOKOL

Kabihu Pola Kodi ("the trunk of Kodi")

1. Bukubani
2. Wei Karoko
3. Nggalu Watu
4. Lawudi
5. Ramba Lodo
6. Wei Yengo
7. Linngyaro
8. Hambali Atur

9. Wei Ratu Rambi
10. Wei Hyati Wyora
11. Pakare
12. Kere Homba
13. Mabaha
14. Bahewa
15. Bondo Gole
16. Mete

17. Ndelo
18. Watu Pakadu
19. Tossi
20. Kalimbu Atur
21. Mboro Mbake
22. Wondo

Kabihu Mbali Hangali ("the other side of the embankment")

23. Wei Kadoki
24. Bondo Maliti
25. Bondo Kawango
26. Malere
27. Malandi
28. Wei Kahumbu

29. Ngi Pyandak
30. Kere Tana
31. Toda
32. Menakaho
33. Lewata
34. Bongu

35. Pou Dawa
36. Bondo Kamodo
37. Bondo Kodi
38. Rambi

KODI BANGEDO

Kabihu Mahemba

39. Hali Kandangar
40. Waindimu

41. Balengger
42. Parona Baroro

43. Manu Longge
44. Kabota

Kabihu Pawungo

45. Mehang Mata
46. Pakare
47. Rangga Baki
48. Nggalu

49. Homba Wawi
50. Watu Lade
51. Ngahu Watu
52. Bondo Tamiyo

53. Hangga Koki
54. Ratenggaro

KODI BALAGHAR

55. Weingyali
56. Wei Hyombo
57. Weinjolo Deta
58. Mahendak

59. Maghamba
60. Weinjolo Wawa
61. Wei Katari
62. Weinjoko

63. Baroro
64. Kaha Malagho
65. Kaha Katoda
66. Kaha Deta

Map 3. The location of traditional territories (*kabihu*) and ancestral villages in Kodi

In 1977, locusts destroyed a large number of gardens, and 1982 saw a plague of mice and the spread of new crop disease. In Kodi terms, such disasters are disruptions of seasonal temporality ("the months of hunger are not the only hungry ones; the months of plenty are also lean"), upsetting an already precarious balance of ecological factors and human activity; they require the ritual mediation of traditional timekeepers to set them right.

The Long Conversation:
Fieldwork Conditions and the Study of Time

I did not come to Sumba to study the perception and organization of time. My dissertation proposal, formulated after reading what few materials on Kodi had been published by missionaries and visitors, focused on the relation of mythology and social organization.[1] Rather, I was only slowly initiated into the topic over the course of seven different periods of ethnographic research that spanned more than a decade (1979–89). I did, though, come with an interest in the cultural construction of the past, and particularly in the narrative definition of precedent, which ethnographic studies had indicated would be expressed in elaborate genealogies in parallel verse (Adams 1969, 1970; Fox 1971).

This past itself was more alive and influential than I had expected, because in the early 1980s the traditional religion of *marapu* worship was still practiced by three-quarters of the population. Spirits of the dead were invited to all important ritual events and fed sacrifices, as well as regularly blamed for inflicting misfortune on their descendants when promises or obligations were not fulfilled. Precedence was invoked as an ordering principle but continually contested and renegotiated. Genealogies were short and alliances unpredictable; hence, the unity of the Kodi people took shape mainly through adherence to the yearly calendar. In sharp contrast to the stratified societies of East Sumba, the Kodi people had no royal

[1] When I arrived on Sumba in 1979, the only ethnographic materials concerning the island available in the United States were the collected essays of the missionary-linguist Louis Onvlee (1973), a series of articles by art historian Marie Jeanne Adams (1969, 1970, 1971a, 1971b, 1974, 1979), and some older missionary writings (Kruyt 1921, 1922; Wielenga 1911–12, 1916–18). Kodi was described in a fascinating but brief article by Van Wouden ([1956] 1977), and some Kodi fables had been published by Needham (1957b). Since that time, however, there has been an explosion of interest and research, including the essays in Fox 1980d and new ethnographic studies by G. Forth (1981), Kuipers (1990), Renard-Clamagirand (1988, 1989), Geirnaert Martin (1987, 1989, 1992), Keller (1988), I. Mitchell (1981), and Keane (1990).

genealogy that ordered collective memory or produced a single master narrative of regional history. Over the next ten years, subsequent field trips led me to question whether the period they called *la mandei la ma ulu* ("the past") was one thing or many different things.

Despite their initial standoffishness, Kodi people proved remarkably open and hospitable once they heard that I had come to study their language and culture. In Java, I had met a Kodi student who arranged for me to spend the first three months of my stay with his aunt, Gheru Wallu, in the market center at Kory in Greater Kodi. A rigorously traditional woman who spoke almost none of the national language, she was also a skilled herbalist, masseuse, and midwife. As my skills in the language gradually improved, I shifted to a new location closer to the ancestral villages along the coast—ritual centers and site of the calendrical festivities. I moved into a small house in Bondo Kodi that had been built for a nurse and set up my own home, living with two local girls, Maria Rihi and Fenina Manu, who helped with cooking and washing. Finally, toward the end of my stay, I spent two months in the distant river valley of Balaghar as the guest of my teacher Maru Daku.

During most of my fieldwork, men served as my "teachers," while women were my "companions." The important men who consented to become my instructors and guides in the arcane world of ancestral custom called me their "student" and "daughter." The women who lived with me in three separate households and helped me with the practical matters of life called me "sister" and "friend." Because of the way my gender and relative youth were culturally construed, my relations with men were cordial but hierarchical. They knew I wanted to collect and compile socially valued forms of knowledge, and they respected my work because I also respected them. Women, however, usually excluded from competitive claims to possess such knowledge, teased me about my earnestness; it was they who gave me the Kodi name by which I am still known there: Tari Mbuku, the name of a female ancestor but also, interpreted in Indonesian, having the double meaning of "looking for a book."

When I first began "looking for a book," I expected it would be an analysis of genealogies and traditional narratives in relation to the system of kinship and alliance. The materials I finally brought together for my dissertation, however, focused on the feasting system and its basis in spirit worship (Hoskins 1984). In turn, feasting was an arena for achieving renown and playing out the politics of exchange, which, I came increasingly to realize, was connected to a very different form of temporality.

The puzzles that eventually became the subject of the present study emerged in conversations with four Kodi "teachers," each of them a "man of knowledge" who controlled a different aspect of local temporality. The first "knew stories," the second "knew history," the third "knew how to sing the words of ritual," and the fourth "held the rites of the year."

Maru Daku, a famous bard and respected elder, was unrivaled in his mastery of Kodi verbal lore ("The book of our customs lies underneath his skin," a friend once said of him), and he was a figure of great authority, if a controversial one. Maru Daku's command of traditional narratives held his listeners in thrall, even when they disapproved of many aspects of his own life. An early convert to Christianity, he eventually repudiated the church leadership and returned to *marapu* worship. His great inventiveness with words was both praised and suspected and (as happens so often in Kodi life) won him an audience but not always followers.

Hermanus Rangga Horo, my second teacher, had been not only the last Dutch-appointed raja of Kodi but also the head of island government for a period after independence. He believed strongly in scholarship and recordkeeping; indeed, the personal notes and journals he kept over the eighty-seven years of his life were the only surviving local archive. I draw on them, and on his own vivid memory of past events, frequently in these pages, as well as on many discussions of custom and local litigation, the problems of governing a remote island only now "breaking into history," and the transformations that had occurred since independence.

My third teacher, Markos Rangga Ede, was a priest and singer who carried out *marapu* rites in his homeland of Bukambero and throughout the district of Kodi. Boasting a baritone so forceful it could "tear apart houses" with its tones, he was a traditionalist leader who served at times during my stay as the ward clerk and ward headman of Bukambero; he was always a strong local personality. For eight years I have followed him to rituals, recorded his songs and the dialogue of orators and diviners, then spent days going over the material with him to understand it in all its complexities.

The highest-ranking priest in Kodi was a "Father Time" figure, the Rato Nale, or "Lord of the Year." In Tossi, the ritual center of the domain, this office was held by Ra Holo, a patient and considerate host to me on my many visits. His own modesty and self-effacing demeanor contrasted strongly with the heavy obligations of his task; as the embattled nature of his position grew ever clearer to me, I came better to understand why he seemed reticent and taciturn on particular occasions. His counterpart in the outlying village of Bukubani, Ra Ndengi, agreed to narrate certain myths and allow me to observe the ceremonies of the new year; he was not, however, as reflective and questioning of his own task as Ra Holo.

Death interrupted the long conversations I began, taking away many of the strongest voices in my fieldwork. Maria Rihi, my "younger sister" and companion in my first home, was tragically killed in an accident at the end of my first year of research. A year later, Maru Daku fell seriously ill and recited a touching last testament to family and friends in my living room (Hoskins 1985). He later recovered and was able to bid me farewell, but I received news of his death as I was preparing my dissertation. His nephew, Ndara Katupu, who helped to compile and transcribe his words, died some months later. My host for return visits in 1984 and 1985, H. R. Horo, died before we returned on a film project in 1986 and 1988. And a graduate student from the Australian National University, Taro Goh, who attended the funeral I describe in chapter 9, died in the hospital of East Sumba six months after beginning his own field research on the island. The loss of these people, sudden and unpredictable because many were so young, haunted me during my writing and analysis, and no doubt contributed to the focus of this work on temporal notions as a response to human mortality.

The "sitting work" of transcribing texts, analyzing them, and interpreting them always took much more time than the "walking work" of traveling to distant villages and attending rituals.[2] It was while sitting with women, chewing betel, stringing cotton thread onto a loom, and untangling recently dyed yarns that I first stumbled on the idea that different temporalities could be the key to understanding much of the ceremonial system and its transformations. The shrewd and often sarcastic commentaries of women who watched from the darkened hearths at the center of Kodi houses encouraged me to look more closely at the ordering of events and lives in time. Their narratives also alerted me to the special significance of objects, because whenever I asked a woman for the story of "her life," I was given instead the story of an object, an exchange valuable, or a domestic animal. Whereas men narrated accounts of how they became the owners and exchangers of wealth, women confided indirectly, telling stories of possessions that had been tied to their own identities and then been taken away.

Because this study examines the public, shared world of the calendar and the annual cycle, it only touches on the more private world of domestic objects, persons, and gendered selves. The wider temporal perspective of the calendar, the exchange cycle, and the encounter with history is not an exclusively male one, but it does give important men a greater voice than

---

[2] Among those who worked with me on the transcription and evaluation of a number of texts, I would like to thank A. W. Bulu, Gregorius Gheda Kaka, Lota Mahemba, Yusup Ndara Katupu, Gideon Katupu, Ndengi Yingo, Radu Yingo, Rehi Pyati, Andreas Ra Mone, and Deta Raya.

their wives or daughters. The more hidden world of household politics and personal memory deserves separate treatment (Hoskins 1987b, 1988c, 1989c, in press). The conversations I had with men centered on time as an encompassing system of order; in those with women it was presented more as a dimension of biographical experience. Eventually, I hope to write about both perspectives.

The Play of Time in Anthropological Writing

Moving from the here-and-now reality of fieldwork to writing about those experiences in an ethnographic monograph creates a discrepancy between personal memory and an analytic account. The mixture of empathy, nostalgia, and guilt that I felt after my departure from the field was processed into descriptions which took various forms—a dissertation, articles, films, and drafts of the present manuscript. I returned to Kodi six times, bringing some of these materials for my former teachers to look over, but few were really interested in the theoretical questions that I address here. Our sharing of the same historic time and space during fieldwork—what Fabian (1983) calls "coevalness"—was replaced by a temporal and spatial distance which made the final writing a retrospective exercise that was mine alone.

The problem of "primitive temporality" that I explore in this study has not generally been linked to the concerns of history, anthropology's own politicized context, or the world economic system. Several recent writers have even questioned whether the argument that other peoples live in different time-worlds amounts to a "denial of coevalness"—an exclusion of them from our own temporal framework and an assertion that they live outside of history (Fabian 1983; Marcus and Fischer 1986; Clifford and Marcus 1986). In my view, this need not be the case; but to free ourselves from such false assumptions we must first get rid of the adjective *primitive*. As Fabian (1983, 18) says, "*Primitive*, being essentially a temporal concept, is a category, not an object of Western thought."

This work is about a specific historical and social system of timekeeping—Kodi temporality. This system is not treated as a subtype of "the primitive"; rather, the conceptual distance between Kodi time concepts and our own is the focus of analysis, not only so that we may delineate differences between "us" and "them," but also to problematize our own concepts, showing them to be neither necessary nor universal. Although the highly contested nature of the past has been the subject of much debate among Western historians, few ethnographic studies address it directly.

To restore the topic of indigenous temporality to responsible examination, I have tried to avoid certain traps in ethnographic writing which recent writers have called to our attention (Fabian 1983, 1991; Sanjek 1991; Thomas 1989). There is, for example, no "ethnographic present" in this book. Descriptions of Kodi life are drawn from historically situated events and persons, who bear their real names, as my Kodi informants requested. The sense of personal engagement and shared experience that I had in the field is revealed through use of the first person in situations where my own involvement was important. This book is not, however, a work of "reflexive anthropology," in the sense that it takes as its primary subject the encounter between the anthropologist and her hosts. My initial feelings of confusion about time are relevant to this theme, but to dwell excessively on each mistake and misunderstanding along my path would be self-indulgent and ultimately solipsistic. Fieldwork is a time when most of us become painfully aware that we are neither objective nor omniscient. In writing about the experience, therefore, I concentrate on how I was ultimately able to make sense of some of these initially alien concepts.

Notions of time are notoriously slippery and hard to grasp. In describing the Western ideas I brought along as part of my own conceptual baggage, I must speak in metaphors. We say, and believe we understand what we mean, that "time is money" and "history moves forward in a linear progression." The people of Kodi say, and tried to explain to me what they meant, that "time is value" and "the presents turns to the past" to seek models for innovation and change. Both of us, in dialogue, often have trouble understanding what lurks beneath the metaphors; we require the context of lived experience to clarify such apparently abstract distinctions. This book tries to provide that context, describing how the past is represented in narrative, objects, and action, and how Kodi calendars and exchange transactions play out specific notions of time. The story must begin with the social groups and categories that I had first thought would be the subject of my study of Kodi. They start to tell us a story about a different way of moving through time—but they are only the beginning.

Social Units in Kodi Society

People locate themselves in time by means of the categories of the kinship system. In Kodi, these categories are preeminently those of ancestors, descendants, and affines. Kinship and alliance are constructed as temporal modes of connection. One mode of connection is established along the patriline, which defines locally resident groups and the worshippers who gather in each ancestral village. A second mode is established along the matriline, with people belonging to named but dispersed social groups somewhat vaguely connected to notions of shared substance, personality, or attributes. Affinal relations constitute a third mode, coursing through the patriclans and matriclans as the "flow of life," by which women are moved to new homes and bear children to continue the descent line into a new generation.

THE HOUSE

The house (*uma*) is the starting point of each individual's location in time. Born as a member of a house in an ancestral village, a man will remain attached to that house throughout his life, will make offerings to its ancestors and heirloom objects, and his bones will come to rest in the stone tombs that circle its central ritual plaza. A woman will, at some point, be transferred by marriage into another house and will come to worship the ancestral community of her husband, but she will retain strong ties to her natal house. Members of the "house of origins" (*uma pa wali*) provide blessings of health, fertility, and well-being for her and her children, remaining obligated to continue friendly exchanges until the final gifts of death, when they finally take back the life they have given to the village by carrying the body of the out-marrying woman and her children to the grave.

The house is both a physical structure and a social group. The tall thatched towers of Kodi ancestral houses rest on a wide bamboo frame that slopes down to a raised floor of unbroken bamboo poles. Many houses are without walls but have inner partitions and platforms for the storage of heirloom objects, which hang from the peaked ceiling. The roof and floor of each house must be rebuilt every decade, and the obligation to "keep the house standing" is the most prominent ceremonial obligation shared by the "people of the house."

The house represents an unbroken line, extending vertically back in time, connecting the current inhabitants with their predecessors and successors. At the top of this line is the founding ancestor, named and propitiated on all ritual occasions, and below him are arranged all that has resulted from his life: his descendants, possessions, ritual offices, followers, and captives. The "masters of the house" (*mori uma*) are those directly descended from this ancestor or else formally incorporated into the house by completing exchange payments (for wives or adopted children). The other "people in the house" (*tou ela uma dalo*) are affiliated to the house through debt, capture, or default, and thus are not part of the house as a corporate unit but only "sheltered" by it. The term is usually used as a euphemism for slaves and dependents, who have no formal membership, cannot participate in house rituals, and must "sit at the edge of the veranda" (*londo la hupu katonga*) when the ancestors are directly addressed.

Ancestral villages (*parona*) are made up of a minimum of four ranked houses and usually contain between seven and thirty named house plots, each connected to a defined descent group (although fewer houses may actually stand in the village plaza, some of which may be in poor repair). A village name always refers to its location ("large hill," "rocky cliff," "edge of the land") or the tree planted in the center of the plaza, which serves as its altar ("leafy banyan," "wide-trunked kapok," "tamarind skull tree"). Direct descendants of the founder are called the "fruits and flowers, sprouts and shoots" (*wu wallada, kahinye katulla*) that grew from this great trunk, the male descendants being the seed-bearing "fruit" (*wuyo*), the females being the "flowers" (*walla*) who go off to bloom in other villages. The female term is anterior but ephemeral; the male one provides continuity into the next generation.

The house built by the village founder stands at the head of the central plaza (*kataku nataro*) and faces the next-ranking house at the "base" (*kere nataro*), with the following two at the "right" and "left" wings (*kapa lawana, kapa kaleiyo*). This division into four quadrants establishes an order of precedence followed in all sacrifices and offerings, as a share must always be given to the four "main houses" (*bei uma*). All other houses originated as the "children" (*ana uma*) of these four founders but may have developed other complex relations to each other in the division of ritual tasks. The houses are given individual names derived from their founder ("Byokokoro's House," "The Foreigner's House"), their ritual tasks ("The Drum House," "The Slaughtering House"), or idiosyncratic characteristics of their appearance ("High-roofed House," "House with Side Posts").

The ancestral village as a unit is exogamous, except for a few exceptionally large villages, which have split into two moieties that can now intermarry. Marriages are negotiated between members of different ancestral villages, and the exchange of bridewealth (livestock and gold from the groom's side, cloth and pigs from the bride's) should ideally involve all the members of a house. The house also owns land and heirlooms collectively and must meet as a corporate group to decide any shifts in its properties.

Houses are associated with genealogies; most persons can recite the names of several important ancestors, which situate them in one of the houses and indicate how they are descended from the founding ancestor. Kodi genealogies are not, however, limited to human forebears. The sacred litany that is repeated at each house ritual, the *li marapu* or "voices of the ancestors," is not only a list of personal names, but also a naming of sacred objects and sacred places important in the history of the house. The "time

line" thus extends the notion of "family history" to incorporate possessions and landmarks that, too, are seen as important predecessors in the
shared past of the community.

PATRILINES AND MATRILINES

Genealogical memory is relatively shallow, usually extending back no
more than four or five generations. Even members of important families
could not remember the names or relationships of people in their great-
grandparents' time, although they might remember the name of certain
important predecessors. The head priest of the calendar, the Rato Nale or
"Lord of the Year," knew the genealogical links that bound him to previous
holders of the office back to the beginning of the twentieth century, but
not before. Descendants of the first two Dutch-appointed rajas could not
produce the legitimating genealogical documents (*silsilah*) that their colonial masters required. The last Kodi raja, H. R. Horo, hired my teacher
Maru Daku to construct an account of his own family history to justify
his right to hold office.

The few important elders or ritual specialists who had detailed knowledge of genealogies were often called in to resolve legal disputes centering
on rights to land or heirloom valuables. Their task shows that in an
important way time is measured through exchange transactions—the careers of objects—and not through the simple succession of generations. It
also shows that the passage of "natural time" cannot be estimated from
genealogical evidence alone. A counting of generational intervals is rou-
tinely used to measure the period of time that has passed in planning a
feast or negotiating a new alliance, but since certain predecessors are often
"forgotten," these accounts serve more to legitimate claims to a long-
standing position than to estimate an actual time span.

Kodi stories about ancestors share the property noted by Paul Bohannan
with regard to Tiv myths and legends in that they often do not distinguish
between the founder of a lineage and his group of descendants. Bohannan
(1967, 265–27) explained that "myths are told as explanation of social
process, not as 'history.'... There are a relatively few stock incidents which
can be applied to any instance of the social process to be illustrated." If we
do not try to use genealogies to reconstruct a Western chronology but
rather to gain insight into an indigenous one, we can make this "explanation of social process" the focus of analysis, probing the unfamiliar
shape and constitution of the Kodi *li marapu* to garner clues about a
different construction of time and history.

The house provides the location and the connection between the person
and his or her ancestors, through the *li marapu* or time line that extends

back to the founding ancestor. The body, especially the blood, contains the substance that links the person to the matriline and a cross-cutting network of "relatives" (*dughu*) who neither live together nor worship in the same house. The term for matriline, *walla*, means "flower" and refers to the "flowering" of a woman's descendants in many different directions. Each *walla* is a named, exogamous group, associated with personal characteristics such as a fondness or intolerance for particular foods, personality traits (brashness, trustworthiness, duplicity), and secret knowledge (the tricks of indigo dyeing, herbalism, love magic).

The *walla* bears the personal name of an ancestress (Loghe, Mbera, and so forth) or the region from which she came. Stories about the origin of matrilines are told in a tone of gossip and scandal, since they usually concern an infraction or violation of a taboo. Walla Gawi, for instance, is descended from a woman who copulated with a goat, Walla Mandaho from one who eloped with a swordfish. The name Walla Wei Kanikiwikyo ("the urine descent line") comes from an infant who urinated on her mother's lap, was severely beaten and finally cast off. Two *walla* are named after related shrubs, Ro Rappu and Cubbe ("potato leaves" and "potato shrub"), which influenced the fetuses of women who developed yearnings for them during their pregnancies. The most dangerous *walla*, Walla Kyula, bears the name of the black witchcraft bird, whose song is an omen of approaching death. Marriage with a woman from Walla Kyula is extremely hazardous, as she is believed to be able to assume the shape of wild animals, fly around at night to prey on the internal organs of her enemies, and suck vital energy from her own husband and children.

Because *walla*s carry many unsavory associations, a person's matriline is often kept secret, to be disclosed only in a giggling whisper behind the house. It provides a link to the past, but a shady past full of suspicion and doubt, not the glorious past celebrated in the *li marapu*. The question of *walla* affiliation surfaces most often in the context of marriage negotiations, where questions of the bride's rank, blood lines, and personal characteristics can become an issue. The rules of *walla* exogamy are much stricter than those of the patrilineal house or village. Because the *walla* is seen as based on a unity of blood, violations of the exogamy rule can provoke not only social sanctions but a rebellion in the body itself. If a woman should be given in marriage to a *dughu*, a member of the same *walla*, the very blood of her womb is said to "rise up in protest," producing high fevers and hemorrhaging. The reaction cannot be mediated in any way, and difficult childbirth, chronic illness, and even death could result.

The patrilineal house and village are socially created corporations united in the worship of a specific group of ancestors, objects, and places. Since patrilineal groups have political, ritual, and jural authority, membership can be transferred by legal fictions and ritual mediation. It is possible, for example, to adopt a potential bride into a new house and village, if necessary, to allow two members of the same village to marry. The problem involves the direction of marriage payments, and thus the definition of social groups through exchange relations, rather than the primordial ties of blood. Violations of *walla* incest provoke supernatural sanctions that threaten the health of the offenders. Violations of incest prohibitions in the house or village can be resolved by the payment of *kanale*, a legal fine that is also used in cases of adultery or a broken engagement.

These contrasts reveal a marked difference in the way relationships through men and women order Kodi society. The patriline provides a *vertical* axis for Kodi social life in three senses: (1) it links people *back through time* by delimiting lines of descent that organize the transmission of ritual prerogatives through the generations; (2) it relates the human order to divinity and to ancestral origins, providing a cosmological justification for the contemporary division of land and powers; and (3) it dramatizes hierarchical relations in both human and spirit worlds at large-scale ceremonies and feasts. The matriline, in contrast, orders social life along a *horizontal* axis: (1) it links people of different patrilineal houses and villages *across space* because of membership in the same *walla*; (2) it forms a personal network of matrilineally related people said to share a common substance (blood) but no ritual or corporate functions; and (3) relationships traced through women work against notions of rank and lineage opposition by providing a cross-cutting system of kin ties that are essentially egalitarian.

ALLIANCE

Alliance links houses and villages and serves as a conduit for the transfer of women, animals, objects, and ritual prerogatives. It is a form of social cooperation and mutual assistance that not only is still hotly contested in Kodi social life, but has provoked a number of interesting contests in the scholarly world as well.

Marriage systems in Eastern Indonesia have long been the focus of research and analysis, ever since Van Wouden's famous characterization of them as "the pivot on which the activity of social groups turns" ([1935] 1968, 2). Early work concentrated on prescriptive asymmetric alliance, which was believed, in the famous "Leiden hypothesis," to be paired with double descent in the original proto-Austronesian form of dual organization. Kodi played an important role in the deconstruction of that original hypothesis. Reports of double descent, "in which both patrilineal and matrilineal clans operate side by side in the organization of the tribe" ([1935] 1968, 163), suggested that the original system might have survived in its most "intact state" there.

Van Wouden himself did two months of fieldwork in the region in 1951. He found, to his chagrin, that the Kodinese differ from many other Sumbanese peoples in that marriage is not governed by a categorical prescription. Thus, a crucial argument in his original thesis had to be modified. His initial disappointment brought him to a more sophisticated formulation of the nature of variation in Eastern Indonesia, stressing the different directions that descent and alliance had taken in societies of the region. While he noted that opposing systems still shared a certain "structural coherence," their historical divergence had become a question "so complex and encompassing that it is doubtful it could ever be properly posed, let alone answered" (Van Wouden [1956] 1977, 219).

Van Wouden's article on Kodi remains an ethnographic classic, not only because it is the earliest description of the region, but also because it signaled an early "opening up" of Dutch structuralism. The goal of comparative research was no longer the working out of a single model (a goal supposedly anterior to the great diversity of present practices), but the understanding of relationships and systemic change along a number of dimensions (Fox 1980a, 6). Recent fieldworkers who have studied asymmetric systems have shown how alliance is essential to the constitution and definition of social groups (G. Forth 1981; Lewis 1988; Traube 1986; Valeri 1980; McKinnon 1991) and the structure of descent is a product of the pattern of marriage.

Although sharing a clear kinship with these societies, Kodi alliance is still "looser" and less consistently articulated than other social institutions. In Lévi-Strauss's terms (1969a), Kodi marriage forms a "complex" system, not an "elementary" one, and it has become increasingly clear that the same is probably true of the majority of Eastern Indonesian societies (Fox 1980b, 329–30). Since alliance is not directed by a categorical prescription, it is endlessly negotiated on the shifting terrain of intergroup relations. Rather than being frozen into an authoritative and enduring "totalizing system," it becomes the focus of local politics and the marker of individual achievement.

The relation of wife-giver and wife-taker in Kodi is asymmetric. The direct exchange of sisters (*pandelu lawinye*), accordingly, is strictly forbidden. The most harmonious marriage is said to be with the cross-cousin (*anguleba*), a category that does not distinguish the mother's brother's daughter (MBD) from the father's sister's daughter (FZD); in both cases, the marriage is valued because it involves a "return" of descendants to the house. In MBD marriage, the son "returns" to the house that his mother came out of, "following her tracks, retracing her steps" (*na doku a wewena, na bali a orona*) to enter again the "door that he came out of, the steps that he came down" (*tama la binye oro loho, la lete oro mburu*). In FZD marriage, the grandchildren will "return" to the *walla* of their grandfather, so that although their mother lives in a separate house and village, the house is once again associated with his matriline.

Both of these ideas of "return" play on the common Eastern Indonesian theme of the reunion of descendants of a brother and sister, which occurs after a generation of separation. The "return of the blood" provides a sense of closure for alliance cycles that is desirable in many societies (Barnes 1974, 248–49; Lewis 1988, 301; Traube 1986, 88), even if it is not always statistically achieved.

A census of 334 households (and 412 marriages) conducted in 1980 showed only 18 cases of cross-cousin marriage (10 with the MBD, eight with FZD) in the administrative ward (*desa*) of Waiha, a relatively isolated region in Balaghar. A survey of exchange activities conducted in 1988 among 50 households in Bondo Kodi, however, showed a much higher incidence: 12 marriages with the MBD and 4 with the FZD. Bondo Kodi is the district capital and the residence of many important families; there, cross-cousin marriage was most likely to occur when the "return" involved a great separation in space, as when the son of a woman who had married into another district or region "followed her footsteps" back to her home region to seek a wife. Informants also argued that such marriages were more common in wealthy families, "who just want to exchange with each other" and do not want to disperse their valuables in new directions.

A prescriptive rule for asymmetric cross-cousin marriage is correlated in Sumba with increased social stratification. Those districts that are most clearly divided into social classes are also said to observe the rule most rigidly. Partly because they are increasingly aware of the diversity of social systems on the island, several Kodi observers provided me with astute commentary on the logic of these transformations:

> Whenever we give a woman to another village, we will keep travel-ing that path for many years to come. If you are wealthy already, you want to give your daughter to someone who will take care of her, who shows his generosity in the bridewealth, and who will con-tinue to demonstrate his respect with later payments. If they are already your wife-takers [*laghia*], their name is good and you can be sure they will help out. Initially, you may ask for less bridewealth because there is already trust and love on the path. But if they are strangers, they must establish their good faith with larger pay-

ments. Otherwise, your valuables will travel down those paths and disappear.

Alliance sets up a mutual lending relationship, and credit is evaluated on the basis of a past history of exchanges. Thus, it is prudent for a wealthy family to marry "close"—among the group of families already linked to them as affines. The "return of the blood" is also a way of assuring the return of valuables, which "follow the path" along with the bridegroom who returns to his mother's village.

A more daring strategy involves investing in outsider groups who have amassed enough wealth to improve their social position through marriage. These groups may include wealthy families from other districts, who want to expand their alliance networks. Marriages that cross district boundaries are increasingly common, as well as prestigious, but they are always expensive. Instead of traveling a familiar path, the bridegroom must "cross over new pastures and cut through virgin forest" (*na palango marada, na dowango kandaghu*). He offers more buffalo and horses to his wife-givers because (as some would say) "he is buying a social position as well as a wife."

Bridewealth payments from the groom's side are calculated in "tails": equal numbers of horses and buffalo, usually from ten to thirty. Each "tail" should be reciprocated from the bride's side with a man's and a woman's cloth, one long-tusked pig for each ten livestock animals presented, and a gold ear pendant. When the bridewealth is over thirty "tails" of livestock, then heirloom valuables such as ivory bracelets, a bronze ankle ring, a gold crescent headpiece, or imported glass beads might be added to the counterprestation. Interdistrict marriages negotiated in the last forty years have often involved bridewealths of a hundred or more livestock, and the shortage of traditional gold and ivory valuables has prompted a shift to new consumer goods—a bed, cupboard, dining table, or set of dishes can now be used to "match" the groom's payment.

Differential bridewealth payments and the "inflation" of such payments by the incorporation of new prestige objects have intensified the degree to which alliance negotiations may appear as a "marriage market" where statuses are bought and sold. As a single performance, in which the families invite an audience to witness and legitimate their claims to an enhanced social position, the negotiation may seem to display this commercial character. But bridewealth is only the starting point of a long-term relationship. A continuing series of obligatory exchanges maintains the alliance for at least two generations, through the marriage of the children produced by the union and the burial of the bride and groom.

Since the position of "wife-giver" (*ghera*) involves ritual duties that extend longer than the lifetime of any individual, the position is passed down from father to eldest son until the final mortuary rites are finished. The funeral involves both a ritual mending of the house and village—the patriline that was torn apart by the death—and a final separation of affines, whose duties to one another are now complete (see chapter 9). It is the last in a series of life crisis rituals that affines must attend, contributing sacrifices and acting as each other's ritual counterparts in promoting life and cleansing the pollution of death.

The proper negotiation of alliance payments requires that a delicate balance be maintained. Self-serving calculation of short-term material benefits is weighed against the expectation of a long-term relationship of mutual assistance. If someone, in marrying, seems too obviously to be furthering a career of social climbing, it is argued that he is trying to "wash himself off with gold" (*pa ihyo ndoka*)—hiding an unglorious past with a new infusion of wealth. While his wife-givers may receive expensive gifts of livestock, the prestige and rank of the woman's house could suffer by association with a son-in-law of lowly origins. Wealth can be converted into status only gradually, by imbuing livestock and gold with social respect and standing. As a general principle, that is, time conveys respectability, because it is associated with the responsible management of wealth and the fulfillment of exchange obligations.

Marriage is particularly important in determining the temporal character of kinship, since each new marriage commits both parties to three generations of exchange obligations. Alliance ties are perceived as vitalizing but ephemeral, the "life blood" that courses through the social body; descent ties, by contrast, are enduring and constraining, symbolized by the swords and spears that pass down through the generations, forming a metal skeleton that extends back to a founding ancestor.

Long-Term and Short-Term Cycles

Both kinship and alliance link individuals, with their own emotional attachments and needs, and social groups. Individuals may develop matrimonial strategies that stress short-term tactical "moves" related to practical goals—assembling the bridewealth, getting assent for a desired match—but these individuals are also part of houses and villages with long-term developmental projects. In Sumba (as in most of Eastern Indonesia) these projects are expressed in terms of the desirability of closing a cycle: the "reunion" of the descendants of the brother and of the sister, the "return" of heirloom valuables that have circulated outside of the house, the "bringing back" of a matriline so that a grandfather and his grandchildren will be of the same *walla*. These projects are articulated within the context of long-term affinal debt, with a temporal span almost always longer than the life span of any given individual.

It is, I believe, the extended temporality of ties based on blood and marriage that makes their regulation more one of long-term projects than short-term strategies. Bourdieu's (1977, 34) opposition of "official kinship" and "practical kinship" criticized anthropologists for basing their theories on the retrospective analysis of genealogies rather than the ongoing strategies of local agents. But the strategic advantage of a delayed return means that the "result" of an alliance in exchange politics often emerges only *after the fact*. Hence, if we accept his position that temporal units achieve power only through their play within a given structure of relations, most of the societies of Eastern Indonesia would have to be said to "play the present with an eye on the past," because they stress the durability of exchange relations over time and through multiple individual relations. An intergenerational model of exchange is needed, in which not individuals but "houses" emerge as moral actors, the transactors in the often rivalrous arena of marriage.

If the "house" is the locus of strategic calculation, it is perhaps not surprising that the Kodi represent this fact by seeming to attribute volition and even calculation to the house and the objects within it. A gold pendant that leaves the house, for instance, is said to "yearn to return home" (*kareiyo balingo*) when it travels to a distant region, and thus to influence human actors to seek new brides from the daughters of its former masters. A buffalo cow received in bridewealth bears a calf who "wants to retrace her footsteps" and go back to the corral left behind, through a son who marries his father's sister's daughter.

The curiously animated objects of Kodi exchange reflect a displaced agency, in which collective strategies are attributed to the valuables and their location instead of to the actors who manipulate them in particular instances. Agency is also sometimes displaced onto the ghostly influences of ancestors, who may tell their descendants they want a cycle to be completed or (most often) want their own place filled by a close relative. The pressure from a deceased wife is cited as a prime reason to renew the alliance by marriage to her younger sister.

Different projects have, of course, different time scales. Just as people must assemble in order for events to "take place," these people must also "take time" from their own lives and devote it to a particular activity. Some institutions and activities, however, carry more "weight" than others (in a metaphor that is as common in Kodi as in English). "The greatest burden," any Kodinese will tell you, "is that imposed by the house." Its duties are the "heaviest" (*rehi mboto*), surpassing even the onerous demands of affinal relationships, and its sanctions the strictest.

Because the house is the temporal center of gravity in Kodi social life, its continuity provides an anchor for more free-floating notions of individual life projects and obligations. Alliance provides the primary means of testing that center and of "weighing" the import of a particular house against its rivals. Thus, it is a mark of prestige and achievement for a house to be filled with "heavy" valuables, which cannot be easily moved along alliance paths. The truly wealthy are those who are able to withdraw their goods from circulation, to sanctify them as "inalienable wealth" (Weiner 1985) and keep them as an exclusive treasure. Few houses ever attain that status in the fierce exchange rivalries of Kodi, and in fact only a very small number of cult houses have supposedly "immovable" objects within them. The accumulation of "lighter" goods, which circulate at marriages and funerals, gives a temporary, shifting sense to status that is always contestable.

Houses strive to appear immobile in time, to hold on to their wealth, and to elaborate and embellish the house site with new objects that are also unmovable. Because of the shifting requirements of swidden cultivation, the locations of gardens and hamlets are constantly being changed; correspondingly, a complex ritual apparatus has been erected to legitimate each change. Movement is required in order to produce new crops, as the movement of women from one village to another is required to produce new descendants. But the striving for immortality is a striving against movement and toward stasis—the always desirable but elusive stasis of the unchanging patrimony.

The objects and the location of the house must define it as enduring through time, since its physical shell—the structure of thatch and bamboo—has to be rebuilt every ten years or so. Because Kodi genealogies are relatively shallow, they do not reflect ideas of the continuity of the house, which always extend further back than four or five generations. In a sense, the objects that the ancestors left behind take their place, "standing in" for the passage of time.

Alliance in Kodi is particularly unstable and shifting, since it serves not as an overarching political structure for the whole society but as a status mover and converter. The directionality of exchanges is not fixed, nor are the social classes in which these negotiations are carried out. Instead, everything is open to contestation and reformulation, and the possibility of status reversals and shifts always looms close at hand. Marriage negotiations are themselves "tournaments of value" (Appadurai 1986), where new power relations are decided and social groups are reordered.

For these reasons, the sense of time that is expressed when people locate themselves in the various categories of descent and alliance is quite different from that experienced by many other Eastern Indonesian societies. In contrast to the extended time frame of Rotinese genealogies (Fox 1980c, 99), Kodi *li marapu* are elliptical litanies of ancestors, objects, and a few place names. And in contrast to the enduring directionality of alliance obligations in Rindi, East Sumba (G. Forth 1981), Kodi marriage ties turn this way and that, ruled more by the shifting balance of rivalrous exchange than by an idea of enduring cycles. The theme of a "return to the source," so central to the ceremonial systems of the Mambai of Timor and the Tana Ai' of Flores (Traube 1986; Lewis 1988), surfaces in Kodi only as the "conservative strategy" of certain wealthy families; it is not given the encompassing religious and metaphysical significance that it has on neighboring islands.

In Roti, Fox (1980c, 100) has argued, the immense depth of genealogies is related to the "social use of history as a means of differentiation," in which the numerous petty rulers who were recognized by Dutch colonial authorities are legitimated and their titles used to maintain claims to power. In Kodi, a much shorter colonial history and a less hierarchical oral tradition has resulted in a time line that lacks a "master narrative" in the form of a royal genealogy that orders the past for all the inhabitants. The result is not a timeless past, but a past that simply is not chronicled in the terms of genealogical charters. It is chronicled, instead, in more loosely connected narratives, dispersed through a number of houses and storytellers, and the objects that they use to remember and commemorate historical events. The main ordering device used is the calendar, which divides the year into ritually marked intervals and synchronizes social activities. The priest of the calendar sits at the center of a complex island-wide ceremonial system, in which the ancestors of the Kodi "lords of the year" (*mori ndoyo*) established the temporal divisions recognized throughout Sumba (see chapter 12).

Ricoeur (1988, 105) has argued that "The time of the calendar is the first bridge constructed by historical practice between lived time and universal time. It is a creation that does not stem exclusively from either of these perspectives on time. Even though it may participate in one or the other of them, its institution constitutes the invention of a third form of time." In the following chapters, we explore Kodi perspectives on the construction of the past, beginning with imported elements brought by the ancestors when they migrated from the west. Time, as part of lived experience and an attribute of the natural world, is said to have a local origin, while the past is made up of many parts, some expressed in narrative, others in objects, and still others in ritual action. While the past is diverse and often contested, it can stand apart from daily life and become an object of reflection. As an abstraction, separated from everyday entanglements, it permits the totalization of hindsight, the retrospective vision of the whole. This vision, then, is called back into question by its involvement in continuing chains of exchange transactions and the encounter with the new, progressive, linear notion of "history."

PART ONE

The Kodi Construction of the Past

1

The Imported Past

Foreign Sources of Power

Brought across the wide seas, carried over the wide oceans
To fall at our feet and be grasped by our hands
The stalk of foreign banana [papaya] now sits at our ancestral hearth
The sweet gourd from overseas is offered to our own forefathers

From a Kodi song about imported heirloom valuables

Kodi is the kind of society that, fifteen years ago, when anthropology had a somewhat different orientation, might have been described as "isolated from history." Sumba remained in the backwaters of the Dutch colonial empire for several hundred years. Sporadically involved in the sandalwood trade of the sixteenth and seventeenth centuries, and later in the export of horses and slaves in the eighteenth and nineteenth centuries, the peoples of this island were never integrated into the Indic kingdoms or mercantile sultanates that lay to the west of them. Until the beginning of the twentieth century, rather, they lived in relative autonomy, divided into many small feuding domains and without a centralized polity or a single indigenous ruler. In the west, each domain had its own language and its own stories of the origins of time and of the calendar, the acquisition of fire, and the development of agriculture.

And yet indigenous social institutions, particularly those that express ideas of hierarchical difference, are conceived of and legitimated in the terms of external political powers. The tension between ideas of local origins and imported authority in fact lies at the very heart of Sumbanese society, inscribing all Kodi social forms in historical space and time. The most important heirloom objects stored in ancestral houses come largely from other islands, and even certain objects that could have been locally made (such as a wooden trough or drum) are traced to a faraway kingdom in the west. Present symbols of local political orders are given a foreign history; their power was "imported," it is argued, and realized anew on the shores of Sumba.

In trying to account for this tension analytically, we are caught between silences in the documentary record and a confusing series of contradictory claims in the oral record. Written sources on precolonial Sumba are extremely scanty, with specific material on Kodi almost nonexistent. As the domain farthest from the administrative centers of Waingapu and Waikabubak, Kodi was the only region not visited by Dutch missionary writers such as D. K. Wielenga, Ten Kate, and Albert C. Kruyt, who traveled extensively throughout the island in the early twentieth century. Louis Onvlee, the missionary-linguist who spent over thirty years on Sumba, visited Kodi only once, for a few days in 1932, and confessed that Kodi was the only Sumbanese language he could not understand (personal comm.). Until the 1950s, when Kodi was visited by F.A.E. Van Wouden and Rodney Needham, there were no published materials specifically concerned with the region.

The history of events in Kodi thus remains largely obscure, at least before the beginning of this century. But we can glimpse certain larger processes, through which ideas of foreign authority were taken up and incorporated into notions of indigenous origins. The imitation and assimilation of incompletely understood foreign powers was sometimes accompanied by a disavowal of their real origins, with foreign objects redefined as "indigenous" and made the basis of local claims to rule.

My treatment of themes in the island's history will focus on the interactions between the Sumbanese and four foreign places, each of which had a significant impact on both the events themselves and the perceptions of the nature of power and its deployment. These are "Java" (more a mythical construct than a reference to the actual island), Bima (on the island of Sumbawa), Ende (on the island of Flores), and Batavia (the colonial capital of the Netherlands East Indies).

Origins from "Java"

The Sumbanese say that their ancestors migrated from the west, crossing over a "stone bridge" (lendu watu) that once connected the island to lands to the west. There are many local versions of the shared mythic tradition of this migration. All of them agree that the first ancestors arrived at Sasar, a treacherous cape along the north shore whose name, in Malay, means "lost" or "off track." In some accounts, the two ancestors had a wooden ship that smashed on the coral reefs and left them stranded on the island. In other accounts only one of them, Umbu Walu Mandoko, traveled to the island by ship, and it was his descendants who settled along the banks of various streams. The other ancestor, Umbu Walu Sasar, often identified as Umbu Walu Mandoko's older brother, came down directly from the sky, riding on his horse; his descendants settled the drier areas

A Kodi woman displays her high rank by wearing imported wealth: ivory bracelets, heirloom ceramic beads, and a bark-embroidered betel pouch. 1980. Photograph by the author.

inland (Couvreur 1917, 209). Both men were originally said to have come "from Java," and to have been driven from their homeland by mysterious circumstances (Wielenga 1916–18, 21:3; Kruyt 1922, 471). Warfare, quarrels between the two siblings, and disputes over their marriages are sometimes cited as reasons for their decision to leave.

These immigrants met an indigenous population, which they gradually displaced by means of a division of powers, a conquest, or the dying out of the original inhabitants. Early Dutch writers generally agreed with Kruyt's interpretation that an "originally democratic society" once existed all over the island. In the east, that society was replaced when a few noble families took power into their own hands, dislodging the traditional religious leaders who guarded the relics of their ancestors (Kruyt 1922, 467). In the west, the ceremonial leadership of a calendrical priest like the Rato Nale ("Priest of the Sea Worms") remained unchallenged, though warfare and political struggles between competing clans raged on. Wielenga noted that many Sumbanese domains are divided into two parts, one older and one younger; he explained this peculiarity by the fact that "one part represented the original inhabitants, who had ownership of the land, and one part were later-comers, who received, with the permission of their elders, a share of the land to live on, or else seized the land without permission through force. In both cases, the older part possessed spiritual powers" (cited in Kruyt 1922, 468). A final possibility was that the original inhabitants might have been almost completely wiped out, with few traces of their presence remaining.

In West Sumba, most domains are traditionally divided into two parts—for example, Lamboya and Patialla, Laura Marada and Laura Letena, Lauli Deta and Lauli Wawa, Kodi Bokol and Kodi Bangedo. It is not clear whether these in fact represent "older" and "younger" parts or are simply geographical divisions that were settled by different clans, with no disparity of rank or genealogical status implied. The names themselves distinguish "pastures" (*marada*) and "mountains" (*letena*), "highlands" (*deta*) and "lowlands" (*wawa*), and "larger" (*bokol*) and "smaller" (*bangedo*; lit., "founded by Umbu Ngedo") divisions. The division between "politics" and "religion" was less clearly established in the west, since there the title given only to a priest in the east (*ratu*) could be used for a chief as well (Kruyt 1922, 469).

All West Sumbanese trace their descent from the ancestors who landed at Sasar, with the exception of the few hundred descendants of an earlier population, called the "Lombo" people in Laura and the "Karendi" in Balaghar. The indigenous people, who are believed to assume the form of wild animals or carrion-eating witches, are recognized as the original owners of the land. Before the migration from the west, they were said to have had no knowledge of fire or agriculture, living as hunters and gatherers of wild forest foods.

The original migration is recounted today in the paired couplets of ritual speech (*panggecango*), a verse form that marks the most important texts in the oral tradition. An invocation of the ancestral journey runs like this:

The ancestors of long ago	Ambu la ma ulu
Came to the distant cape of Sasar	Na duki ela haharo malango
From another land, the foreign land	Wali la hambali cana, tana dawa
The forefathers of ancient time	Nuhi la mandeiyo
Came to the adze-shaped stone bridge	Na toma la kataku lendu watu
From across the seas, the strange land	Wali la hambali lyoro, tana ndimya
When dawn came over Gaura's coast	Ba na mahewa helu nggaru
When day broke on Lombo's land[1]	Ba na madomo a tana lombo
Off to Kodi went Lord Ngedo	Otu la Kodu umbu ngedo
And to Rara went Lord Wango	Mono Rara umbu wango
. . . to Ede . . . and Manola	Ede umbu Koba, Ibbila Manola
. . . to Manekka . . . and Lombo	Kairo Manekka, Roto Lombo
. . . to Karendi, Bukambero, Weyewa	Karendi Bukambero, Pittu Waiwewa
. . . to Gaura and Lamboya	Nggaro Umbu Tola, Lamboya Patialla
. . . to Rua and Wanokaka	Rua wu Wungo, Yongga Wanukaka
. . . to Lauli and Lawonda	Lauli Anakalang, Lawondo Bolobokat
To Kambera of a different language	Kambera Heka Hili
To Kanata of different speech	Kanata Heka Taki
. . . to Melolo and Kabata	Talinjaka Malolo, Kabata Dola Ngapu
. . . to Laura and Tana Righu	Mboro Palamedo, Laura Tana Righu

Much of the passage cannot be translated, since it consists of a series of place names and names of ancestors, which blend into one another. The division of Kodi Bangedo is said to have been settled by the descendants of a Lord Ngedo (*umbu* being an East Sumbanese title for a nobleman, and Ngedo remaining a common name in the area), but little else is known of such an ancestor. The other place names are recited in a sequence that suggests an itinerary from Kodi into the highlands (Rara, Ede, Manola), across various eastern boundaries (Karendi, Bukambero, Weyewa), down to the south coast (Rua, Wanokaka, Lauli, Lawonda), and then, with a final detour to East Sumba (Kambera, Kanata, Melolo, Kabata), returning to the northern coast (Laura, Tana Righu). These verses must be recited at rites bearing on the distant past, when the souls of ancestors of the whole island are invoked. The "strange, foreign land" of *tana dawa, tana*

---

[1] *Lombo* means "end" or "point" in Kodi, but this reference of an ancestral migration "as the day breaks over Lombo" is often interpreted as referring to an origin from the island of Lombok, which lies three islands west of Sumba (after Flores and Sumbawa).

ndimya is usually glossed as Java and Bima (one of two sultanates on the island of Sumbawa), though it may also include Lombok, Bali, or Flores. A similar series of couplets recited in East Sumba mentions Malacca, Singapore, Makassar, Ende, Manggarai, Roti (Enda), Ndau, and Savu (Kapita 1976b, 13).

The "Java" that is evoked as the origin of the Sumbanese should not necessarily be taken in its literal sense. As one of the earliest chroniclers noted, "The Sumbanese call everyone who comes from overseas a foreigner (*tau jawa*), so the category includes Europeans, Arabs, Chinese, Javanese and inhabitants of other islands in the archipelago" (Couvreur 1917, 213). The great lord who ruled over the foreign kingdom from which the ancestors came is ambiguously rendered as Rato Ndimya, Rato Dawa, and his kingdom is not so much Java or Bima but any distant land to the west. Sumbanese oral tradition contains many narratives about heroes who traveled to this distant land; the presence of Javanese krises, heirloom porcelain jars, Indian *patola* cloths, and other imported finery suggests that relations with these distant states took the form of trade and perhaps tribute.

Written records offer only a few scattered references to substantiate the existence of a tie between Java and these outer islands. In the *Nagarakrtagama* (conventionally dated about 1365), Sumba is named as a subject of the Majapahit Empire (1294–1478). A fleet of Gajah Mada sailed to Dompo, Sumbawa, in 1357, and apparently laid some claim to the island, though there may never have been any physical landing on Sumba (de Roo 1906, 185). It is not known how much contact there actually was with Java at that time, and no Hindu or Buddhist remains have been found. The main resource that attracted traders since the seventh century was sandalwood, whose fragrant bark was used to make incense, fans, and clothes chests and was much sought after by Chinese merchants. In 1522, Magellan's chronicler Pigafetta mentioned sailing past "Cendana," or the "Sandalwood Island"—which, later maps indicate, must have been Sumba (de Roo 1906, 187).

The sandalwood trade attracted other European powers to the Timor archipelago, prompting competition for control of the waters. In 1566, Portuguese traders settled on the neighboring island of Solor and built a fortress to protect Christian converts from Moslem sea raiders. The fortress was attacked and captured by Dutch forces in 1613, which sparked an intense rivalry (Fox 1977, 63). In 1636, a Dutch ship was wrecked on "the unknown island of Sandalwood," and some of the men were left behind, but no expedition was sent to look for them (de Roo 1906, 188). The Portuguese of Larantuka built a small fort at Tidas, on the southern

coast of West Sumba in Wanokaka, but its dates and use remain mysterious. In 1726, the government in Batavia recognized the presence of the
Portuguese on the island; the fort itself, however, was not spotted until
1902 (de Roo 1906, 188).

Local legends often associate the ancestral migration to Sumba with the
fall of the Hindu-Buddhist kingdom of Majapahit. Mythologies of aris-
tocratic origins are extremely widespread in Indonesia, and it can hardly
be true that all the peoples of the outer islands were descended from exiled
Javanese princes. Nevertheless, the legend of Majapahit does have a long
history on the island. Colfs, writing in 1880, reported: "Every evening a
light can be seen in the direction of Monboro: the natives there say that
it is on the tombs from the Modjopahit period which are there" (cited in
Needham 1987, 21). No actual tombs with Javanese inscriptions were
found at that time, though, nor have any been discovered since. In Anakalang, Alfred Buhler was told that the ancestors descended from the sky
to settle first at Majapahit, later migrating from there through Bima and
Flores until they eventually reached Sumba (1951, 57).

Present-day speculations about the origins of Sumbanese ancestors
often include "the Majapahit" as a category of the prestigious past. In
Kapunduk, East Sumba, I was told in 1988 that the noble families of the
eastern part of the island had immigrated from Majapahit, and this was
why they still had so much gold. In Kodi, some people speculated that
Pokilo and Mangilo, the brothers who founded the ceremonial system,
were from Majapahit, but the members of other clans were not. When a
film crew from Java filmed scenes of horse battles on Sumba using local
riders as extras, there was additional speculation that the ancestors of the
Sumbanese must have been from Majapahit, because they also were horsemen. Such conjectures, however, should most appropriately be interpreted
as reimaginings of the past, and not oral tradition. As Geertz (1973, 398)
has noted, Majapahit assumes the mythical status of *illo tempore* in much
of Indonesia: a glorified time of origins that may not correspond to any
actual historical time or place.

The Sultan of Bima

The sandalwood trade was administered by the sultan of Bima, whose
claims to control the island appear in the records of the Dutch East India
Company. In 1663, a merchant named Van Heijst reported that the sultan
of Bima was having troubles delivering Sumbanese sandalwood because
of the complicated political situation at the time. The sultan said that the
Sumbanese had been his subjects "from antiquity," but "now it seemed

that they wanted to become independent." He then asked for assistance from the Company to crush the rebels so that the trade could continue. The Dutch were willing to help only on the condition that they be paid with the profits of the sandalwood, but they would not promise to build a fortress on the island. The planned military expedition never took place, however: the sultan had to travel to Makassar, and when he returned the Company ships were deployed elsewhere (de Roo 1906, 189).

In 1675, further correspondence from the Company to the sultan affirmed that "from ancient times these lands have belonged to the King of Bima and his viceroy Turilia Gampo, and the Company has no plans to interfere with this dominion, but simply wants its contract to be fulfilled." The sultan said that Portuguese Christians from Larantuka had been fomenting unrest among the local population, forcing him to wage war against insurrections on Sumba and in his other possessions, even though he realized that the Dutch and the Portuguese were supposed to be at peace. The authorities in Batavia answered that they would have nothing to do with such internal strife: "The ruler of Bima can do as he likes in the areas that he controls, but the Company can give him no help; however, the authorities recognize that he must wage war on Sumba, because he has enemies there" (de Roo 1906, 190–91).

It is not clear how the situation was resolved. In 1726, a Dutch merchant named Engelbert suggested there may have been an alliance between the ruler of Melolo, East Sumba, and the "Black Portuguese"—Portuguese-speaking mestizo Christians, later known as the Topasses (de Roo 1906, 193; Fox 1977, 63). The documents indicate that there was some strain in Sumba's tributary relationship with Bima, which was accepted in some regions but resisted in others. Each sultan claimed a much larger territory than he was really able to control, because he wanted to direct trade and impose taxes. Thus, the claim that Sumba belonged to Bima "from antiquity" was more rhetorical than real, even though it did reflect a long-established trading pattern. Yet the Dutch policy of using the coastal sultanates as intermediaries for dealing with distant islands had the effect of strengthening the sultan's hand, since he retained control of the export market. In 1775, Tekenborgh wrote that several domains along Sumba's northern coast had close relations with Bima, which included marriage alliances and gifts of "people" (i.e., slaves) supplied when needed to the Bimanese court (de Roo 1906, 228). The people of Memboro were most intensely involved in trade with the sultanate, and as a result appeared "more civilized" than peoples of the rest of the island.

Accounts collected from Sumbanese informants indicate that Bima and Java were associated with prestigious trade relations, titles, and imported objects, but people did not see themselves as the subjects of a foreign power. At the beginning of the twentieth century, Wielenga heard that strangers from *tana ndima* had settled in Kodi and Laura and intermarried with local people (Wielenga 1916–18, 20:139). In 1920, Kruyt was told that the people of Laura still remembered paying tribute to the sultan of Bima. The eastern part of the island, his informants said, had been dominated by Bima much earlier, but the "more democratic" domains of the west had had only sporadic contact. The "more refined" and "articulate" people that he met along the northern coast were supposed by him to have developed these superior skills as a result of a long involvement with Bima (Kruyt 1922, 472).

As in the somewhat mythologized depiction of Java and Majapahit, Sumbanese accounts represent their relations with outside powers in terms that suggest relative equality, not subjugation. Indeed, a profound ambivalence is expressed in stories about both European traders and the Bimanese, as in this one, collected by Kruyt in Weyewa in 1920:

> In the old days, the Sumbanese were friends with the "white foreigners" and the Bimanese. They crossed the stone bridge which went from Sasar to the other side. Both groups once came to visit a harvest feast, and followed local custom by engaging in a calf-kicking contest. The foreigners won the first time, and many Sumbanese suffered broken legs. When they moved to boxing, however, the Sumbanese defeated their guests, making blood stream down their faces. Finally, the Sumbanese and their guests started shouting insults at each other, and the foreigners left. A little later, the Sumbanese found an eel. They sent a messenger on horseback to invite the others, but he took so long that the Sumbanese went ahead and ate it up. When the guests finally came, the eel was gone. The Bimanese were furious and became violent. In the end, peace was reestablished, and they agreed to share a meal. The Sumbanese gave them meat that they would not eat (perhaps the Bimanese were already Moslem, and the meat was pork). They became angry again and went home. As they returned, they told their hosts, "We'll get our revenge!" The revenge came in the form of a smallpox epidemic, which killed many people.
>
> (Kruyt 1922, 471)

The story cannot be interpreted literally, since it collapses a mythical time when Sumba was still connected to the other islands of the Lesser Sundas with an event of recent history, the smallpox epidemic of the late nineteenth century. Relations with these foreign groups are cast in the idiom of contests, which later lead to quarrels and the angry departure of the guests. The Europeans did not return, and although the Bimanese came back, they were unable to share a meal. The final explanation interprets the epidemic introduced from other islands as a punishment for violations of the host-guest relationship: because of cultural differences, exchanges of food were not possible, and a reciprocal relationship could not be maintained.

In a somewhat similar vein, the East Sumbanese nobleman Oembu Hina Kapita has written an antiquarian folk history that contains an account of the fifteenth-century Bimanese viceroy Turelia Nggampo, who came to Sumba to establish a power base there:

> This power cannot be compared with that of Dutch colonialism or the Japanese occupation, but was only a recognition of the superior power of the Sang Aji Ruma Mawa Ndapa, since the local rulers of Sumba maintained their own authority. The sovereignty of the Great Raja of Java and the Raja of Bima was not visible, but remained always in the hearts and memories of the people of Sumba, and became the stuff of myths and legends about the *hanggula ratu jawa, hanganji ratu ndima*, "the crown of the Javanese ruler, the hajji title of the Bima ruler." . . . These titles were given to local nobles, as synonyms that also preserved a difference in sense. The *hanggula* was the one who had been in power but was no longer active, while the *hanganji* was the one who was still ruling and still active. The prince who was no longer active was also given the title *karaingu*, coming from the word *karaeng* in the language of the Bugis or Makassarese.
>
> (Kapita 1976b, 17)

It is interesting that Kapita here transposes the contrast between the two foreign sources of power to a differentiation of indigenous types of rulers: the distant but all-encompassing power of Java is presented as the senior, passive party and opposed to the closer and more immediately effective power of Bima. He also brings in a title taken from the rulers of the South Sulawesi kingdom of Goa, which was also used by the related rulers of Sumbawa (Andaya 1981, 164). The combination reveals the complex lineages of foreign powers who were evoked by Sumbanese nobles in claiming an authority legitimated by "great lords" who lived overseas.[2]

[2] Kapita's folk etymologies can be compared to historical evidence on the derivation of these titles. *Sengaji* was a title used in the Moluccas in the seventeenth and eighteenth centuries to refer to "a village head who had almost the same rank as a raja" (Knaap 1987, xx). Ellen (1986) gives it as a title in the sultanate of Ternate. In Manggarai, once the tributary of Bima, *sengaji* refers to the "Highest Being" (G. Forth 1981, 444).

The people of Memboro claim the closest ties with Bima; indeed, a section of Manua Kalada, the ritual center of the domain, is still called Nggaulu Ndima ("the Bima enclosure"). The houses of Bimanese mercenaries who once served the raja of Memboro were located there; also, a number of Sumbanese were said to have migrated to Bima, where they guarded a great gun called Kambeku at the mouth of the Bima river (Needham 1987, 22). Kapita reports an encounter between foreigners from Bima and an indigenous wild spirit which has resonances with Kodi oral traditions: In the village of Sangu Mata, the Bimanese started to excavate a channel when they met a spotted snake with a human head. Terrified, they abandoned their undertaking and returned home (Kapita n.d., 10). The snake resembles Pala Kawata, a spotted python-man who is said, in Kodi, to have defended the island against intruders and even accompanied the culture hero Lendu overseas in the search for life-renewing powers, which resulted in his return with the sea worms (see chapter 3, text #1).

Both "Java" and "Bima" are often cited as the ultimate origins of titles, objects, and finery. Traditional political authority was legitimated by reference to gifts received from foreign powers. Javanese rajas made gifts of fine silk Indian textiles—the *patola* cloths—to subsidiary local rulers, including those on Sumba. Although few of the cloths survive today, they have been extensively copied on local *ikat* textiles. In the eastern part of the island, they shaped decorative motifs once restricted to the nobility (Adams 1969), and in Kodi they were the model of the man's loincloth and funeral shroud (*hanggi wola remba*). Traditional rulers were called "lords of the silk headpiece and the *patola* cloth" (*ratu hunda rangga, ratu ruu patola*), indicating that ownership of the textiles symbolized claims to office. In East Sumba, sumptuary rules made the double-dyed, rust-and-indigo cloths a noble prerogative. The more diverse textiles of the west expressed claims to rank through complexity of design, the icon of gold ear pendants, and the use of deep indigo backgrounds. Wearing an ivory-handled sword or dancing with a gold pendant strung around the neck likewise served as a statement that one had noble ancestors. These particular usages must be placed in the wider context of the archipelago in colonial and precolonial times.

Moslem Mercenaries: A Predatory Expansion over the Seas

The coastal sultanates of Sulawesi, Sumbawa, and Flores figured importantly in trade with the eastern islands from an early period and became intensely involved in local politics in the eighteenth and nineteenth centuries. Many heirloom objects in Sumbanese houses are traced to contacts with *dawa ronda* (literally, "foreigners in cotton sarungs"), a category referring to all the Moslem seafaring peoples who came to the island. The Sumbanese construction of the past is heavily vested in these "history objects" traded from the west, but before we can understand their involvement in local events we must examine the cultural heritage they represented.

Given the importance of military conquest to many of these sultanates, it is hardly surprising that a great many of their sacred objects were weapons, most famously the Javanese kris, swords, spears, and even cannon. Some of these were captured from the enemy, others were acquired through trade, marriage alliances, or the miraculous "discovery" of an unusual and thus apparently spiritually potent object (Andaya 1975, 120).

In his study *Conceptions of State and Kingship in Southeast Asia*, Robert Heine-Geldern describes the importance of regalia in Southeast Asian political life, including the idea that certain objects, such as the royal sword of Cambodia, had their own magical force. This attitude reaches its most developed expression in the Malay Peninsula and Indonesia, where it culminates in "the curious conception prevalent among the Bugis and Makassarese of Celebes, according to which it is really the regalia which reign, the prince merely governing the state only in their name" (Heine-Geldern 1956, 10). The regalia were conceived as immortal and immobile, defining the center of power and geographical space, while the ruler was mortal and mobile, serving, says Shelley Errington (1989, 129), as "a kind of mouthpiece" in contrast to the "stable silence" of the object. Only after his death did the ruler acquire the full sanctity of his objects, for then his own clothing, teeth, and personal effects could join the store of valuables that formed the heirloom treasure of the kingdom.

In the oldest Bugis kingdom, Luwu, royal objects served as placeholders for the titles and responsibilities the ruler could bestow on his subjects (Errington 1989, 124). Titles that included ritual obligations were attached to sacred objects and were given for the recipient's lifetime (Errington 1989, 200). Each family, noble or not, had its own collection of "leavings from the ancestors," which were passed on through the generations and cherished as talismans of the power of the past.

Errington's interpretation emphasizes the stability of local inherited objects both as representations of power and as assertions that descent and "white blood" qualified a ruler to claim authority through sacred objects (1989, 125). Writing about the southern Buginese state of Bone, Andaya (1975, 120) presents an image of much greater political turmoil and change, in which the transfer of sacred objects (*gauking*) could legitimate usurpation or even conquest: "The ruler could be deposed at any time, but the gauking and the rest of the regalia would continue to be accorded the highest veneration in the community. A ruler without the arajang (regalia) had no authority to rule whatsoever, whereas the arajang retained its power by virtue of being considered the representative of the gods on earth."

In 1666–69, the Company fought a war against the kingdom of Goa in South Sulawesi, then one of the most powerful and extensive empires in the history of the archipelago. Just three years earlier, Goa had conquered Bima, and a huge migration of Makassarese to Sumbawa began. A thousand men in twenty-eight ships arrived in 1664, followed a short while later by eight more (de Roo 1906, 243). Fearing the political campaigns of the Buginese prince and Dutch ally Arung Palakka, the refugees fled to the south. Some of them settled in Sumbawa and Flores, intermarrying with coastal Moslems in Bima and Ende, while others roamed the seas from one kingdom to another disrupting normal processes of trade and government (Andaya 1981, 217–18). In 1675, a large community of Makassar refugees was reported to have formed under a Daeng Mamanga at Ende on Flores, and roving bands of Makassar, Bugis, and Mandar refugees started to move farther eastward (Andaya 1981, 163–64). Invited by Arung Palakka, by then the conqueror of Goa, to return home, they refused, suspecting they would be enslaved by the victors (Andaya 1981, 217). Their presence had a great impact on the Sunda seas:

> These refugees constituted an unstable element within the area. They cast their lots with one or another factions within a particular kingdom, thereby creating unnatural or transitory governments which survived at the pleasure of the refugees. Such arrangements bred resentment in the local populace and the eventual expulsion of the refugees. They were then cast adrift once again seeking a home and an ally and making every ambitious leader in a kingdom vulnerable to the attractions of such a powerful group of armed warriors.
>
> (Andaya 1981, 217)

Sumba at the time was a tempting target: since the early fifteenth century, traders from South Sulawesi had visited the island, and by the early 1600s there was a steady market on Sumbawa for products obtained on Sumba.

The character of trade in the Sunda Seas had changed significantly by that time. Although Sumba continued to be called the "Sandalwood Island" by European mapmakers of the sixteenth and seventeenth centuries, its supply of the white fragrant wood quickly dwindled, and most trade interest shifted to Timor (Fox 1977, 61). In the eighteenth and nineteenth centuries, the island's main exports became living things: horses, buffalo, and human slaves. The new "commodities" involved foreign traders much more intensely in local politics and colored perceptions of outside powers with a new dimension of terror.

The Makassar-Endehnese appear in colonial documents relating to Sumba in complaints about "pirates" who raided Dutch ships and competed with them for control of trade in the Sunda Sea. Company officials soon realized that their own chances of exploiting Sumba for slaves depended on the exclusion of these rivals from the area. De Roo (1906, 195n.2) presents the Dutch perspective clearly:

> The Makassarese power in those times made the waters of the Timor archipelago unsafe not only because they committed piracy and captured slaves, but also because they sold imported goods more cheaply than the Company and paid higher prices for local products, as well as selling gunpowder, lead, and rifles to the enemies of the Company. . . . These Makassarese over the years caused great pain and suffering to the Company. Now and then, when their actions got completely out of hand, military expeditions were mounted against them, which would temper their outrageousness for a while but were not enough to stop it completely.

Sumba, in fact, was to remain an intermittent battleground for the two competing forces for the next 150 years.

In 1750, Van den Burg concluded an oral contract with Sumbanese rulers along the northern coast, binding them to trade exclusively with the Dutch East India Company, and not with the Portuguese or the Makassarese. Presents of weapons, beads, gold, and a flag and staff were distributed to those who consented, from ten different regions of middle and East Sumba (de Roo 1906, 196; Kapita 1976b, 21). In 1755, a second written contract was signed with the raja of Mangili, East Sumba, in Kupang, and the Dutch sent an official named Beynon to investigate conditions on the island. He described it as very large, sparsely populated, and disrupted by constant regional warfare; the export of sandalwood, cotton, slaves, and livestock, he concluded, would not be safe until the whole region was pacified (de Roo 1906, 204–5; Kapita 1976b, 21).

The year 1753 saw an intensification of Makassar slave trading activities, and a large raid was conducted in 1758, with hundreds of people captured in the eastern areas of Melolo and Kanatang (de Roo 1906, 196n.2; Needham 1983, 38). The refugees also began to work as mercenaries for local rulers: they supplied forces to the raja of Lewa in central Sumba, for example, for an attack on his enemies in Melolo, accepting fifty-five slaves in payment (Needham 1983, 20). By 1775, fleets of thirty to forty Makassarese praus came into Sumbanese ports each year; the island had become their "general rendez-vous or nesting place" (de Roo 1906, 227; Needham 1983, 21).

The holdings of the Company passed into the hands of the Netherlands East Indies government in 1800. In 1820, the Dutch ship *Pamanoekan*, under the command of J. Batiest, was on its way from Java to Makassar and became stranded on Sumba's western coast, in the region of Lamboya Patialla. Taken prisoner by the local people, Batiest and his men stayed on the island for many months, until an Endehnese ship passed by and took them to Makassar (de Roo 1906, 240). The captain's description of his time on the island, recorded by J. D. Kruseman, trade commissioner of the Timor area, provides the earliest glimpse of daily life in West Sumba and the shifting political situation. The Sumbanese that he encountered drew a very sharp distinction between outsiders—people from beyond their own island or domain—and insiders—those who shared their feasts. The members of the *Pamanoekan* crew seem to have experienced both states, one when they first arrived, the second after they had spent some time in a single village. In the words of Batiest:

> Concerning honesty and faithfulness, the people are prone to great extremes. Men who not only robbed the survivors of the Pamanoe-kan of everything they could take, and even cut their clothes off their bodies and led them as slaves to the mountains, would not steal even so much as a piece of firewood from a neighbor, even if he needed it very badly. At and during harvest time, the homes are often empty for months, and although nothing is hidden, nothing is missed. . . . If they can steal something from a foreigner, they will boast about their skill and delight in their accomplishment; but once the same foreigners have become united to them as members of the clan, sharing a meal of goat meat sacrificed to the deity, then they will have nothing more to fear, and they and their belongings will become just as safe as the life and goods of a native. The people are in fact very friendly, so much so that their goodwill seems almost a contradiction of their fierce appearance. They would not kill a for-eigner or enemy lightly, and would never strike an ally or friend.
>
> (Kruseman 1836, 70–71)

Batiest reported that West Sumba had "a society without kings or chiefs," led by elders of the hereditary nobility who gained their followers through skill in speaking and daring in warfare. Slaves were kept in noble house-holds, but they "ate from the same dish as their masters" and worked and rested beside them. He described his hosts as brave, generous to a fault, and very impressive orators, who ruled through persuasion at large, consensus-based tribal councils and did not coerce others to accept their authority (Kruseman 1836, 72–74).

The hereditary nobility was recognized primarily in council meetings, where their speech was granted the most authority and their eloquence could be demonstrated: "Such meetings always take a long time, even when the case at hand is relatively clear, because a speaker must always be answered by someone else who interprets his words, and the people believe that no important issue should be resolved too quickly. Large gatherings also give them a chance to display oratorical abilities, and this is a society in which rhetorical skill is a source of great pride" (Kruseman 1836, 74). Celebrations were held for the rice harvest, coconut harvest, and alliances with neighboring districts, but there is no mention of the swarming of the sea worms or the *pasola* jousting (see chapter 5). A lunar calendar is suggested, however, by references to the "fasting month" of October, in which sacrifices are dedicated to a spirit who protects ancestral graves (Kruseman 1836, 82).

Domestic life was characterized as "a truly rare example of morality and chastity among Orientals as is found nowadays only in the most remote corners of the world" (Kruseman 1836, 70).[3] People were industrious and kind, if a bit cowardly by Batiest's standards. Although he found Sumbanese warriors strong and cruel in their appearance, their wars seemed "almost child's play," involving much strutting and shaking of spears with relatively little bloodshed (Kruseman 1836, 74). Each side carried swords and spears in a battle formation, but stayed at such a distance that their weapons rarely struck anyone. When someone was injured, the battle was immediately stopped and sacrifices were made to compensate those who had suffered losses.

Relations of traditional hostility between domains did affect travel and communication, however, even if they rarely resulted in the conquest of territory. Heads were taken in wars waged against neighboring domains, in a pattern of continuing enmity for which there was no historical explanation:

> The Sumbanese do not know much about their own history. The current generation is even ignorant of the cause of the wars between

---

[3] Social customs may have changed since Batiest's time. In the 1970s, the domains of Lamboya and Wanokaka had one of the world's highest reported rates of gonorrhea, which the local doctor attributed to frequent changing of sex partners before marriage (Mitchell 1982a, 12). However, it seems most likely that Batiest's remarks concern the absence of prostitution or homosexuality, a state that continues to the present.

Laboya and Manukaka [Wanokaka]. But there is such enmity between these domains that whenever someone crosses the borders set
by the ancestors, armed or unarmed, man, woman, or child, they
must be captured and are put to death immediately. . . . The only
exception is made on the occasion of death feasts, where relatives in
the enemy territory may be invited with a white banner to join in
mourning for a shared ancestor.

(Kruseman 1836, 75–76)

Respect for the dead and for the spirits of the deceased was the primary
idea behind all of the traditional feasts, which were led by the elders of
the clan in the center of the village. The sequence of events was much the
same as is still found on Sumba: guests were greeted with offerings of
betel nut, entertained with singing, dancing, and oratory, and fed large
platefuls of rice and shares of the sacrificed pigs, goats, and water buffalo.
The description of elaborate shared ritual celebrations prompted this early
observer to a nostalgic evocation of the vanished world of antiquity:

One can hardly imagine the feelings a civilized European has when
he sees all this! One sees a mixture of manners, customs, and habits
which bring to mind so many past eras and make one go back to the
time of our own ancestors, when men lived in a state of natural
happiness, such as the era of the Romans, who celebrated in their
camps, hanging their weapons in the trees as they tired of victory,
removing all memory of war and destruction from their minds while
they gave themselves over to the innocent pleasures of a sacrificial
celebration under Italy's warm beautiful sky.

(Kruseman 1836, 81)

The account appears idyllic, especially when contrasted with reports from
East Sumba in only a slightly later period—the late nineteenth century,
after 1860, when slavery was forbidden in the Netherlands East Indies and
the Dutch forces tried to regain control of the Sunda seas. At the time of
Batiest's visit, however, isolated western districts like Kodi and Lamboya,
many days away from the centers of trade, were to remain sheltered from
the most intense raiding for only a few more years.

In 1843, an Arab horse trader, Sharif Abdulrahman, founded the port
town of Waingapu at the best natural habor on the north coast of Sumba.
He was "an extremely enterprising but sinister character" (Needham 1983,
24), well connected to both the Dutch resident Gronovius and the Endehnese. Authorized to develop the export of horses from Sumba to Java,

Flores, and Sumbawa, he was soon also involved in the burgeoning slave trade (de Roo 1906, 248).

Endehnese communities rose up along the northern coast and soon were deeply involved in local politics: in 1860 Etto, the crown prince of Ende and married to the daughter of the Sumbanese chief at Patawang (de Roo 1906, 245), sent ten ships and five to six hundred men to help the raja of Kapunduk wage war against his enemies in the interior. The Dutch resident attacked and sank the ships at Kapunduk, then signed an agreement with four local rulers who said they wanted to be freed from the oppression and molestation of the Endehnese. Sharif, though married to Etto's sister, advised the Dutch to expel the Endehnese in order to stop the slave trade, perhaps because he feared them as trade competitors and a challenge to his own supremacy (de Roo 1906, 266; Needham 1983, 28).

In 1861, the export of slaves to Lombok and Sumbawa was reported to be dying out because it was no longer profitable, but the Endehnese were now plundering the interior, burning villages and capturing people to sell them to Sumbanese rulers on the coast. "The spread of the Endehnese plague not only outside Sumba but now into the interior has become even worse than it was before," lamented a Dutch report on the slave trade (de Roo 1906, 245). Because the Dutch were stronger on sea than on land, this new development threatened their already unstable control of the island's politics.

The Makassar-Endehnese have been presented as the villains of the island's history, "the scourge of Sumba" who caused tremendous suffering wherever they went. Needham (1983, 39, 49) shares the interpretation of many Dutch writers when he says:

> It does not call for great imaginative powers to conceive how the Endehnese domination of Sumba would have proceeded if it had not been forestalled by the Dutch intervention, or what would have been the condition of the island if the Endehnese had wreaked their will without restraint or limit. . . . The history of Sumba presents the example of a land formerly ravaged by the slave trade but eventually liberated from the terror of forcible transportation to distant countries.

It is useful to remember that the Dutch also participated in the slave trade until 1860 and were not sharply distinguished from their rivals by local populations, who suspected all outsiders of coming as robbers and marauders (*penyamun*). The leverage exercised by these outside groups depended on warfare, slavery, and island instability, which created conditions ideal for ambitious local leaders to form alliances with the Endehnese, Dutch authorities, or Arab horse traders to further their own political goals.

External and Internal Slavery on Sumba

Slavery seems to have had a rather different meaning in the closed, indigenous context described by Batiest in Lamboya of the early 1800s relative to the "open market" in which human beings were traded as commodities along the northern coast at the end of the nineteenth century. Samuel Roos, the first Dutch controller sent to the island in 1862, wrote that slavery was an indigenous institution "so deeply ingrained in the Sumbanese character that it would be hard to bring it to an abrupt stop" (1872, 11). He noted that a ruler's power depended on his control of slaves, who provided a fixed pool of labor for the cultivation of wet-rice fields and whose status was marked by ritual and legal subordination. A very large number of people were slaves: Gregory Forth (1981, 462) found that nearly 38 percent of the population of Rindi was of slave descent, and of them over 90 percent had been attached to the noble clan. Village heads from Kapunduk and Lewa estimated in 1988 that fully 75 percent of their populations was descended from slaves.

Slavery in the eastern part of the island resembled the "closed systems" of other parts of upland Southeast Asia (Reid 1983, 161–63). Slaves were inherited, connected to noble houses, and identified with those houses' paternalistic power. The nobility themselves were called the "mother moon and father sun" (*inya wula ama lado*)—those with dominion over the area—and their hereditary servants were the "feet of the sun, the feet of the moon" (*wisi wula, wisi lado*). This form of slavery implied an obligation on the part of the master to assist his subjects, by finding them wives and homes, paying their bridewealth and (in the colonial period) their taxes, and providing clothing and food as "a kind of poor relief" (Versluys 1941) when times were hard. Hereditary slaves (*ata pa helu* or *ata memango*) were never sold, sacrificed, or used for hard labor, and they could be transferred from one house to another only if they accompanied a noblewoman as the "bearers of her *sirih* pouch." Referred to as "children in the house," these servants were often invested with important ritual duties. At funerals and important ceremonies, hereditary slaves were dressed in gold, fine textiles, and ivory, and they paraded the finest ornaments of the house.

Quite different was the fate of war captives, outsiders who were taken prisoner and could be used for ritual sacrifices. Called the "feet of wild pigs, paddy gathered on horseback" (*wisi wari ruta, pare pa mandara*) (Versluys 1941), they were treated as casually acquired plunder or booty. Reports from precolonial times say war captives were killed at the funerals of important nobles in East Sumba (Kruyt 1922, 540). In West Sumba, some domains were linked in gruesome exchanges of sacrificial victims for ritual purposes. In Anakalang, a Weyewa girl was purchased and sacrificed so her skin could be used to cover a sacred drum; and in Lauli, a Wanukaka captive was strangled as an offering to a python spirit (Kruyt 1922, 540–43). In Weyewa, captives were sacrificed whenever a sacred house was rebuilt (Kuipers 1990, 20–21). In Kodi, I photographed the skulls of sacrifice victims buried under the pillars of the headhunting house (Uma Katoda) in Ndelo (see p. 313) and was told about the sacrifice of young slave girls to cover the "drum with human skin" (Hoskins 1988a).

The demand for victims for ritual sacrifices, however, could never have been as great as that for live captives in the late nineteenth century. Certainly, the development of an export trade in human beings changed the nature of raiding and regional warfare profoundly. In oral histories, my Kodi informants recalled the 1880s as a time of escalating violence and attacks between one domain and another. Headhunting, a ritualized form of traditional enmity between domains, was accompanied by a new greed for captives as sellable property. A nobleman traveling to the coast to sell some of his own captives risked ambush and decapitation himself, as in the locally famous case of Rato Malo, whose head was stored in the Kodi village of Ratenggaro for thirty years before his son negotiated for its return (Hoskins 1989a). Other cases I heard of concerned raids on Weyewa and Tana Rio, from which prisoners could be transported to Wai Kalo to be sold to the Endehnese. Headhunters who traveled along the south coast, to Gaura and Lamboya, were more isolated from the trade and were locked in a cycle of vengeance killings that seems to have been linked to patterns of political achievement within the society (Hoskins forthcoming [1]).

The intensification of slave raids and the export of human captives in the second half of the nineteenth century arose because of the mercantile rivalries of Endehnese traders, Dutch colonial officers, and corrupt middlemen like the Arab Sharif. While they did not invent the sale of human beings in the area, they certainly seem to have developed it to an extent unimaginable in the precolonial context. The impact of slave raids was felt most heavily along the northern coast, which Resident Gronovius claimed in 1855 had been almost totally depopulated by slave raiders (cited in Fox 1977). In the more fertile interior and southern coastal areas, the impact was more one of destabilizing local politics, since a few indigenous warlords obtained monopolies on gunpowder and firearms, which they used to raid others.

The peoples of West Sumba, organized into ceremonial confederations but not under the rule of a single noble lord, were more successful than those of East Sumba at defending their autonomy. Although the Endehnese traveled throughout the interior, they were never able to establish permanent bases in the west or make alliances with important local rulers. One Endehnese soldier told the Dutch controller A. L. Couvreur that the bodies of people of West Sumba "could not be pierced" and that special magical preparations protected them, produced by their "secluded priests" (*ratu sepi*) (Couvreur 1917, 213, 215).

Moslem mercenaries were both admired and feared for their control of a superior technology of war and sea travel; consequently, some uneasy alliances were formed despite cultural differences. Two ancestral villages in Kodi, Manu Longge and Wei Hyombo, were founded by Moslems and contain Islamic burial stones in their centers. The descendants of these early ancestors later "converted to paganism" by eating pork with their fellows at *marapu* feasts. A great many other villages have a house called the Uma Dawa, or "Foreigner's House," where people from other islands lived and intermarried with local families, eventually becoming officially adopted. One Florinese visitor, a man remembered only as Rato Daing,[4] became the brother-in-law of the first Kodi raja, Loghe Kanduyo, and the father of the second, Ndera Wulla. He sailed away from the island before his son was born and never returned, but left behind a legacy of alliances with foreigners that his son was to repeat.

At the start of the twentieth century, when the Dutch tried to dissolve the Endehnese communities of the northern ports of Waingapu, Memboro, and Wai Kalo, a number of Endehnese moved into Kodi, establishing the village of Pero (Needham 1968). Now four generations old, the community of six hundred Moslems is distinguished by its architecture (Bugis-style wooden bungalows instead of tall thatch towers over a bamboo frame), Islamic cemetery, and involvement in sailing and trade. Most men make a living from fishing and livestock sales, while women weave sarungs with commercial dyes, not the traditonal Kodi indigo. A few wealthier merchants own motor-powered boats that can travel as far as Ende. There is a small mosque, and in the 1980s eight of the most prominent family

---

[4]The name is in fact a coupling of two different titles. *Rato* is the Kodi title given, usually posthumously, to leaders in feasting or warfare, while *Daeng* is a title for middle-level Bugis or Makassarese nobles, which has the literal meaning of "older sibling" (Errington 1989, 197).

heads had made the pilgrimage to Mecca. Like their predecessors, present-day *dawa ronda* are suspected of transporting contraband and violating government regulations on dynamite fishing, but they have been able to negotiate compromises with local authorities that allow them to continue in these activities as long as they are not overtly disruptive.

Batavia and the Dutch Colonial Project

Dutch traders and colonial officers remained a distant presence for the Sumbanese until the beginning of the twentieth century. Like the early rulers of Java and Bima, they claimed dominion over the island but for a long time made no moves to impose state control. When the colonial army finally arrived to enforce rules against slave trading, regional warfare, and the plundering of foreign ships, they were greeted as "the foreign mother and stranger father" (*inya dawa, bapa ndimya*), whose paternalistic power was conflated with that of earlier kingdoms that had intermittently legitimated local rulers in return for tribute. The Dutch came bearing prestigious gifts, gold and silver staffs of office that were conferred on prominent Sumbanese, to create the offices of *raja* or *bestuurder* (ruler) and *raja kecil* or *onderbestuurder* (subruler).

The goals of Dutch colonial policy for Sumba were not articulated until the late nineteenth century because the island was judged to be of little economic value, remaining "scantly regarded and neglected" (Fox 1977, 164). In the provincial capital of Kupang, the first person to pay much attention to the island was Resident Gronovius, who wanted to expand the horse trade and bring Dutch planters to settle the land, giving them land on credit to cultivate coffee, sugar, cotton, pepper, and tobacco. Although the project was never realized, his suggestion that Christian Indonesians from other islands be encouraged to migrate to Sumba was prophetic:

> To the idea of colonizing the Sandalwood Island, I still remain devoted. My stay there and my travels through the island convince me that such an undertaking would be crowned with success. There would be great blessings in this for the development, civilizing and protecting of a dumb but good-natured population, who are now the prey of usurious traders, pirates and insignificant but vexatious rajas. I would hope that if the Government agreed to such an undertaking, a colony of Rotinese and Savunese would be transferred to Sumba.
>
> (Gronovius, cited in Fox 1977, 164)

Christian Savunese began to settle on Sumba in the 1800s, though not initially because of Dutch policy. A royal marriage alliance between rulers on the two islands was the reason for the first colony, established at Kadumbu on the northeast coast in 1848 (Wijngaarten 1893). Only a few Rotinese ever came, but later in the nineteenth century a considerable number of Savunese mercenaries were brought by the Dutch to help "pacify" the island and control wars between local rulers.

Dutch policy at the turn of the century was based on an assessment of the "character" of different populations on the islands and their usefulness for carrying out the colonial project. The Savunese had developed a reputation for bravery and skill in battle and so were recruited into the army. It also seems the Christian converts on Savu may have been pressured to leave the island and seek their fortunes elsewhere (Fox 1977, 172). Although armed and often uncooperative, they appeared to the Dutch more controllable than the Moslem Endehnese. But the Savunese settled only in the region of Melolo, where they maintained a bounded, endogamous community, while the Endehnese continued their predatory expansion throughout the western parts of the island, cementing military alliances with local rulers by intermarriage.

The Sumbanese of this time were often depicted as naive victims of the two invading forces. The Dutch resident Humme in 1876 described the Sumbanese as "timid and cowardly . . . never having left his island, [he] considers any foreigner a dangerous wild animal from which he quickly takes flight" (cited in Fox 1977, 171). Unfamiliar with firearms, the local population was quickly terrified into leaving the territories conquered by the Savunese and was unable to take them back. Soon, however, Sumbanese were purchasing firearms from both the Endehnese and Savunese, as well as hiring foreigners as auxiliary troops in wars between domains. The Sumbanese rulers were described as living "mainly from warfare which they conduct in an inhuman fashion," intent on capturing slaves for export (*Koloniaal Verslag* 1877, 37).

The Dutch policy of encouraging Savunese migration after 1890 should be interpreted as part of the wider *Islampolitiek*, which aimed to produce a buffer between Dutch-dominated areas and areas where Islam had diminished Dutch influence (Bigalke 1984; Kipp 1990). The Dutch feared the political power of Islam and did not trust any of the Moslem seafaring peoples in the region. They therefore allied themselves with the Savunese, defending their presence on the island with military power. In 1875, the ruler of Batakepedu tried to drive both the Dutch and the Savunese from his territory. After an attempted negotiation, the Dutch gave the Savunese ruler a gunboat to transport armed men and weapons; they crushed the

Sumbanese rebels, forcing them to accept the presence of foreigners along the coasts (Fox 1977, 172).

The Savunese settlement in Melolo carved out an ecological niche on the parched northern coastline by tapping the sap of the lontar palm. Associated with Christianity and education, the "Savunese foreigners" (*dawa haghu*) traveled to the western part of the island as schoolteachers and village evangelists, bearing a religious message in the form of the Malay Bible. Local Kodi perceptions were that the supernatural arsenal of the Savunese included black magic and witchcraft (*marango*). Because of these suspicions, to this day few Sumbanese will eat the small brown patties of lontar sugar produced by the Savunese. Their link to an alien faith practiced by white people also supposedly gave them access to magical procedures that made the skin invulnerable to bullets, caused abortions and miscarriages in one's enemies, and involved sacrifices to the spirit of wealth.

Mistrust, however, is combined with a recognition of a shared cultural heritage and a long history of contact between the two islands. Of all the foreigners, the Savunese were and still are the closest to the Sumbanese. Savu is also often referred to as the "younger brother" of Sumba, for it is said that after the ancestral migration across the stone bridge at Sasar, one junior member of the party continued on to Savu. It should be noted that the younger brother in these narratives is usually more clever and more enterprising than his seniors. While Sumbanese commentators acknowledge the industry and ambition of the Savunese, they often disparage their relative deficit in honesty and loyalty. Haghu, the local designation for Savu, is a common name given to Kodi children; it is also the name of the hero of a series of entertaining tales about a crafty younger brother who makes his own fortune, rising from abject orphanhood to great wealth.

In Kodi oral tradition, the arts of metalworking and indigo dyeing were brought to the island from Savu as part of a complex of occult techniques passed down through the generations. A number of Kodi ancestral villages contain a house named Uma Haghu ("Savunese House"), where Savunese ancestors are recognized and metalworking and indigo dyeing are practiced. The spear used in divination is addressed as *mone haghu*, or "Savunese man"; it is told to "cut through" to the source of trouble and root out the reasons for ancestral displeasure (Hoskins 1988a). The secret combination of dyes used to make the darkest form of indigo is a heritage from a Savunese woman, whose "blue arts" included knowledge of herbalism, contraception, and infertility cures (Hoskins 1988b).

As they gained a greater knowledge of Sumbanese society, Dutch visitors began to speculate that the power of the wealthy warlords was counterbalanced by that of an indigenous spiritual authority, the *ratu*. Several hundred years of more intensive involvement in the related polities of Flores, Timor, and Roti had prepared them to encounter the recurrent social phenomenon of dual leadership and established a pattern for incorporating it into local administration:

> A common feature of many of the political systems of the Timor area is dual sovereignty—a division between a person endowed with spiritual authority and one or more persons who exercise political power on behalf of this spiritual authority. . . . In the signing of treaties, therefore, it was often the executive figures of these various territories who obtained the recognition of the Dutch as rulers and legitimate representatives of their states. Not infrequently, these recognized rulers did not have the authority to command the recognition of inhabitants of their own territories, who either opposed them or recognized some higher traditional figure. Local legends to this day abound with stories about this kind of confusion over legitimate rule.
>
> (Fox 1977, 68)

Reading the accounts of the earliest administrators, Roos and Couvreur, in fact, we often see them struggling with local categories and trying to understand how they could be used for the purposes of colonial administration.

Both Roos and Couvreur were concerned to determine the relationship between military power and genealogical precedence as bases for leadership, and each provides a somewhat different view of the raja as either the head of a descent group or a master of force. Roos (1872, 8–9) argues that descent is an important criterion for social and ritual status, but real leadership must be achieved through conquest:

> The rajas should be considered not so much as kings but as the most important person in the domain, where the aristocrats and wealthy warriors remain the main actors, as long as they can remain in power through the control of slaves. The Raja of Tabundung, the head of the so-called royal line from which the most important rajas are descended, is poor. He lacks the power to enrich himself at the expense of others; he is not feared. But the rajas of Batakapedu and Kawangu (Sudu), who rule through robbery and murder, are feared and obeyed, and there are many others like them.

Couvreur (1917, 215), by contrast, argues that the power of the conquering rajas was balanced by a different kind of hidden, supernatural power exercised by the *ratu*, saying colonial officials had to be especially cautious in dealing with this figure:

> The *ratu* . . . performs ritual offerings that can bring calamity to the community, so it is necessary to treat him as a friend. . . . In everyday life, he is completely ordinary, a poor little man whose appearance gives no clues of his importance. . . . But the *ratu* can, if he wants, act as the medium of mystical power in its supreme form, exercising a great influence, greater even than [that exercised by] the chief of the domain; hence, if the chief seems personally weak, or the times are troubled, one should keep a close eye on the *ratu*'s actions. During these periods, colonial authorities on Sumba have discovered that it was not the weak chief of the domain but another person, who never showed himself and was always in the background, who had the greatest influence. That was correct; the authority had simply stumbled onto the *ratu*'s existence, since the *ratu* in West Sumba is always isolated or in seclusion.

The power of the "hidden *ratu*" was mysteriously associated with the power of the indigenous population to resist outside domination. The conventional interpretation, presented by the missionary Wielenga and endorsed by Couvreur in his colonial policies, was that there had been a diarchic division of powers between the "priest" (*ratu*) and "noble" (*maramba*):

> The *ratu* was originally the sovereign. He was the authentic ruler, but then the spiritual and worldly functions became split. The *ratu* was obligated to live in mystery and isolation, and thus lost his worldly power. He delegated it . . . to another related family or descent line, but in the same clan. . . . So the *marapu* of the *ratu mangu tana* are found in a subordinate house in Middle and East Sumba, but in the west they are not subordinate.
>
> (Couvreur 1917, 217)

In the end, though, it is difficult to reconcile this version with the diversity of ritual divisions found in Sumba today, where a clear division between "spiritual" and "worldly" functions is not so clear.

The role of the *ratu* was, even in these early accounts, concerned not so much with "spiritual" affairs as with agriculture and the calendar. His office expresses the concerns of the whole population to avert plagues, provide rain, and assure the success of the rice crop. He was opposed to the warrior, the master of force, who was not purely "worldly" in his orientation, since he used a vast array of magical weapons, potions, prayers, and charms to enhance his skill in battle. What distinguished them was the fact that the *ratu*'s power was based on concerns *shared* by everyone, having to do with fertility of the land and crops, while the warrior had the *differentiating* attributes of a conqueror, who stands out from his companions by his skills in battle.

An important difference between the eastern and western halves of the island, which operated with fundamentally different political institutions, came into play here as well. In Kodi, an independent priesthood maintained a certain autonomy alongside the various military leaders. Because the smooth operation of the complex calendrical cycle was essential to the well-being of everyone, the Rato Nale retained the highest ceremonial rank in the domain—if only by means of a relatively fragile and diffuse form of ritual authority. In the eastern domains where the Dutch had had greater contact with local rulers, this independent priesthood had largely been incorporated into the political power of the nobleman. In Umalulu, the *ratu* retained only a few shreds of their former autonomy (Kapita 1976b); in Kapunduk, they were assimilated to slaves (Adams 1974); and in Rindi, the priestly function had almost completely merged with other duties of the nobility (G. Forth 1981).

The program to bring "civilization" (*beschaving* in Dutch) to the island had to begin, therefore, with a change in its leaders, who had to become convinced of the necessity to submit to a central administration and co-operate with it in efforts to control the local population. As Couvreur (1917, 219) states, "Once we know who and what these leaders are, we understand that we can only rule with and through them. The rajas, noble chiefs, and heads of descent groups (*kabisus*) must have our full attention, and also the *ratu*. The first three to be used in governmental administration and information, the *ratu* only as a source of information, since he can play no direct role in government." The Dutch decision that the authority of the *ratu* was not "governmental," despite its great importance, was crucial to future interactions with figures such as the Rato Nale, who controlled the center of the Kodi polity through control of the calendar.

As the first civil administrator to take effective control of the western part of the island, Couvreur implemented a colonial policy that shifted the meaning of diarchic terms and brought them more closely into line with Western notions of the division of church and state, religion and politics. As the origin narratives of chapter 3 show, the precolonial division had a quite different foundation, for the *ratu* was the guardian of important objects and the passive center of the cycle of time. In Kodi, the polarity was established between the passive ritual authority of the *rato marapu*, the priest whose seclusion within the village protected the crops and the rhythm of the seasons, and the *rato katoda*, the war leader who used his magical powers to raid neighboring peoples and appropriate their vitality for his own people. The competition for life and political power was played out between domains through the taking of heads and the capture of prisoners. The power of the Sea Worm Priest was centrifugal: it spiraled outward from him, the unmoving center that held together the round of seasons and agricultural activities. The power of the headhunting leader, by contrast, was centripetal: it turned inward to the center, bringing the trophy heads back into the domain and placing their fertile, vital energies at the disposition of the victors.

In making contact with the peoples of West Sumba, the Dutch tried to displace the value of the *ratu* and the "founding objects," which represented the indigenous polity, by offering their own alternative: the gold staff of the office of raja. In doing so, they were implicitly playing upon a contradiction that existed within the ritual objects controlled by the *ratu*—for many of them were imported, appropriated objects, taken from an acquisitive, conquering power, then used to contain the threat of external domination and reabsorb its charismatic power into the center of the polity.

Distant Wealth and Its Distribution

The relations of the various foreign populations on the island to the sources of wealth and power are evident in a Kodi version of the "money tree" story: In the "foreign land" (*tana dawa*), a tree grows that bears fruit of gold, silver, and copper. Since the Dutch were the first to gather this fruit, they got the gold pieces. The Moslem sailors were the second, gathering many silver *rijkdollars*. The Savunese were the third, collecting copper coins which they ate in the form of lontar sugar. When the Sumbanese came, the tree had already been stripped bare, and they were told to travel back to their own island to "work the land and weed the grass" (*dari cana, batu rumba*), because the riches of those who do not labor had already been plundered by others.[5]

Before Dutch control of Sumba became a reality in the early twentieth century, foreign powers were seen primarily as sources of wealth. Trade was the paradigmatic form of the precolonial encounter, and when efforts were made to establish political alliances through signed contracts with

[5] Witkamp (1912, 486) gives another version of this story, presented as the speculation of his East Sumbanese host about the source of money for the Dutch and others. He does not, however, mention the Endehnese and Savunese in this context.

local rulers, the local perception was that they were bound to a new trading agreement, not to a sovereign political state. The legitimation of foreign powers was sought by means of gold and silver objects, some conferred directly by the Dutch on local people, some stolen from shipwrecks.

A story I heard about a sword with a golden handle illustrates this theme. Sometime near the end of the nineteenth century a ship anchored off the bay at Rada Kapal to trade food for metal and cloth. A man from the hilltop village of Ratenngaro spotted one of the sailors carrying the sword and decided to tempt him by sending his beautiful daughter bare-breasted to greet the newcomer. She offered him her betel bag, and the sailor immediately grasped at her breasts. Then her father and brothers grabbed the man and took him prisoner. "According to our custom, he has committed a great offense and must pay a fine," they insisted. The Endehnese ship captain agreed and forced the man to give up his sword. It was called *katopo huhu ana*, the "sword of the daughter's breasts," and remained as an heirloom in the village for many years. At the time of my fieldwork, it had been pawned to the former raja to pay a gambling debt. "If I still had the sword in my possession, I could have been a raja too," the family of its former owner insisted. "The glimmer of the gold was as bright as that of the raja's staff."

Whether its acquisition is legitimate or illegitimate, accomplished by delegation or by conquest, an important foreign object conveys power and represents an ability to command, or at least to exert a certain mystical influence over events. In the following chapters, we will see how objects become attached to narratives, to ritual offices, and to social action, through a process in which the object becomes an actor in history and history itself becomes embedded in the object.

2

The Local Origins of Time

The Day, Month, and Seasons

What, then, is time? If no one asks me, I know. If someone asks me to explain, I cannot tell him.

St. Augustine

The past, in many of its most important aspects, has been imported to Sumba. The ancestors came originally from a faraway land to the west and had to cross the sea to come to the island where they made their home. Valuables which they brought at that time, or traveled to other places to acquire later, are the markers of wider historical processes that bind the whole region together. The past is also concerned with the creation of hierarchical difference, and with the acquisition of objects that distinguish one person from another.

Time, however, is considered a local invention. The ancestors arrived a long time ago, in an age of origins (*e nawu*) before people knew the experience of death, or loss, or temporal variation. According to the narrative traditions, it was only after they came to the island that the divisions of time came into being and time units were perceived and named. Perception of the passage of time and of mortality are universals that transcend hierarchical differences and reveal what is shared by all human beings.

"Time" in the English sense cannot, however, be given a precise translation in Kodi. Kodi has a host of words to designate English ideas such as "one time" (*heimihyango*), the "present time" (*henene*), the "time of day" (*piri a lodo*), and the "time of year" (*piri a ndoyo*), but none of these has the all-encompassing scope of the English word *time*. This is not to say that time is not a category of Kodi experience, or not something that can be the subject of reflection and speculation. Rather, this fact only underscores the fact that in English we collapse a number of separate concepts to make our own category of "time," whereas in many other cultures these notions may be kept more rigorously separate. This separation does not give these cultures a sense of "timelessness"; instead it allows them to distinguish different aspects of time more carefully than we do ourselves.

The experience of time takes two major forms, which could be said to be universals in human perception: sequence and duration (Goody 1968, 31). In Kodi, these are labeled with the terms *katadi* and *mandeinya*. Sequence designates the order in which acts are performed and can be approximated by the English notions of "steps" or "stages" along a continuum. The experience of duration refers to the relative span of events and the intervals between them and is indicated in English with phrases such as a greater or lesser "length of time." The English terms are spatialized, reflecting a need for images of physical objects in space (a ladder, a pathway, a length of string or cloth). In contrast, the Kodi terms are more abstract. Physical "lengths" are designated with another term, *maloyo*, so the term for duration, *mandeinya*, has a uniquely temporal reference. Similarly, although sequences often unfold across space, the term *katadi* does not presuppose a spatial referent; images of steps, ladders, and pathways (*lete*) may be used in metaphoric speech, but for simply expressing temporal progression they are unnecessary.

The distinction between sequence and duration is especially interesting because it separates discrete actions that can be repeated and arranged in a particular order, on the one hand, from continuous and indivisible ones, on the other. Sequence assumes the possibility of repetition; duration implies that some processes may be irreversible. Leach (1961) argues that the union of these two logically distinct notions in a single category of time is due to a Western religious heritage: by equating the irreversibility of time with the possibility of its repetition, we deny the commonsense truth of our own mortality.

Kodi narrative traditions dealing with origins of the day, month, and year reflect this problem. They present time, in the sense of duration, the experience of time slipping away from us, as coming into being with the genesis of oppositions such as night and day, the waxing and waning of the moon, and the wet and dry seasons. The narratives argue, with keen phenomenological insight, that our awareness of time passing appears only with the knowledge of our mortality. When we come to realize that our days are numbered, then we seek actively to number them, and systems of time reckoning come into use. Sequence, the possibility of ordering events and counting them, becomes relevant once our own duration becomes short-lived.

Time is concretized in notions of the day, month, and seasons by peoples all over the world, since these reflect natural oscillations that are part of all human experience. Artificial intervals such as the week, the epoch, the historical age, or the period, by contrast, are not universals, and in places like Kodi they are in fact relatively recent conceptual imports. Now that many Kodi speakers are fluent in Indonesian, they use words like *masa* (period) or *jaman* (era) that have a long and complex history in many Malay cultures and religious traditions (McKinley 1979). These terms have no local equivalents, however, and generally refer exclusively to the period since the Dutch colonial conquest, when "history" broke into local time. The stories told about the local origins of time differences reflect on the "natural" categories that are part of all time experiences and how these diverge from "historicized" categories that follow a particular path to reach the island.

When the Kodi say that time did not begin until their ancestors arrived on Sumba, they give a primacy to their own social experience and endow it with cosmological significance. Aside from such narratives, ultimate origins or eschatological issues receive little formal attention. The past, in most of its aspects, is treated relatively realistically in Kodi narratives. Only through their accounts of how time started do Kodi narrators place themselves, at least briefly, at the origin of a world order.

It has often been noted that a local view of the world is, primarily and most importantly, a view of time. The perception of how time passes is also a perception of life and what it has to offer. As a preamble to our wider discussions, then, let us turn to Kodi stories about the origin of time.[1]

The Day

THE ORIGINS OF NIGHT AND DAY

Once, very long ago, the world existed as an undivided continuum. It was neither dark nor light, but always murky. People lived for a while, and as their bodies wore out they would shed their old skins and rejuvenate. They went through cycles of youth and old age, but they did not

---

[1] All narratives have been translated by the author from a recorded text, usually with the assistance of Kodi commentators who transcribed parts of the text and helped with the rendering of ritual speech. Some repetition has been edited out, but I have made no substantive changes in the telling. Passages recited in ritual speech have been printed in a format that highlights the use of parallel verse (and also its special status as the most authoritative and "unchanging" section of the story). All narrators were older men, with minimal schooling, who "owned" the story concerned. (See the discussion in chapter 3 of narratives that are "held" or "grasped" by a specific owner.)

The first rice and corn harvested from each garden is cut by a woman and placed in a special basket to be given to the priests who control the oscillation of wet and dry seasons. 1984. Photograph by the author.

die. The sun was close to the earth, the sky was not far away, and people could easily go up to the heavens.

One day Mbora Poka built a house that was taller than the houses of any his fellows, and because the sun was so close, the thatch on his house tower caught fire. "Couldn't you move the sun a little farther away, at least part of the time, so that our houses will be safe?" he asked the Creator.

"Yes, I can create a division of night and day, so the sun will be absent half the time. But with that division come other divisions. People will no longer grow old and then rejuvenate. Their own lives will come to an end, and they will die."

Not long after that, Mbora Poka noticed that his own body was not returning to its youthful form, but starting to grow old and brittle. Gradually his limbs began to rot and disintegrate, and he became the first victim of leprosy [*mboghi mopiro*, "decay while still alive"]. Finally he sat down under a banyan tree near the river and heard the cry of a blackbird [*kula*]. This signaled that his time had come, and he became the first Sumbanese person to die, and also the first ancestor.

Since that day, all other persons have also grown old and died. At their funerals, we repeat his name, saying we must all come to the same end:

Now we must all die	Henene maka na mate kaheka
Like Mbyora at the banyan tree	Mbyora la maliti
We cannot push back	Nja pa weinggelango a
The tides of the flowing river	A were wei lyanggaro
Now we all pass away	Henene make na heda kaheka
Like Pyoka at the *waringin* trunk	Pyoka la kadoki
We cannot escape	Nja pa hundarona a
The border of all human life	Likye loko mbaku

This was also the beginning of the reckoning of time, when people began to count the months and number the years [*baghe a wulla, ghipo a ndoyo*], because the period that they spent on earth was now limited. The living and the dead became divided, and people began to bear children as the replacements of those gone before, the breath that is born again [*dadi cou pa helu, hungato pa dadi*]. The living tried to make bargains with their ancestors: they promised to give feasts and sacrifices in order to extend the time given them on earth, and so exchanges began with the invisible world.[2]

Narrated by Temba Palaka, Wei Walla, Bukambero

[2] This story is clearly related to the Weyewa myth about Mbyora Paku presented in Kuipers 1990, 36, but it differs from it in several important ways. In the Weyewa variant, Mbyora Paku does not build a house that catches fire but simply asks for the Creator to let the Sun and Moon "live and die again" because the earth is too hot. His actions cause not his own death but that of a respected elder, and he does not suffer first the deterioration of leprosy and then the knowledge of his own demise in the blackbird's song. In some other variants, the earth's heat continues until it is shot out of the sky by Umbu Tindu, in a story with obvious relations to

The last lines announce several important themes in Kodi attitudes toward time: timekeeping is a calculation that emerged only as a form of struggle against mortality; exchange is the key manifestation of this struggle on the ritual stage; and the creation of descendants is the only effective way to assure one's continuation after death. The finiteness of human life provided the first measure of other finite entities, like days, months, and years. Progressions, intervals, and cycles are given meaning through narrative, which makes the relation between parts intelligible. The sense of loss and incompleteness that resulted from the division of the living and the dead becomes the prime motivation for the performance of rituals.

Another aspect of this story is its highlighting of the disruptive influence of individual striving. Mbora Poka's attempt to build the tallest house was a form of hubris that eventually dislodged the self-renewing continuity of human life. His competitive urge to stand out from his fellows brought about the curse of human mortality, a curse only partly mitigated by the possibility of continuing life in the form of future generations. Even today, it is recognized that tall house towers attract lightning and risk the destruction of whole villages by fire; they are nonetheless built, material proof of the leadership of particular individuals who dare to defy the gods' authority to control the heavens.

The origin stories provide a way to understand both the uniqueness of distinct and irreversible events and the order and structures by which they can be apprehended. The stories must be understood in a creative tension with the commonsense vocabulary used to talk about time, where these abstract concepts are applied to the contexts of daily life and realized in human experience. Ritual time operates on somewhat different principles from the mundane time of routine activities. Before we turn to deliberate divisions and manipulations of Kodi temporality, it is necessary to examine the terms of ordinary speech that characterize daily life.

Time and tense are not always marked in Kodi expressions, and certain conversations are carried on with some vagueness about actual sequences of events. If precision is desired, it can be accomplished by careful use of modifiers such as "already" (*mengeka*) and "not yet" (*nja pango*), and by a particle, *kya* (or with a direct object, *nikya*), which indicates a completed action. But one can also choose to speak in a "timeless world" to a much greater degree than is possible in English. As a general rule, it is easy to

---

the Kodi account of the origins of the phases of the moon (Kuipers 1990, 54). Another related story about the origins of differentiated time from a shattered unity appears in McKinnon 1991, 38–62.

specify the exact temporal location of events occurring within a few days of present time, but increasingly difficult to specify either their location or their duration as they become more distant.

Although the notions of sequence and duration are not spatialized, an overlap of spatial and directional terms in the vocabulary does order "before" and "after" as "in front of" and "behind." Ancient times are not referred to as "far away from the present" or "distant," but as having "come in front of" (*la ma ulu*) specific events in a particular sequence. Generations that follow in time come "behind" (*ha muri*) and follow the preceeding one in space. Metaphors referring to the future may use spatial segments when a specific pathway or journey is indicated. Thus, a man may say, "I haven't yet come to that point" (*nja ku duki pyango*), in referring, for example, to a sequence of rituals that he is planning to sponsor, but one cannot speak in more general terms of the "times that lie ahead of us." In fact, it is extremely difficult to discuss the future in any abstract terms. The Indonesian phrase *waktu yang datang*, itself a rather ungainly way of designating the times to come, cannot be rendered into Kodi at all. The future, in the end, can only be suggested by speaking about the world of great-grandchildren (*nuhi*), who are categorically merged with their great-grandparents and thus only uncertainly oriented in the future.[3]

Spatial metaphors come into play in the set of terms that refer to what we might call "process"—that is, change over time, which is conceptualized and represented as movement in space. The "development" of a particular set of plans and their realization are described as their "walk" (*halakona*) on a journey that goes from a former state to a future one. The oriented and irreversible aspects of time, thus, are projected onto space, but those which are not given direction by human motivation are expressed in a language that is at once more neutral and more abstract.

MARKERS OF THE DAY

The Kodi word for "day," *lodo*, as in many other Austronesian languages, also means "sun" and refers to the period between sunrise and sunset. There are also terms for "yesterday" (*wei myalo*), "last night" (*wei hyudo*), "the night before last" (*wei hyudo ihya*), "tomorrow" (*meraho*), "the day after tomorrow" (*haromo*), and even the day after that (*haromo ihya*). The twenty-four-hour period is referred to as "a single day and night"

[3] This would seem to be another difference with the Rindi vocabulary for time in Eastern Sumba, which G. Forth (1983, 47) describes as "a series of spatial segments articulated by a number of points of transition."

(*hawu lodo, hawu hudo*), but when periods of several days are counted they are generally counted as nights.[4]

Ritual intervals, such as the period set aside to plan a feast or the reburial of a body in a stone grave, are always counted in years, which are metaphorically referred to as "nights." Thus, if a feast is planned in three years' time, it is stated that it will happen "after two nights" (*menge du hudo*). Sometimes informants explicitly linked the concept of "day" to the dry season (*mara tana*) and that of "night" to the rainy season (*righuto*), making clear the assumption that all major rituals occur after the harvest and usually toward the end of the dry season.

A great many expressions are used to distinguish stages of the day and night. These are particulary densely concentrated at points of transition—the ritually efficacious early hours of the dawn, and the darking time of dusk. A series of terms reported by informants described the light spreading over the land: *Na mangahaka*, "the horizon becomes light"; *delakoka a tana*, "the lay of the land becomes perceptible"; *ice ura manu*, "the lines on the hands are visible"; *na hundaka a lodo*, "the sun appears"; and *mbara kapahudo*, "the morning is close by." The term for the morning hours, *kapahudo*, means literally the "edge of the night," which extends until the chill of the early dawn has passed. From 7:00 to 8:00 A.M., the sun's rays begin to bring heat as well as light, and people come out of their houses to "warm themselves in the sun" (*pa dirungoka a lodo*), wrapped in sarungs and mantles. By eight they have "finished sunning" (*menge pa dirungoka*) and begin to do their errands.

The position of the sun in the sky is pointed to with the index finger extended to refer to periods of the day. Both the sun and the moon are perceived to rise in an arc, then to "sit" (*londo*) briefly at the zenith before they begin their descent. The rising sun is called the *lodo koko*, and the setting sun the *lodo malo*. At about ten in the morning the sun grows "boughs" of heat that pull it to the top position (*na karangga dinjaroko a lodo*). The moment the sun "sits" is *dinjaro lodo*, "high noon" or the "center of the day"; this is also the time that the heat from the sun is said to "sting" with special intensity (*mbati a lodo*). The climax of ritual combats, such as the mounted battle of the *pasola* or traditional boxing, is timed to come at midday, under the "biting" sun. This is when "the sun steps on the shadows" (*pandali ngingyo lodo*) so they appear small. Later

[4]This agrees with Nilsson's (1920, 300) contention that primitives count days by nights, although G. Forth (1983, 48) insists that this is not the case in Rindi, Eastern Sumba. However, he does not cite data about ritual counting of intervals of ceremonies, and does concede that nights are usually counted rather than days when Rindi people state how long a lengthy journey should take.

in the afternoon the shadows grow longer, and the sun lowers its "feet" (*witti*) as rays reaching down to the earth and "pushing the shadows" (*na tularongo ngingyona*) along the ground.

When the sun moves lower in the sky it is said to "look down into the ocean" (*na tangera a wei myahi*) with slanted rays in preparation for its final descent. Near the horizon, the sun begins to "sit askew" in the sky (*na tangera hoka a lodo*), and its "feet" dip into the water (*ndallu ndikya ha wittina a lodo*). Sometimes it is described as "pausing over the waves" (*mangga ela panu mbanu*) or dyeing the waters red with its evening glow (*na raraka a wei myahi*). It sets halfway (*tama hapapa*), and then entirely (*tama hambolo*).

Evening begins with a period of twilight, when the sun has set but the darkness is not yet complete (*nja hudongo pango*). This period is the time of stealing and ill deeds—hence the expression "they used the twilight darkness, the obscurity of the dawn" (*na waingo hudo ndoko, lodo ndango*) to refer to deception and subterfuge. It is opposed to the "full night" (*hudo mbolo*), when ritual singing begins (usually about 10:00 P.M.), which is said to coincide with the first cock's crow (*hakuku handoko*). The first few hours after darkness has fallen are called "those in which sleep is still light" (*manduru pa lete konggo a hudo*), a time when people can be easily disturbed. These are followed by the deeper, darker hours (*na kapandu pohi myalo*), when sleep is heavier. Midnight is the "center of the darkness" (*taloro hudo*) and is marked by the second cock's crow, but it is not as symbolically charged as the early hours of the dawn (*mari myeraho*), when the morning star Venus is about to make its appearance. The approach of the star is described in spatial terms. At about 2:00 A.M., it is "still far away" (*marou pango a motoroma rara*); by 3:00 A.M. "it is approaching" (*na tukeka*), and the third cock's crow is heard; by 4:00 A.M. "it is close" (*na maranda*), and about half an hour later "it appears" (*na hundaka*).

This moment marks the key transition from night into day. It is when signs are expected from the invisible spirits that they have heard the prayers addressed to them. Such signs may take the form of a flash of light in the sky (a falling star), a large crashing noise, or a shaking and rumbling near the bamboo "spirit ladder" (*pahere*), erected in front of a house where rites are held. In Kodi prayers, the moment is designated as

The time that tomorrow's sun appears	Ba na hunda a lodo koko
As we lie on pillows facing its rise	Yama ba ma luna luna lodo koko
The time that the evening sun ascends	Ba na tama a lodo malo

Until we sleep with our sides turned away	Yama ba panape lodo malo
No longer sitting in the light of the full moon	Njama londo pango ela kandeghu wula taru
No longer sleeping in the darkness of the deepest night	Njama manduru pango ela kapandu pohi myalo

After the morning star has risen, the next stages of the dawn are marked by the cries of the *kadoko* bird, who sings once "to tease the young men" (*kahele mone*), arousing them to defend their women and children); a second time to "tease the older men" (*kahele malupu*); and a third time to mark the real dawn of the next day (*delakoka*). The rooster must then crow four times (*hakuku hambatango*) to confirm the song of the *kadoko* bird and stir the other domestic animals from their sleep.

THE TIME OF DAILY SOCIAL ACTIVITIES

In addition to a vocabulary of descriptive markers that focuses on the transition between day and night, the Kodinese have "chicken time" and "buffalo time," which are further delineated with references to routine tasks in caring for domestic animals. Dusk, for example, is called "when the chickens go up to their perches" (*ba na detango a manu*), and the period just before dawn is "when they come down" (*mburu a manu*). Midmorning is when "the buffalo go out" (*pa loho a karimbyo*) of the corral to pasture, and midafternoon is when they return (*pa tama ka-rimbyo*). Such markers are as common in everyday speech as is reference to light or darkness.

Although many other daily activities occur with similar regularity, they do not function as time markers. Fetching water and building a fire are a part of every morning, as is pounding paddy for the morning meal, but these are not used to designate temporal sequences. It is the coordination of human activities with the more or less independent movements of animals that is used to generate a sequence of time markers. The importance of domestic animals, especially buffalo, as markers of social and biographical time for longer sequences is further explored in chapter 7.

Evans-Pritchard (1940, 101), noting that the Nuer have as many points of temporal reference between 4:00 and 6:30 A.M. as for the entire rest of the day, claimed that these moments are more finely partitioned because they are important in directing economic and domestic activities. In Kodi, the density of temporal reference at these points seems related to ritual as well as economic concerns. The early stages of dawn are the time of symbolically significant transitions—when messages sung and spoken by human orators reach their destination in the upperworld, when dream conversations with an ancestor may occur, when visions of medicines or magical phrases are transmitted. Kodi village dwellers are early risers, and they often witness sacrifices to the highest *marapu* performed just after the appearance of the morning star, waiting for the light of the sun's first rays to interpret the liver or entrails. Divinations performed at this hour are the most significant; when asked why, Kodi priests told me that our consciousness is most receptive in the early hours when darkness fades into daylight.

NUMBERED DAYS AND NAMED INTERVALS

Traditionally, no intermediate unit of time between the day and the month was specified. Upon the introduction of markets during the Dutch colonial administration, "weeks" began to be been counted in cycles of market days (*lodo paranggango*) or, for churchgoers, Sundays. The days of the week are not named but instead are counted—"the first day" (*lodo ihya*, Monday), "the second day," and so on. Government regulations often shift the days the market is held, sometimes scheduling two different days (say, Wednesdays and Saturdays) for these gatherings; moreover, the frequency of and interval between markets are not necessarily constant. Thus, when someone speaks of an event as having happened "three market days ago," it could mean three weeks or only a week and a half ago. Markets are held in four different locations in Kodi (Bukambero, Kory, Bondo Kodi, and Waiha), so the counting of market days varies regionally. Appointments and time references are made in terms of market cycles, and the name of the market's location is specified if there is any doubt about which one is meant.

Cycles of Sundays refer to the custom of "entering the house of the seventh day," a Kodi term for the Christian church. An analogy between the Christian proscription on Sunday work and the Kodi ritual silence for the period of the "bitter months" has created a more common reference, with Sunday referred to as the "bitter day" (*lodo padu*) and churchgoing as "entering the bitter house" (*tama uma padu*) (Hoskins 1987c). The term is not meant to be derogatory of Christian teachings, but only to stress the local perception that Christianity, too, involves restrictions and that a separate demarcation of sacred time obtains in the Christian religion. Since not only churches but also schools and government offices observe Sunday as a day of rest, the cycle of "bitter days" is becoming increasingly common as a term of temporal reckoning.

The Month

The moon is the most important unit in Kodi time reckoning. Its variability is explained in another story of an initial, enduring entity that was broken apart as a result of human action:

THE ORIGINS OF THE PHASES OF THE MOON

Two brothers in the village of Toda, Myondo Manda and Pyati Lando, were famous hunters. They traveled to Ngahu, a high cliff in Bangedo, and from there they threw their spears into the heavens, trying to see whose spear flew highest. One of the spears caught on the edge of the moon and a piece of it broke off and fell to earth. They caught it in one of their hunting nets [*kareco londo laka*] and carried it back home to show the others.

Rato Pokilo and Rato Mangilo, in Tossi, saw the moon glowing in their net and said, "How beautiful! What is it?"

"It's the moon," said Myondo Manda and Pyati Lando; "we struck it with our spears and captured it in this net."

"But you cannot leave it here," said Mangilo and Pokilo. "If this piece of the moon is not returned to the sky, it will always be dark, and we won't be able to sing or dance in the moonlight or travel home from long journeys. Give it to us and we will return it."

"What do we get for giving you the moon?" asked Myondo and Pyati. They were promised that each year they would receive the first fruits of the harvest. Everyone who made a garden in the territory of Bali Hangali would have to honor the people of Toda with a small sacrifice of a chicken or dog and a gift of a knife and a spear. This showed the control that Toda once had over the moon, which they surrendered to their older brothers in Tossi.

Mangilo and Pokilo took the moon down to the seashore and released it into the sea at sunset. It rose as just a small sliver at first, but gradually grew fuller and fuller, until it became very full and red, then began to diminish again. From that point on, the moon was always variable, waxing and waning, "dying" and coming back to life. The net that had contained the moon [*kareco londo laka*] was taken back to Tossi and stored beside the great gold breastplate that belonged to Mangilo. The home of the treasures was called

Village of the ancient mother jar	Parona inya pandalu ndongo haghu
Village of the father moon net	Parona bapa kareco londo laka
Tossi of great renown	Tohi lendu ngara
The spreading red banyan	Wei marongo rara
Mangilo and his gold breastplate	Myangilo la marangga

Baraho the sitting ruler	Byaraho maboto
The urn that cannot be moved	Ngguhi nja pa dadango
The plate that cannot be lifted	Pengga nja pa keketo

The people of Tossi watch the moon, while the people of Toda use the moonlight to sing and ask the spirits for better harvests and more descendants.

Narrated by Rangga Pinja, Toda

In this story, the theme of mortality and loss is applied to a heavenly body as well as a human one. Wounded by human attack, the moon now suffers the same processes of aging and death that people do. It differs from people, however, in being capable of regeneration. The regenerative power of the moon is also for the first time connected to objects: the net used to capture the moon, whose guardians are now in the ceremonial center of Tossi. The idea that some persons are privileged controllers of time is introduced here.

The narrative suggests other associations if we consider it in the context of related mythological traditions. The shattering of the moon and its fall to earth are common themes in other parts of the island, where they are associated with ties between the moon and precious metals. The Sumbanese often say that the sun is fashioned from gold and the moon from silver. Although gold and silver are found on the earth, they are said to be deposited there when a star falls from the sky (G. Forth 1981, 441). A creation story from Lewa in central Sumba tells how two suns and moons were forged by the founding ancestors from stone cliffs on the fifth level of the earth. At first both were hung in the sky, but since it was too hot, one sun was removed and set aside. The two moons got into a quarrel over a woman, and one of them struck his counterpart with a dibble. He in turn was stabbed with a knife. The stabbed moon fell to the earth and died, while his companion still bears the scars of the battle at his home in the sky (Kapita 1976b, 219, 230–31).

The life and death of the moon are associated with the life and death of human beings in everyday life as well. For example, it is widely believed that a person should die at the same lunar phase in which he or she was born—that is, that the cycle must be completed. Similarly, it is considered inauspicious to plant crops when the moon is at its fullest and appears "red" (*taru rara*—that is, just as it begins its decline) or when it is not visible and "dead" (*mate wulla*) (see also G. Forth 1981, 208). The net that captured the moon is treated as one of the most precious heirlooms of Tossi because the moon itself is seen as a wealth object, but one that had to be returned to the sky. Because the people of Tossi helped to return the moon to its proper place, they established a special relationship with it that in turn gives them a privileged position in the calendrical rites. The story about knocking down the moon is also about the exchange of wealth and the potential violence involved in dislodging a wealth object from its original home. (This exchange theme is further developed in the story of the origins of the wet and dry seasons in a trade of fire for water; see below.)

METHODS OF MOON COUNTING

The phases of the moon are described and distinguished by both laymen and ritual specialists, though the degree of specification varies widely. Gregory Forth (1983, 54) recorded a list of twenty-nine named phases from one informant in Rindi, Eastern Sumba, but notes that for most people "the total seems to be incidental to the classification; for some Rindi denied knowledge of the number of nights, or days, in a month, while others claimed there were thirty" (1983, 53). Many Kodi informants provided terms for the full moon (*wulla taru*) and for five or six phases of waxing and waning, but usually they (like the people of Rindi) enumerated the rest simply as "several nights when it gets darker" (*piri hyudo na kapandu taruhinikya*).

Dogs are believed to be able to see the new moon before it has become visible to human beings. In the calendrical rites, invisible spirit dogs (*bangga marapu*) patrol the village of Tossi and the beaches where the sea worms will swarm, and may bite anyone who offends the taboos of the yearly festivities. The first phase of each new moon is when "it is seen by dogs" (*pa ice bangga*), and the death of the old moon (*mati wyulla*) is signaled by dogs barking. The new moon, moreover, is associated with new plans and new projects and the budding of fruits and garden crops, as expressed in this couplet referring to an intention that has not yet surfaced in open speech:

If a new moon appears in the tree	Ba nei jongo a wulla wudi hyungga
If a jackfruit emerges on the branch	Ba nei jongo a nangga wudi jadi

Kodinese share the feelings of many other agricultural peoples that it is better to plant crops when the moon is waxing and still "young."

As the moon travels on its path, it has several "resting places" that mark its journey. At the first quarter, it hovers so it can be seen "looking up from the village gate" (*tangara binye*). Three days before it reaches its fullest point, it is dangerous and inauspicious (*wulla nja ndaha*); during this period, wild creatures of the land and sea are particularly active, and people should not venture out to hunt or fish. As the moon becomes almost completely full, it becomes auspicious again. The *wulla mburu manu*, or "moon that comes down with chickens," marks the beginning of a good time for feasts and night dancing, which continues as the full moon becomes "red" (*taru rara*) and stays in the sky until sunrise.

The full moon signals a period of intensified nocturnal activity and amorous conquests. In ritual couplets, illegitimate children are called "children of the light of the full moon and the fleeting darkness of the evening" (*ana kandeghu wulla taru, kapandu pohi malo*), and the erotic charge of this phase of the moon often features in haunting love ballads. After the full moon "sits" at its zenith (*londoka a wulla*), seven dark nights are counted to determine the day the sea worms will swarm for the *nale* festivities. This event marks the beginning of the period of license. The moon then becomes "old" and "slender" (*wulla malupu, wulla malaka*) and begins to amble uncertainly toward its death. The aging moon rests briefly on the high plateaus to the east (*mangga la panuna*), then shifts into an uncertain existence where its visiblity is open to debate (*wulla pa palumungo*, the "contested moon") before disappearing.

The Seasons

There are only two "seasons" in the Kodi year: the dry season (*mara tana*) and the rainy one (*righuto*). The division is presented in traditional narratives as stemming from another incident in which human actions played a role, provoking an alternation between periods of abundant rainfall and others of drought. In this story, the theme of exchange comes most prominantly to the fore, and is negotiated by a wily cultural hero.

THE ORIGINS OF THE WET AND DRY SEASONS

When the first ancestors first came to Kodi, they were still connected to the upperworld of the sky and its inhabitants. Relations were not good, however, for the Kodi people wanted to plant gardens, but their crops were constantly being eaten by a huge boar. The boar belonged to Rato Byokokor, the giant gatekeeper of the flood gates of the heavens. He lived in the sky beside a dam that controlled rainfall, along with his brother Manjalur, and they were called

Byokokoro by the dam on the river	Byokokoro kori lyoko
Manjalur who only stands guard	Manjalur nduka ndende

One day, the boar ran into the garden of Lete Watu of Wei Kahumbu.[5] Lete Watu was not afraid of anyone, so he threw his spear at the boar and struck it. The wounded boar ran home, scrambling up a series of stone steps [*lete watu*] that led to his master's home in the sky.

Lete Watu followed him to the upperworld and found the bloody boar dying in front of Rato Bokokoro's house. "This pig was destroying my gardens," he said. "I have a right to take his meat."

"This was my favorite boar," said Rato Bokokoro. "We will eat you instead, since you have killed him." His words were unclear, because Rato Bokokoro had a harelip and could not talk distinctly.

The two were about to fight, but Lete Watu was too clever to allow that to happen: "Don't eat us, elder brother. We will bring you something else to eat, as compensation for your loss. Then we can be at peace, since your boar will no longer be destroying our gardens."

He brought one of his own buffalo and killed him so they could share a meal together and make peace. They decided to divide the meat from both animals equally.

As soon as the two shares were distributed, the people in Rato Bokokoro's party immediately began to chew at the bloody carcass with their jagged teeth, while those who came with Lete Watu set about cooking their share in a large pot. In a short time, the smell of the roasting meat began to travel over to Rato Bokokoro's house.

"What do you do to make that meat smell so good?" the harelipped giant asked.

"We cook it with fire," answered Lete Watu, and handed him a piece of the cooked pork. Rato Bokokoro noticed that not only was the meat superior in taste, but it was also much easier to chew.

"How do you make this fire?" he asked. "You must give me the secret. We are always hungry here because it takes us so long to chew the meat."

Lete Watu said, "I will give you the secret to relieve your hunger if you will help us to relieve our thirst. On land, we can make fire whenever we want, but our crops are parched and dying because there is not enough rain. You are the gatekeeper of the flooding waters from the south [*mandoko*], so if you can give us the tools to make rain, we will give you the tools to make fire."

They exchanged the objects needed to start a fire and start the rainy season. Lete Watu gave Rato Bokokoro a *kohe*, a wooden tool whose two sticks could be rubbed together to make sparks, and showed him how to use it. Rato Bokokoro gave Lete Watu his "toys": a gourd filled with water from a sacred source [*tabelo wei hyari*] and, to Ra Hupu, his com-

[5] Lete Watu is a familiar trickster figure who appears in a number of Kodi myths. His Weyewa counterpart, Yanda Mette, has a somewhat similar adventure, as reported in Kuipers 1990, 14–15.

panion, a bamboo pipe with more of this water, along with lightning stones. "This is the water that will feed your crops," he said, "and here are the lightning stones that will punish any infractions of the rules of planting and harvesting." These objects can still be found in Wei Kahumbu and Bondo Kodi.

Lete Watu told Rato Bokokoro to be careful in storing the fire tools, because any stray sparks could destroy the flammable thatch of Sumbanese houses. Rato Bokokoro told Ra Hupu and Lete Watu to use the power that they had over rainfall wisely, and not to ask for rainfall more than once a year, so that when it came there would be enough to nourish the crops until they were fully grown. In this way, it became the task of the rainkeepers to maintain the seasons in the proper balance.

"These tools are yours," he said, "but whenever you pray for rain you will have to say my name and my brother's name, because we are the owners of the rain waters." Then Lete Watu and his party went home to earth.

A short time afterward, Rato Bokokoro's village caught fire because they did not use the tools properly. "You have cheated me, Lete Watu!" He called. "What you have destroyed by fire can also be destroyed by water!"

And he sent a huge flood, which washed over all of the first Kodi villages and destroyed their homes.

Because of Rato Bokokoro's anger, he does not always keep his part of the bargain. Sometimes the rains are insufficient or unpredictable, not coming in the months that they were requested. Sometimes the rivers flood and the young crops are destroyed, other times the ground is parched and the dust is so thick nothing can be planted until very late. A house named after Rato Bokokoro has been built in Tossi, and it faces the House of the Sea Worms, which controls the calendar. But its master does not always heed the pleas of those who make offerings to him.

Narrated by Gheda Kaka, Wai Kahumbu

In each of the stories about the origins of temporal divisions, human action destroys an initial plenitude that can be restored only partially and elliptically. Mbora Poka's ambitions lead to his own death, but he gains the power to help succeeding generations. Myondo and Pyati return the moon to the sky, but now its cycle is variable and inconstant. Lete Watu receives the tools to ask for rain, but he antagonizes the guardian of the heavenly waters. The destruction of an original unity is replaced by a more complex and confusing concatenation of particulars.

The beginnings of separation and opposition are also the beginnings of organized exchange, through ritual prayer and obligatory offerings. In these stories, the origins of time are linked to the beginning of mortality and to the consequences of human ambition: Mbora Poka's unusually tall house, Pyati Lando's skill with a spear, Lete Watu's ability to trick Rato Bokokoro with his words. An original unity is violated by the disruptive power of an individual who wants to stand out. In its place, an oscillation is established—the cycle of day and night, of wet and dry seasons. This in turn may also be disrupted by efforts to gain control over the seasons and the heavenly bodies. Compromise and accommodation are the hallmarks of exchange, which is given the paradigmatic form in these early narratives of a negotiation between a clever, forceful invader of someone else's space and the earlier, superior, but more passive power.

In the first story, Mbora Poka dies as a result of this ambitions, but he thereby becomes the first ancestor. In the second, the two brothers from Toda achieve an important role in harvest ceremonies through a temporary disruption of the flow of time. The theft of the moon interferes with the division of day and night, requiring the leaders of Tossi to intervene; the wounded moon is returned to the sky, and its hunters secure increased ritual importance by acknowledging the temporal authority of their seniors. Finally, the story of Lete Watu's victory over Rato Bokokoro describes the dangers of human guile. Although he tricks the sky giant out of valuable tools, what he receives in return is ambivalently charged: division is presented as the necessary precondition of exchange. There is a certain familiarity to the contrast between the cultured, smooth-speaking Lete Watu, who possesses the art of fire-making, and the more primitive, animal-like Rato Bokokoro, who controls the natural power of rain-making. Unlike in the famous lowland South American myths of fire stolen from the jaguar (Lévi-Strauss 1969b; T. Turner 1985), the cultural art is not taken from the creatures of nature but traded against another art, one dependent not on cunning but on access to heavenly waters.

I interpret this opposition as a version of the diarchic divide: Lete Watu, representative of the human intruders, takes on the role of the younger brother and addresses Rato Bokokoro, lord of the skies, as his elder brother. It is a gesture of respect and deference and at the same time potentially derisive, since it is often asserted in Eastern Indonesian diarchies that "the older brother is stupid."[6]

Lete Watu's use of the kin term creates a framework of ranked sibling-ship, in which cannibalism can be avoided and a mutually beneficial exchange relationship can be established. Rato Bokokoro is, if not fully human, at

[6]For other cases, see Traube 1986, 51–65, on the Mambai of Timor; Schulte Nordholt 1971, 262–74, on the Atoni; and Lewis 1988, 17–19, on the Tana 'Ai of Flores (where the opposition between older and younger siblings is transposed to female and male, with a similar symbolic valence).

least potentially so, and he is won over by Lete Watu's offer. But he is too careless to handle fire properly, so eventually he loses his house and his sympathy with the "younger brother."

Rato Bokokoro is one of the original inhabitants of the island, a race of primitive hunters and herbalists from whom present-day witches (*tou marongo*) are supposed to be descended. Although they had detailed knowledge of medicines and the healing properties of roots and barks, these people did not know how to grow gardens. Their ability to open and close the gates that dam the flow of waters from the sky was for them a trivial skill used only to avoid getting wet when returning from a gathering trip to the forest. For an agriculturalist, by contrast, it is the supreme power, the determiner of feast or famine, and not to be used casually. Rato Bokokoro is stupid to surrender his rain-making toys to someone else who values them much more highly than he does himself. Yet despite his blunder, he retains a hold on power. His "toys" must be ritually manipulated in seasonal prayers, where his name is repeated in invocations to coax a bit more rain to fall.

The story ends with the uncertainty of reciprocity from an antagonized exchange partner. Because of Rato Bokokoro's anger, the stone steps that once connected the heavens and the earth have been withdrawn, and the stone bridge that once connected Sumba to Bima and Java to the west has been washed away. Separation and exchange have replaced unity and sharing.

In a universe of diverse origins and disparate peoples, the problem is no longer how to divide basic resources, but how to reallocate them once they have already been distributed. The shifts and changes that occur over time are henceforth irreversible, and there is no unbroken cycle returning to the origins. Detailed and elaborate narratives associated with the founding of the calendar continue the theme that valuable ritual objects (such as the trough to catch the sea worms) are initially seen as mere toys, undervalued by their original owners and only later recognized as important, once they have been put in the proper place.

The Beginnings of Time and the Construction of the Past

The division of wet and dry seasons defines the year as a seasonal cycle, but in this story they have not yet been elaborated into the twelve named "moons" of the Kodi calendar. The wet and dry seasons exist as simple opposites, the "repetition of repeated reversal" that Leach (1961, 126) believed to be characteristic of the "primitive" conception of time.

At the end of these three stories we come to a conceptual period in which "time" as an experience of discontinuities could be said to exist, but it is still incompletely "cultural" in that it is not marked by the collective festivities and memories of the calendar. This fact was expressed to me in the field by a storyteller who said that after the exchange of fire and water and the division of the moon, "there were months, but they were not yet Kodi months, and there were years, but they were not yet Kodi years." That is, they had not been classified within the tradition handed down by the ancestors and were not part of a ritual sequence (*katadi marapu*). I interpret the storyteller's statement to refer to the fact that "the past" as a cultural category refers not simply to time itself as an abstract entity, but to a specially constructed understanding of time in which the experiences of previous generations are put into a meaningful framework.

The cultural variability of the past has been the subject of much recent debate, which also concerns the notion that particular cultures may perceive duration in very different ways. The debate has often centered on whether there is a universal form of time perception, with duration as its basis, or whether all time concepts are culturally relative. Durkheim ([1912] 1965), Whorf (1964), and Geertz (1966) have been presented as the defenders of the relativist position, holding that all such concepts are socially determined, while Bloch, Turton and Ruggles (1978), and Appadurai (1981) suggest instead that "all speakers must at some level apprehend time in the same way" (Bloch 1977, 283) in order to communicate with each other and be capable of eventually changing the prevailing conceptual order.

The debate has started out on the wrong foot, however, by failing to distinguish between "time" as a perceptual experience with certain universal features, on the one hand, and "the past" as a culturally constructed image of a particular society projected backward onto previous generations, on the other. Certainly, at one level, the people of Kodi perceive days, months, and annual seasons in much the same way as peoples all over the world. Because of their closeness to the equator and the climatic conditions they experience as gardeners and stock-keepers, they have not developed a quadripartite notion of fall, winter, spring, and fall. The binary opposition of wet and dry seasons they use is commonsensical for any resident of an equitorial zone. The vocabulary just elaborated for speaking of time in relation to diurnal cycles and social activities uses a number of different time scales, each of which classifies time in relation to specific purposes (agriculture, animal tending, ritual stages).

In everyday ways of talking about time, events are correlated with each other through proximity and by reference to the life cycle of specific individuals. Great cultural importance is placed on sequence, since the order of birth, of building houses, and of acquiring valuables determines rank in a ceremonial context. Attention to sequence produces a memory of precedence, but not one of chronology: the *relative* position of an event (as before or after another event) is remembered, but it is not situated in reference to an absolute time scale.

The particular characteristics of Kodi notions of time, in other words, do not lie in a fundamentally different concept of duration, or in the absence of duration in favor of repetition, but instead in the plurality of temporal scales and their relationships. Rather than being subsumed in a single sequential chronology, these different ways of expressing the passage of time coexist for the numerous special purposes that they serve. The portrait that we have drawn of Kodi time before the creation of the calendar, hence, is of a diverse but not necessarily confusing series of time concepts, applicable in different contexts.

The calendar itself, as we shall see, provides a loose integration of the notions of day, month, and season and is the first step toward the synchronization of different cycles and processes in a shared chronology. As I use the term, a chronology refers loosely to an independently calibrated gauge of events over time through which various time scales can be brought into meaningful relationship with one another. I do not restrict the term to actual dating systems; it is, rather, a more encompassing frame of reference, one that, in Kodi, is articulated in traditional narratives.

The coexistence of a number of varying temporal frames is characteristic of the intellectual systems of many non-Western societies. Robin Horton (1967, 176–77), for example, describes the time systems of many African groups as equally particularistic, piecemeal combinations of loosely connected segments:

> In traditional Africa, methods of time-reckoning vary greatly from culture to culture. Within each culture, again, we find a plurality of time-scales used in different contexts. Thus there may be a major scale which locates events either before, during or after the time of founding of the major institutions of the community; another scale which located events by correlating them with the life-times of deceased ancestors; yet another which locates events by correlating them with the phases of the seasonal cycle; and yet another which uses phases of the daily cycle.

The distinction between special-purpose time scales and a more encompassing chronology is similar to the distinction between special-purpose primitive money and our own multipurpose money: a common currency is not needed until it is necessary to generalize across contexts that under normal circumstances are assumed to be separate (Maltz 1968). A multiplicity of time scales is also found in the West, of course, in that we can speak of events occurring during the Kennedy administration, at the end of the summer, and during someone's adolescence; the important difference here is that these expressions can also be rendered in dates, while those of many other societies cannot.

Kodi "time," therefore, is plural and not necessarily consistent, and builds on notions of duration and sequence, both of which have correlates in the natural world (the movement of celestial bodies, the changing of the seasons, the waxing and waning of the moon) and in human biological experience (the processes of aging, death, and reproduction). These notions of time are then brought together in the ritual calendar, to which we turn next. From the story of the creation of the calendar we start to see the construction of a "past," or rather several "pasts," which reveal Kodi understandings of their own heritage and its imprint on present-day life.

3

The Past in Narrative
The Creation of the Calendar

> Apart from the practical value of the calendar it is used in order to supply
> the framework of a narrative account of the year. Whenever one of the old
> men is asked about the moons he does not give a sober account, but will
> proceed at once to recite a story in which he gives the successive names in
> a more or less detailed and flowery description of what takes place in each.
> An intelligent old native will make it clear that not everyone knows the
> names of the moons, that only those having to do with gardens and
> knowing how the year runs are acquainted with them.
>
> Bronislaw Malinowski,
> "Lunar and Seasonal Calendars in the Trobriands"

Malinowski's description of the Trobriand response to questions about the
calendar in a sense replays my own field experience. When I first began
my investigations and traveled to speak to a couple of respected older men,
I was encouraged to focus on the calendar, "the Kodi months and the Kodi
year," which might give an overarching structure to the vast project of
recording Kodi tradition. "If you don't know where to start," an old man
advised me in an early conversation, "start with the sea worms. That is
where we start ourselves."

The enumeration of month names was also an occasion for enumerating
an annual round of social activities, the times of feasting and the times of
famine, and also, I was to discover, the division of ceremonial tasks among
ancestral villages and the location of objects that represent the historical
process of acquiring these rights. The creation of the calendar at a consensus meeting of the ancestors provides the narrative frame that orients, to
a certain extent, all Kodi storytelling about the past. All accounts of how
crucial social institutions came into being are in some way related to the
structure of the sea worm festivities and the divisions of the year. Knowledge of the calendar is focused on a few important ritual centers, invested
in named religious officers (the Rato Nale, or "Priest of the Sea Worms"),
and seen as something of a "native science."

Having said this much, however, it should be added that there is no
"master narrative" of the origins of Kodi society or the calendar. The

stories that exist are "owned" by certain houses and "attached" to objects within them, and told by their descendants in full recognition of their partial and partisan content. An idea nevertheless persists that, scattered through the memories of a great many different storytellers, there is a common, encompassing story line that—although contested and debated in many of its details—is both inscribed on present-day social institutions and part of a shared, narrativized past.

This chapter represents my attempt to reconstruct that shared story line, through the presentation and analysis of seven different texts. Each one, collected from a descendant of an ancestor involved in the story, was considered a relatively "legitimate" version of a portion of the past, but each was also the subject of other interpretations and counterclaims, which I discuss alongside it.

Kodi thinking about the past is expressed not only in narratives, but also in exchange valuables, the architecture of villages and gardens, the names of places, and movement through the landscape. A feature of the narrativized past, however, is its malleability—and this feature is also its undoing, for stories are given less credence than many other forms of evidence because of local recognition of their almost infinite variability. It is important, therefore, to begin with considerations of genres of narrative and their relation to knowledge about the past. Once we have situated narrative in the context of other forms of "traces" or "signs" left by the ancestors, we can better understand how these particular stories are fixed in time and place, and why debates still rage about them.

A sense of temporal positioning, of how human acts have been ordered in time, is clearly crucial to problems of legitimacy and historiography in Kodi. The origin narratives discussed in this chapter convey an ambivalent attitude toward the locus of authority, often defined by contrast to the locus of action in a diarchic division of agency. In the colonial period, this ambiguity came into play in reshaping authority, moving it away from the ritual centers and into a newly defined "political" sphere, separated from the officers of the calendar. Later transformations of exchange trans-actions and the "new order" penetration of the state into local affairs disturbed indigenous ways of talking about the past, leading to a new authoritative discourse in "history" (*sejarah*)—a progressive, oriented vision of a discontinuous past, informed by the rhetoric of a new national future.

None of these transformations has brought about a complete change: the different forms of historical consciousness developed, respectively, in precolonial times, the Dutch period, and the years since independence still coexist in dialogue with each other. By studying their complex interrelationships we can analyze the processes of formation and interpretation that lie behind them.

Genres of Stories About the Past

Knowledge of the yearly cycle and the control of time is a key strategic resource of the local polity. Calendrical knowledge is concentrated in the most prestigious genre of storytelling, the recitation of narratives that are "attached" to persons, objects, or locations. These narratives usually concern origins, and knowledge of an object's origins can carry power over that object. No ancestral relic can be addressed without pronouncing its special couplet names; yet it is both dangerous and inappropriate to pronounce these names without an understanding of their sources and significance. The classification of a narrative as "fixed" or "grasped" by a particular person, therefore, implies certain standards of authentication and legitimation that do not apply to other genres.

Kodi storytellers recognize four categories of narratives,[1] which are differentiated by their relations to space and time: "stories from long ago," *ngara kedoko e nawu*; "stories performed with songs," *ngara kedoko lodo*; "stories that are held or attached," *ngara kedoko pa ketengo*; and "the voices of the ancestors," *li marapu*. "Stories from long ago," which make up the first group, happen in a distant, bygone era that is roughly similar to the "once upon a time" frame of Western folktales. They refer to an age when trees and animals could still talk, people did not yet die, and the Kodi did not yet live at their present village sites. They include animal fables of a vaguely philosophical and speculative character (Needham 1957b, 1960), accounts of how people acquired shared human characteristics, and the stories about the origins of days, months, and seasons that we have

[1] These four genres can be compared to Adams's (1970, 1979) enumeration of three similar categories in East Sumba: harvest myths told in the fields, clan myths told on the porches of clan houses, and chanted texts in ceremonial language performed inside the clan house for the invisible audience. Her list marks a similar progression from unmarked, ordinary language to more fixed, invariant speech but does not differentiate between the "stories from long ago" and the "stories performed with songs." Christine Forth's (1982) dissertation on Rindi oral narrative concentrates on nine orphan (*ana lalu*) stories that I classify among the "stories performed with songs," though her texts are much briefer than the Kodi ones. Kuipers (1990), writing about Weyewa ritual speech, notes a similar progression toward invariance and greater textual authority in the movement from divinations to misfortune rites to feasts of fulfillment (*woleko*), but his discussion focuses only on genres of couplet speech and does not include vernacular narratives.

"Stories that are attached" can be narrated only by their rightful owners, who usually prefer to speak on the wide verandas of their ancestral houses, where they can request permission from the dead to tell each tale. 1985. Photograph by the author.

already surveyed. They do not refer to social divisions between people, houses, or territories, and can be told by anyone in an informal context.

"Stories performed with songs," in the second group, are elaborate performances that alternate vivid scenes of dialogue and action with commentaries sung or chanted in ritual couplets. Their recitation requires a specialized, and usually paid, storyteller, who speaks for an entire night. Moreover, because the stories are sacred, they must be preceded by the sacrifice of a chicken to the ancestors to ask permission. They feature standardized heroic protagonists: the male figure is called Ndelo in the greatest number of stories, though occasionally Rangga or Haghu; the female figure is almost always Kahi or Leba. The story typically begins with the birth of the protagonist and usually concerns orphanhood, abandonment, and a struggle to recover a lost position of privilege. It is punctuated by long songs of lament, in which the hero's or heroine's trials and tribulations are recast in poetic couplets. It ends with a happy resolution, usually a marriage or a triumphant feast of celebration. Although these stories may "belong" to a specific village, they can be told by a number of talented storytellers, and are a form both of entertainment and of edification.

The third genre comprises stories that are "attached" to persons, places, or things; often, therefore, they are called in Indonesian the "property" (*milik*) or "legacy" (*warisan*) of a particular descent line. They are highly sacred, but need not be told in an elaborate style, and at times are in fact quite truncated in their presentation. Although they contain short passages in couplets, they are narrated in the vernacular and are more "realistic," even "historical," in their content than stories in the first two groups: that is, they take place in actual, named locations, concern the ancestors of the storyteller, and have a minimum of supernatural elements. They may be jealously guarded, so that not everyone is allowed to listen in when a performance occurs. These stories document how people and objects came to their present homes and contain historical "evidence" in the form of references to named valuables, places, and persons.

The fourth genre, the *li marapu*—"voices of the ancestors"—is a chanted, relatively invariant series of couplets that is performed only when actually invoking ancestral spirits. Recited almost exclusively beside the sacred pillar in an ancestral house, these narratives refer elliptically to the events of the "attached stories" but do not elaborate on them. Their purpose is not to explain the past, but simply to evoke it, using a chain of place names, ancestor names, and the names of sacred valuables to "travel back" to the *marapu* and summon them as an invisible audience for a ritual event.

The genres are distinguished by the conditions of performance, their "truth frame," and the community they address as an audience. While the first two groups are considered part of the heritage passed down through the generations, it is expected that a narrator may change or at least embellish their story lines to achieve the proper effect. In contrast, the "attached narratives" are supposedly invariant, and a narrator must assert that he is doing his best to repeat the tale as he heard it from his father or grandfather. The *li marapu*, as ritual invocations, are so rigidly structured that a mistake in pronouncing the couplets could necessitate the paying of a fine or, in an extreme case, result in physical danger to the speaker: if someone speaks wrongly in an important ancestral house he risks illness and even death, sanctions from the listening ancestors who decide that their voices have not been properly rendered.

Each genre has characteristics of what Bakhtin (1981, 84) has called the *chronotope*: "In the literary artistic chronotope, spatial and temporal indicators are fused into one carefully thought-out, concrete whole. Time, as it were, thickens, takes on flesh, becomes artistically visible; likewise, space becomes charged and responsive to the movements of time, plot and history." The chronotope defines generic distinctions as different relations to time: in the first category of narratives, the relation is reflective and generalizing; in the second, time is used to edify by means of dramatic tension, comedy, and song; in the third, an authoritative but partisan vision of a sequence of legitimating events is provided; whereas the fourth is characterized by a definitive and invariant ritual text.

The "stories from long ago" and the "stories told with songs" recall the romance genre in many ways, taking place in an abstract adventure-time where no significant changes occur. At the end of the story, the initial equilibrium that had been destroyed by chance is restored, and everything returns to its own place. For some storytellers a psychological development occurs, with the hero or heroine becoming more knowledgeable as a result of these various experiences, but it is not characteristic of the genre as a whole. The songs are repeated, sung once at each stage of the protagonist's travails; their very repetition reinforces the idea of an unchanging time frame in which the individual simply moves through a series of stages. The space of the "stories with songs" is also abstracted: although specific villages are named, the same story can be told by different storytellers in different locations. Thus, the narrative itself is not fixed to particular locations but simply uses them as a frame for the action.

The "stories that are held or attached," by contrast, occur in concrete space, with great importance given to named locations and features of the landscape. The time that they contain is a time of sequences and orders, but not yet a "chronology"—in the sense of a time situated in relation to an external time scale, such as the passage of years. Nonetheless, such a chronology could be said to be emergent in the form of the stories them-selves, since they are about the origin of a single external time scale: the ceremonial system that synchronizes events to provide a unifying cycle for social life in the domain.

The *li marapu* are conceived not as narratives *about* the past but as the actual voices of the ancestors—that is, the past speaks directly in the present. The spirits play a ventriloquist's role, "placing" the words into the mouth of the speaker and requiring that they be pronounced correctly. As he chants or recites these couplets, the priest is said to be a simple mouthpiece of the spirits ("the lips told to speak, the mouth told to pronounce," *wiwi canggu tene, ghoba tanggu naggulo;* see Hoskins 1988b). There is no loss of consciousness on the part of the speaker, who does not become possessed. He remains responsible for his words, and this responsibility is immediately checked by the ancestor for whom he speaks, who can punish any errors that misrepresent him or other traditions.[2]

The Politics of Narrative Collection

The methodological problems that I encountered in trying to piece together this collection of narratives illustrate cultural attitudes toward the ownership and guardianship of the past. Members of the community who were interested in my project warned me that I would be told many lies and that I should insist on seeing the objects to which each narrative was attached in order to validate its legitimacy. They also told me to listen only to the "masters of the house" (*mori uma*) when collecting its narrative traditions and to pay no attention to the "talk on the veranda" among those less directly involved. Some of my taped narratives were given to me in confidence, with a request that they not be shared with rival groups. Most storytellers, however, were willing to let their words be widely known, because they were proud of their claims and wanted others to recognize them.

My informants disagreed about whether this project should be a simple compilation of diverse stories told in different villages or should result in the distillation of an authoritative "history of origins." I soon became convinced that no single "true version" existed, but the project was haunted by the possibility that such might have existed in the not too distant past. Although aware of discrepancies, my Kodi informants liked to imagine that a unifying canonical text could be pieced together "if only a few more old men were alive today, those who really knew." With this aim in mind, they applied themselves with particular rigor to the criticism of the texts collected.

The future use of these materials was also of great interest. One of my assistants, a former schoolteacher named Guru Katupu, proposed that at the end of my stay I leave a notebook of the complete texts, in Kodi and Indonesian, in the district office where it could serve as a reference work

[2] The frequency of these punishments was much debated. Ritual speakers are often older men, and when one of them dies abruptly after an important ceremony speculation inevitably arises about whether he might have "said something wrong" in the course of his oratory. A number of both speakers and singers, moreover, are blind. One such singer, Ra Kambura, told me that his loss of sight allowed him to concentrate on listening to the spirits and thus protected him from error. Another, Rangga Pinja, who lost his sight some four years after I met him, interpreted his blindness as a punishment not for mistakes he had made in speaking but because one of his sons had been convicted as a thief and blemished the purity of his descent line.

for generations to come. The suggestion was vetoed by his mother's brother, Maru Daku, who noted that there were people who might want to destroy such a record, much as they had burned local government archives in the past. He proposed instead that printed versions of individual narratives be given to those who had provided them to me, and that these be stored in their own ancestral houses, "so those spirits could watch over them and protect them separately." The younger man here was affirming a belief in a master narrative and a synthesis of Kodi traditions, while his senior was cautioning him against the possible consequences of forcing a consensus that did not exist. I decided on a compromise: the documents I left in the district office listed the names of the spirits worshipped by all the people of Kodi, in the shared ritual traditions of the harvest and rites of affliction, but it did not include partisan versions of the acquisition and distribution of sacred objects.

Real historical time and space can never be completely assimilated into expressive forms. Each of these four narrative genres offers a lens through which we can view a Kodi construction of the past, but none is absolutely definitive: even the "attached stories," which carry the greatest authority, are challenged and contested. The Kodinese see history as materialized in the house and its possessions. Narratives about ancestral exploits are themselves placed among the "possessions" of a house and are permanently attached to it, subject only to the variations of memory in its descendants. Remembering becomes a sacred duty, and ancestors can punish those who remember them falsely or neglect what they have said. This is why I was told to listen only to people who were as permanently attached to these houses as the narratives were: if one of them were to deceive me, he would suffer the consequences, because these stories are "heavy" enough to crush offenders who play games with them.

Presentation of Texts

For the purposes of exposition, I present seven narratives, each identified as the product of a specific narrator and clan. They are arranged in a sequence that corresponds roughly to the one in which "the events" are said to have unfolded, but there is no occasion in Kodi when all of these narratives would be told together. The central narrative—the one most widely known, though in abbreviated form—is text #5, concerning the founding of Tossi by Mangilo and Pokilo, the Sumbanese equivalent of Romulus and Remus, two orphaned boys who stumble into possession of the sea worms and the most important valuables in the domain. The other texts all refer to this one in some way, usually by including Mangilo and Pokilo themselves or by "anticipating" or "repeating" some of their actions.

I have chosen the fullest and most lively texts to present as a first version, but I follow these with a discussion of alternate versions, to convey a sense of both the common ground and areas of disagreement. Leach's early (1954b) reminder that mythic discourse provides "more a language of argument than a chorus of agreement" can be explored in terms of the controversies surrounding these texts.

TEXT #1: THE COMING OF THE SEA WORMS TO KODI

Lendu Myamba was the first Sumbanese to bring the knowledge of certain things from across the seas. He came to the island along with many others in a migration from the west, crossing over the stone bridge [*kataku lendu watu*] at Cape Sasar and entering from the north coast. After a few years, the first settlers began to experience hardships. Their garden crops were not large enough, and there was nothing to eat during the hunger season. Lendu set off to look for new sources of food [*mandara*]. He was accompanied by Pala Kawata, his mother's brother, who took the form of a giant python.

They traveled across the western seas to the splendid kingdom of Rato Ndimya, a foreign lord who had tremendous wealth. Lendu hoped to secure powerful valuables and magical knowledge from him, but first he had to perform a variety of trials. When he arrived at the palace of Rato Ndimya, he was treated as an honored guest, and a large water buffalo was slaughtered in his honor. The meat was not skinned or separated from the bones but chopped up and cooked all together. Then he was told to eat the huge pile of flesh, skin, fur, and bones so that his host would not be offended. Realizing that he could not do it alone, Lendu prayed to his mother's brother Pala Kawata, who told him to ask to be served by the palace gates. When the huge plates of meat were brought to him, the python slithered up behind, opened his mouth, and swallowed it all whole.

In the second trial, Lendu had to play *buke*: a post as slender as a hair was set up fifty meters away, and Lendu was told to hit it with a small sharpened bamboo dart [*karaki*]. He again called on his mother's brother, who gave him a piece of sticky resin to put on the dart. When he set the dart flying straight, the resin made it head for the hair-thin post and stick there, so that there was no doubt that it had struck fast.

The third trial was the board game *kule*, played with two rows of eight holes and twenty-four *dedap* seeds. The goal was to arrange eight in a row, and even though the number of seeds was not great enough,

Lendu managed to win with the help of Pala Kawata, who magically created new seeds from his mouth.

Once he had passed all of these trials, Rato Ndimya announced that he had been searching for a son-in-law to marry his beautiful daughter Nyale, and Lendu had proved himself worthy. "But what," he asked, "did you come looking for on this long voyage?"

"I was searching for eternal life," answered Lendu. "I have grown tired of hard garden work in this dry land."

"Alas, there is no eternal life," said Rato Ndimya, "but I will give you a gift of returning life, to renew the land with fresh waters. I will give you the sea worms [*nale*], spirits from the deepest ocean who will bring you fertility and the birth of new generations. Each year, if you receive the sea worms well and they are abundant, your rice harvests will be good and your descendants will be plentiful."

With the help of Pala Kawata, Lendu produced a magnificent bride-wealth payment of gold valuables, which he presented to the foreign lord. Rato Ndimya's daughter was told to prepare to return with him as his bride. She was dressed in all of her finery and sat beside him as he was given a series of farewell gifts.

The most important gift Lendu received was the *karaba rica*, a small trough to hold the worms and preserve them with ginger and spices. The worms themselves were not inside the trough, but he was told that they would come to meet him on a specified day of the year when they swarmed along the western beaches. They would continue to come to the island as long as they were greeted with a ritual combat on horse-back called the *pasola*. He also took with him the megapode bird [*wondo*; a long-legged forest fowl that builds large mounds of mud in which to lay its eggs] and several wild tubers, caterpillars, and honey. These were all wild foods that could be eaten in times of famine while waiting for the harvest of garden crops.

As Lendu's ship prepared to return home, Rato Ndimya's daughter refused to come with him. She threw herself into the ocean instead, her body parts breaking up into many tiny small pieces, which would wash up along the beaches of Kodi in February—red pieces from her rosy, betel-stained lips, blue and black pieces from her long flowing hair, golden pieces from her smooth skin. If he found the right spot in Kodi, he could release the sea worms from his trough and call the other worms to swarm and reconstitute the lost body of his sweetheart in the sea.

Lendu and Pala Kawata returned to Sumba, following along the same pathway as the first ancestors:

They came to Cape Sasar far away	Duki la Haharo malango
The road that they traveled	A lara li pa lini

Past seven layers of fences	Nggallu pitu wala
They arrived at the stone bridge	Toma la kataka lendu watu
On the path that they followed	A annu li ha mane
Past stone walls up to the knees	Kanale cadu kuha

They followed the northern coast to the region of Bukambero, where the megapode bird was released. She immediately began to gather up bits of mud to make a huge nest to lay her eggs. The nest was as tall as a high-towered house, so the bird was called Wondo Cabeka ["the great house builder"]. Her eggs were incubated in the mud nest until they hatched into a man and a woman, who became the first inhabitants of an area called Ngundu Ngora Tana, Pyapo Ndara Lewa ["the cape of land stretching out, the round cheeks of tall horses"]. They took the wild foods brought from overseas and settled there.

Lendu observed the techniques that the megapode bird used to construct her house and taught the other Sumbanese to build their own homes in the same fashion—standing on wooden piles with tall thatch towers, so that their finest heirlooms could be stored in the tower. He himself build a large house with a great tower in the interior of the district of Bukambero.

Narrated by Temba Palako, Pati Merapati, Bukambero

This narrative marks the beginning of a sequence of events. The descendants of Lendu and the children of the megapode bird are the present inhabitants of Bukambero, numbering some four thousand; their home is at the northern edge of the domain of Kodi, and although most them are fluent in Kodi, at home they speak their language (*paneghe bukambero*), which is most closely related to Laura. Because Bukambero is a marginal territory, however, this narrative is a potentially controversial part of the corpus of the "Kodi past." As the first architect of Kodi villages, Lendu had an important role to play in defining the region's cultural identity, but he is not acknowledged as a founder of Kodi. In Tossi, people play down his importance, stressing the fact that Lendu received the sea worms overseas but (as we shall see) was not able to keep them for himself.

Lendu's courtship of the daughter of Rato Ndimya, who later metamorphoses into Inya Nale, the female spirit of the sea worms, recalls the Javanese tradition of Nyai Lara Kidul, Goddess of the South Seas. She became the special protectress of the House of Mataram after a similar series of events:

According to Mataram tradition, she was a princess of Pajajaran who had been driven from the court when she refused a marriage arranged by her father. He laid upon her a curse: she was made queen of the spirits with her place beneath the waters of the Indian Ocean, and would only become a normal woman again on the Day of Judgement. . . . After Senapati [the perhaps mythical founder of Mataram] had spent three days with her in her underwater palace, the Goddess promised him the support of her spirit army.

(Ricklefs 1981, 38)

Like the Javanese princess, Inya Nale is the female consort of the "ruler" of Kodi and can be summoned to appear only by those who possess certain sacred objects (green cloth in Java, the sea worm trough in Kodi). Her unwillingness to marry Lendu is sometimes interpreted as showing that he was not an appropriate leader for all of Kodi, thus requiring the transfer of the worms to others.

While the people of Bukambero are acknowledged to be the custodians of an ancient and in many ways powerful form of knowledge, other people in Kodi are profoundly suspicious of them and of this version of the origin of the worms. Lendu is recognized to have had the worms in his possession at a certain point, but versions told in Mete and Tossi say that it was in fact Temba and Raghe who brought the worms from overseas. Another form of secret knowledge that Lendu is widely believed to have brought to the island is not mentioned in this myth: the knowledge of secret poisons (*pawunu*), which find their way into food served to guests in Bukambero and which work, like witchcraft, to consume the internal organs of the victim and transfer all his strength and vitality to the witch who has afflicted him. All the people of Bukambero are suspected of being involved in witchcraft, though most deny that the occult arts are practiced by more than a tiny number of the indigenous inhabitants. The descendants of two matriclans (Walla Kyula, Walla Ngedo) and the patriclan of Wei Wyalla Pati Merapati are particularly notorious for their knowledge of poisons, herbs, and wild foods.

In the narrative, Lendu receives *nale* in disguised form: the gift of the daughter is in fact the gift of the worms. Lendu believes that he is receiving a human bride, but in fact he receives only the shattered pieces of her body—the sea worms which will bring him the renewal of life that he seeks. The trickster is thus, in one sense, tricked, since he does not get what he bargained for and his most precious gift cannot be used in his own homeland but must be passed on.

The text introduces a symbolic trope that we will encounter in other narratives as well: the idea of an original location which in some way proved unworthy. This trope is useful because it is open to multiple interpretations, and the tension between different versions is often not resolved. Thus, from the perspective of this storyteller, the narrative establishes the ritual priority of Bukambero, since the worms were brought by Lendu from overseas. From the perspective of other storytellers whose narratives follow, however, it establishes only that Bukambero was the first of a series of different locations for the worms on Sumba, but not their definitive home. In denying the consequences of the story told in Bukambero, the people of Mete and Tossi incorporate many similar elements (especially the idea of a series of games and trials) into accounts of subsequent events.

TEXT #2: THE JOURNEY OF THE SEA WORMS
AND THE FOUNDING OF TOSSI

Since Lendu lived in the interior and could not release the sea worms near his home, he traveled out to the coastal region, passing through the deep forests of Honde Ryara. There he met two small boys, Mangilo and Pokilo, who were living all alone in a "Monkey Shack" that served as an outpost for hunting monkeys and wild pigs. Mangilo and Pokilo saw the worms and thought they were a plaything—a bauble made of cotton, a skein of colored strings [*maghana lelu, mangguna hario*]. They wanted to play with them, but Lendu was not sure that he should surrender them. He invited them to come stay with him in Bukambero.

A little while later, Temba and Raghe came by. Temba and Raghe had migrated from islands to the west, sailing to the northern promontory of Sasar, where their wooden boat was smashed to pieces on the stone bridge that then linked Sumba and Sumbawa. Their father was Tana Mete ["Black Land"], their mother was Ndabi, and their descendants were also "black" [i.e., members of the village of Mete]. They traveled to the island of Sumba with many other companions, but they were the first to reach the western tip of Kodi. They sailed around the island to the east, past the southern districts of Anakalang, Wanokaka, Lamboya, and Gaura, and eventually to Kodi. They stopped in Balaghar and set up a stone, called the Temba Raghi stone. Near the western tip of the island they stopped and planted a garden at Kule Ndako, the "Wandering Board Game,"[3] named after a game they played on their trip.

One day they wandered farther inland and discovered there were other people living in the area, who did not have gardens or cook their food. They were hunters, skilled in herbal medicines, and eaters of raw foods, who knew many poisons and occult secrets. They lived with the

---

[3] *Kule* is a game played by inserting *dedap* seeds into a piece of wood in particular formations. It is traditionally associated with the sea worm festivities, and it is taboo to play it in the period preceding the arrival of the worms.

wild animals and wild spirits of the region [*marapu la kandaghu*], and some of them were said to be witches and eaters of human flesh. Temba and Raghe made a peace pact with one of them, an old woman who lived in a hut made of bitter creepers [*warico lolo kapadu*]. She had no fresh water, only brackish water, and no cured tobacco or dried areca nut, only fresh leaves and fruits. But she lived in a fertile valley and was willing to let them live beside her if they promised not to harm her or her husband. Temba and Raghe cut off bits of their fingernails and hair and scraped a bit of flesh from their tongues to be put into a bamboo flask as proof of their pact. They settled at the upper end of the village, in what became Mete Deta, and the old woman and her descendants settled in Mete Wawa. But the village was still empty and lonely.

Temba and Raghe invited Mangilo and Pokilo to join them in settling the new territory of Kodi. But Lendu and his brother, Atu Awa, were reluctant to part with them. Temba and Raghe played a trick on the boys to persuade them to move to the coast: they filled their drinking gourds with coconut water and offered them to the boys.

"Where does this delicious water come from?" asked Mangilo.

"It comes from the coast, where every day you can drink this sweet liquid," Temba and Raghe said. They did not tell them how parched the region could be in the dry season, or that fresh water was not available for much of the year. Each day, they fetched new coconuts to feed to the boys so that they would agree to join them in their new home.

Temba and Raghe wanted to adopt the boys, but their guardians in Bukambero did not agree. "If you take them away like that, you will be stealing our younger brothers, and that will be the beginning of an unending enmity, like that of cat and mouse. Our people will come to take heads from your people, and your people will come to take heads from ours."

"No, we do not want that, so we will give you something to compensate you for the food and betel nut that you have given to raise them." Lendu Myamba was given a huge gold breastplate, the *marangga bali byapo* ["breastplate of both sides of the river," the couplet name for the Kodi territory], to secure his blessing. That breastplate is still to be found in Wai Walla, Bukambero, as proof of the fact that the masters of the Kodi calendar spent their youth there. It also assures the people of both regions that they are not strangers to each other, and cannot take heads on the warpath.

Lendu had to provide a countergift for the gold valuable that he had received, and he also wanted to provide the boys with something that would bring them good fortune in their new home. He decided to give them the "plaything" they admired so much, but it came with ritual requirements.

"My home is too far from the seashore," he said, "so I will give these worms to you so you can play with them like cotton baubles, amuse yourselves with string games. But there are also responsibilities. Once you release the worms into the sea, they will come back each year on a specific day, and you must count the years and measure the months to determine the proper day. They must be greeted with a mounted battle, the *pasola*, so you must find a village site where the horses can run without hurting their feet. You must teach the others to observe the taboos that come with welcoming these special creatures, and then you will receive good harvests and many descendants."

Mangilo and Pokilo took the worms close to the sea shore, but as the boys played, the worms got washed away in the river water.

"Where are the sea worms?" Temba asked.

"They have disappeared," the boys answered.

"Then go look for them, all over Kodi if necessary!" said Temba.

They searched all along the coast, and found that the worms had been caught by the roots and trunk of a banyan tree at Kawango Wulla [the "Moon's Banyan," near Tossi]. The worms were rescued and taken out to the sea at Kawoto, near the western tip of Sumba at Cape Karosso. But the land there was too rocky for horses to run without hurting their feet. Then they took them to the midpoint of the coastline, Halete, in the center of the line of ancestral villages called Pola Kodi, "the trunk of Kodi." There, the worms swarmed in great numbers and washed up on a sandy beach where they could be easily collected. A large flat grass field lay beside the beach, perfectly situated to receive the thousands of horses and riders of the *pasola*. The site was renamed Kapambolo Nale Hari, Karangga Rica Marapu ["Platform for Sacred Sea Worms, Beam of Spirit *Pule* Wood," the present site of the *pasola* combat]. This was the best site for the sea worm woman [Nyale] to be reborn.

When the trough was placed at this site, in the shade of the Kawango Wulla tree, the next day they found on the beach a great porcelain urn that had washed up from the sea. The urn was filled with cool, fresh water, which Mangilo and Pokilo drank, surprised that it was not salty after being tossed for so long by the waves. "This will be our village," they said, "and here will be the home of the sea trough and the urn that cannot be lifted." It was clear that after this long journey, the sea worms would remain at this site, which is where Pokilo and Mangilo built their own village, Tossi.

Narrated by Guru Kedu, Mete, Pola Kodi

This narrative uses the trope of a journey to establish both a series of areas that have some residual rights to participate in sea worm rituals and the primacy of the two oldest villages in Kodi, Mete and Tossi. Since it was collected from a descendant of Temba and Raghe, it places them in the spotlight, stressing the events that made them the "first to claim the land, and first to build a village" (*kapunge tana, tandai parona*). However, as in the story of Lendu from Bukambero, this narrative finishes with the sea worms being passed on to another owner. In some versions told in Tossi and Wai Kahumbu, the trip overseas to obtain *nale* is carried out not by Lendu but by Lete Watu, the trickster who exchanged fire for water in the narrative about the origin of the seasons (see chapter 2). Lete Watu was the younger brother of Mangilo, who later split off to found the village of Wai Kahumbu.[4]

The long search for the proper place to hold the horse jousting combines practical considerations with political ones: the form of *pasola* is taken as a heritage from the overseas kingdom of Rato Ndimya, linking the promise of fertility that comes from the worms' swarming to a ritual condition that these visitors be welcomed with a proper spectacle. Lendu, Temba, and Raghe surrender their earlier rights in order to place the worms in a new location that is not merely close to the sea but at the very center of the line of ancestral villages along the western coasts.

The relationship of Mete and Tossi in this narrative is that between an adoptive father and his young sons. It contrasts sharply with the one we see in text #5, where Mangilo and Pokilo turn on their earlier benefactors and usurp the site of the "unopened land and round stones" (*mboka tana, mbola watu*) where the ancestors first settled. But let us first turn to two other stories of change and disruption in the times of the earliest settlements.

TEXT #3: RA HUPU AND THE DISRUPTION OF THE REGION

After several years, the region grew more inhabited, but it became unsafe. Settlers along the western beaches began to notice that their pigs and chickens were disappearing mysteriously. The raids escalated, and soon not only small animals but also horses, buffalo, and even people were perishing. The trouble was caused by Ra Hupu, the younger brother of Mangilo.

When Ra Hupu was just a boy, he began to throw small nets of cotton string in front of the house. He threw the nets at grasshoppers, as a game. But when he caught grasshoppers, poor people began to die here and there. Their souls were caught in the webbing of the magical nets.

[4] Lete Watu strongly resembles the Weyewa figure of Yanda Mette (Kuipers 1990) and is also associated with two brothers, Anda Mangu Langu and Mete Mangu Dulu, who were, in some accounts, the first Sumbanese to arrive on the island. Some say, using a folk etymology derived from Indonesian Malay, that Anda, the elder brother, went first into the tides, while Mete "first waited" (Ind. *mangu dulu*), then followed him. Others say that Langu and Dulu were the names of the wives who accompanied these two brothers to the new land.

His spirit was fierce, it was not good, so he could not control this magical power. When he grew up, he bought thread of many colors—black, white, yellow, and red. He wove nets from this thread, and smelted heavy weights for the nets from gold.

This time, when he went down to the seashore to cast his nets, they were powerful enough to endanger not just poor people but important ones. He would cast them in the sea and catch the bearded *manduli* fish and the *mangata* fish with a straight tail [couplet name for the nobles and wealthy men who became his prey]. Ra Hupu grew into a huge man with a forelock of yellow hair who could breathe flames of fire. When others objected, he went on a rampage to punish them, sending out lightning bolts or fierce winds, which blew so furiously that all their tender young crops were destroyed.

The people of Kodi decided to meet in Tossi to establish a system of order that could control his rampages. "We must send you off to cool your head. You will go into exile in the next valley, where you will live at the corner of the river and the edge of the tides," said Rato Mangilo.

The meeting was held in the Uma Batango (Council House) in Tossi, presided over by Temba and Raghe, known as Temba who established the villages and Raghe who owns the land [*Temba tandai parona, Raghe kapunge tana*], since they were the founders of the region who established the first rights to land. All of the lands in Kodi were divided between the ancestral clans and houses, and a single mother-father village had to be chosen to keep order and oversee the annual cycle of the months.

At this meeting, Ra Hupu was banished to the other side of the river, to "soak his head and cool his liver" in the fresh waters that flowed down from the highlands. He was told to

Go off to the creeping bamboo vines	Otu bandikya ela onggolo lolo
Go off to the small bitter plants	Otu bandikya ela padu katapa
Home of the wild hens and white songbirds	Pandou tagheghe, pandou katara
The large coconut leaves	Nuha kalama
The twigs of *ledo* wood	Paworo ledu
Stand at the long snout of the tides	Ndende ela manumbu mara
Sit at the corner of the river	Londo la kabihu loko
Watch over the pike fish	Kandi ha kamboko
Guard the realm of the shrimp	Dagha ha tana kura
Cutting the meat separately	Roponi ha kabiyo
Heaping the rice on his own	Hanggani ha ngagha

With these words he was exiled to the other side of the embankment [Bali Hangali], where he and his descendants would live on their own territory, separate from the original villages of the "trunk of Kodi" [Pola Kodi] but still acknowledging their ritual preeminence. He was forbidden to steal from his fellow Kodinese, but his fierceness and fire were given a new focus in the skull tree erected in the center of his village, where the heads of enemy highlanders could be hung. On the warpath, his magical weapons and control of the winds could once again be used—but in Kodi they would not be unleashed for as long as the Sea Worm Priest [Rato Nale] remained confined during the month awaiting the swarming of the worms.

When he established his residence at Mba Ronggo, Ra Hupu moved into the territory of Pala Kawata, the python who had helped Lendu overseas. Pala Kawata came originally from the highlands, but in certain years he would visit the drier regions of Kodi, bringing with him abundant rains and unusual fertility. Pala Kawata took a fancy to Ra Hupu, so he adopted him as his nephew and moved his own residence farther upriver to the gates of the river and the source of the swamps [binye loko, mata rende]. The descendants of Ra Hupu have preserved a special ritual relationship with Pala Kawata, so that if they need more rainfall they can ask for it by shaking the trees at Mba Ronggo in the early hours of the dawn, or by making offerings of betel and chicken feathers at the sites associated with their ancestral names.

Narrated by Ngila Pati, Bondo Kodi, Mbali Hangali

This text serves largely to justify the land rights of the people of Bondo Kodi, who established rights to all the territories that border on the river. This right is expressed socially by the fact that they must receive the heads of all sacrificed buffalo and pigs throughout this region. It also comments, obliquely, on the problematic trope of first owners versus later owners that we noted in the first two narratives, since in this text Temba and Raghe preside over the consensus meeting, but it is held in the Council House in Tossi.

Ra Hupu, like Lendu, is an adventurer who is allied by fictive kinship with the python. While all sides agree that Ra Hupu was powerful and disruptive, his descendants stress the ways in which his magical powers could be put to the service of others—in obtaining rainfall or enemy heads, for instance. Detractors emphasize the losses suffered by his fellow villagers, which led to his exile. Because Ra Hupu and his descendants still control lightning and rainfall, members of other villages must go to them and present a sacrificial animal to request that rites be performed to bring rain or control lightning bolts.

The text views the central consensus agreement that established the ceremonial system from the periphery, the outermost edge of Greater Kodi. It also presents a part of the rituals of agriculture, whose more complete version is found in the next narrative.

TEXT #4: THE CREATION OF RICE AND OF THE BITTER AND BLAND MONTHS

The early settlers of Kodi were having a hard time making a living. While the soil was rich and fertile, rainfall was erratic, and long periods of hunger plagued the first generations who opened up gardens there. A diet of root crops, corn, vegetables, and beans was not enough to fill their bellies or to give them the sense that they had eaten at all.

Pala Kawata, the giant python who lived in the highlands, decided to make the supreme sacrifice to feed the others. His own daughter, Mbiri Koni, was nearing marriageable age, but she found none of her suitors to her liking. One day he came home and told her to dress up in all of her best finery. She put ivory bracelets on her wrists, a string of colored ceramic beads above them at the forearm, a gold *hamoli* pendant around her neck, and wrapped herself in fine indigo textiles dyed with intricate patterns. She presented herself to her father, glowing with girlish beauty, and he led her off into the center of his garden plot to meet her new "husband."

When they arrived at the platform built to hold the rice seeds, he took out his small harvesting knife and killed her. Then he cut her body into small pieces and buried it throughout the garden. He rinsed the blood from his loincloth, wiped his knife clean, and concealed it in the folds of his waistband. He went home to his wife, without a word about what had happened.

After their daughter did not return for two or three days, her mother grew very worried. "Perhaps someone has carried her off without our permission," she said. "Perhaps she has eloped."

"No, my wife," Pala Kawata answered. "That will never happen. Your daughter may not be visible now, but she is with you in the gardens, and she will show her face after four days."

On the fourth day, the mother went out into the gardens to call her daughter. "Ooooo, Mbiri Koni, where are you?"

"Here I am, Mother," came the daughter's voice, but she was nowhere to be found. Finally, the mother went to the seed platform and called again. "Ooooo, Mbiri Koni, where are you?"

"Here I am, Mother," answered the daughter's voice, "don't you recognize me? The mother turned in confusion to her husband, who told her: "Your daughter's body has returned to us in the small green sprouts that you see just breaking out of the ground at your feet. Her ivory bracelets have returned in the white tubers at the side of the garden, her ceramic beads in the beans, her gold pendant in the corn ears beside the rice. She has been transformed into the garden crops to save us all from hunger."

Her mother was so distraught she refused to eat any of the new crop. She became the old woman who guards the upright stone at the entrance to each garden plot [waricoyo ela watu kareke] and stayed in the garden with her daughter. Each year, when the rice seeds are planted, we say that Mbiri Koni has died and her mother goes into mourning for her.

We, the Sea Worm Priests, are also in mourning—we follow the rules of kabukuto kalalu, we sit in silence and brood. We wait throughout the bitter months, and do not allow anyone to beat the gongs or disturb the young crop. Then, when the rice crop is tall and golden and full [pa ihi; lit., "pregnant"], we hold the sacrifices to allow the harvest to happen. Once the sacrifices are done, the month is bland [kaba] and the crops can be eaten.

Narrated by Ra Ndengi, Rato Nale, Bukubani

Different versions of this story play on the changing identity of the "knife" and the person who wields it. In one, the girl meets a handsome young man, Rato Malogho, who is in fact a field rat. She marries him and becomes pregnant by him, but when he tries to take her home to his village under the ground, she cannot fit through the hole. He kills her and drags her body in piece by piece. Once she is completely underground, she remains there for four days before being reincarnated in the form of the rice crop. In another, Mbiri Koni is sacrificed by her brothers and sisters who migrated to the island with her, but her erstwhile suitor is so saddened that he chooses to become a field rat in order to join her underground.

In all these versions, the fate of Mbiri Koni clearly parallels the fate of Inya Nale, the foreign beauty whose body was transformed into the sea worms. Each is a bride whose body is dismembered and transformed to create a resource needed by the whole region. The "gift of a woman" in marriage is thwarted, but a symbolic equivalent—the source of fertility and vitality—is substituted.

In the following pivotal text, we learn of the consensus agreement that leads to the regulating of the harvest by the priests of the sea worms.

TEXT #5: THE KODI MONTHS AND THE DIVISION OF RITUAL TASKS

When the leaders of Kodi gathered to divide up the lands and the various ritual tasks, they did so by using the divinatory powers of objects. Four ritual objects were brought to this meeting to make the selection: the

kule game with eight holes, the *buke* stakes and darts, the *kadiyo* top
made of buffalo horn, and the *kalayo* discus. These were all divination
tools which the first ancestors brought with them from Sasar.

Representatives of each of the ancestral villages played each other in
the traditional children's games:

They played the *kule* board with eight holes	A kolekongo kule pando pato
They won the *buke* game with four sticks	A talerongo buke pato ghaiyo
Throwing the top of buffalo horn	Watani a kadiyo kadu kari
Tossing the discus of round seed	Watani a kaleiyo mbombo
To set up interdictions in the groves	Tana roto waingo hemba
To establish taboos in the village	Tana weri waingo napu
With the spear of planting	Mono dikya a tonda nambu
With the wrapped land and stones	A kambolo tana, kambolo watu

Mangilo and Pokilo defeated all the others, easily smashing their
opponents' tops and outdoing them in contests of skill and strategy. This
established their right to serve as the "mother-father" figures of the
region.

There was then a division of power between the two brothers based
on birth order. Mangilo, the older one, was told:

You guard the immovable urn	Yo na daghi a ngguhi nja pa dadango
You watch the plate that can't be lifted	Yo na kandi a pengga nja pa keketo
The hen who broods over her eggs	Bei myanu na kabukutongo taluna
The sow who calls to her young	Bei wyawi na karekongo anana
Hold onto the knots in *dewang* leaves, the knots of pandanus leaves	Kete bandikya ha kawuku mboro, ha kawuku panda
To count the years in the sea worm land	Tanaka ghipo ndoyo ela tana nale
To measure months in the bitter land	Tanaka baghe wulla ela tana padu
Holding the sacred trough	Ketengo a rabba rica
Grasping the wooden trap	Ketengo a keko nalo

Given the most sacred of the ancestral heirlooms, Mangilo retired
into relative seclusion. He served as the guardian of the calendar and the
yearly seasonal cycle, but took no active part in enforcing the rules that
he established.

Through his calculations, the times of planting and harvesting were
controlled and agricultural activities were coordinated throughout the

region. No one could hold feasts once the preparations of the gardens had begun, and none of the tender young plants could be picked before they reached maturity. Rato Mangilo received the lightning stones used to direct lightning bolts at offenders of these prohibitions, and promised to remain in strict confinement in the months preceding the coming of the sea worms.

Rato Mangilo then named the twelve months of the Kodi calendar [see table 1]:

The first month of preparations before the sea worms came was called [1] Nale Kiyo, and it was during this month that he performed sacrifices to make the tree crops of *pinang* and coconut ready for the harvest [*kaba wei kapoke*; lit., "bland waters on the sprouts," since water from the sacred urn was poured on them]. The month of the worms' arrival was called [2] Nale Bokolo, and it was when the *pasola* combat was staged. It was preceded by offerings of betel nut on the tombs of one's ancestors [*hengapungo*] and followed by the sacrifice of a chicken in each lineage house [*tunu manu nale*]. Then came [3] Nale Wallu, for the "remaining" [*wallu*] worms of the second swarming. [4] Bali Mboka, the "return of small buds," marked the beginning of the harvest season, followed by [5] Katota Lalo, the "small red flowers" of a common bush, and [6] Katoto Bokolo, the "large red flowers." Feasting on a large scale was not supposed to begin until [7] Rena Kiyo, the preparations for celebrations, then [8] Rena Bokolo, the larger celebrations. Feasting could continue through the period called [9] Padu Lamboya, but had to stop once the priests had performed the sacrifices necessary to start the Kodi "bitter months," or [10] Padu Kodi. Silence had to be observed throughout [11] Habu, the "nesting" [*habu*] season for birds, and [12] Mangata, the month when the white flowers of the *mangata* bush were visible.

His younger brother Pokilo received a fast-traveling horse [*ndara halato*] and was given the task of patrolling the area to guard against theft or trespassing onto another man's gardens. He was told:

You are the horse with the upright tail	Yo a ndara ndende kiku
You are the dog with the black tongue	Yo a bangga mete lama
Who roams past the posts in the region	Na halato kataku loda
Crossing through the fields	Na doda marada
Who roams past the posts in the area	Na halato kataku pada
Parting the elephant grass	Na pepe kapumbu
Seeing the crossed boundaries	Na haranga manumbu likye
Seeing the gardens that stretch too far	Na haranga mangora mango

His was the task of roaming through dangerous border territories, mediating between litigious parties, and leading war parties, if necessary,

Table 1. The Kodi Months and Agricultural Calendar

	Rains/Wind	Hunting and Fishing	Crops	Ceremonies
Nale Kiyo "small seaworms" (January)		Octopus collected at low tide	First corn crop matures Coconut and *pinang*	*Kaba wei kapoke*: "bland young shoots of *pinang* and coconut" *Kaba wataro*: corn made bland
Nale Bokolo "large seaworms" (February)	Heaviest rains and wind	Sea worms swarm along the beaches		*Nale* festivities *Pasola* jousting
Nale Wallu "leftover worms" (March)				
Bali Mbyoka "return to growth" (April)	Thunder, cold winds	*Ipu* fish swarm in the bay		
Rena Kiyo "small blossoms" (May)	End of rains Dry season *mara tana*	Mice hunted in the fields	Rice crop matures and is harvested Second corn crop matures	*Kahale kaba pare*: harvest rites to make rice bland and edible
Rena Bokolo "great blossoms" (June)		Wild pigs and monkeys hunted in the forest		*Yaigho* singing ceremonies *Dari Uma* house building

Month	Season	Crops	Ritual
Katoto Waharongo "cottonwood blossoms" (July)		Tubers, beans, vegetables	*Woleko* buffalo feasts *Gharu Watu* stone dragging
Nduka Katoto "full cottonwood flowers" (August)	Burning fields before the first rains	Mangoes, papayas, diverse fruit	Largest-scale feasts and celebrations
Padu Lamboya "Lamboya bitter month" (September)	Beginning of the hunger season *wulla malamba*		*Padu* planting prohibitions
Padu Kodi "Kodi bitter month" (October)	First rains of the wet season (*righuto*)	Planting rice, corn Weeding fields, planting other garden crops	
Habu "bird's nest" (November)	Heavier rainfall	Intensive work in the gardens	
Mangata "flowering white shrub" (December)			Period of ritual silence: the "bitter months"

against invading groups. He was the "master of force" whose powers counterbalanced the elder "master of time."

Then they divided up into separate villages. Each man of importance was told to establish his own village so that they would have enough villages to intermarry. The villages took the name of the site they occupied, and the tree which served as their altar. The *lara marapu*, or "path of the ancestors" recited in each village, began with Temba and Raghe, the founders of the land, and then went on to name those who dug the first pillar holes and put together the foundation stones at each village site. The indigenous spirits of the earth [*tagheghe mori lyodo, wondo mori pyada*, "forest fowl lord of the region, megapode lord of the area"] also received invocations and sacrifices, as did the deputy hamlet deity [*inya mangu tana, bapa mangu loko*] in the gardens.

There were twenty-four villages formed from the "trunk of Kodi" (Pola Kodi), and seventeen on the other side of the embankment (Mbali Hangali). All of these villages come together now to sacrifice chickens to the sea worms and offer the first fruits of the harvest to Toda.

Narrated by Ra Holo, Rato Nale, Tossi

This version of the central narrative of the division of powers and the establishment of the calendar was obtained from a 1980 interview with both the Rato Nale of Tossi and a retired Kodi minister, Pendita Ndoda, who was descended from the Sea Worm House and helped with translations and transcriptions. It is the closest thing to a "charter" in the Malinowskian (1954) sense for the Kodi ceremonial order as it exists today. Parts of this narrative may be strongly contested, however, and there are many different interpretations of its relevance to present action.

The most widely known and quoted part of this narrative is the division of power between Rato Mangilo and Rato Pokilo. These couplets provided the first model of a diarchic divide, which was then repeated, in subtly different ways, in a number of other areas. The Kodi assertion that it provided an "unchanging template" is at least partly supported by the fact that the only previous recording of the narrative, by Onvlee and Kapita in 1932, cites the couplets in almost exactly the same form as I heard them in 1980, even though the wider political situation was quite different at that time. A consensus that Tossi had the role of ceremonial leader because of its control of the calendar remains, along with ideas that Bondo Kodi has access to rain magic and Toda receives the first fruits of the harvest. All other ancestral villages are the *ari ana*, or "younger siblings and children," of these founding villages and trace their ancestry to their founding figures.

Beyond this core template, however, interpretations of the events that occurred at this distant meeting vary widely. The first alternate interpretation that I will develop emerges from the background to Onvlee and Kapita's visit to Kodi in 1932, and illustrates what was at stake in manipulating versions of the ancestral agreement. The Kodi transcripts of texts recorded by Onvlee and Kapita include a version of this story, narrated by Haghe Tyena of Mete and Rehi Kyaka Ndari of Tossi, that repeats the peace pact between Kodi and Bukambero established with the transfer of the breastplate and adds that the first gardens were made at Kule Ndako. These tellers also said that Temba and Raghe brought sacred stones with them from their homeland to the west, which they used to consecrate the land and make it "bland" (*pakabaya*) enough to cultivate (Onvlee and Kapita 1932).

The interview was dominated by Raja Ndera Wulla, the district ruler at the time, who summoned the two storytellers to give their account, but "insisted on speaking first while all others remained silent," saying that he had invited the others "to confirm his accounts, in case there were suspicions that he had made misleading statements" (Onvlee 1973, 57). The primacy of Tossi had to be stressed in his presence, and ambiguities about its position played down. The raja finished the interview with an invocation of his ancestor, Rato Pokilo, and an assertion that "I was given the land of Kodi from the beginning of the earth and stones, and if I now command, it did not begin when I first held the Raja's staff, but because Pokilo and his descendants have always been those who commanded from the time of our ancestors and forefathers" (Onvlee 1973, 59).

In a later recollection of the 1932 visit, Onvlee reports that Haghe Tena came to see him privately in Waikabubak and "presented a story in which the relationships were rather differently represented" (Onvlee 1973, 59). Mangilo and Pokilo received the sea worms and their ritual offices as a gift from Temba and Raghe, who sought them out as companions in order to defend themselves against enemy attack. Mete was the oldest village and the real "elder brother," whose authority was based on the "unopened land and the round stones" (*mboka tana, mbolo watu*), while Mangilo and Pokilo were just boys who received these important ritual offices without knowing what to do with them. Haghe Tena described them as "locusts scampering on cassava leaves, bats balancing on banana leaves" (*papa enggena kabala rou katete, pa pandeta panighe rou kalogho*), meaning, as Onvlee (1973, 60) says, "they did not have themselves to thank for the good place that they currently occupied."

Reinterpreting this account with the benefit of hindsight, I would classify it within the same trope as the Bukambero story. We have, on the one hand, a group that maintains its prior rights to the worms as a source of traditional authority, and on the other, a group that stresses the significance of the transfer while implying that the first site was unworthy. During my own fieldwork, tensions between Tossi and Mete were muted, presumably in part because Tossi was no longer the center of district government. But I did record a narrative about how the people of Tossi tricked the people of Mete into abandoning their original village site and moving a short distance to the north. The source of this story, however, was not Mete, but another faction within Tossi: the storyteller was himself a descendant of Rato Mangilo and told the tale as an example of the cleverness of his ancestors, who used their superior ritual position to appropriate the most sacred village site in the area.

TEXT #6: HOW TOSSI AND METE CHANGED PLACES

The place where Tossi is now located once belonged to Mete. It is the oldest village site in Kodi and was founded by Temba, who built the first villages, and Raghe, who owned the land. Tossi was originally located to the north of them, and it was founded by Mangilo and Pokilo.

One day, as he took his horse to the *pasola*, Rato Mangilo rode past Mete and began to think: "Here we are, the guardians of the most sacred objects in the land, but we do not have the best village site. It would be much better if we were right at the edge of the *pasola* field, so as soon as we untied our horses we would be ready to ride out to receive the sea worms." He thought and thought, but found no solution. So he told Rato Pokilo to call Lete Watu.

Rato Mangilo told him: "I want you to figure out a way for us to change places with Mete, so they won't be closer than us to the field."

Lete Watu answered: "If you want to exchange villages, first go to a feast and tell them not to give any meat or rice to the people from Mete. When they ask why they haven't received their share, tell them that it has been a long time since they held a feast. Goad them into agreeing to feed the others, because once they hold a feast in their own village, we can outwit them and take over their village site."

Embarrassed by what they heard at the feast, Temba and Raghe of Mete planned a two-day feast [*woleko*]. They invited people from Kodi, Bangedo, Bukambero, and Karendi. Lete Watu built a platform outside the village gates to receive them, so they wouldn't enter the village. They all received food and betel at the gates and then settled down to sleep. Lete Watu called over four or five people and told them to take the swords of the Karendi and Bukambero people and stab all the pigs, horses, and buffalo. After killing the animals, they put the swords back in their scabbards and did not wipe off the blood.

The next day, the guests were horrified to see that all the animals were already dead and rotting, and Temba and Raghe were deeply embarrassed. They called out, "Stop the dancing, stop the slaughter. What has happened here? Who killed all these animals?" Their bodies were so numerous they couldn't be counted. Everyone gathered together and members of each region were asked. "No, we didn't do it," they all answered. They called Lete Watu to the village gates, and he suggested that they look at people's swords to see if they bore traces of blood. They looked at the swords of Kodi, Bangedo, and Balaghar and found no blood. They looked at the swords from Karendi and Bukambero, and they were full of blood. The people of Karendi and Bukambero were ashamed and ran away to settle at the farthest ends of the domain.

Then Lete Watu said, "This feast was a failure. There must be a curse on this village site:

It is as if there were	Hengyo ailyoloka ba nengyo
Mice under the heirloom Savunese urn	Loti kyambu ndunga haghu
Tickling the body hairs of the nobles	Wulu heghu ratu
It is as if there were	Hengyo ailyololoka ba nengyo
Termites in the pillar rings and	Wano kamba lele
Wood pests in the house posts	Kambilya pungu pongga

The village site is no good. If there is anyone else who would agree to come here, I would advise you to trade with them."

At this point, Rato Mangilo said: "Perhaps we are the ones who should help you out, since we are the mother-father village, the mother of the water jar and the father of the moon net. If you wish, I promise to drag the funeral stone that we have prepared for Temba until it stands by the former site of Tossi. And we will cut down the great tree of Tossi that stands by our house and replant its sprouts at our own new village site down here."

So they agreed, and the two villages changed their sites, with Temba moving back, away from the *pasola* field, and Tossi moving down. They sacrificed a buffalo and pig to establish themselves in the new location and banish the curse that afflicted the site. Mangilo brought the sacred water jar and the moon net and made his new home the place

Of the sacred priest who sits	Hola pyondi rato bihya
Counting out the years	Na ghipo a ndoyo
Of the ancient water jar	Hola habelia tana ndongo
Measuring the months	Na baghe a wulla

| In the pastures to tie the horses | La marada pangu ndara |
| By the bay to bind the ships | La menanga horo tena. |

Narrated by Ra Katupu, Tossi, Pola Kodi

This narrative accounts for two things: the estrangement and isolation of two peoples who intermarried with the indigenous peoples of the area, the people of Bukambero and Karendi; and the displacement of Mete at the oldest village site. In both cases, it celebrates the triumph of crafty newcomers over earlier inhabitants.

The narrative told in Tossi about the acquisition of the sea worms does not refer to a change in village sites. The location of the Kawango Wulla, or "Moon's Banyan," is assumed to be unchanging. It now stands near the present village gates, at the entrance to the *pasola* field, about two hundred feet from the beach. If the waves once washed up at its roots and deposited sea worms there, marking the spot on which the village was to be constructed, one wonders why Mangilo and Pokilo first chose to build their houses farther inland. Ra Katupu, the narrator of this version, reconciled it with the story told by the Rato Nale by saying that "Mangilo and Pokilo were young boys when they first came, and still ignorant. Once they grew up, they saw that Temba and Raghe had a better location, and so they decided they wanted it."

Contradictory assertions about the centralization of Tossi's power, said to be unmoving yet at the same time continually tested and reaffirmed, emerge in the events of the early twentieth century (see chapter 4). Before the colonial period, such assertions cannot be directly associated with remembered history, but political processes contesting Tossi's position through often conflicting interpretations have left traces in narratives such as this one. The emphasis on trickery and guile is much less evident in the next narrative, which details the agreement to extend the calendrical system beyond the Greater Kodi valley to the distant region of Balaghar.

TEXT #7: THE CREATION OF A BRANCH OF
THE SEA WORM FESTIVITIES IN BALAGHAR

Many years after the first settlement of Kodi, the population filled the territories of Kabihu Pola Kodi and Kabihu Mbali Hangali, so people moved across the river into the valley of Bangedo and even farther across an estuary into Balaghar. Since they were still descended from the original founders, they still had to travel back to Tossi and Bukubani for the calendrical rites.

One day, Pyunggero, from the village of Wainjolo Wawa in Balaghar, asked for a meeting with the elders of Tossi. Rato Mangilo and Rato

Pokilo, now old men, attended, as well as Temba and Raghe, Ra Hupu, and many others. Pyunggero stood to make a speech;

I ask permission to tell you, Mangilo	Di moka diyo, henene, Mangilo
That although we strike to the same beat	Mono ba na hama douka a tuku
And row to the same rhythm	Mono ba na mera douka a bohe
As our older brothers who establish taboos	Ghagha a kapada mburu weri
And make offerings to the sea worms	Ghagha a katende ngara nale
We beg you to consider the fact that	Pa we kimi ngara yama
At *nale* we cross the river	Nduka nale mono dowa kiyo loko
At *padu* we ford the bay	Nduka padu mono palu menanga
To gather all in one granary	A kambango mangoto
Bringing *nale* chickens to mother	Ngandi manu nale la kaha inya
At the net of heirloom valuables	Ela kareco londo laka
To assemble in one rice sack	A lepeto makaha
Bringing *padu* chickens to father	Ngandi manu padu la kaha bapa
By the ancient water jar	Ela pandalu ndunga haghu
Give a twig of the sacred branch to	Wo kini ana kahanga bihya
The children of the ship at Wei Lyala	Tangguna ana tena wei lyala
Give a piece of the taboo stone to	Wo kini ana watu mburi weri
The children of the village of Weinyapu	Tangguna ana wei nyapu

He was asking the officials of Tossi and Bukubani to delegate their powers to people in Balaghar, who would serve as lower-ranking ritual officers but would be able to preside over their own ceremonial calendar. If they agreed, there would be a division of territories expressed as a separation of the food served at feasts, which would henceforth be "meat cut up separately, rice heaped in a new plate" [*ropini kabiyo, hanggani ngagha*].

Rato Mangilo and the elders of the main ritual villages in Pola Kodi considered this request, but said that it would be necessary to test the leaders of each of the villagers in Balaghar, as they had been tested themselves, to see who was capable of controlling the calendar:

So that we can know who is able to	Tana peghe nggama ngara na tutu a
Hold up the taboos on the land	Ketengo a kapada mburu weri
And the offerings to the sea worms	Mono a katende ngara nale
Let us cast ropes on the headrest	Tanaka ta magholo la luna baka
So that we will recognize the one who	Tana tandi nggama ngara na tutu a

Can make rice and water bland again	Ketengo a kaba weiyo, kaba ngagha
Let us have a divination at the pillar	Tanaka ta urata la pongga baka

The method of divination that was required for this occasion, however, was not the usual interrogation with a spear or reading of animal entrails, but once again the playing of children's games, which combine elements of skill and chance to determine the best candidates.

So a competition was held, first with the *kule* board and the *buke* darts. The representatives from Balaghar played against the officeholders in Tossi. Rato Mangilo played *kule* against Lere Ura, from Waingyali, the oldest village in Balaghar. If Rato Mangilo had won, it would have been a sign that the spirits of the heirloom objects concerned—the holy branch and sacred bough, the ancient water jar and the net of valuables—were not in agreement and could not be moved. But Lere Ura won, taking all of Rato Mangilo's seeds. Pyunggero played *buke* against Rato Pokilo, and defeated him.

The people of Tossi called for a rematch, this time with the tops and discus [*kadiyo, kalayo*]. The new series was played by Lete Watu, from the village of Wainjoko, and Rato Jadi, from Kaha Malagho. Once again, the challengers won—but they won a victory that was divided between two players, rather than a simple conquest on all fronts. So the sacred prerogatives of Rato Mangilo to control the annual calendar and the agricultural rites were divided between two villages in Balaghar—Weingyali for the *nale* offerings, and Kaha Malagho for the *padu* offerings. Likewise, the powers of Rato Pokilo to control the borders and control the rains were divided between Wainjolo Wawa and Wainjoko.

Lere Ura from Waingyali received a small trough to hold the sea worms and a trap to scoop them up, just like the ones that Lendu had brought from overseas and given in turn to Mangilo. Rato Jadi of Kaha Malagho received a twig from the sacred kapok tree (Wei Marongo Rara), which stood by a source in Tossi, where offerings were placed to begin the ritual silence of *padu*. Rato Pyunggero received a fast-traveling horse [*ndara halato*], of the same descent line as the one used by Rato Pokilo, which he could use to patrol the region and enforce land boundaries. Lete Watu received a bamboo tube used to ask for rain [*onggolo ura*]. All of these objects were brought back to Balaghar, and feasts were held to consecrate them in their new home.

Narrated by Maru Daku, Wainjolo Wawa, Balaghar

This text legitimates the transfer of the sea worms to a new region by "summarizing" events from many of the earlier narratives, especially text #5, and placing them in a new context. Perhaps because of its skill in borrowing elements from the familiar stories of the founding of Kodi, this narrative provoked the suspicion of various local people who listened to it on tape. Their ambivalence may reflect an uneasiness about the legitimacy of the Balaghar rites. Despite the acknowledgment that the source of their calendrical ritual was the older "trunk of Kodi," many people in Greater Kodi dismiss the smaller *nale* rites held in Balaghar as insignificant, asserting that nothing of importance was transferred.

The villages of Balaghar were the most remote in all Kodi for most of this century, since no road reached them until 1988. As a result, this most recently settled region remained a bastion of tradition, where less than a fifth of the population had converted to Christianity. The calendrical rites of Balaghar, though they are derivative in terms of the mythical mandate, are performed with very full participation of the population and a passionate involvement, which contrasts with the more desultory performances in Tossi, now a village of many converts and extensive contacts with schools and government agencies. It is precisely because of the continuing importance of ancestral rites in Balaghar that many people suspected this detailed narrative was an "invention of tradition"—a bit too finely wrought to be genuine.

The narrative was collected from one of my finest informants, Maru Daku, who was among the first Kodi converts to Christianity in the 1920s but then returned to traditional worship late in his life (Hoskins 1985). Although he was recognized as one of the best ritual speakers in the region and a skilled compiler of ancestral lore, he also provoked mistrust and criticism. As someone who had been a practitioner in both systems, the Christian and the pagan, he was said to have been punished by his ancestral spirits and the Christian God for "worshipping two sets of gods"; this charge diminished his credibility in reciting the most sacred stories. His gift for rhetorical flourishes was seen as "adding too many spices to the stew" and thus concealing the basic flavor and consistency of their original form.

Since each time a story is narrated it takes a slightly different form, Maru Daku's critics may simply have been accusing him of being too effective at his task of providing coherence. "He has been studying our own stories," they said, "and so he knew what to put in his account to make it sound good." Maru Daku answered his critics with the physical evidence referred to in the narrative: the sea worm trough in Weingyali, the sacred banyan in Kaha Malagho, the bamboo tube in Weinjoko. A narrative attached to an object can be proved true if the object is efficacious. Few other challenges were mounted.

Problems of Legitimacy, Authenticity, and Hierarchy

Consideration of these seven texts opens up numerous questions about the bases of ceremonial authority in narrative. Almost all of the texts contain, in some form, a trope embracing a tension between an earlier owner of a sacred object or site and a later one. The earlier owner can claim primacy, the later can try to show that he has achieved control. All of these narratives speak of how Kodinese ancestors have gradually gained a certain mastery of their surroundings through a social consensus about the proper use of objects with magical properties.

This transfer of power involves one of two processes: delegation by an older authority to a younger executor or usurpation through trickery. The first stresses genealogical priority and ascribed position, the second individual action and achieved rank. Often, the difference between the two is a matter of interpretation. Thus, the descendants of Temba and Raghe say that they gave the sea worms to Tossi out of generosity and a desire to help two orphaned boys. The descendants of Tossi, by contrast, say that they deserved the gift because of their superior skills in games, which allowed them to trick their benefactor into giving them even the site of his own village. The people of Bukambero, for their part, say that they originally acquired the sea worms but knew they should pass them on to people who lived closer to the beach. And the people of the coastal villages maintain that they were always the rightful owners, so their use of false accusations to drive out the earlier inhabitants was justified by hierarchical privilege.

The differences between the two modes reflects the variety of interacting oppositions that constitute hierarchy. The locus of authority is opposed to the locus of action, and the production of asymmetries of power emerges as "not a principle but an outcome, the result of the application of several principles" (Fox 1989, 52). The "order of precedence" produced by the calendar thus comprises heterogeneous components, which include genealogy, spatial location, personal qualities of skill or bravery, and fortuitous circumstances. Power is conceived not as a single entity but as something that is immanent in a plurality of existing social relations (Foucault 1978).

Power is transferred in these narratives by means of three specific devices: descent (reckoned through persons, places, or objects), game playing, and offerings to obtain the fertility of the land. Descent is established either by the birth of the ancestor within a particular line or by the breaking apart of a whole object into parts that can be moved. Breaking off a sapling from the great tree at Tossi and planting it in Balaghar, for instance, establishes a plant line of descent, which substitutes for the absence of a human line of succession. The part is always less than the whole, however, and the transfer is thus of a diminished and subservient power. When descent is the criterion of transfer, an accompanying idea of devolution, of a lessening of status as one moves away from the source, is implied.

Such is not the case with things acquired through games and contests. Playing at tops and discus, the *kule* board and the *buke* darts, is a very serious business. In the ritual formulas still pronounced today, priests say they are only children who "hold the top's string, grasp the discus's net." They evoke children's games to protest their innocence and inexperience in relation to the ancestors, but also to remind their listeners of the primordial contest in which their ancestors emerged victorious. The theme of "playing" at ritual is related to the idea that the process of acquiring ritually charged objects is also part of the human process of learning and maturation. Mangilo and Pokilo, the ancestors of present-day calendrical priests, appear first as small children, tempted by the sea worms as playthings but not yet responsible enough to control them. They must first find the proper site for their village, then prove themselves through games. Once they have achieved the maturity to serve as the masters of time and of force, they agree to pass on some of their ritual prerogatives to junior deputies—but only in a divided and diminished form.

As the proper locations are sought and the proper intervals established, the need for rain and new crops arises. In several cases, the "proof" that one's ancestors had legitimate control of a certain territory is established by a ritual demonstration that rain can be obtained to nourish the land. The art of rainmaking is hardly a trivial one in a land as parched and prone to drought as Kodi. Rain is associated with disruptive, rebellious ancestral figures: Ra Hupu, Lete Watu, Rato Bokokoro—a thieving fisherman, a playful trickster, an easily duped guardian.

The power of the rainmaker is at the opposite pole from the power of the lawgiver, in a relationship similar to the elder brother/younger brother polarity that binds Mangilo and Pokilo. It provides the basis for the ritual cooperation of older source villages—the locus of authority—and younger peripheral villages—the locus of action. Rainmaking is represented as a violent assault on the heavenly kingdom, which explains why in mythic accounts it is associated with warfare and headhunting. The control of seasonal rains, thunder, and lightning is invested in stable, unmoving ritual authorities, whereas the disruption of these powers is a necessary infusion of energy associated with the young, mobile manipulators.

Time within the mythic narratives is constructed in relation to temporal sequences in the annual cycle of ceremonies. It is a common theme throughout Southeast Asia that a period of mourning is ended with a celebration of the renewal of life. Both Nyale and Mbiri Koni are female sacrificial victims whose bodies are transformed into food. Since the harvest of the sea worms anticipates the harvest of rice, Nyale's reincarnation precedes Mbiri Koni's; indeed, the spectacle of many-colored sea worms actually *depicts* the abundance of the harvest in iconic form.

Although the past is given great value, simple priority in time is not enough to assure hierarchical supremacy. An analysis of these narratives shows that no one single principle is dominant; rather, several principles must be used in combination. The "order of precedence" that finally emerges bears the traces of past conflicts and negotiations, which are not totally obscured in an idealized collective past.

Different Tellings of the Tales: Historicizing These Narratives

In my opening remarks, I noted that the narratives are composed of a mixture of prose and poetic couplets. Most of the action happens in the prose sections, as well as all of the conniving, scheming, and trickery. The couplets in verse represent primordial statements, "contracts" that supposedly have been passed down, unaltered, from one generation to the next. Examining the records we have of the tellings of these narratives, we find this claim to be justified to a certain extent, but it also becomes clear that the continuity of the literal form of a traditional couplet is quite separate from the continuity of its interpretations.

Since there are no occasions on which all of these narratives are brought together to be performed, compared, or heard, their general consistency is impressive. Despite minor differences, members of all villages agree that Tossi was the ceremonial center and that the most powerful objects were stored in certain ancestral houses, though they may have followed a long and circuitous route to reach them. I suspect that the reasons for the generally high degree of consistency lie in the fact that the Kodinese are very interested in their own history and enjoy discussing and comparing stories.

Conclusions about the current political position that are drawn from these stories, however, vary widely, for the narratives are themselves involved in historical processes and reshaped by them. It is, for example, interesting to compare the views of Kodi's past as recorded by Onvlee and Kapita in 1932, by Van Wouden in 1951–52, and by myself in 1980. Three of the seven narratives in this chapter (nos. 2, 3, and 5) were also recorded, in clearly recognizable form, by Onvlee and Kapita; they deal with the settlement of the region, the exile of Ra Hupu, and the division of tasks in Tossi. The couplet sections that detail the division of tasks between Rato Mangilo and Rato Pokilo appear almost verbatim in their transcriptions. Although the 1932 texts are somewhat more disjointed than the ones I was given—briefer, choppier, less detailed—this may be because I told my informants I would try to construct a longer, continuous political history from the stories they shared with me. In soliciting the narratives I specifically asked about relations to other stories I had heard, requesting that the narrator make these explicit. My texts were recorded on tape, which allowed the narrator to speak at his usual rhythm without having to pause while words were transcribed. In practice, however, narrators often paused after speaking to repeat the verse passages, checking that I got them right because of their greater importance.

Van Wouden's account of his stay in Kodi does not include texts, but it has many references to the political order and ancestral precedents.[5] He was told that Mahemba, Pawungo, and Balaghar, the three *kabihu* of Kodi Bangedo, were all equal and "each of them separately performs the *nale* ritual," but in Kodi Bokol the villages of Mbali Hangali were superior to those of Pola Kodi. Bukambero had a controversial status. Some people described its inhabitants as "unimportant people who retreated into the hills," while others said it was "a venerable *kabihu* from Sasar" (Van Wouden [1956] 1977, 5).

Within Mbali Hangali, Van Wouden describes a division between two halves, also called *kabihu*, of which one, Bukubani, is associated with "religion," and the other, Barada, is associated with *adat*, or "custom": "The ancestral house of the first section is called the office for religious affairs, that of the second is the office for customary law." He continues: "The meaning of religion for Bukubani is clear. In the first place it refers to the celebration of the *nale* ritual. The most important functions of the *adat* are the determination of the calendar and the ordering of the seasons. Furthermore, Barada was seen as the meeting place of all Kodi Bokol. . . . It may be noted that the sections of the two halves of Kodi Bokol intermarry" (Van Wouden [1956] 1977, 6). The passage is obviously a version of the division of power between Rato Mangilo and Rato Pokilo, and reflects the fact that within Tossi there is a division between Tossi

[5] In my discussion of Van Wouden's article, I have adopted his spellings of Kodi names to be the same as my own to avoid confusion. For the record, he wrote Bukambero as Buka Mbero, Bukubani as Buka Bani. I have followed the spellings currently used by government officials and the literate inhabitants of these areas, although it is reasonable to assume that the names were once binomials.

Bukubani (descendants of Rato Mangilo) and Tossi Barada (descendants of Rato Pokilo).

When I discussed these passages with Kodi informants in the 1980s, however, they were unanimous in denying (1) that *nale* rites had ever been conducted in Pawungo and Mahemba and (2) that the division of Bukubani and Barada existed outside of Tossi itself. The supposed "superiority" of Mbali Hangali could be interpreted as the superiority of Tossi as a ceremonial center, but it did not imply inequality between the peoples of the other villages of Pola Kodi and Mbali Hangali. Bukubani and Barada are the two "halves" of Tossi, representing the descendants of two founding brothers whose progeny can now intermarry. While they are descent groups, not *kabihu*, they do represent a complicated ritual division of powers (see chapter 4 for further discussion of later developments). These errors on Van Wouden's part were linked, I believe, to the political situation in Kodi in 1951–52 and possibly reflected misunderstandings of the facts as they were presented by local informants.

Van Wouden had great skills as an ethnographer and insight into Eastern Indonesian social formations, but he came as the guest of the current district administrator, Hermanus Rangga Horo, and stayed in his house. Horo, who continued in his position after serving as the third raja during the brief Dutch return to power in the late 1940s, came from the region of Bangedo. During the period of his administration, a small *pasola* had been performed in the grasslands between his ancestral village of Rangga Baki and Ratenggaro. The performance was a display of his power and influence, but it was not linked to offerings at a separate *nale* house or to any independent ritual control of time or the calendar.

Despite Van Wouden's position as a guest and the fact that he stayed only two months, his article is extremely valuable. It is not surprising, however, that he accepted an interpretation of the Kodi polity that, consistent with the aspirations of his host, emphasized the ceremonial independence of Horo's homeland Bangedo and did not acknowledge the priority of Tossi or its links to a large number of external, even foreign sources of power—the distant lands of Java and Bima, the earlier populations of Bukambero and Karendi, the competitive structure of neighboring regions. Van Wouden's ([1956] 1977, 19) conclusions about the structure of the Kodi polity can be quoted to illustrate a compelling, if inaccurate, vision of a totalizing polity:

> Kodi Bokol can certainly be considered a community that we could call a "tribe." It has a single *nale* house. There are clearly defined oppositions and an explicit division of ritual tasks between its con-

stituent parts. Both these oppositions and ritual divisions are the expression of a total unity. Virtually all marriages are contracted within the community. If the sea were to swallow all of western Sumba except for Kodi Bokol, it would leave a completely self-sustaining unit in terms of social and religious life. Only the ritual contests with Bangedo would be missing.

In fact, in the 1950s, Kodi Bokol already had a long history of marriage alliances with Endehnese visitors, borrowed heirloom objects from overseas, and wars and confederations with neighboring domains. The *nale* cult was itself divided between two ritual houses, in a tense balance of powers that will be the subject of the next chapter. Even in his misunderstanding of the rather confusing assemblage of stories about the past that were presented to him in 1951–52, Van Wouden pulled out a theoretical insight of considerable force. He noted that loose ends remained for the area of Bangedo, which broke up this totalizing vision into competing claims. Turning away from his earlier view that each Eastern Indonesian society could be viewed as a "closed society with a fixed number of groups," expressing "a specific type of social structure characterized by double descent," he came to see that regional variations were "complex and encompassing historical and sociological questions" (Van Wouden [1956] 1977, 148) whose dynamics were inscribed in a wider network of relations of insiders and outsiders, local traditions and foreign influences.

4

The Past in Objects

The Colonial Encounter

Vaygu'a [shell valuables] are not indifferent things; they are more than
mere coins. All of them, or at least the most valuable and the most coveted,
have a name, a personality, a past, and even a legend attached to them,
to such an extent that people may be named after them.

Marcel Mauss, *The Gift*

Objects are not what they were made to be but what they have become.

Nicholas Thomas, *Entangled Objects*

Local knowledge of the past is organized not only in narrative, but also in
the visual and tactile traces left by past events: heirloom objects, features
of the landscape, the special relationship established with a particular
animal or location. This chapter begins with the "archive of the past" that
is found in the Kodi world of objects, examining first the principles by
which that world is constituted and then how certain objects have changed
in their relations over time. The origin narratives presented in the last
chapter all deal with the period when Kodi society was coming into being,
the period "of former times and earlier peoples" (*la mandei la maulu*),
which is nevertheless perceived as homogenous with the present and
described "historically" rather than "mythically."[1] In examining the role
of objects to represent the past, we move into the realm of remembered
time and documented historical events, for at issue now is the shifting
diarchic balance established between an object identified as "indigenous"
and one brought by Dutch conquerors. This chapter probes two related
questions: first, what is the historiographic function represented by objects, and second, how is their picture of the past subject to reinterpretation? Resolving these issues also engages the political tensions of diarchy,

[1] Following Valeri (1990, 164), I distinguish between a mythical past where events
happen that are no longer possible in the present (as in the Kodi stories "of long
ago," *e nawu*) and a historical past that can be exemplary for the present but that
can also be questioned and challenged. The mythical past has a transcendent and
unquestioned character that keeps it "walled off from all subsequent times" (Bakhtin 1981, 15); thus it is not a direct force in shaping patterns of present action.

118

or dual rule, which is variously described as involving two different figures—passive and active, female and male, indigenous and external, "spiritual" and "worldly."

The two questions are related in their resolution, as important objects are endowed with features of gender and agency that place them in complex and changing dualistic contrasts.

History Objects and the Reification of the Past

A number of the most important ritual objects are described as "history objects" (Ind. *barang bersejarah*), a term that corresponds to the Kodi expression "the traces of the hands, prints of the feet" (*oro limya, oro witti*), which sees these things as the physical marks left by the ancestors. Although many have a utilitarian function—a water container, a weapon, an item of clothing, or an ornament—their most important role is to mark a particular historical moment. They are used didactically, as "evidence" of the past and a reminder of what has been lost, giving a permanent, external form to contingent events and preserving the memory of a promise, a covenant, or an alliance.

These objects are material signs of the past that exist not only as expressions *of* history but also as objects *in* history. They can even help to *make* history by "choosing" their proper location and exerting a mystical force on their human guardians to assure that they end up there. Some "history objects" fit the wider category of heirlooms or the more narrow one of regalia: they legitimate the claims of whoever may come to own them and as repositories of magical power are sometimes believed to affect the processes that they represent.

Most of the "history objects" I studied on Sumba were imported items that came to the island through trade. They included porcelain ceramic urns and plates, gold jewelry, swords, and gongs, which were stored high in the lofts of traditional houses, removed from circulation in exchange. Through a ritual dedication they became the "possessions of the ancestors" (*tanggu marapu*), attaining a status at which they were equated with persons. At each important ceremony they had to be addressed in prayer with respectful kin terms and fed with rice and animal sacrifices. If they were sold, mistreated, or lost, they could curse their former masters and exact supernatural revenge. Power objectified in a concrete object preserves an impression of stability even when the object comes into the possession of a rival; thus it can legitimate usurpation while maintaining a fiction of continuity.

A few, however, were objects of local manufacture, including a spindle that once pierced through the heavens (*kinje maniki*), a drum covered with human skin (*bendu kalulla toyo*), and a fiddle and flute (*dungga mono pyoghi*). Stones used to summon lightning or earthquakes were found in the local area, but their power was revealed to an ancestor by a special vision. Some villages kept not an object but an animal, a horse or dog given a ritual name who served as the "placeholder" for a ritual office. Others had stories of exchanges with crocodiles or pythons, coded as marriage alliances, which entailed a totemistic prohibition on eating the animal's flesh.

When I began to ask the people of Kodi about their past, the first stage of my investigation was not to establish a line of dates and periods, but to make a map and a catalog. The map showed the location of each ancestral village, and the catalog listed the heirloom objects or totemic animals located there. A summary of this catalog (table 2) notes the location of the forty most important named possessions in Kodi. Although many other important objects are also kept as reminders of the past in Kodi villages, for this catalog I limited myself to objects given ritual names, invoked along with the ancestors, and "fed" at sacrifices. I included only objects or spirit-animals that were addressed as ancestors, anthropomorphized to become part of the invisible community that "listens in" at each ceremonial occasion.

These forty possessions are distributed among thirty-one ancestral villages, out of the total of sixty-six villages found in Kodi. Thirty-five villages (many of them small and only recently founded) had no significant heirlooms and worshipped "using only the names of their ancestral founders." Almost all of these villages were "attached" to larger and older villages with a store of heirloom objects, drawing on the power and prestige concentrated in the "mother village" (*bei parona*).

A Kodi interpretation of the catalog is that it provides "evidence" (Ind. *bukti*) of the veracity of the narratives presented in chapter 3: Tossi's ritual preeminence, for example, is "proved" by the fact that it has the largest concentration of sacred objects. The redistribution of other objects to outlying villages, with separate posts for harvest offerings (in Toda, Bondo Tamiyo, and Kaha Malagho), metalworking tools (Wei Yengo and Wei Hyombo), and the skull tree (Ndelo, Bondo Kodi, Kere Tana, Bongu, Lewata, Ratenngaro, Parona Baroro, and Kaha Katoda) all display the narrative pattern of delegation from the source to an executor. The bush knife that belongs to the village of Watu Pakadu and its associates deserves a special explanation. The story is told that Landa Deta, the founder of this village, was a famous healer who was treating a pregnant woman at the time of the first division of ritual tasks and territories. Since he missed

Among the sacred objects stored in the ancestral village of Toda is an heirloom spindle that once connected the heavens to the earth by a line of cotton thread. 1988. Photograph by Laura Whitney.

the demarcation of traditional boundaries, he was allowed to make his gardens in all of the tabooed areas, being given a special knife that "cuts without waiting and chops without hesitating, since it does not recognize the crown of sacred land or respect the forelock of forbidden ground."

The "evidence" of objects, however, sometimes contradicts the narratives. Why are the urn and plate entrusted to Rato Mangilo in Tossi now found in Bukubani? How has the skull tree given to Bondo Kodi spread to six other villages? How have metalworking and rain magic traveled into other regions? The answers to these questions are usually offered in other narratives, which tell, for instance, how the nephew of a famed headhunter in Bongu or Kaha Katoda achieved so much renown that he was allowed to cut off a sapling from the earlier skull tree and plant it in his own village. In some cases, though, a more complex accommodation has occurred, in which supposedly "unmovable" objects have been moved. The most important of these is the great porcelain urn "discovered" by Mangilo and Pokilo near the site of Tossi. When I pursued the question of the urn's location, I found that it had been moved only relatively recently, as a result of events during the colonial encounter.

Table 2. Catalog of Objects and Animals in Kodi Villages

In Pola Kodi, Kodi Bokol

Tossi	the sea worm trough (keko nalo/rabba rica)
	the platform for calendrical offerings (kapambalo nale hari, karangga rica marapu)
	the Savunese water jar (pandalu ndunga haghu)
	the net that captured the moon (kareco londo laka)
	the gold breastplate given to Mangilo (mangilo la marangga)
Mete	the earthquake stones (ngundu watu ndandaro, kalembu tana opongo)
	the spindle and twiner (kinje nambu ndende, pote kaleku tana)
Bukubani	the lightning stones (watu kanduruko kanduku, kabalako habaka)
	the urn and plate (ngguhi njapa dadango/pengga njpa keketo)
Ndelo	the skull tree (kere katoda, ndende andung)
Watu Pakadu[a]	the bush knife of Landa Deta (monggo njana mangga/teba njana rema, njana peghe a lindu tana hari, njana tanda hungga tana bihya)
Wei Yengo	metalworking tools (tuku merang gawi, palu longo meha)

In Mbali Hangali, Kodi Bokol

Toda	the spindle (kinje maniki, pote kalehu)
	the harvest offering post (kahele timbu rongo, kareka watu ndende)
Bondo Kodi	the python of rainfall (ra bobo, pala kawata)
	thunder and lightning plates (kanduruko kanduku, kabalako habaka)
	the skull tree (kere katoda, ndende andung)
Kere Tana	the skull tree (kere katoda, ndende andung)
	the spotted spirit dog (bangga nggoko, bangga bela)
Wei Lyabba[b]	the chicken of the sun and moon (myoko manu lodo, tara manu wulla)
Bongu[c]	the skull tree (kere katoda, ndende andung)
Rambi	the shrimp and pigeon (kura kamone hori, rowa hamondo kataku)

[a] and the related villages of Hambali Atur, Nggallu Watu, Ramba Lodo, and Bondo Gole

[b] and the related villages of Ngi Pyandak, Malandi, Malere, Bondo Kawango, Bondo Kamodo, Palikye Tana, and Mahemba

[c] and its associate, Lewata

Table 2 (*continued*)

In Pawungo, Bangedo	
Pakare	the earthquake stones (*ngundu watu ndandaro, kalembu tana opongo*)
	the crocodile and octopus (*woyo pala lari, kawica mbila tamaro*)
Hangga Koki	the drum made of human skin (*tamburu kuru, taranda kenda*)
	the fiddle and flute (*dungga ndaha liyo, poghi njaha ndalu*)
Ratenggaro	the skull tree (*kere katoda, ndende andung*)
Bondo Tamiyo	the harvest offering post (*kahale timbu rongo, kareka watu ndende*)
Watu Lade	the grass snake and python (*maghu nipya, maghu kaboko*)

In Mahemba, Bangedo	
Waindimu	the urn and plate (*ngguhi njapa dadango, pengga njapa keketo*)
	the net that held the moon (*kareco londo laka*)
	the Savunese water jar (*pandalu ndunga haghu*)
Balengger	the harvest offering post (*kahale timbu rongo, kareka watu ndende*)
Parona Baroro	the skull tree (*kere katoda, ndende andung*)

In Balaghar, Bangedo	
Waingyali	the sea worm trough (*keko nalo, rabba rica*)
	the platform for calendrical offerings (*kapambalo nale hari, karangga rica marapu*)
Kaha Malogho	the harvest offering post (*kahale timbu rongo, kareka watu ndende*)
Kaha Katoda	the skull tree (*kere katoda, ndende andung*)
Wainjolo Wawa	the spirit dog (*pyunggoro marapu, labirri wangge rowa*)
Weinjoko	rain magic (*lete watu la kaheku loko, hambi cana la manumbu mara*)
Wei Hyombo	metalworking tools (*hyaghu tuku bahi, palu teko doro*)

The story of the urn reveals a present division between the functions of objects as traces of ancestral heritage and their new involvement in a more disruptive, discontinuous "history." The conceptual framework for this discussion therefore begins before the colonial encounter itself, in the constitution of an "imported past" in the form of ritual treasures brought from faraway places.

The Location and Transfer of Objects in the Past

In the traditional ceremonial system, the authority of objects came from their priority in time, expressed by an arrangement in space. The oldest objects were stored in the ceremonial house at the head of each village square, with younger ones in ranked positions at the base and sides. A consciousness of the past was produced and transmitted by visually encoding notions of precedence, sequence, and order; in this way, residues of ancestral migrations became guideposts for future generations. The location of these objects is probably the single most authoritative form of historical evidence on Sumba: land disputes can be resolved by the revelation of an heirloom sword, political struggles can focus on the proper name for a plate or jar, and ritual offices are defined not by the persons who hold them but by the objects that are manipulated.

A. L. Couvreur, the Dutch district officer (*controleur*) who commanded during the period in which Kodi was effectively brought under colonial rule, wrote that the relics of the *marapu* included "ornaments, bits of gold, and sometimes other terrible rubbish as well," noting that a colleague of his once found a disheveled and filthy copy of the Koran in a sacred basket stored in an ancestral cult house (Couvreur 1917, 207). While he considered the Koran an anomalous ritual object for a community of pagan ancestor worshippers, I argue that it is in some way paradigmatic. These "history objects" represent an effort to appropriate an incompletely understood external power—one often coming from Hindu or Moslem states—into a very different symbolic world. It was the *power* of the Koran that Sumbanese villagers fetishized, but not the content of Islam.[2] Dutch of-

---

[2] The category of "fetish" has not been used in Indonesian ethnography, though the magical importance of objects has often been noted and the tradition of family heirlooms, or *pusaka*, is widespread throughout the archipelago. Fetishism was a classic problem of nineteenth-century anthropology, but in this century only art historians, psychoanalysts, and Marxist economists have continued to use the term. If I venture, tentatively, to join this motley crew, it is in order to propose an *analytic* alternative to a term that has suffered from pejorative connotations. Pietz (1985, 14) notes, "The discourse of the fetish has always been a critical discourse about the false objective values of a culture from which the speaker is personally

ficials also had their own version of fetishism: they deliberately introduced the gold staff of office as a substitute for indigenous heirlooms, using the prestige of imported objects to reweight and reorder indigenous political systems under colonial rule.

Couvreur (1917, 215) acknowledged the power of traditional objects when he wrote that the person most likely to cause trouble for a colonial officer was not the chief but the secluded priest: "Although he stays in the background, he exercises a great mystical influence," and his guardianship of land and heirlooms can have important political consequences. The passage probably refers to the Rato Nale of Tossi and his guardianship of the urn, since it was importantly involved in the largest and most sustained armed resistance to the presence of the Dutch on the island.

THE URN AS A RITUAL OBJECT

The urn involved in these events is made of glazed porcelain, probably produced in South China during the Ming period and one of a large number of ancient high-fired ceramics traded widely throughout Southeast Asia from as early as the eleventh century into the nineteenth (O'Connor 1983, 402). It is decorated with blue dragons (perceived as "pythons" locally) and contains sacred water, used to heal wounds in warfare or ritual jousting, and ancient coins, pieces of gold offered by people who have come seeking its blessings. The urn is classified as a female object within the rules of the Kodi ritual division: in the apportionment of powers between the two brothers, its hollow, curved shape made it appropriate to store in the "mother house" of Rato Mangilo, while the roaming horse of Rato Pokilo had to be male, expressing as it did qualities of virility and mobility. The elder brother was told to behave like a woman, remaining confined inside the house for four months before the sea worms came, "brooding" over the new year "as a hen broods over her eggs, as a sow calls to her young," showing nurturing, maternal concern for the young rice crop. The stallion ridden by his brother followed the same food taboos as the priest, avoiding corn and tubers and eating only rice.

---

distanced." In other words, *they* have fetishes, *we* know better. But it can also be used to refer to the attribution of mystical powers to objects in a historical context of shifting political realities. The genesis of fetishized relations in the colonial encounter expresses different perceptions of value between the colonizers and the colonized and a problem of translation that is, in turn, presented as a displaced agency or consciousness from persons onto things. Fetishized objects occupy a historically particular cross-cultural space. They are found at the intersection of ideas of descent from an indigenous founder, on the one hand, and power from an external force, on the other—an intersection that in Kodi can be represented by tension between the ancient urn and the new gold staff.

The hard, shiny surface of imported porcelain is so different from locally produced earthenware that many people in Southeast Asia trace their origins to a cosmogonic act: the miraculous excretions of the Ceramese divinity Hainuwele (Jensen and Niggemeyer 1939), a gift from the heavens in northern Luzon (Cole 1912), a formation from the clay used to make the sun and moon in Borneo (Bock 1881, 198). Assessment of the age of such jars using objective criteria—form, glaze, decoration, and physical properties of the body—is a developed tradition in many isolated tribal communities, each having its own rigorous standards of connoisseurship (O'Connor 1983, 405).

On Sumba, most ceramic pieces are perceived, realistically, as imported objects, though no one could trace their provenance back to the kilns in South China, Vietnam, or Thailand where they were probably manufactured. In this case, although the origin narrative says the sea worms came from the court of the sultan of Bima, the urn was not traded for but *discovered*. It appeared magically on the island and "chose" Mangilo and Pokilo to serve as the priest and defender of the calendrical system. The urn washed up on the sand at Tossi to mark the location of the sea worms and the site where the rituals of the Kodi new year could be carried out. The historical ties that brought trade goods like the urn to the shores of Sumba are thus displaced from the imported object itself to the sea worms. This mystification of the urn as an "indigenous" object is related to its distinct appearance and to earlier ritual uses of jars on the island.

The physical properties most admired in the urn were its hardness, the smoothness and whiteness of its surface, and the ring of its body when struck. Almost all objects of local manufacture on Sumba were only semidurable: even the finest *ikat* textiles would eventually tear, even the firmest mats would disintegrate, and none of the local ceramic ware was anywhere near as hard and fine. The imported urn was valued because it was an irreplaceable object, the only one of its series. Its "voice" was compared to the deep sonorities of imported gongs,[3] its smoothness to the surface of a tortoise shell, its roundness to the seeds of the *dedap* tree.

---

[3] There are many other reports of imported porcelain jars that talk. Cole (1912, 12), for instance, tells the story of a jar called Magsawi by the Tinguian of Abra that could speak softly in very low tones; it also went on long journeys by itself and was married to a female jar owned by the Tinguian of Ilocos Norte. The famous jar of the sultan of Brunei was said to have howled dolefully the night before his first wife died and to have heralded misfortunes of all sorts by emitting strange tones. Its cries may have been the result of air draughts thrown into resonant reverberations by the peculiar form of the mouth of the jar. Usually covered with brocade, it was uncovered only when it was consulted, so it spoke exclusively on solemn occasions (Cole 1912, 11). Among the Datu of Borneo,

Archeological research has shown that long before the import of high-fired ceramics, urn burials were made on Sumba, dating back as far as the first millennium B.C.[4] Contemporary peoples have no memory of these rites; today they bury their dead in large stone megaliths or earthen graves. But ideas of the sacredness of pots and their relation to the afterworld persist in the sacrificial offering placed in the urn to "ask for blessings" and assure the safe voyage of the soul. The urn was said to have descended directly from the upperworld, the land of the dead, and to have assumed its position as the symbolic anchor of the Kodi year.

The narrative tradition that the urn presented itself to its proper owners established a paradigm for attitudes toward ritual heirlooms found in many other parts of Southeast Asia. Imported ceramics are not "mere handy crockery"; rather, they are marked by "a potency that makes them active agents" (O'Connor 1983, 403). Kodi ritualists recognized this fact when they placed the urn in the house of Rato Mangilo, at the head of Tossi, naming it "the urn that cannot be moved," and laying an heirloom porcelain plate on top to close off the sacred opening, called it the "plate that cannot be lifted."

THE URN MEETS THE STAFF

In 1909, when the Dutch took effective control of the island of Sumba, they asked the people of Kodi to choose a leader to serve as an administrator and representative to the colonial powers. This leader would be presented with the gold staff that created the colonial office of raja, the native administrator of each "self-governing region." A meeting of elders from all the ancestral villages was held in Tossi, in the Council House established by Rato Pokilo, and they agreed to choose this leader from the home of the urn, the most sacred object in the domain. Hence Rato Loghe Kanduyo,

---

villagers brought gifts to the sultan and received water from the sacred jar to sprinkle on their fields and thereby assure plentiful harvests. The "voice" of heirloom plates among the Hua Ulu of Seram is an important characteristic of their value, used in calculating bridewealth (Valeri 1980).

[4] An urn field at Melolo in East Sumba was excavated by van Heekeren in the 1920s and 1930s. Many round-based urns were found with unburnt secondary burials of broken bones, as well as adzes, stone bracelets, shell and stone beads, and smaller votive pots. The smaller pots were highly polished and had elegant long-necked flasks, some depicting human or animal figures with incised geometric designs filled in with white paint. Polished pots of the same type are found today in Lamboya and Memboro, but not in Kodi, where ceramic work is much cruder. Van Heekeren now (1972) dates the urn field to the Southeast Asian Neolithic (about B.C. 1000), but in his first publication of the results (1956) he estimated it as early Metal Age (B.C. 500–A.D. 1000). Heine-Geldern (1945, 148) favors the Metal Age date.

a famous orator and warrior descended from Rato Pokilo, was selected to be the first raja, serving as a spokesman and mediator vis-à-vis outside forces.

His selection was legitimated by an argument involving the genders of the urn and staff and the idea of their complementarity. The urn, a hollow cavity with generous curves, was a female object containing fertile, life-giving water. The staff was classified as a male object, because it was long, firm, and could be used as a weapon; it was therefore included in the category of spears, swords, and metal goods presented as the male gifts of bridewealth. Because the holders of both objects were members of the village of Tossi, the two objects could be properly balanced, along with the two kinds of powers. The male staff served as the "husband" of the female urn. This symbolic marriage linked the two offices, making the representative of the Dutch colonial administration into the junior partner in a division of powers, since the holder of the staff (called the *toko*, the native term for raja, from the Indonesian *tongkat*) owed ritual deference to his senior, the priest of the sea worms.

CONTESTED CLAIMS: THE STAFF SEPARATES FROM THE URN

The gold staff that Rato Loghe Kanduyo received was stored in the Council House in Tossi and, as local people tell the story, wasted no time in causing trouble. As an officer of the Netherlands East Indies government, the new raja was supposed to explain its civilizing mission to his people as well as provide labor for bridge- and road-building projects to improve communications. Two years later, in 1911, rumors circulated that Dutch soldiers had enslaved noblemen to work on these projects, insulted the raja, and raped a local woman. An armed rebellion began with the ambush and killing of four soldiers by headhunters from outlying villages, who fled into the forest with the guns captured from the soldiers. The Dutch forces retaliated by burning the raja's village of Tossi, after which they took refuge with his rivals in another river valley.

To avenge the burning of his village, the raja gave permission for military attacks to continue. He took the traditional symbols of governmental power—the urn and plate—off into the bush and hid them. Yet he did bring the Dutch staff of office with him when he rode, in a procession bringing gold and livestock, to meet the Dutch commander and negotiate a peace payment. Instead of talking to him, however, the commander pulled him from his horse, bound him under the house, and made him march to a distant prison, where he soon died. This brutal punishment of the first native ruler united almost all the population in opposition to the Dutch presence. Three years of fighting followed, with rebel forces hiding in the interior and attacking the colonial army periodically. The Dutch, deciding to starve out their enemies, then forced everyone to move to coastal villages and leave their gardens behind. Finally, pressured by famine and hardship, the rebel forces surrendered and were sent into exile.

This first sequence of events shows the consequences of differences between local understandings of governmental power and those of the Dutch colonial forces. The Dutch expected to find rulers who could command the population and thus concentrated power and wealth in the man chosen as raja. By contrast, Kodi perceived the raja, at least initially, as a mediator and spokesman, who would speak for them in negotiations with outside forces but who had no authority to act without a meeting of elders from each village.

The creation of a Kodi polity, and after that of a regional resistance movement, was one of the unintended consequences of the colonial encounter. Because no single ruler preceded them, the Dutch had to establish the legitimacy of the first Kodi raja themselves. Rato Loghe Kanduyo died in the process of his transformation into a raja, and his nephew Ndera Wulla made the first claims to a new and different form of political power.

STOKING THE FLAMES OF CONTROVERSY

Once order had been restored, the captured staff of office was given to Rato Loghe's nephew and adopted son, Ndera Wulla. He had taken the urn and plate to Bukubani, the garden settlement farthest from the Dutch fortress, and stored them with descendants of Rato Mangilo who had planted coconuts there. Washed in coconut water to cleanse them after their journey, they were placed beside the lightning stones which were Bukubani's most important heirlooms.

Tossi was rebuilt during the next few years as Ndera Wulla prepared to assume political control of the area. On the day he was officially installed in office as raja, he decided to place the gold staff in his own house and bring the urn and plate to join them. A procession was formed from Bukubani to the Council House, where he lived, to bear these sacred objects and place them under his guardianship. Many people criticized the move, because the urn and plate had never been stored anywhere except in the Sea Worm House, and they speculated that his uncle's own problems had occurred because the staff did not get along well with the urn. They said the urn, which was supposed to be unmovable, had already been moved too many times.

In 1927 and in 1936, the village was burned again, first by a powerful Javanese trader, who resented efforts to control his activities, and then by rivals of the raja within the village itself. In the second fire, flames spread quickly to all of the houses, and the urn and plate were damaged by the blaze. Charred and cracked, the two old porcelain dishes were taken to the bush to be repaired. Special sacrifices had to be performed to "mend their bones and lift up their souls" after this incident, and repeated prayers were offered to the ancestors Rato Mangilo and Rato Pokilo pleading for unity among their descendants.

At the end of this rite, a special meeting was held to discuss the location of the urn. The raja's rivals, who came from the division of Tossi Bukubani, argued they should have been the ones to hold the office of raja. They particularly resented the fact that the urn and plate had been moved from the Sea Worm House into the raja's house, since he had no hereditary right to them. "This is why our village keeps burning," they said; "the ancestors will not protect us if we do not keep things in the proper places." As a compromise, it was decided that the urn would not go back into the raja's house, but neither would it be placed in the Sea Worm House of Tossi, where it had been scarred by fire three times already. Instead it would be entrusted to the outlying village of Bukubani. There, safely removed from the ritual center, descendants of Rato Mangilo would look after it and offer it sacrifices of rice and meat. Tossi was not surrendering its authority over the objects, but only delegating it to the house of another priest. Subsequently, a new Sea Worm House was built and ritually dedicated in Bukubani, specifically to store these objects. Later, once the political struggles had cooled, the urn could be reclaimed—but probably not while the office of raja remained in Tossi.

The annual festival of the sea worms brought all the people of Kodi back to their ancestral villages to sacrifice chickens to the souls of the dead, collect the sea worms, and participate in a huge ritualized jousting combat on horseback. It was still performed in Tossi, as were the calculations that determined the start of months for planting and harvesting and the four-month ritual silence.

In the late 1930s, these rites were led by a priestess, Mbiri Koni, who bore the name of the rice spirit. She had been chosen to succeed her husband at a divination that occurred during the period when Tossi was deeply divided politically. Because the diviner read her name in the entrails of sacrificial animals, a reading confirmed by spear divination, her anomalous selection was explained as the "will of the ancestors," who this time, exceptionally, favored a high priestess over any of the male descendants of the house. We should note, however, that the role of priest, though symbolically female, became literally so only *after* the raja developed a strong concern to depoliticize the functions of that office. Once the supreme ritual leader in the domain, the Sea Worm Priest became, in the

1930s, little more than a religious functionary who performed standard rites in the raja's village. Raja Ndera wanted a Tossi priest to continue to lead the region in these ceremonies, but he did not want the ritual leader to emerge as a political rival. Thus, there may have been a strategic advantage to this choice of an older woman, widowed and past childbearing age, as the new priestess of the Kodi year.

Consistent with the constraints placed on the office, Mbiri Koni was a rigorous traditionalist who refused to have anything to do with foreign authorities, withdrawing into seclusion whenever Dutch visitors came to the village. She understood that to retain her authority she could not display it openly, and to continue as a guardian of tradition she could not speak to foreigners. The selection of a female priestess thus *intensified* and further *polarized* a diarchic division that had already been shifting in a certain direction. It brought the division between the functions of the urn and staff more into line with Western notions of a division of church and state, emphasizing spiritual power at the cost of secular influence.

Separated Powers: The Japanese Occupation and Independence

Conflicts did not end with the relocation of the urn, but they came to be defined in different terms. The next few decades were ones of great turmoil and suffering. Eight thousand Japanese troops arrived on Sumba in 1942, whereupon they forcibly inducted local people to work on airstrips for a planned invasion of Australia. They required that local rulers supply them with large amounts of food and decimated local herds to feed the occupying forces. A number of people went hungry, most had no clothing, and few seemed to accept the Japanese message that they had been sent to liberate them from the oppressive institutions of Dutch colonialism.

During the Japanese occupation, the cycle of calendrical rites and government functions in Tossi was interrupted by the deaths of both the high priestess and the raja. In some local interpretations, the deaths were linked, as the guardians of the land and government both succumbed to their inability to relieve the suffering of their people. Raja Ndera Wulla was replaced by his administrative assistant, H. R. Horo, who came from Rangga Baki, across the river. The Japanese forces administered Indonesia through the Dutch-established hierarchy of native leaders. Their decision to appoint Horo followed the rules set by the colonial powers that preceded them, but as a consequence it moved the office of raja away from the "mother-father" village of Tossi and gave it to the rival territory of Bangedo.

In 1945, the independence of Indonesia was declared, and five years of fighting followed to keep Dutch forces from returning to power. Sumba remained protected from most of the violence of that struggle. With no military opposition at all, the new Kodi raja, now presiding over a Council of Rajas in the port town of Waingapu, simply ordered the raising of the new Indonesian flag to replace the Dutch one. In the first elections after independence was realized in 1950, Tossi recovered its position of political leadership when Martin Calei, a descendant of Rato Mangilo, was elected to the new parliament and later nominated to assume the position of regent (*bupati*), administrator of the whole island of Sumba.

In 1958, Tossi was burned again. In the same year, Martin Calei, having lost the regency election by a single vote, fell seriously ill and died, as did his mother and father in rapid succession. The series of catastrophes was interpreted by Raja Horo as punishment sent to his Tossi rivals by their own ancestors, who did not approve of the mixing of ritual power with careers in local government. "This is what was needed," he told me, "to teach them that some people wear the high feathered headdress and the black plumes and can be warriors and government leaders. The others, the members of female houses, are the ones who control the seasons, the time of planting and harvesting. They must stay confined to protect the whole region and should not try to wander off to the capital city. The holder of the staff cannot be the same person as the holder of the urn."

This formulation of the diarchic divide was the one used in 1949, when Raja Horo received a new gold staff from Dutch officials, during their brief return to the island before independence was realized. He stressed the legitimating power of objects at a time when the prerogatives of Dutch-appointed rulers were being increasingly called into question. After independence, traditional rulers were left in ceremonial positions and respected, but virtually all power was taken from them: a new nationalist rhetoric asserted that because all of Indonesia was once a "village democracy," past hierarchies and inequalities were the creation of a "feudal" colonial system and should be abolished.

The early 1960s were a time of great disorder and turmoil throughout the country, expressed in Kodi by the burning of seven important ancestral villages—not only Tossi, but also Rangga Baki, home of Raja Horo, and five others that contained significant wealth and heirloom objects. Some of the suspected arsonists were described as "communists"; yet they, too, were engulfed in the flood of violence that spread over the country in 1965, after generals crushed a reported coup. At this point it is unclear just where local politics stopped and national politics began. Anyone who seemed to wield power or privilege was the object of assaults, with quick retaliation a foregone conclusion. The result was to paralyze not only the national political system but also the local ceremonial cycle.

The office of Rato Nale in Tossi remained vacant for much of the sixties as villagers tried to summon the resources needed to perform a ceremony calling back the soul of each of the destroyed houses, which would permit them to be rebuilt. No one dared to assume the politically dangerous position of high priest lest further arson and attacks be the result. For almost a decade, therefore, Ra Ndengi alone performed the calendrical rites, "holding the year" in place from his secluded home in Bukubani. The lapse in ritual performance created a sense of social fragmentation and a loss of hierarchy. People no longer gathered for large-scale festivities, feasting and jousting to welcome the sea worms, but simply prayed in their isolated garden huts.

In 1972, a divination was held in the newly rebuilt Tossi, and Ra Holo, the grandson of Mbiri Koni, was selected to become the new head priest. He was reluctant to take the post because of his youth and ignorance, however, protesting with a verse that argued he could not perform the rites properly:

I am just a child playing with tops	Yayo pimoka a ana lereho kadiyo
I am just a boy who spins stones	Yayo pimoka a ana pokato kalaiyo
I don't know the long narratives	Nja ku peghe a ngara kedoko lawonda
I don't remember the strange verses	Nja ku ape a lawitti wanokaka

He was finally persuaded that his authority would be buttressed by Ra Ndengi, who acted as his senior in the ritual installation. The trials and humiliations of the urn itself (and, by extension, the ancestors who acquired it) were cited in words he reported they used to convince him to accept:

How can the master of the house	Mono pena a mori uma
Not raise his buttocks for this	Inde kede a kere mu
How can a member of the village	Mono a pena a ihi parona
Not step with his feet to help	Inde pangga a witti mu
A heavy burden for the land of sea worms and prohibitions	Mboto wadjomoka a tana nale a tana padu
Because the urn has been moved	Oronaka na pa dandango a ngguhi
The yellow forelock burns with shame	Na merina a hungga rangga rara
Because the plate was lifted	Oronaka na pa keketo a pengga

The foreign lime ship is profaned	Na kabana a tena kapu dawa
What will happen to Tossi of great renown	Mono pena Tohi lendu ngara
If the new day dawns	Ba na mahewa a helu
And all the dead mothers and fathers	Mono ngara ha inya mate bapa mate
Are given no rice to eat?	Inde woni ngagha ha muyo?
What will happen to the golden banyan tree	Mono pena a wei maronga rara
If the light breaks over the land	Ba na mandomo a tana
And the dead grandparents and forefathers	Mono ngara ha ambu mate nuhi mate
Are given no water to drink?	Inde woni weiyo pa inu?

The spirits of all the ancestors were seen as angrily demanding that sacrifices again be offered to them so the prestige and importance of Tossi would be restored. Ra Holo was anointed with water from the sacred urn, but allowed it to remain at its present location in Bukubani. He and the leaders of Tossi agreed that since the urn was the senior object, its ritual authority was greater than the genealogical priority Tossi had over Bukubani. As long as they guarded the urn, the people of Bukubani would be the "older brothers," and Tossi the "younger brothers," in the public context of calendar rites.

Since Indonesian independence the raja's gold staff has no longer been used and is kept as a family heirloom by his descendants. The "immovable urn" has found a new home, one now, after sixty years, recognized as its legitimate location. Once again reassuringly immobile, the urn can anchor the ritual polity and exert some of its mystical power to hold together the year and the people as expressed in its mythical mandate.

Interpreting and Criticizing Sources on the Kodi Past

At this point, I pause to reconsider the role objects play in constituting "evidence," in addition to and sometimes in contrast to the "evidence" of narratives and ritual action. The competing claims made in origin narratives often concern the identity of the ancestor who first acquired a certain valuable, since the valuable's present location is well established. Differences concerning the story of the sea worm trough on its journey to Tossi are all of this kind. A second kind of competing claim concerns *why* an object found its way to a particular village, and on this question a greater variety of interpretive strategies are possible. Some argue that the transfer was legitimate, some that it was the result of a theft, some that eventually the object will "return home." Others say that if it has stopped moving, this in itself is evidence of the superiority of its new location.

Competing versions of the story of the urn express differences of opinion on who was really an agent in historical change, and whether the potential for agency invested in objects had changed over time. The people of Bukubani said, "We have always been the older brothers," but this was denied by those in Tossi, who reminded them that Bukubani was once only a small garden settlement where the descendants of Rato Mangilo grew rice and corn. Before a ritual house was constructed for the urn it was not even consecrated as a site for ancestral offerings, much less the calculation of the beginning and end of the ceremonial year. But if Tossi's leader argued, "We are the only mothers and fathers," members of other villages objected that they were exaggerating the contingent event of receiving the Dutch staff of office and neglecting the disputes that led to its loss.

The disagreements concerned interpretation more than the sequence of events. Debates centered on the issue of whether the urn could still play a role in determining its proper home. In the distant past, the great urn was said to have washed up on the shores of Kodi and found its way into the hands of Mangilo and Pokilo almost as if it moved of its own volition. Some people assert that such movement was possible only in the past, and now when objects are shifted it is only because of human actions. Others, however, still read a divinatory significance into the trials and tribulations of objects like the supposedly immovable urn. It was "not happy" that Tossi had become so divisive, that quarrels about who should hold the raja's staff had disturbed the unity of the center of calendrical ritual for the whole region. The fact that the urn was moved when these conflicts escalated, so that it reposed more peacefully in Bukubani, was no accident. "The urn knows," they would say, "where it is supposed to stay."

A sacred object can become reanimated if its authority is violated in a particularly extreme way. Events that occurred in 1986, when a smaller ceramic urn in the village of Waindimu was stolen, were interpreted as supporting this position. The urn was taken to remove the gold coins placed there by people seeking blessings, and when it suddenly disappeared Moslem thieves from a nearby fishing village were suspected.[5] The wealthiest Moslem merchant owned a small motorboat, which left port a few

[5] Most people agreed that "no Kodinese could have done it" because of their respect for ancestral taboos. Even converted Christians offered testimony of the power of sacred objects, which they said did not violate the rules of conversion because it was an inherent power, not mediated by ancestral spirits.

days after the disappearance, apparently carrying the urn to sell to traders on Flores. A huge storm came up, the boat was smashed to pieces, and the urn drifted back with the waves to the same area where it was originally discovered. Emptied of its contents and cracked on one side, it was recovered and carried into the village, where sacrifices were performed to call back the soul dislodged by this act of violence. The urn's guardian said that the soul of the urn had "taken its own revenge": the thieves were financially ruined, and shortly afterward the merchant went mad.

The lessons taken from these events were these: a sacred object in the right place brings good fortune on its owners and thus legitimates their ownership, whereas the loss of an object is a sign of moral weakness or deception. Possession here is more than nine-tenths of the law; it is itself a form of mystical justification.

The smaller urn was stolen while I was compiling the competing versions of the past of its "elder sibling" in Tossi. The people of Bukubani argued that since the urn now sits soundly in the Sea Worm House of their village, it should have always been there. The past, in their view, showed only a record of error that is better eclipsed by memory. When I first interviewed them, they made no mention of the historical events I have detailed, saying simply that the urn had been entrusted to Rato Mangilo and that his descendants continued to be its guardians. Their silence on the issue seems to conform to the classic anthropological view that unwritten history is largely fictive history, with myths recited as charters to justify present institutions (L. Bohannan 1952; Malinowski 1954). But a closer look at the situation reveals that this apparent presentism is illusory: they were fully aware of the difference between the urn's past location and its present one, but interpreted the fact that it remained in Bukubani as vindicating their own position. If the urn did not belong there, it would have left.

From the people of Tossi I heard two arguments. The descendants of Rato Mangilo in Tossi Bukubani said that the power of objects to determine their own destinies held true only for the primordial period of the ancestors, and now it is human beings who are the actors on the stage of history. Objects serve only as historical evidence for certain attributes, such as rights to an office, but the mythical, magical past is finished. In this view, explanations that attribute meaning to an object's location can only be retrospective. "The true home of the urn was established in the distant past," they said "and nothing can change that."

A second group, descended from Rato Pokilo in Tossi Barada, claimed that sacred objects continue to exert a mystical influence on the behavior of their owners (or their violators) to legitimate processes of innovation.

In some ways, this is the more historical view, because it focuses on the changing relation between an object and a particular temporal context, saying the location is not determined absolutely but must always be viewed relative to shifting circumstances. Their version of this argument, however, gives a different spin to the idea of magical choice. The gold staff of office, in their perspective, proved to be the more powerful than the urn during the colonial period, so the loss of the urn to Bukubani became necessary to preserve a transformed diarchic division of powers, in which Tossi emerged triumphant. In other words, although control of ritual time was the supreme office according to the cultural values of the past, in the socioeconomic world of the Indonesian new order, access to government offices is of much greater significance. The emergence of new cultural forms always involves the incorporation of the outside by the inside, in which the signs and substances of foreign powers are taken and made part of new local systems. While the office of raja is now denigrated as a relic of feudal colonialism, the active, secular orientation given by the staff has enabled other people from Tossi to hold administrative offices and to seek education overseas.

The differing views of the power of objects are evoked as interpretive strategies, not as mutually exclusive representations. Each side might choose in a different context, for example, to argue that the movement of some other object had no ancestral sanction; the fact that the urn itself is now "settled" in its new home would have no bearing on that case. With regard to the urn, the ultimate test is the well-being of the people of Bukubani over time: if they continue to prosper and enjoy good health, the favor they have found with the ancestors who brought the urn and with the spirit dwelling in the urn itself is proved. But if they are struck by illness or misfortune, the location of the urn can be called into question again in a traditional divination.

The attitude of "spiritual empiricism" invoked here is similar to that contained in the phrase "History will be the final judge": that is, the past receives its fullest legitimation in the events that follow it. Because precedents are evaluated by their effectiveness under new conditions, current events provide a retrospective justification for past claims.

The System of Objects and Knowledge of the Past

I began by addressing two different questions, one historiographic, the other ethnographic. The first had to do with the forms taken by a historical knowledge invested more in objects than in persons—a "great things" approach to ordering the past, instead of one based on "great men" or "great women." The second involved the conundrum of dual sovereignty, or diarchy, where powers were shared between two persons or two objects on uncertain terms.

In answering the first question, I argue that the focus on objects as markers of past traditions creates an *impression of stability*, which seems to represent enduring offices and relationships as less open to variation than a person-centered genealogical model. At the same time, this stability can be illusory, for the offices and relationships do not in fact remain unchanged, even though the objects that represent them maintain a reassuringly ancient appearance. The traces of the past left in objects can be manipulated, as can other forms of historical evidence, but they remain, from a Kodi point of view, the "material that needs to be explained."

Objects belong to history as a heritage of the past, an uninterrupted process that reveals the continuity of culture over time. This contrasts with the discontinuous history of recent years, called by the Indonesian term *sejarah*, in which a new ideology of process is associated with the ephemeral importance of persons. In written histories, individual heroes are introduced as the protagonists of a novel form of narrative, set on the stage of irreversible historical changes. Thus Wona Kaka, the military leader of the rebellion against the Dutch forces in 1911–13, is cited as a "historical figure," while people like Ra Holo and Ra Ndengi (as well as their predecessors in the office of Rato Nale) are seen as placeholders in roles whose real meaning is defined by ritual objects.

The authority of the past depends on the existence of cultural standards of validation—a native historicity of some sort. A repertory of rules for appropriate action, such as those involved in the political constitution of diarchy, can be revised and adjusted by reweighting certain elements to respond to new historical conditions.

The traditional anthropological view of dual sovereignty presumes a static separation of powers, in which persons or objects interact to reproduce an established cultural pattern. It is unrealistic, however, to believe that diarchy in the past presented an unchanging template of complete consensus. Rather than portraying the "ragged Forces of History shattering the crystal Patterns of Culture" (Geertz 1990, 326), I maintain that the diarchic pattern constantly shifts to accommodate the importing of foreign models of rule—which often come, through trade routes, in the form of foreign objects. Ideas of hierarchy and wider social orders (whether those of Moslem sultans, Dutch administrators, or Indonesian nationalists) are incorporated into indigenous traditions and change their values. The relation between the urn and staff as tokens of office appears as a dynamic process, in which unities dissolve into oppositions, with a single opposition reproduced in a new context or else reunited with its counterpart at the opposite pole. The once supreme inner, spiritual source has been marginalized and made subservient to an outer, active executor, showing how the pervasive duality of power in Eastern Indonesia is always and intrinsically contestable, unstable, and politically constructed. The opposition articulated in metaphors of gender or seniority must repress internal ambiguities in order to stress certain differences at the expense of others. An initial pairing of male and female objects, for example, is now expressed more commonly in terms of elder sources and younger executors, and the cultural value of the distant past competes against the attractions of a new social and political order.

The value of the urn was an object of contention because an externally introduced trade item came to be used as a symbol of indigenous rule. The urn stood for the immutable and undeniable power of the great courts to the west of Sumba, yet it was used to legitimate the much more restricted powers of the indigenous timekeeper, the priest of the calendar. While the priest was never a ruler, he was the supreme ritual official of the area and exercised hierarchical control over the social organization of time.

The power of the foreign state was both recognized and denied in the process of offering sacrifices to the urn. A splendid imported object was made the center of the indigenous polity, described as the immovable anchor that held the calendar in place. The fresh water originally found in the urn after many days in the sea was replaced with the water from local sources. Once it had been stored in this sacred vessel, it became a medium of blessings and ritual cooling. The Chinese dragon, a powerful mythological animal for the urn's creators in South China or mainland Southeast Asia, was transformed for these islanders into a python, the giver of rainfall who sacrificed his own daughter so that the people might have rice. The original meaning of the iconography was lost on the way from China to Sumba, but its reinterpretation reflected the historical conditions that brought it to the island. The imagery of fertility and power was invested with a specific sense of distant sultanates and indirect rule, an aura of remote authority and diminished capacity for action.

Objects in Movement and Objects in Place

This drama of the disruption and reabsorption of colonial power through the rearrangement of sacred objects prompts an evaluation of the role of objects in Kodi exchange and the meaning of an object's movement. When the names "urn that cannot be moved" and "plate that cannot be lifted" were given to these objects, they assumed a distinctive place within the world of Kodi valuables. They became *objects that stay in place*, and as such were sharply distinguished from the objects that move almost incessantly along traditional exchange paths.

Most wealth objects, even those of great value, are supposed to circulate in transactions between affines. Decisions about when to keep them and when to give them away are motivated by thoughts of possible gain or loss, but not by the threat of supernatural sanctions presented here. The gold ear pendants (*mamoli*) used in bridewealth transactions move incessantly, up to nine or ten times a year.

The goods exchanged at marriages are opposed by gender: wife-takers give "male valuables"—swords, spears, gold pendants, and livestock (horses and buffalo)—while wife-givers present a countergift of "female valuables"—men's cloths and women's sarungs, pigs, cooked food. In the context of marriage exchanges, male goods are durable, forming the metal skeleton of the patriline, while female ones are perishable—food that must be consumed, textiles that must be rewoven each generation. The meeting of male and female in the world of objects parallels the marriage of man and wife, since the man's group will acquire descendants from it and an identity that will endure through the generations, while the women's group will "give life" but achieve no continuity from daughters who marry out.

The urn and plate are paradoxical because they are both female valuables and durable ones. Their inalienability places them at the top of a hierarchy of valuables, mobilized in the more encompassing struggle to achieve a lasting influence over time and escape the risks of loss involved in the exchange game. For stability and immortality are not finally achieved until death, when a man is placed inside a stone grave and his finest wealth objects are sealed up with him. Death removes a person from the risks of exchange and begins the process of his transformation into an ancestor, a *marapu*, whose grave will be decorated with carvings of the gold jewelry, gongs, and buffalo horns he owned in life. To play the exchange game is to struggle against time, trying to achieve immobility and permanence through the acquisition of wealth that can be transformed into the stable value of a splendid tomb.

The object which is "turned into an ancestor" (*bali marapu*) by a ritual consecration that makes it inalienable is consciously used as a "vehicle for bringing past time into the present" (Weiner 1985, 210) and making history visible. It acquires a peculiar temporal identity, becoming an anachronism, lifted "out of time" to sit above it. Like the pen used to sign the Bill of Rights or a hat worn at a famous battle, this object must be *taken out* of history in order to represent it. The treasure kept in each lineage cult house is a miniature museum, segregating particular objects to protect them from being caught up again in the flow of historical contingencies. But the ancestral patrimony is, at times, disturbed, pulled back *into* history by irregular events—theft, breakage, burning. On these occasions, the assault on the object is a deliberate assault on the history it represents, as well as an effort to undermine precedent and dismember memory.

The ways in which objects are embedded in history and the politics of representing the past have only recently come under scrutiny (Parmentier 1985, 1987; Thomas 1991). Throughout the Pacific, exchange valuables have become complexly entangled in local politics and colonial expansion. The contingent meanings that become attached to these things must first be analyzed within the framework of an indigenous system of objects and their relations before broader conclusions about reciprocity and regional interactions can be made.

5

The Past in Action
The Rites of the Kodi Year

Truly, carnival is the denizen of a place which is no place, and a time which
is no time, even when that place is a city's main plazas, and that time can be
found on an ecclesiastical calendar. . . . What we are seeing is society in its
subjunctive mood . . . its mood of feeling, willing and desiring, its mood of
fantasizing, its playful mood.

Victor Turner, *The Anthropology of Performance*

Calendrical rites have been described as attempts to abolish time, to annul
the past and to return to a primordial era of cosmogonic regeneration. For
Mircea Eliade (1954, 85), they represent "archaic man's refusal to accept
himself as a historical being . . . to grant value to memory and hence to
the unusual events that . . . constitute duration." In the ceremonies of the
New Year, he sees a revolt against the irreversibility of history and a claim
that "past" and "present" can coexist, the ancestors once again being the
contemporaries of the living. The *nale* festivities held to welcome the sea
worms in Kodi display many of the features of the "rites to regenerate
time" that he describes: they follow the narrative sequence of privations,
chaos, then a restoration of order; they involve ceremonial combats between opposing sides, a dissolution of the barriers between the living and
the dead, a "carnival" atmosphere, and a great feast of commensality.

But Eliade is wrong in saying that rites of reversal do away with the
past. The point of all these actions is not to destroy the past but to revitalize
it, to reflect upon it and reenact it imaginatively, recognizing a continuity
of tradition in cultural heritage. The roles that people assume in the
ceremonial context are those of ancestral personae, whom they personify
on a stage where the present "plays" at recreating the past. The actors are
conscious of shifting roles, and the ritual frame allows them to travel back
in time while still remembering their own personal, contingent relations.

In moments of liminal separation, they display an ironic distance from social convention—singing bawdy songs, crossing lances with their seniors on the playing field, defying the formal etiquette of most ceremonial events. But they do so in full awareness that this temporary "time out" will soon come to an end and they will reconstitute ordered social relations with a final sacrifice and shared meal.

The rites of the Kodi year involve an oscillation between constraint and excess, strict discipline and Rabelaisian rejoicing, which helps to define the polarities of both social life and the year. The *nale* festivities and *pasola* battle provide a unifying, centering focus for Kodi collective life, defining a shared order and ritual discipline for the whole domain. But they also offer an occasion for contests, both physical and verbal, that reveal underlying tensions—between juniors and seniors, women and men, members of peripheral villages and the ceremonial officers of the source.

The outer frame of the calendar is set by prohibitions. As outlined in mythic narratives, the autochthones are excluded, displaced by the descendants of Rato Mangilo and Rato Pokilo, who take over the center. The rites of the year bring people together, assembling them into a totality that observes a single annual rhythm of activities and acknowledges a single source of fertility in the *nale* spirit that comes from the sea. At the same time, the songs and ritual combat are made up of many voices and many riders, playfully celebrating the physicality of their encounters, exchanging courtship banter and blows in the mounted combat. The restrictions of ritual prohibitions give way to the risky pleasures of a game, and regulation ends in revelry.

The creation of the year is enacted at four ritual performances: (1) the start of the ritual silence at the "roasting of the bitter chicken"; (2) the playful period of courtship songs and games played along the beaches; (3) the sea worm collecting[1] and the crescendo of *pasola* jousting; and (4) a feast of chicken and rice to honor the dead souls in each village. Over the last century, the form of these enactments has changed, as has the significance of the historical reimagining they attempt to achieve. In moving from narrative to action, we see how ideas of ancestral precedence have also served as the basis for innovations and changes in ritual sequence.

---

[1] Sea worms collected on Kodi beaches are marine annelids of the Eunicid family (*Leodice viridis*), commonly known as the *palolo* in much of the Pacific. Rituals to greet the sea worms are reported from the neighboring Indonesian islands of Savu and Lombok (Fox 1979a) and more distant Pacific islands such as the Trobriands (Malinowski 1927), Fiji, and Samoa. The significance of the sea worms for the indigenous calendar is explained in chapter 12.

The "Bitter Chicken" of the Four-Month Ritual Silence

The ceremony to begin the ritual silence of four "bitter months" (*wulla padu*) is a simple one, conducted first in the Sea Worm House in Tossi, then in Bukubani, and later in Hangga Koki in Bangedo and Kaha Malagho in Balaghar. In 1980, I witnessed the rite in Tossi, as raw rice was scattered to dedicate a chicken from each house in the village, with these words:

Since the year is beginning	Maka a kabondi nya ndoyo
And the rains will start to fall	Mono a kawungo nya ura
We ask to plant a few seeds	Wokandi ha wini we kingoka
We want to sow a bit of rice	Tonda ndi ha pare we kingoka
So we brought you this chicken	Maka henene a manu
Slinging the gizzard on the shoulder	Na wyunggangongo wutena
Lifting his crest like horns	Na kyadungo lalerona
To say there will be no more loud laughter	Nja do kingyoka na kendero takeka
And no more careless giggling	Na madico lamera
You won't hear the sounds of flutes	Nja pa rongo li pyoghi
You won't hear the singing of fiddles	Nja pa rongo li jungga
We will all be off digging the land	Onikya la dari cana
We will all be off weeding the grass	Onikya la batu rumba
Bringing the hoes to work the land	Dukindi ha pangale haka tana
Carrying the knives to cut the bushes	Tomandi ha katopo teba rama
So that now	Tana henene
What we place at the edge of the posts	Pa tane ela tilu wu katuku
Let it come up like little chicks' feet	Pa witti ana manu we ki byandaka
What we set beside the seed platform	Pa tane la londo wu pawini
Let it rise like calves' shoulders	Pa wonggo ana ghobango weki byaka
The one with a shrimp's waist	Hena a kenda kura
Silences the fiddle's song	Na riri we kingyoka a li pyoghi
The one like a banyan blossom	Hena a walla kawango
Quiets the flute's sound	Na leta we kingyoka a li jungga
There will be none who go a node too far	Nja do kingyoka na dowa handalu
There will be none who overstep one joint	Nja do kingoka na pala hawuku

The spirits were assured that the human community would follow the

Before the *pasola* battle can begin, the Rato Nale, or "Priest of the Year"
(here, Ra Holo), must circle the playing field on a consecrated horse. 1980.
Photograph by the author.

calendrical prohibitions, and in return they were asked to provide an
abundant crop for the next harvest.

Small offerings of a bit of chicken meat and cooked rice were placed in
eight different locations in the house, drawing different domains of social
life together meaningfully and relating them to the cycle of the seasons.
The first share went to the right front corner of the house and the base of
the main pillar, conduits to the Creator and the Great Spirit of prosperity
(*marapu bokolo*). Then other offerings were made to the Elder Spirit
(*marapu matuyo*) at the rock and tree altar in the center of the ancestral
village, to the spirits of the dead along the front veranda, to the spirit of
hunting and of domestic animals in the rear corners of the house, to the
place where wealth objects are stored near the hearth, and to the guardian
spirit of the gateway. In this way, the prohibition was spread to different
domains of social life, and ancestors, affines, animals, and men were bound
together to concentrate their energies on producing a successful harvest.

The prohibitions of the bitter months forbid noisemaking and a wide variety of activities that could endanger the growth of young rice plants. These include children's games, large animal sacrifice, and the manufacture of white substances that might seem to compete with the production of full, white grains of rice. The prohibitions were summarized by the Rato Nale thus:

You cannot make any noises, such as	Pa heringo a puni-puni
beating the drums and gongs	bendu tala
playing the flute and fiddle	poghi dungga
rhythmically striking bamboo floorboards	katendango katonga
You cannot sing the refrains of group songs	Lodo hanggelico
or personal ballads	lawitti
sing to drag stones or house pillars	bengyo watu, bengyo pongga
recite traditional narratives	ngara kedoko
You cannot play games with the top or discus	Mangguna kadiyo kalaiyo
play with bamboo darts or seed boards	mbuke kule
play hide and seek (outside)	kambuni kandaba
play search and find (in the house)	kambuni kaloho
You cannot cut pandanus leaves	Ghoto panda
You cannot dye white thread	Betingo kamba
You cannot tattoo the arms and legs	Ta kamandu
You cannot put bells on horses' bridles	Ta langgoro ndara
You cannot boil salt	Pandende mahi
You cannot bake limestone	Tunu katagha
You cannot spear pigs, slaughter buffalo	Ndakuro wawi, teba karimbyoyo
cut goats' throats or beat dogs	ropo kawimbi, palu bangga

The complex list of prohibitions defines precisely those activities that, as *nale* festivities approach, will be permitted and even joyously engaged in. The origin narratives describe the sea worms as having been won through a series of contests, so the repetition of these contests (the top and discus, jousting, and beachcombing) serves to regenerate the vitality and fertility of the year. By means of temporal regulation, apparently frivolous children's games become a means for recreating the social order.

The period of the bitter months is a time of intense agricultural activity, when fields are prepared and the new crops of corn and rice are planted.

Most people live in their garden huts, usually located several hours or even days from their ancestral villages. They devote all day to preparing their gardens, with none of the distractions of ritual gatherings.

By late December or early January the crops have been planted, and the phase of preparation for the New Year starts with the moon called Nale Kiyo. The priest of the sea worms, Rato Nale, begins to "brood," adopting a pose of immobility and spiritual concentration, which is also ritually enjoined on the female mourner at funerals (*kabuku kalalu*). He "sits like a hen on her eggs, like a sow sheltering her young" (*bei myanu na kabuku tongo taluna, bei wyawi na karekongo anana*). By remaining totally inactive, he controls the forces that activate the seasons, keeping the calendar in place and maintaining time as it has been culturally constructed. Symbolically female during this period, he provides a model of self-discipline and self-control that rules by example rather than by decree.[2]

The whole region would be in danger if the Sea Worm Priest were to violate any of these restrictions. Should he leave his house, fierce winds would tear apart the tender young rice plants. Should he eat any of the taboo foods, lightning bolts would strike the fields. Should he fail to control the calendar and coordinate feasting within a seasonal pattern, a tidal wave would engulf the whole coastline and destroy the ancestral villages. As the master of time, the priest of the sea worms represents the collectivity, both the land and the people, and should he fail in his duties, all would suffer.

From Taboos to License

As the young rice sprouts grow stronger, however, and as the time of harvest approaches, a lessening of these constraints begins, expressed in rites to make the early-ripening crops "bland" or "sweet" (*kaba*) and harvestable for the festivities to come. The first marker of the relaxation of taboos is a small ritual named for the "sweet waters of the young sprouts" of the areca and coconut palms (*kaba wei kapoke*). A chicken is sacrificed with a prayer by the Rato Nale requesting that the people be allowed to gather their stores of areca and coconut to receive guests. Fresh branches full of young areca nuts will be placed as offerings on the tombs

---

[2] The rule is that he may not "cross over" into the women's part of the house, and his wife, in turn, must prepare his meals in a special area where no corn is allowed, and she cannot join him, as she usually would, to sleep in the right front bedroom. Except for this period, the Rato Nale has a normal family life. Ra Holo, at the time of my research, had a wife and five children, while Ra Ndengi had three wives and eight children.

of the recently dead on the morning that the sea worms arrive, and the coconuts will be processed into the thick cream used to cook chickens and rice for the festive occasion.

The full moon of Nale Kiyo, approximately three weeks before the predicted sea worm swarming, is when young people begin *kawoking*, wandering the beaches at night singing to the spirit of rice, calling her back from overseas to return to Sumba and provide a bountiful harvest. During this period it is taboo to fish or spear octopus along the seashore, so the beaches are deserted during the day but full of bustling, giggling nocturnal activity. Children bring out the tops, discus, and board games that were forbidden during the bitter months and scamper in the sand playing games of hide and seek. Young boys meet to practice *patukengo*, a form of traditional boxing, in which teams hold on to a single rope and swing their fists at each other to force the other side to let go. Groups of girls gather to watch them, and sing the bawdy *kawoking* songs: short compositions in light verse (*lawitti*), which comment ironically on the upcoming *pasola* and its ethic of male bravery. They are answered by choruses of boys, who take up the same themes but turn them around to mock female resistance. The wordplay focuses on ordinary objects (the spindle, the loom, the sword, the trough), which are anthropomorphized and made to speak for their owners in comic fashion. The obscenity of the everyday offers a veiled commentary on male-female relations, represented in the homespun idioms of weaving, hunting, fishing, and scavenging along the beach.

Among the most common are two women's songs, which purport to treat the appropriately feminine domain of weaving but in fact comment on male propensities to seek other wives:

Rolling three threads at the same time	Ombolo katalu
You say you want to take three at once	Talu ngole ambu wemu
But you won't be able to handle it	Inje laghu la katalu
Even if you want three you can't hold them!	Talu ngole dogho damu!
The weft that holds up two threads	Wunango kadungo
You say two on the same pole	Kadungo deke ghaiyo ambu wemu
You can't take two of them at the same time	Inje deke la kadungo
The pole can't do it even if it wants!	Dungo deke ghaiyo dogho damu!

The ending of both these ditties, *dogho damu*, has something of the sense of "you silly little thing," and is used in instructing children. Thus, on one level the song instructs young girls on the proper technique for arranging threads on the loom, but its allusion is to men who try to satisfy two or three women at the same time and are not up to it.

The mockery is flirtatious at the same time that it is critical. During this period of nighttime revels young people are allowed the freedom to initiate liaisons, which they consummate, discreetly, in the darkness of the dunes. But although the songs play a role in courtship, they also serve to warn young girls against agreeing too readily to the demands of their suitors. A whole series of songs carry explicit messages to deflate male strutting and posturing, asserting that young men are not always as irresistible as they seem to believe:

Do not shake yourself senseless	Ambu tara tara mu
Like a centipede in the road	Kalipye ate lara
"I'm the one whose liver [heart] is desired," you say	Di ate ngguba wemu
But you're not the one my heart intends!	Kana nja ku ate danghu
Do not squeak so in excitement	Ambu diki diki mu
Like the mouse at the headrest	Malogho taku luna
"I am the one whose throat is desired," you say	Di koko nggaba wemu
But you're not the one my throat longs for!	Kana nja ku koko danghu
You rustle around and grope	Na kayighu na kayeghuka
Probing the *sirih* pouch for fresh fruit	Yighu yeghu kondo a rou uta
But only old yellow ones, dead ones	Rou uta rara, rou uta mate
Not enough to turn one's mouth red!	Kira njora mali njora!

The fondness of men for young girls, newly fertile, is mocked in the last verse, which asserts that they would do better to turn their attentions to the older women who might be more receptive. Implicit warnings against polygamy and age differences are found in the assertion that an older and important husband "cannot keep giving fresh betel" to satisfy his wife, especially if he has other wives to "feed."

Three other songs dwell on the heroic image of the *pasola* rider as he departs for the field of combat, dressed in a high-peaked bark headcloth and carrying a tall saber with a horsehair fringe. His costume celebrates his virility, as do the jangling bells around his horse's neck, but the songs suggest that on his return from the combat these objects will look much less impressive:

Why are the bells on your horse's neck broken?	Pena ba na mbera a longgoro koko ndara mu?
You say the sound was piercing	Nggubu wemu
Even sharper, even stronger	Rehi liyo, rehi calo
Until they came out of the pastures	Oro loho la marada
Bogged down in exhausting mud!	Nola njenduko haghogha!
Why did the handle of the saber snap?	Pena ba na mbata mbekatungga pandi ceko?
You say it was once so strong	Ngguba wemu
A bearded saber, a lordly upright saber	Teko ndari, teko rato
Until it came from the forest of pig's swamps!	Oro tamani kandaghu la kapore koko wawi!
Squeeze tightly on your Kodi stallion	Kapiridi kiyo ndara kodi
Still a little tighter there	Hodi kyapiridi kiyo
Press hard so the stallion rides straight	Kapi pandaha wadi kiyo a ndara kiyo
Still firmer to keep your loincloth from slipping	Hodi kyapa la mangeria hanggingo
So the horned peaks of your headcloth will stay erect!	La maderia kadu mete!

These attacks on male virility present its splendor as only momentary and its weapons as weak.

Although the majority of the songs are sung by women, groups of young men can compose their own replies, such as the following verses:

Sniffing about like a young bitch	Palaka pa kabondi byangga
What moves in her black belly	Mete pugha kambu
Lifts her white tail high	Wala kiku damu
The one with white face marks	Bela mata
Who calls to each passer by	Ba na kangakopaleko yila
To join her in the sand dunes!	Paraduana halaiyo!
Following her through the dunes	Maneya la halaiyo
I see no more footprints in the sand	Nja ku ice oro maneya la halaiyo
Only traces of bodies rolling	Lighoboro kambona ihi mbanu
Getting up dirty from their games	Ba na kede la mangguna

The image in the first verse of the unattractive but sexually voracious woman finishes with a description of the trysting in the sand that often ends the evening.

The coy girl who refuses all her suitors until it is too late is the subject of another set of verses:

The tips of long grass are yellow	Lombo ngingo rara
They look dry and dead	Ngingo mate ghabu wemu
Not the juicy tips of young grass	Inja lombo ngingyo moro
Just old dead grass, you fool	Ngingyo mate doghu damu
Passed over by the young bay stallion	Na pa li kahiri balinya a kamone ndara rara
Who wanders to seek new pastures	No ba na halato manapa
Nibbling here and there	Bono wilu bono walinya
Left behind on top of the cliff	Na pa hangula tadu ngamba
With the low-lying thorn weeds	Ha kaparico kadada ria kadada

The girls reply to these verses with short ditties describing unsuccessful attempts to catch them and seduce them, using the idiom of the *pasola* battle and the male activites of hunting and fishing:

However hard you try to mount it	Ghalio apa halio
Trying again to mount the hero's horse	Helu halio kalete ndara njelo
You slip off the horse's slippery side	Kaka kuku hiya mbali ndara
And the poor hero falls off	Njelo kaka douka luka
The hero is left to walk!	Kako njelo douka luka!
However hard you chase after it	Ghala apa wemu
Thrusting here and there	Na bananada helu ananda
Trying to spear the pig	La manghila gheghu wawi
Not a single pig is speared	Kana wawi inja ghena
Even a sick pig is not speared	Wawi hyadu inja ghena
You return all ashamed	Nduka luka bali kyaba
Returning empty-handed, returning shy	Bali pengyo, bali meke
Your spear thrusting was all in vain	Nduka luka hengyo banda
Vainly trying to be a big man!	Banda bei kabani!
However much you splash about	Ghala apa wemu
Holding the trap for river shrimp	Na bawiluko maghogha kura loko
Scooping again and again in the river	Helu panda wiluko kura loko

Not a single shrimp do you catch	Kana kura inja ngole
Not even a dead shrimp lies in your trap	Kura mate inja ngola
Catching nothing, you burn with shame	Inja ngole nduka douka
Returning empty-handed, returning shy	Bali kyaba, bali meke
Not as it would suit a big man	Inja hengyo bei kabani

Shrimp and pigs are symbolically female animals, yet here they escape the traps and weapons of the hunter/fisher; even the horse, a man's closest companion, slips from his grasp and leaves the "hero" without a mount. Njelo Kaka, the name given to the "hero" in this ditty, is the protagonist of a series of myths of male achievement, but in the context of women's bawdy songs he is degraded and humiliated—closed off from the impenetrable façade of the woman's body and made into a grotesque parody of the dismembered organ.

The courtship of young boys and girls is supposed ultimately to summon images of agricultural fertility and abundance, reflecting the idea that the sea worms bring back the lost soul of the rice crop and capture it for the harvest. The link is made most explicit in one more serious song, which echoes the prayers of the Rato Nale:

Come to swarm	Mai tami ghu tana wemu
Come to wriggle	Mai tame ghurango
You the mother sea worm	Yo inya nono nale
In the trough that doesn't leak	La karaba nja manama
The trough of *rica* wood	Yila rabba rica
Come to swim	Mai tadidu tana wemu
Come to flop about	Mai tado dikyongo
In the trap that doesn't spill	La keka inja dori
The trap made of *nalo* wood	Yila keka nalo

The *nale* and *pasola* celebrations link human and plant reproduction, and provide a propitious time to begin an affair, which will come to fruition in the period of harvesting the mature crops of rice and corn.

At the end of the evening, the tone turns serious again, and a haunting ballad is sung to summon the distant *nale* and place the teasing and enticing courtship songs in perspective:

| There is really only one woman | Nduka pinja pinja naka |
| The mother of the distant sea worms | Inya nale nono |

Whom we call until our throats are hoarse	Pa kawula mbera koko
Hoarse from begging her to come	Koko mbera denga kinja
To the edge of the tides at Hanjongi	La kahiku la Hanjongi
There is really only one man	Nduka pinja pinja naka
The father of the damp *ipu* fish	Bapa ipu mbaha
Whom we beckon until our hands break	Pa pangede limya mbata
Breaking from stretching them out	Mbata limya denga kinja
To the depths of the male ocean!	La talora limbu mone!

All of the songs are, in a sense, addressed to the spirits of the sea: the Mother of the Sea Worms, who swarm for these festivities, and her consort, the *ipu* fish, which swarms in March or April along the same beaches.

The revelries of *kawoking* continue for about ten days, until the moon waxes and the nights become dark. Starting on the darkest night, the Rato Nale then begins his official count. On the seventh day after the new moon appears, the sea worms should swarm.

The Sea Worm Swarming and Pasola *Jousting*

On the morning of the swarming, hundreds of people go down to the beaches with traditional woven dippers, ceramic jars, and plastic buckets. In the early hours of dawn, the tiny, multihued worms swim to the surface of the tides and begin to discard their genitalia after reproducing. The sea fills with colorful, pastalike strings, some only a few inches, others several feet long. Men, women, and children eagerly scoop the soft, wriggling bodies up, collecting them in a great number of containers. By the time the sun has risen to its midday position, the worms are largely gone, as they dissolve quickly in the harsh light of day. By then, though, the kitchens in the ancestral villages are full of *nale*, which are flavored with ginger and garlic and prepared as a condiment, a pungent mixture vaguely resembling anchovy paste. Prized as a delicacy, a rare and wondrous food from the sea, the worms will be eaten in this way along with the chicken and rice offered to the ancestors after the most heated battle of the *pasola*.

The spectacle of a mounted battle with spears, mandated in Kodi mythical narratives for the entertainment of these unusual supernatural visitors, begins with the massing of thousands of riders in full ceremonial garb. Men and boys arrive wearing several lengths of red, orange, and yellow cloth tied around their heads and under the chin, supporting tall peaks reinforced with bark cloth or cardboard inserts to stand erect. Draped in mantles of indigo textiles and wrapped in loincloths (nowadays worn over shorts), they grasp their mounts with bare legs, stirrupless in the traditional style. Their horses are decorated with bells hanging from their bridles, cloth banners tied to their manes and tails, and sometimes even added tufts of horsehair at the neck and foot. No saddles are used, but colorful back pads are secured by a cinch around the chest. Members of the core villages of Pola Kodi—"the trunk of Kodi"—are pitted against the more recently founded villages of the other side of the river and the embankment (Bali Hangali, Bangedo). The two sides gather to face each other on the field, awaiting the arrival of the Rato Nale to start the event.

Although the Rato Nale does not participate in the jousting, no one can ride out until he has circled the field. He rides the Ndara Nale, a special horse raised from the herd in Tossi, which follows the same prohibitions as its master: it is not allowed to leave the village for the period of confinement, cannot eat corn or tubers, can never be bought or sold. The taboos observed by the Sea Worm Priest and his mount are supposed to protect the other horses and riders on the field, preventing serious injury or death. Although the shedding of some blood is part of the logic of the event, water taken from the heirloom urn is said to cure wounds of anyone who has not violated the calendrical taboos.

Participants in the *pasola* represent both ancestral personae who confront each other across the terrain of an early ritual division and ambitious individuals who want to impress others with their horsemanship. The contest is a forum for the display of personal feats of bravery and skill, but it produces champions rather than winners. While great riders are noticed and applauded by the crowds, no score is kept, and there are no final victors. The emphasis is on a display of vitality and fierceness—which of course is open to multiple interpretations. Not surprisingly, given the contentious nature of Kodi life, both sides usually return with claims that they have bested their opponents.

The combat warms up gradually. For the first half hour of the combat the event is more a parade than a contest as riders circle the field in long, easy, loping strides that allow the jingling bells on their horses' halters to ring out, while those watching can observe them and identify individuals by their colorful dress. The best riders do not enter the field until later, leaving the terrain open to younger riders who let their horses run loose before the spectators. Once the field has been trampled, the more experienced horsemen begin to challenge their rivals with verbal taunts: "Where are you, the counterpart with bent knees, the partner with parted hair?" they will shout, using the couplet that refers to opposing sides in warfare or alliance—*papa ndende kundo, nggaba horo longge.* "Come to meet me in the wide pastures," they cry; "come to clash spears on the grassy field."

In the nineteenth century, the combat was conducted with real spears, and blood was quick to flow, but since the period of Dutch colonial control only blunt bamboo lances have been permitted. The goal of the jousting has thus shifted primarily to trying to unseat one's opponent, making him fall from his horse or causing the horse to trip. Groups of five or six riders set off in a formation, charging toward the other side and then circling back, with the famous champions in the lead and younger apprentice riders bringing up the rear. Short bursts of intense activity alternate with more leisurely circling of the field, followed by a sudden and concentrated attack.

The first blunt lances rarely strike their mark. It is only the most experienced riders, daring to get close to their opponents, who strike the head or flanks. Falls occur most often in the middle of the battle, when the rider is in great danger of being trampled by passing horses. Broken ribs, blindness, and neck injuries are frequent, occurring almost every year. Deaths from blows to the throat, eyes, or skull have occasionally occurred, but are rare, and are always explained as the result of a taboo violation.[3] The dangers experienced by the riders are a way of testing their adherence to traditional norms and values, which ensure them protection, not to mention a forum for competitive display.

Three combats are held, but only the middle one is of great ritual significance. The day before the worms swarm, a small "training session" (*dongu ndara*) is held in late afternoon in front of the village of Bondo Kawongo. This is said to "soften the horse's feet" and prepare the mount for the later combat. The middle combat, held the next morning at the westernmost field by the village complex known as the "trunk of Kodi," is the most intense, climaxing in the generation of ritual heat that coincides with the sun's ascent to its highest point in the sky. The combat continues for three or more hours, and is called to a halt when the Sea Worm Priest circles the field on his horse. People then return to their ancestral villages to roast a chicken to their ancestors and make offerings. In late afternoon,

---

[3] In 1980, a man was killed at the *pasola* in Wanokaka, and it was explained that he had defied the taboo against fishing along the seashore in the month before the sea worms swarmed. His wife reported tearfully that he had set out to spear an octopus, claiming that he was strong enough to resist the ancestral law. When he insisted on taking part in the ritual combat afterward, he was struck at the base of the breastbone, and the lance opened up his windpipe.

they gather near Tossi for the last and final battle, which helps to "cool down" the excitement of the morning and dissipate remaining aggressive feelings.

The *pasola* has been interpreted by some contemporaries as a substitute or exercise for war, remembering the not-too-distant period at the beginning of this century when the island was torn by tribal warfare and mounted parties of warriors took the heads of highland peoples. Nowadays it expresses an aggression that is more properly interpreted as reflecting the tension within the region between hierarchical ritual order and egalitarian competitive exchange. On the *pasola* field, a certain kind of supremacy, one based on history and precedent, is challenged by another, and in many ways more pervasive, mode: that of ostentatious achievement. Young men ride to make a name for themselves by impressing girls and prospective in-laws, and older ones display their ability to command, marked by the following they have among their juniors and the fine possessions that they have acquired.

The finest riders at the *pasola* often come from Tossi, the "mother-father village" of the whole region; but men from more recently founded villages on the other side of the river that have emerged as Tossi's rivals in a wider political context are also coming to dominate the proceedings. In the 1970s and 1980s, the informal leader of Tossi's horsemen was Tari Nggoko, a descendant of the first Kodi raja. Rangga Baki and Ratenggaro, the home of the third Kodi raja and a famous center of headhunting rites, are now the main challengers from Bangedo.

A champion, or "rooster" (*maghailio*), is someone who has not been unseated in several years of riding across the field but who has caused many others to fall or bleed at his hands. The greatest champions may hold this title for ten or twenty years. None of them can hold it forever, however. The glory of the *pasola* rider is ephemeral. "So far," a current champion told me, "I have dodged all their lances and none of them has struck me down. But when my time comes, I will know that I have grown old, and cede my place to the younger men." The *pasola* is an arena in which daring younger men can challenge and even defeat their elders, defying the usual deference due to those senior in rank and social position.

Today, close police supervision is needed to keep the ritualized violence from erupting into actual battles or skirmishes on the sidelines. It is forbidden to wear bush knives onto the *pasola* field, to throw stones, or to charge directly across the opponent's lines, although angry riders do at times give chase. Hundreds of frightened horses and spectators retreat hastily if a rider loses control of his mount and breaks out of formation.

The *pasola* resembles other ritual combats found throughout Indonesia,

Local people walk down to the western beaches in the early hours of the dawn on a date determined by the Rato Nale to collect the sea worms and bring them back for a sacrificial meal shared with the ancestors. 1988. Photograph by Laura Whitney.

such as Balinese cock fighting (Geertz 1973), Savunese rock-throwing battles (Fox 1979a), Minang buffalo duels, and other animal combats involving elephants, tigers, bulls, or oxen (Reid 1988, 1987). R. E. Downs argues that all of these confrontations began with the dualistic opposition of two groups within the society, who engage in "a ritual struggle representing the two halves of the universe" (Downs 1955, 59). Many present performances are interpreted by him as having lost this original meaning: "Often they would seem to have degenerated into mere sporting events indulged in at the time of general festivities, without any consciousness on the part of the participants of their religious significance" (Downs 1955, 55). As for the *pasola*, the struggle of opposing principles is still clearly tied to the constitution of the ceremonial system as presented in traditional narratives, though the particular form of the combat was probably imported from Java.

Consistent with the Kodi idea that the *pasola* was introduced from a splendid kingdom to the west, the Malay epic *Hikayat Hang Tuah* mentions jousting as part of the entertainment at the Javanese court of Majapahit. The first detailed description of the weekly tournaments (*senenan*) held in the squares near the royal citadel comes from a Dutch account of the events in Tuban, and is summarized by Reid (1988, 187):

> About four in the afternoon the younger braves of the court would converge on the square after parading through the city on their magnificently attired horses. There they would engage in a series of charges and manoeuvres, one generally pursuing the other down the length of the field, with the aim of knocking each other off their horses with blunted spears. In reality, this happened seldom, and most attention was paid to the horsemanship displayed in the constant wheeling and turning on the square. The king was always present for these occasions and, at least in Mataram, took part in the jousting.

The similarities with present-day *pasola* are very strong, and the Kodi combat shares the aspect of serving as a "metaphor of war in which young aristocrats displayed their qualities" (Reid 1988, 188). Before 1600, the tournaments seem to have been quite bloody, as provisions are mentioned for the families of victims (Ma Huan, 1433; cited in Reid 1988, 187). The "knights" of Java were described by Tome Pires in 1515 as proud horsemen who often provoked deadly combat on an individual basis: "The noblemen are much in the habit of challenging each other to duels, and they kill each other over their quarrels, and this is the custom in the country. Some of them kill themselves on horseback, and some on foot, according to what they have decided" (cited in Reid 1988, 187).

Jousting tournaments declined in Java as warfare became less frequent, and they were gradually replaced by animal combats. The coupling of human and animal combat suggests that the blood of one has often been used to represent the blood of the other. Ritual cock fighting on Savu is held in conjunction with ceremonies to welcome sea worms, and Savunese explanations of the combat closely parallel the *pasola*: "It is a struggle between classes of spirits represented by men, the spirits of the land the spirits of the sea; and it is a substitute for warfare between clans and villages" (Fox 1979a, 165).

Sumba, in a way, is similar to the societies of classical Greece and Sparta, where athletic champions were often political and military leaders as well. This seems to have changed somewhat with the suppression of interregional warfare in the 1920s, as well as the institution of present government policies controlling feasting. In effect, an informal and competitive political system is increasingly being replaced by an externally appointed administrative hierarchy in which horsemanship is no longer an important factor. Thus, the *pasola* is being promoted now as a folkloric celebration and a way of entertaining visiting dignitaries; it is no longer a religious rite and the basis of the Kodi polity.

Roasting a Chicken to the Dead: Sacrifices in the Ancestral Villages

At the end of the second *pasola* battle, people return to their ancestral villages to prepare a meal. A somewhat chaotic scene follows, as hundreds of chickens are sacrificed to those who have most recently died, whose graves were scattered with betel nut in the morning. On this occasion, all the various members of a house unite with their lineage brothers on an equal footing, without the hierarchical divisions of the feasting season. Instead of competing to see who can bring the buffalo with the longest horns or the largest pig, participants at the *nale* feast all come with a single chicken, which they share with their ancestors. The markers of rank and seniority are conspicuously absent as everyone shares cheerfully and generously in the reserves of rice set aside for the feast, flavoring their meat with small tasty servings of the sea worms themselves, spooned on the side of the plate as a relish.

The *nale* feast is the only one in which everyone can be included because no embarrassment is involved if one cannot bring an adequate contribution. It gathers together all the members of a house and can, as a result, be an occasion for the telling of mythic narratives and the singing of songs forbidden for so long. It can also be a time to discuss new projects for the dry season: the erection of a new stone grave, the building of an ancestral house, the giving of a feast. The *marapu* must be informed of these projects through sacrifices, and may also be told of changes in residence or group composition, recent marriages, or a preference for male or female descendants. At this gathering, "no one is afraid to come with empty hands, and no one must go home with an empty stomach." Defined by its simplicity, the feast is also generalized and shared.

The entrails of chickens sacrificed at the *nale* feast are read for auspices of the coming year. If they contain black spots or red flecks, it is a sign of disease or death in the house. If they are twisted or crossed by membranes, there may be stealing or adultery among the descendants of a particular ancestor. But if they are straight and firm, suggesting the straight flow of blessings from previous generations into the present, the signs are positive and everyone can celebrate.

In the most important ritual villages, private household sacrifices are followed by a public meal attended by male representatives of each cult house. The first share of chicken and rice is dedicated to the sea worms, and other portions are set aside at the clan altar, household altars, and on the tombs of important ancestors. Because this food is specially consecrated as *ngagha nale* or the "rice of the sea worms," it requires a personal purification before it can be eaten. If any participant has committed theft, adultery, trespassing, the stealing of rice souls, or the breaking of food taboos, he must first confess to the Rato Nale before partaking. The price of spiritual cleansing seemed too high to several of the delegated representatives whom I observed, for many chose not to eat their share of the meal. They respected the ritual context of commensality, but denied its power to regulate their lives.

Time, Carnival, and Disruptive Revels

Mikhail Bakhtin, writing about the folk culture of the Middle Ages and the Renaissance, notes that

> the feast is essentially related to time . . . to moments of crisis, of breaking points in the cycle of nature or in the life of society and man. . . . As opposed to the official feast, one might say that carnival celebrated temporary liberation from the prevailing truth and from the established order; it marked the suspension of all hierarchical rank, privileges, norms, and prohibitions. Carnival was the true feast of time, the feast of becoming, change and renewal.
> It was hostile to all that was immortalized and completed.
>
> (Bakhtin 1984a, 9–10)

The *nale* festivities can be interpreted as a carnival-like feast, bringing an end to the bitter months of prohibitions and marking the ritual calendar, much as carnivals in Europe marked the last chance to indulge in revelry before the privations of Lent. Incorporating elements of obscenity, rivalry, and ribaldry, *nale* involves a temporary dissolution of hierarchy and the playful defiance of order.

The sharing of the *nale* feast celebrates a particular temporality—the repetitive, regenerative time of bodily processes—and an ideal of equality and common substance. It contrasts in this respect to the feasts of the dry season held for stone draggings and house buildings, and with celebrations of those who have taken new titles or achieved competitive renown. In Bakhtin's (1984a, 10) terms, the ladder-of-prestige feasts are "consecrations of inequality," focused on the display of wealth and regalia to communicate differences in rank and genealogical order. At the *nale* feast, by contrast, economic differences are invisible, for each family sacrifices only a chicken. The pretense of immutability that is maintained at other occasions is challenged by a festive laughter, and hierarchies are contested by dissident voices. The great leaders of the ritual centers may be knocked off their horses by younger challengers, and arrogant husbands may be prodded and teased by women's clever puns and songs. In playing with apparently fixed categories of social discourse, participants show them to be ephemeral and relative, a revelation that may prove less threatening than reassuring. The ritual framework defines a space within which license is possible, and places parentheses around established verities. The *nale* festivities are a time of laughter and excitement, when the tensions between men and women, between established ritual centers and peripheral ones, and between old and young are parodied with droll abandon.

There are several possible interpretations of the combination of ribaldry and reverence in the *nale* celebration. One, dating back to Frazer, is based on the linking of human and plant fertility, with the rite anticipating the harvest and using magical principles to make the young crop more abundant. A second, drawing on the work of Victor Turner, interprets the egalitarianism as expressing "communitas," an intensified sharing and dissolution of differences, as Geirnaert Martin (1987) has argued happens in Lamboya rice ritual. But in these cases the veiled hostility marking the exchanges between riders and between men and women singers seems out of place. The ritual discipline required by the Rato Nale and the respect shown for the sea worms and the spirit of rice contrast sharply with the disrespect and even mockery directed not only at human failings but also at other participants.

I would therefore propose a third option, which is to see the *nale* festivities as exploring and celebrating the regenerative powers of differences—between men and women, juniors and seniors, past and present. If, as Bakhtin (1984a, 10) says, laughter is the enemy of hierarchical structures, then the ribaldry can be interpreted as asserting the heterogeneity of ritual participants and their resistance to official authority. The Rabelaisian flavor of the exchanges along the beaches reveals a various lines of conflict between source and periphery, between the values of control and those of joyful release. This confrontation is muted in much of the festivities, but surfaces in the songs and combat, and is never finally resolved.

The deference rendered to the authority of the Rato Nale would seem to be an exception to this defiance of ritual order. It is, however, an exception that proves the rule, since his authority is maintained only by identifying it with immobility and passivity. Because he cannot act, the Sea Worm Priest can serve as the anchor of the traditional calendar. Because he cannot speak, his preeminence cannot be challenged with verbal taunts. The fragile consensus of heterogeneous groups collected together for the occasion can be held together only by an empty center, where power is retained by an image of powerlessness. As we saw in the last chapter, the timekeeper has on many separate occasions been forced to surrender his authority over other concerns in order to preserve his ritual position as one beyond controversy; the *nale* festival is just such an occasion.

The carnivalesque aspects of the *nale* celebration do not represent a mere moment of antistructure in a dialectical process of structure-making (V. Turner 1969). Rather, they express divergent political sentiments, bringing opposing forces into contact to affirm their power to generate a new whole. The dualistic opposition of the sexes and of the two sides of the *pasola* is an effort to order the relationship between "antitheses that cannot be allowed to become antipathies" (Maybury-Lewis 1989). While the principles they represent may seem contradictory, their combination can be creative rather than destructive. A balance of contending forces is assured by allowing them to meet in the bounded arena of institutionalized "play." The authority of the Rato Nale, the ultimate encompassing frame for the calendrical rites, is not challenged; yet his ascetic discipline and withdrawal enable others to enjoy a time of cheerful, chaotic disorder. My argument is not that the carnival-like celebrations of *nale* reinforce the serious institutions and rhythms of society, but that they make them possible to live with.

A Century of Pasola Performances

The implication of the *pasola* in larger historical processes is evident if we examine changes in its performance over the last century. At the end of the nineteenth century, when Sumba was still caught up in internal warfare, the *pasola* was performed on a relatively small scale, with only the participation of those people who lived in the ancestral villages of Kodi Bokol and Bali Hangali.

The fathers and grandfathers of contemporary riders were horsemen whose skills were valued not only as entertainment (for both humans and spirits) but also as part of the practical arsenal of warfare. In the late nineteenth century, Rangga Baki and Ratenggaro were locked in a deadly pattern of murders, feuding, and livestock raiding. The two villages, however, suspended their hostilities at *pasola* time, when they rode together against their opponents from Tossi and source villages of the "trunk of Kodi." One of the region's main *pasola* champions and fiercest warriors, Rato Muda of Rangga Baki, was said to have been approached to serve in the colonial administration. He refused, saying, "I still have my brother's blood to avenge"—meaning that he could not serve as a peacekeeper under Dutch rule.

The season for headhunting, local feuding, and warfare was July through September, after the harvest and toward the end of the dry season, when agricultural activity was at a minimum. *Pasola* falls at the other polarity of the calendar, in a time of agricultural cooperation, when people live in dispersed settlements near their gardens so they can weed and harvest the crops of the rainy season. Thus, although the ritual contest held near the beach provided a forum for impressive, competitive displays of force, it was stringently distinguished from actual warfare.

The *pasola* always has two opposing sides, but their composition has shifted over the years. The origin narrative pits the villages of Pola Kodi against Mbali Hangali. In the 1920s, shortly after the Dutch pacification, the people of Bangedo came to join in the fray, riding with their neighbors from Mbali Hangali. During the rule of the first two Kodi rajas, Rato Loghe and Ndera Wulla, the performance of the last battle, on a field close to Tossi, became a celebration of the power and influence of the Tossi rajas. As the largest village in precolonial Kodi, Tossi produced both the finest horsemen and the largest group of riders taking part in the ritualized combat, establishing a reputation that still lives on in the present.

In the 1930s, Dutch colonial officials decided to encourage the growth of the *pasola* as a "stabilizing" celebration of the unity of the polity and invited participants from the whole region. They proposed new rules that would forbid the use of sharpened spears and substitute blunt bamboo lances. Less blood was spilled, but more riders dared to join in, and a new group of challengers from the regions of Bangedo and Balaghar formed to test the skills of the Tossi riders. Since a separate rajaship also existed on the other side of the river, what was at stake in the combat became a struggle for symbolic domination of the whole area.

In 1945, upon Ndera Wulla's death, power passed into the hands of H. R. Horo of Rangga Baki, Bangedo. At the ceremony inducting him into office, he ordered the first performance of a mock *pasola* on the field between Rangga Baki and Ratenggaro. In the 1950s, this "new *pasola*" was repeated in conjunction with the calendrical rites to celebrate his power and demonstrate the horsemanship of the people of Bangedo. The ritual combat held outside Tossi remained, however, the most important one, and the one that has consistently drawn the largest number of participants.

Raja Horo was criticized by many people in Kodi Bokol for imitating the form of the *pasola* without an appropriate ritual mandate. As the climate of criticism of local rulers grew more intense, a new rhetoric opposing the Dutch-appointed rajas as "feudal" emerged in the newly independent state of Indonesia. When Raja Horo became the district head (*camat*) of Kodi, he stopped performing the *pasola* near his own ancestral village in an attempt to allay attacks by rivals in Tossi. The fires that raged in the early 1960s destroyed the villages of Rangga Baki, Ratenggaro, and Tossi, but did not stop the *pasola*, which apparently became all the more violent as the region seemed on the brink of significant social change. The bloodshed of 1965 was much more limited on Sumba than in most of Indonesia, but it upset an image of larger stabilities and turned local inhabitants back to their own ritual system to seek an equilibrium.

At the same time that the people of Tossi were rebuilding their cult house and designating a successor to the office of Rato Nale, the *pasola* was becoming recognized as a form of local "art" that should be "developed" to entertain outside visitors and even attract tourists. In the 1970s, government funds were allocated to establish temporary housing for visitors and arrange for charter flights at the time of the *pasola*. Official efforts concentrated on the *pasola* held in Wanokaka in March, since it could be reached in an hour and a half from the regency capital of Waikabubak, while Kodi required a full day of travel and, by the end of the 1980s, the road to Kodi was still not paved. But news of busloads of foreign visitors who came to watch the performances began a subtle transition in the way the Kodinese themselves viewed the procedure, moving it gradually from the category of "ritual" into that of "spectacle." In particular, it shifted the relations between the riders and the onlookers, for in a ritual the onlookers are also participants, whereas onlookers at a spectacle become disengaged and are transformed into a mere audience. At the *pasola*, the subtle interplay between young men and the women who both mock and praise them with bawdy songs was thus replaced by a greater separation, and the carnivalesque elements of an all-embracing revelry became domesticated into passive observation.

In his analysis of the differences between carnival and spectacle, Bakhtin (1984a, 7) argued that "carnival does not know footlights": its performances are not framed by distinctions between actors and outsiders, performers and spectators. The subversive force of laughter confronts this boundary and dissolves it. In the past, this may also have been the case at the *pasola*. I was told that skilled women singers would continue to tease the riders with bawdy verses even when they were on the playing field. Men were the main actors on the stage, but women could challenge them.

At present, however, this behavior would be inadmissible, because the *pasola* has been framed as a spectacle, with official police forces hired to maintain order. Women remain on the sidelines, participating only by ululating (*kaghilikongo*) in imitation of the excited cries that used to greet victorious war parties returning from headhunting raids.

The new official staging of the *pasola* has also changed its relations to calendrical rituals and to the forms of temporality enacted in the performance. Summarizing Bakhtin's notion of the disruptive power of carnival to move through official time, Holquist (1984, xviii) notes that "the sanction for carnival derives ultimately not from a calendar prescribed by church or state, but from a force that pre-exists priests and kings, and to whose superior power they are actually deferring when they appear to be licensing carnival." This force, which we could term a vital physicality, is represented in the narratives and songs associated with *pasola* performances. The presence of carnivalesque elements was related to their power to evoke regeneration, to assert that because complete repetition is impossible new life must come from the death and rebirth of the body, in all its grotesque forms.

Official development of the spectacle has focused on a more clearly defined "stage," elaborate costumes, and orderliness but has not yet sought to change the vulgarity of the verses women sing. The songs are described as "traditional merrymaking" in the official publication on the *pasola*, and visitors have the impression that they, like the priests' prayers, are respectful invocations of the ancestors. The boundary-crossing of the bawdy songs remains a key characteristic of their power and gives them a pivotal role in commenting on male-female relations. Without the ability to disrupt the spectacle and "steal the stage" in a carnivalesque parody, the role of women in the rite is greatly curtailed.

Rites of Regeneration

The stages of the *nale* celebration reflect the familiar pattern of rites of passage that move from order into a liminal period of disorder and then back to a new, regenerated social order (Van Gennep 1960; V. Turner 1969). They enact the past by creating a context in which people can assume the roles of ancestral personae, but at the same time that they constitute temporal relations they also offer a site for their disruption.

The *nale* festival presents a conjoining of male and female, where the complex centered on female symbols of rice, sea worms, and fertility is brought to meet male symbols of horsemanship, warfare, and virility. The songs that anticipate the *pasola* show an insolent lack of respect for male spheres of achievement, and remind the men that all this prancing about on stallions must be followed by sacrificial offerings to a female deity, the great Mother of the Sea Worms, Inya Nale.

The complementarity between men and women is contested and challenged, but only to a certain extent. As Turner (1969, 176) has argued, most "rituals of status reversal" provide reversals that are only transitory, and may finally reaffirm "those categories which are considered to be axiomatic and unchanging both in essence and in relationship to each other." He maintains that ritualized hostility can actually serve to reinforce a pattern of complementary but fundamentally unequal cooperation: "Cognitively, nothing underlines regularity as well as absurdity or paradox. Emotionally, nothing satisfies as much as extravagant or temporarily permitted illicit behavior. Rituals of status reversal accommodate both aspects." However, since ritual performance heightens an awareness of the past and the heritage of the ancestors, its temporal sequence can lead in either of two directions: it can, in "successful" performances, reconstruct the fragile hierarchy of the original ancestral consensus or, in "confused" ones, contribute to its dissolution.

Writing on Western historiographic practice, R. G. Collingwood (1946, 282–302) proposes that the historical method is based on an imaginative "reenactment of past experience" in which documentary evidence is reconstructed into a coherent interpretation. In a nonliterate society, where "documentary evidence" takes the form of tombstones, heirloom urns, and sea worm swarmings, ritual provides the locus for an imaginative reflection upon the past. The material traces of the ancestors are assembled for collective examination, their names are repeated in prayers and invocations, and their continuing power is "tested" through propitiatory offerings. This ritual experience is, in the end, a form of self-knowledge. By playing ancestral personae, participants come to rethink their mode of relationship and may find the means to change things.

The conflicts that underlie these festivities surface in the temporal opposition of order and disorder and the hierarchical division of source and executor. The *nale* season begins with months of prohibitions, restrictions, and ritual silence. All joyous, noisy behavior is suppressed to concentrate the population's attention on the activities of planting. The Sea Worm Priests, as descendants of the elder brother, bear the heaviest taboos and remain immobilized in their houses, while the descendants of Rato Pokilo roam around, training their horses for the *pasola* but avoiding the sacred field of combat and the sands near the sea. Breaking any of the first set of taboos on the priests would endanger the coming rice harvest ("shaking the tender grains loose off the stalk"); breaking any of the second set would be personally damaging to the individual violators (who could suffer illness or injury) but not to the region as a whole. The hierarchically superior elder descent line is identified with the unified territory, while the junior descent line represents the more particular concerns of its separate members.

As the time of the combat approaches, the complementarity of senior and junior houses is contrasted with male/female complementarity. Women offer an irreverent commentary on the male prestige system with their *kawoking* songs, even as they prepare to travel as spectators to a glorification of the male qualities of bravery, flamboyance, and daring. The ritualized confrontation "frames" an arena within which juniors may challenge seniors and women may tease men. At the end of the game, these differences are reabsorbed into a wider order as the Sea Worm Priest stops the combat and all participants return to their ancestral villages to sacrifice chickens to their ancestors. Male heat is "cooled" by symbolically female ritual officers; the excitement of the play is transformed into an injection of fertility and vitality for the whole region.

Occasionally, however, the ritual transformation does not succeed, and the reconstruction of a fragile hierarchy dissolves into chaos. The *pasola* can provide an occasion for outbursts of real violence between parties at odds with each other, so it is now heavily patrolled by the local police and army. In 1980, a rock fight broke out between the people from the villages of Rangga Baki and Tossi. In 1981, swords were bared and one person was struck with the edge of a bush knife in a fight that occurred beside the playing field. In 1988, women's teasing songs on the way to the spectacle in Wanokaka provoked the brutal murder of a woman by her former husband, who left her body at the edge of the playing field. Although individual acts of violence are prohibited by the rules of the game, they are (like brawls between players or spectators at football games) expected and hardly a structural anomaly.

The assembly of large numbers of people in communion with the spirits of the dead and the forces of fertility provokes a combustion of vital forces, which can regenerate the ceremonial system for the coming year or degenerate into a chaos of conflicting claims. These dangers are inherent in the performance of "ritualized violence," since it is still, in a very real sense, actual violence. The ceremonial frame that should serve to contain aggressive behavior may also promote and encourage it. Male exhibitionism is intensified by the undercurrent of mockery expressed by female spectators. The daring of representatives of the peripheral, younger-brother villages is exacerbated by the constraints on timing and ritual control invested in the "mother-father" villages of Tossi and Bukubani. The *pasola* represents a chafing under certain types of authority and an opposition of principles of ascription and achievement, which can prove explosive.

As a reflection on the past and an enactment of the ceremonial divisions outlined in traditional narratives, *nale* and *pasola* celebrations encourage a reimagining of historical relations, in which the continuity of the Kodinese cultural heritage is displayed by the flexible and contested nature of such ritual confrontations. The antagonistic mode of this central ceremony of unity reflects a social conflict between equality and inequality. Although the competitive struggles of warfare and feasting may be provisionally absorbed into a more encompassing ceremonial whole, they always threaten to break out of these boundaries. In fighting fiercely against each other, the Kodinese acknowledge a mutual origin and a set of shared values. Only through this violent and dangerous game can ritual equilibrium be restored and the idea of an unstable but essential cosmic balance maintained.

Disparate Voices in a Unified Calendar

The multitude of voices heard in the bawdy songs sung along the beaches and the many antagonistic confrontations of clashing lances on the *pasola* field are juxtaposed to a single evocative silence: that of the Rato Nale, sitting immobile on the veranda of his ancestral house. He does not participate in the fray, but has the power to begin and end the combat by circling the field on his horse. He does not sing teasing songs, but he leads the groups who entreat the spirit of the sea worms to return to Kodi.

The exuberant, carnivalistic display of vitality that occurs at the time of the Kodi New Year is made possible by the ascetic withdrawal of the Sea Worm Priest, the "Lord of the Year," whose disciplined passivity contrasts so sharply with the revelry and license of all others. In this respect, despite all the Bakhtinian echoes of subversion, the participants still acknowledge a particular kind of superordinate, all-encompassing authority. This authority derives from the Rato Nale's power to begin and end the year, providing an indigenous control of time and the cycles of the seasons.

The position of the Rato Nale is at present an embattled one. His authority to set the dates of the performance and regulate its occurrence is being challenged by officials of the Indonesian government, who are imposing an external calendar as an arm of a secular, universalistic, bureaucratic state. The complicated ramifications of these changes will be discussed in chapter 12. Before coming to them, however, we must first understand that the ritual reenactment of the past, in all its diverse and disputatious aspects, is itself a political act. While many people in Kodi are anxious, confused, and divided about what to draw from the past and how to sustain it, when they gather together to make *nale* sacrifices and ride on the *pasola* field they are united in a collective effort to keep a part of their past alive. Retaining ideological control over tradition is extremely difficult. It involves an ongoing process of compromise, reinterpretation, and adjustment to new circumstances. The unity of the Kodi people is expressed in the calendar and in the rites of the New Year, which provide the basis of Kodi cultural identity and Kodi polity. With the present threat to such unity, these reenactments become all the more important as feasts of becoming, change, and renewal, which continue an ancestral heritage into the future.

Exchange Sequences and Strategies

6

Exchanges over Time

Continuities Between Past and Present

Promises made by our grandfathers bind us to the land
But the land is often shaky
Commitments made by our forefathers tie us to the stones
But the stones are often shifting.

> A Kodi comment on the negotiability
> of exchange obligations

In part two, I explore the role that time plays in the determination of exchange value. Looking at data from the colonial period through the 1980s, I examine the importance of temporal intervals in individual and collective strategies of exchange in marriage, feasting, and funerals. I do so in order to offer both a critique of the "colonial perspective" on notions of interest and exchange and a contribution to contemporary debates about temporality. Bourdieu's axiom that the play of time transforms ritualized exchange into a game of strategies is treated critically in two different ways. First, I show its validity for understanding the *tempo* of various transactions and what is at stake in decisions to delay or speed up the schedule of payments. Second, I show its limitations for gaining a more complete understanding of the temporality of exchange. A perspective drawn from the perceptions of an individual actor reveals only part of the complex interactions that take in social groups as well as the objects that represent them. Two sorts of time must be considered in constituting exchange value: biographical time, the time span of an individual life; and intergenerational time, which includes the relations of ancestors and descendants. A temporal depth greater than that of the individual life cycle is needed to understand relations of spheres of exchange, monetary and nonmonetary markets, and the long-term strategies of the house and village.

To understand how time is involved in the constitution of value, I first examine exchange in its historical context. J.I.N. Versluys, a Dutch tax collector who did research in Kodi and two other districts, sought during his time there "to identify which aspects of social life money has started to play a role in, and where the traditional household economy of exchange persists" (1941, 435). All people who paid taxes in West Sumba in 1940 were asked where they had received the money they paid in taxes: who had given it to them and what sort of relationship they had to this person, or what activities (trade, labor, market sales) they had undertaken on their own to get the money.[1] Respondents were also asked how long they had had the money that they paid as taxes, and estimates were made of how often the money had changed hands before being paid in taxes.

To a large extent, Versluys's study was designed to measure the success of Dutch colonial policy, since taxes were deliberately introduced not only as a means of obtaining revenue, but also to "stimulate independent economic initiative" and "sharpen economic insight" (1941, 453, 466) through the use of markets and to promote what were considered the "social benefits" of involvement in monetary trade. These "benefits" are explicitly identified by Versluys as greater individualism, entrepreneurial spirit, and movement away from the "structures of dependency" that tied large numbers of the population to "semifeudal" lords. Since at the beginning of the century, and still to a large extent today, money came mainly from wages and payment for services rendered to the government and the mission, liberation from one sort of dependency was replaced by a new dependency on these external sources of revenue. In effect, taxation was designed to introduce the Sumbanese to the view that "time is money," as was the practice of rewarding discrete periods of labor with precisely measured exchange values. The values of a traditional "moral economy" were to be deliberately transformed into a new system of wage labor (Scott 1976, 97–98)—a transformation, in effect, from a "pure subsistence economy" to a "cash economy."

Versluys, though, came to realize that the traditional Sumbanese economy was not one of "pure subsistence" at the time that colonial control became a reality on the island. It was in fact a complicated system with several spheres of prestige exchange, the use of livestock and foodstuffs (rice and corn) as measures of value, significant ways of protecting and storing value and creating boundaries around certain kinds of wealth that

[1] He received 996 responses from Umbu Ratu Nggai, 438 from Lauli, and 324 from Kodi. The larger number of responses in some areas than in others is attributed to the persistence of the clerk in asking these questions and the requirement that the survey not stand in the way of the process of actually collecting taxes (Versluys 1941, 443). Versluys admits that "it is possible that not every person told the truth," since, for instance, no one reported that they had received money from illegal gambling. Yet most of them would have had no reason to lie, and local officials (the head of the *kampung*) found the results fit their own ideas of Sumbanese exchange.

Wife-givers and wife-takers are invited to all feasts and honored with gifts of betel, rice, and raw meat, though they are usually expected to contribute pigs or buffalo to the slaughter. 1980. Photograph by the author.

were considered "inalienable" (Weiner 1985). His account of Sumbanese forms of mutual exchange highlights a number of features of the indigenous economy that have remained constant over half a century; it fails, however, to perceive the significance of time in constituting value in ceremonial exchange. As a snapshot of alternate modes of defining interest and obligation, dependency and generosity, it provides glimpses of a style of life admired by Versluys even as he tried to dismantle it. As a historical document, it allows us to look into the past and discover an enduring pattern of relations not visible to its chronicler.

Hierarchy, Regional Differences, and Exchange

Versluys (1941, 433) argued that the process of shifting from a "traditional" to a "monetary" economy could not be studied as a simple progression because "it is necessary to consider local differences even in an otherwise fairly homogenous society." Sumba at the beginning of the twentieth century was divided into about twenty indigenous domains. Those in the eastern part of the island were ruled by a single lord, usually addressed as *tamu umbu*, who was the head of stratified, autocratic polity. In the western domains, no such centralized ruler existed; instead one found a shifting, achievement-oriented competition between "big men" who established their power bases from ancestral villages but did not rule over their fellows:

> In the east . . . life is centered on the big houses of the aristocrats, who live with their servants or slaves in a relatively autonomous fashion. . . . Stock breeding is of great importance, and the population is sparse. . . . In the West, on the contrary, we see huge plains of wet rice fields and a great many swidden gardens, often layered along the steep slopes of low-lying mountains, and a much denser population. There is greater economic equality, since livestock are distributed over a larger number of owners, and this accords with the total social structure, where the figure of the aristocrat who can live as a separate entity with his family and servants is much rarer.

The presence of servants as part of the household was "a strong reminder of the time the ownership of slaves dominated all life on the island in both the social and economic senses" (1941, 436). In the west, inherited servants were much less common, but there were many war captives.

The theme of slavery as a sign of "feudal" rule by local despots is frequent in accounts by Dutch colonial writers. Versluys presents an unusually nuanced picture, even suggesting ways in which new forms of dependency and "enslavement" were created by money. Many people in West Sumba, for instance, contracted a form of voluntary servitude to a particular noble because they were unable to fulfill certain economic obligations. Although they could be commanded by the noble, they reserved the right to buy back their freedom later with a payment of livestock (1941, 447). In the precolonial period, this form of debt bondage was primarily associated with young men who were unable to get the livestock to pay their bridewealth. When their sexual relations with a girl were discovered, they had to accept temporary servitude, either to her father or to a wealthy patron who received rights to the children produced from their union.

After the colonial administration was established, the need for cash on certain occasions became as pressing as the need for livestock to pay traditional fines or bridewealth. Verluys (1941, 447) says that in Wanokaka he heard of people who became debt bondsmen in order to get the money they needed to pay taxes, giving their labor to a wealthy man until they could achieve economic independence through the payment of one or two buffalo as a parting gift. In trying to eradicate old-style debt bondage to the traditional lords, therefore, colonial officers universalized indebtedness to another, all-knowing higher authority—the state; in that way they may in fact have intensified the dependency of some members of the population.

Albert C. Kruyt was the first to note the ambiguity of the term *ata*, which means both "human being" (in many western dialects) and "slave" (in East Sumba and Kodi). He argued (1922, 507) that it can refer to the whole population, since "*ata* are . . . the paupers who put themselves under the guardianship of the rich to be protected and fed by them." Although his formulation conflates the idea of dependency with debt bondage, it does highlight the diversity of the senses in which the term is used on the island. As Reid (1988, 132) has noted, "most of the Southeast Asian terms which early European travelers translated as slave could in other circumstances be rendered as debtor, dependent or subject."

The social and economic meaning of this kind of dependency is visible in Versluys's statistics. In the domain of Umbu Ratu Nggai, which lies along the border between East and West Sumba, 46.6 percent of the people who paid taxes received the money from a "dependent" source: 10.2 percent from a relative, 15.7 percent from the sale of livestock by someone else, and 20.7 percent from a master-servant relationship (1941, 449, 453). The author notes that this "patriarchal system" also functions as a form of "poor relief," since it is a way of caring for those who are economically disadvantaged, but it does so only at a price. (As he notes, "here poor relief is not the same as philanthropy!" [1941, 453].) By contrast, the two western districts showed a much greater degree of economic independence: in Lauli, "dependent" sources accounted for 13.5 percent of all taxes paid, with master-servant relations accounting for less than a single percent (1941, 455); in Kodi, the percentage of "dependent" payments was only 6.5 percent , and master-servant relations were less than 1 percent (1941, 459). In those regions, markets and large-scale exchanges of traditional goods developed much more quickly.

Versluys describes the indigenous institution known as the *paranggana*, or "barter gathering," which existed in western districts and was deliberately encouraged and codified on a weekly schedule by the colonial government. These gatherings were arranged between two groups, usually one of them from a mountain area and another from the coast, with the meeting taking place at the intersection of two roads. Because such groups were intermittently at war, the meeting had to be arranged beforehand by intermediaries, and a buffalo was sacrificed on the first occasion to provide a commensal meal. On subsequent occasions, the gathering had no ritual marking but consisted almost entirely of exchanges of tubers from the mountains against salt from the coast (Versluys 1941, 463). After several years a somewhat greater variety of products would be exchanged—coconuts, indigo, and lime from the coast, and beans, corn, and vegetables from the mountains. No prestige goods were exchanged, only subsistence products, the purpose being to avert famine.

Between 1920 and 1930, the colonial government organized twice-weekly markets in Bondo Kodi (attended by about six hundred people) and at three locations in Weyewa (Elopada, Waimangura, and Palla, attended by four hundred, eight hundred, and two hundred people, respectively) (Versluys 1941, 464). Market day came to play an important role in social activities, as it still does today. Versluys describes most of these encounters as occasions for barter, not monetary purchase. In fact, the idea of monetary equivalents had an influence mainly as a "measurement of value" rather than a "means of trade." A woman would arrange small piles of *sirih* piper or salt on a mat, for instance, and describe each pile as "worth one cent," but she clearly did not intend to sell them only for money. Instead she would exchange them against sticks of tobacco, jars of paddy, or groups of vegetables assessed in the same way. For small transactions, unhulled rice and corn were often used as equivalents, because they could be easily measured, though the fixing of prices was often inconsistent (1941, 465). Versluys (1941, 466) saw the effect of markets as salutary;

> The opportunity to sell very small amounts of goods gives people a chance to use small surplus goods profitably. It appears that besides the large amount of money that is brought into circulation, the buyers and sellers are getting used to measuring value and countervalue accurately. Markets also create the opportunity to obtain daily necessities in an easy way. If for some reason the amount of money should diminish, thus forcing people back to the direct trade of barter for goods, one thing will remain: the fact that *economic insight is sharpened*—and this is caused by money, but does not depend on it. (my emphasis)

I will return to the issue of how economic insight has been sharpened (or dulled) by the presence of money later. For the moment, it is significant that Versluys interprets the results of his survey as showing the greater entrepreneurial skills and aptitudes of the people of West Sumba. In Kodi, he argued that one could already discern a "free trade market where people can buy and sell goods individually and handle their own money" (1941, 461). The degree of individual autonomy was in sharp contrast to areas like Umbu Ratu Nggai, where all the money went into the hands of a few persons who spent it outside the indigenous sphere.

Versluys (1941, 461) was careful to add that the money supply was still quite small in Kodi, but since it circulated, there was potential for economic development and a weakening of the structures of dependency: "A widely developed retail trade creates the possibility of reducing economic differences, and thus also the degree of social differentiation, because when the chances for single persons to obtain money are greater they can, with time, also gain power and influence."

Taxes were much higher (and money much scarcer) under the Dutch than is true at present. Versluys gives as an example a poor man asked to pay two and a half Dutch guilders for the head tax, an amount equivalent to half a small water buffalo, about one year old, or a calf of several months (1941, 480). It is likely that a poor man would not own any water buffalo, though he would probably have a horse and a few pigs and chickens. He would of course be loath to sell his only horse to get tax money; instead he might ask for credit from someone else who was selling livestock, either by giving him several chickens or a pig (the full value of his taxes) or *promising* to give him an animal as soon as he was able to get one (Versluys 1941, 439).

Most often, one among a group of brothers would sell a large animal, and the money would be shared among them to pay taxes in a given year. The next year, it would be someone else's turn. Versluys notes that "market exchange of livestock focuses on big and beautiful animals, in general used for breeding, which means that small animals have hardly any monetary value because they are only used for local exchanges. Money is of much less importance as an equivalent in smaller transactions, where payment is made with paddy or a local textile and a pig" (1941, 438). Livestock traders at the time were almost without exception also shopkeepers, and generally Arab or Chinese. In general circumstances, they were interested in offering payment in kind—store goods such as clothing, lengths of fabric, and bush knives. Usually when livestock were sold, however, they were sold for money, "for the simple reason that the seller wants to receive money, and the shopkeeper will not always be able to give goods of the same value as livestock" (1941, 428). Since most Sumbanese would not want more than a simple jacket and a length of cloth, only 20 percent or so of the purchase amount was paid in kind.

It can be argued that partly as a result of Dutch taxation policies, demand for money was of two kinds: either a large amount of money would be wanted, which was then used for a specific purpose, such as to pay taxes, or else a very small amount (one or two Dutch cents), which served as a standard of value and means of exchange at markets. Between December and April, the "tax collection season," everyone had to find some way to get money. In hierarchical areas like Umbu Ratu Nggai, large livestock owners would buy a number of smaller animals from many poorer people, profiting immensely from the exchange because of the very low rates at that time. In regions like Kodi, it was more common for a number of people of modest means to rotate in paying taxes, with a single group member selling one impressive animal to a Chinese shopkeeper and dividing the money with the rest, only to be on the receiving end for the next several years.

The average price paid for a buffalo in 1940 was 15 to 30 Dutch guilders, and for a horse, 20 to 50 guilders. West Sumba exported 1,163 buffalo and 367 horses in 1940, and probably sold about 600 more to the eastern part of the island (where they were not registered, though they did require a certificate of sale). The number of buffalo and horses that entered the money market, however, was still only a small percentage of those that changed owners in that year; moreover, the movement of animals and goods in the indigenous sphere was much more extensive than their movement to outside buyers. The rules of exchange for indigenous transactions were very different.

Even in the most "individualistic" and "democratic" areas of Sumba, Versluys described a series of institutions that constrained exchange and operated independently of the market or monetary sphere. Preeminent among these institutions were bridewealth, feasting, and funerals. Versluys argued that raising bridewealth was both a "stimulant for the circulation of values" and an area of "resistance to the spread of money," since nowhere on the island was money used in bridewealth payments (1941, 466). Fifty years after he wrote this sentence, the resistance of the Sumbanese to the idea of paying bridewealth with cash is still strong, even though almost all of them are aware that cash payments are now common among the Savunese (a significant minority population on the island) and in many other Indonesian populations (Sherman 1990; Singarimbun 1975; Rodgers 1981).

For a Sumbanese of simple means, payment of his own bridewealth remains the largest single transaction in which he must participate, and one that can keep him in the shadow of debt and obligation for most of his life. No girl can move to her husband's house without a minimum payment of ten "tails" of livestock (five horses and five water buffalo) and a gold ear pendant. The effective "social minimum" is usually the bridewealth paid for the girl's mother, which can be augmented if the girl is educated, has special skills (such as weaving or dyeing thread), or if a punitive payment is made to compensate for a violation of the normal rules of courtship through elopement or broken promises.

It is often said that the value of the bridewealth should be equivalent to that of the countergift (*lipyoko*) paid by the woman's family in pigs and cloth. The usual formula is for the groom to receive two large tusked pigs, one presented alive and one killed for serving to the guests, and pair of woven textiles, one man's cloth and one woman's sarung, to reciprocate his initial payment of ten head (five horses, five buffalo). However, only the bridewealth is publicly agreed on in a formal negotiation; the size of the countergift is determined by the bride's parents, who "look at the livestock" and examine their own resources and feelings to decide what they will give. If they want to be generous, they can include ivory bracelets, a bronze ankle ring, colored beads, a riding horse for the bride, or even one or two slave girls as servants "to carry her *sirih* pouch" (*kaleku mboro*). But they can also easily fulfill the minimum with small pigs and cloths of poor quality. Hence, the "balancing" of payments between wife-givers and wife-takers is always a subject for comment and often for invidious comparisons. Versluys (1941, 486) provides some examples of strategic manipulation of the countergift:

> In the case of a match that gets a father's full approval, the value of his countergift will be approximately equal to that of the bride-wealth, or sometimes even higher. But if his daughter insists on marriage with someone else whom her father does not like, he will show his disapproval of this son-in-law even as he gives in by demanding a very high bridewealth and giving almost nothing in return. This also means that he considers the bonds between him and his daughter to be broken. But if a father approves, and he still presents a countergift that is of much less value than the bridewealth, he will be held in contempt by his daughter's in-laws [his wife-takers], and she, I'm told, will never hear the end of it.

The matching of the bridewealth and countergift is an ideal for prosperous families, and often the subject of boasts. In the 1970s and 1980s, some families started to give furniture, modern clothing, and other "household goods" as additional "signs of love" (*tanda manawaro*) for their daughters. The gift of land on a usufruct basis has long been part of the wife-givers' "generosity." Poor families, by contrast, may be more accepting of a countergift that is less than the bridewealth; this, Versluys (1941, 468) noted, occurred often as "an exception that is tolerated in practice." Then too, the father might use a "moral" value to substitute for an "economic" one, arguing that he had taken good care of his daughter for many years, and this affection will have to take the place of a generous countergift.

A high bridewealth did not, therefore, mean a windfall for the bride's parents, but it did help to establish the social status of both parties. Many bridewealths in Kodi today run to thirty or forty "tails," and a few (those contracted with people from other regions) to over a hundred. In a strict sense, some people argue that anything over the minimum is not really part of the bridewealth but "trading" (Ind. *dagang*); that is, it is linked to the wedding gifts but really part of a more extended system of credits and debts.[2]

Continued "trading" and mutual assistance was expected between the two groups for a great many years. A wife-taker should always be available to provide horses or buffalo for any ritual occasion at which they are needed, and will always be reciprocated with pigs and cloth. When payments were still being made on the agreed-upon bridewealth, these reciprocal gifts were figured as part of the countergift. If the bridewealth had been fully paid, the two parties could continue for as long as both had the means and the occasions to exchange. According to Versluys (1941, 469), the consensual nature of this continued trade assured that it remained equal over time:

> Since it is a mutual exchange of marriage gifts which changes gradually into a trading relationship, one can assume that the value of given and received goods is neither onesidedly social nor onesidedly economic in structure. . . . Marriage is very important from an economic point of view because in this way a continuing relationship between families develops, or, if this relationship already exists (which, given the popularity of exclusive cross-cousin marriage happens quite often), it is strengthened.

Alliance in fact defined the exchange pathways for "almost all trade" in East Sumba, and was "a very important part of the circulation of goods" in the west. Versluys suggests that the mobility of the goods needed for bridewealth—water buffalo and horses—was greater than that of all other items, even if these were also goods of great value. In several places he

---

[2] Versluys does not indicate in his text that this term carried a derogatory connotation in 1940, but certainly by the 1980s it was not flattering to describe affinal exchanges as "trading," since that emphasized calculation rather than mutual benefit. In my interviews, the Indonesian gloss preferred by most informants was *saling membantu*, or "reciprocal assistance," and this was used to describe all exchanges that involved gifts and countergifts between groups related by marriage. Anthropologists usually distinguish between "trading" and ceremonial exchange (however motivated by strategic considerations), so I have put Versluys's references to "trading" in quotes.

asked how many times an animal had changed ownership over a period of two years. In Lamboya, one water buffalo had had nine owners, two of them for periods of almost a year and the rest for only one or two days. In Memboro, a water buffalo had changed ownership twenty times, and a horse thirteen times (1941, 469); in these cases, periods of ownership varied so greatly they could not be expressed in an average.

Despite the large markets developed in the 1930s and people's familiarity with the use of money, Versluys concluded that "the traffic in goods is doubtless much more important in the west than the monetary system" (1941, 480). He argued that the standard of value for all items worth more than a handful of coins—including land, gold jewelry, horses, and fine textiles—remained the water buffalo. As a result, the concept of "water buffalo" had been made abstract. The "normal water buffalo," as a unit of account, referred to a year-old animal, whose value Versluys estimated in 1940 at 5 guilders (1941, 480). When buffalo were used as a means of payment or exchange, adjustments were made on the basis of the buffalo's age, as measured by the horn span. Versluys says nothing more about the "sliding scale" of values given to livestock because of this calculation; I, however, will return to this important point later.

Wealth was measured in the number of water buffalo a person had, and buffalo were also the standard used in reckoning debts, loans, and interest. Versluys's notes provide insight into the tempo of transactions during the colonial period, as well as the economic value given to the passage of time.

Land could be purchased with buffalo, and small plots of garden land often changed hands. The most favored transaction involved a father-in-law and his son-in-law, for that allowed the daughter to live close to her parents. In such cases, no separate purchase was made; rather, the land was seen as the countergift to reciprocate the bridewealth, called "a pig that will not get sick, a cloth that will not tear" (*wawi nja kapore, kamba nja ma diryako*). If a nonrelative wanted to buy land, however, a price was fixed based on the size of the field, its fertility, and its geographical position relative to water. Prices varied enormously according to the seller's needs at the time and what the buyer could afford to pay. In Kodi in the 1980s, land was often given over for use for a very minimal payment but with the expectation that buffalo would be provided to the owner of the land when he needed them on ritual occasions. Versluys mentions that a few large wet-rice fields were considered "family heirlooms" because rice from those fields was used to feed the spirits in the house (*marapu uma*). Such fields were supposedly inalienable, but if a family was in desperate straits it might "pawn" the fields to a wealthy neighbor. Although in reality this usually meant a final renunciation, the buffalo received from the buyer were formally considered a "loan" provided against the value of the land, with no permanent transfer of ownership involved.

The lines between "borrowing," "giving," and "buying" were indistinct; indeed, one term might be used to describe the first stages of a transaction (when something was only "borrowed"), while another, used retrospectively, would describe its final result quite differently. Euphemisms were also often used, which allowed relatives to assist each other without forcing the requesting party to admit the full extent of his need. The advantages of transacting with kin lay in the studied vagueness of terms:

> When a Sumbanese speaks about "borrowing" he may often in fact mean "buying." If someone needs a water buffalo, he will "borrow" it, often from his sister's husband, but there is no strict rule. Both parties will then agree at that time on the day the countergift must be presented. The value of both things is usually fairly equal. But again and again one detects a certain vagueness in these agreements, and it is very common that the outcome of the agreement differs somewhat from what was originally agreed upon.
>
> (Versluys 1941, 475)

It was very hard for an outsider to determine what the actual debt situation was between the two persons concerned, especially if they were closely related. All transactions between affines would be described as giving and receiving gifts, but that did not mean they did not know exactly who still owed whom. Furthermore, although affines were not supposed to charge interest, the presentation of many small gifts of cloth "to ask for more time" was common practice.

The strategic advantage in all exchange transactions lay with the person who stayed at home and received a visitor with a request. This pattern, taken from the situation of bridewealth payments, was also applied to other situations of borrowing or selling. The person who came with a request took full legal responsibility for following through on the transaction, since it occurred at his initiative. Thus, if a man needed to sell a buffalo and visited a prospective buyer, the price would be much lower than if the buyer had come to him to request the sale. The price of all livestock plummeted during tax collection season, simply because people needed money. The Sumbanese recognized this process in the popular saying "When the buffalo looks for cash, he is cheap, but when the money looks for the buffalo, he is expensive" (Versluys 1941, 438).

A more extreme example of this imbalance comes from a legal case concerning an accusation of fraud when a gilded silver ear pendant was sold for the price of a solid gold one. The buyers claimed they had been cheated, but the sellers argued that the buyers themselves had come and asked if the pendant was for sale and then confirmed the agreement with a meal. The judge agreed that the sellers were innocent because they did not take the initiative and offer to sell the pendant (Versluys 1941, 475). Kodi commentators on this story told me that it showed you must "do your research first," gathering facts about any animal or valuable you might want to purchase before negotiations begin, because the initiator of any contract is liable to conclude it, even if it has involved misrepresentation or fraud.

Since money was a scarce commodity, it could only be borrowed from acquaintances, and the rules were usually strict in terms of amount but lenient in time. The normal rate of interest was 25 percent per loan period, which could be a week, two weeks, or a month. In practice, it was common for the borrower to declare that he would pay the money back in six to ten days, or at the most a month. The short time limit was supposed to demonstrate his good faith, but in most cases repayment took much longer. The interest rate remained constant, however, and was not particularly high in view of the extended time period over which it actually ran (Verluys 1941, 27).

Paddy could also be borrowed—either seed paddy to plant or stored paddy to eat in times of famine. The usual expectation was that for one woven sack (*sokal*) of paddy, two would be given in return after the following harvest, along with a bunch of areca nuts and a stick of tobacco. Sometimes, if the people were very needy and their supplier had adequate stores of paddy himself, paddy that was to be eaten carried no requirement of an interest payment. If the paddy was borrowed to use as seed, however, the price difference in selling rice before and after the harvest had to be considered; thus, the double refund was justified. Versluys (1941, 474) notes that "seed paddy is borrowed only in very poor times, since otherwise the person would have saved the seed for himself." During periods of great hunger, paddy would not be borrowed to eat, because it was considered a luxury food, appropriate mainly for feasting and receiving honored guests. Famine instead sent people off into the forest to look for wild tubers and root crops. Hence, "if paddy is borrowed in order to eat, one can safely assume that there is still a relative abundance left" (1941, 475).

"Interest" was levied only when the borrowing party sought something that was relatively rare. The amount was almost always determined by the giver, and the requester had to agree to his conditions or there would be no transaction. Close family members were forgiven debts much more readily than outsiders, but the criteria varied, with the greatest amount of "forgiveness" occurring at funerals. Gifts of cloth that friends and neighbors brought to contribute to the dead person's shroud were not usually reciprocated, though ideally when wife-takers brought horses, goats, or buffalo for the slaughter they would be compensated. According to Versluys (1941, 476), the rule was that if the bereaved family simply accepted what their guests brought, their obligations could be forgiven at a later date; if, however, they specifically *asked* for a contribution—a pig or buffalo, say, to serve at the funeral feast—the debt would remain and require a countergift.

Less Than Revolutionary: Money and the Traditional Economy

Much anthropological writing about economic change has concerned the impact of money on traditional worlds. Paul Bohannan (1967), for instance, argued that the Tiv traditional economy comprised three spheres of exchange—which, following Raymond Firth (1965), he called the spheres of subsistence goods, of prestige goods, and of goods of "unique quality"— until the British forced the Tiv to abandon the use of brass rods for bridewealth in favor of coinage ("general purpose money"). At that point the distinctions between spheres were destroyed, "making everything exchangeable for everything else" (P. Bohannan 1967, 127). The use of money converted a multicentric economy into a unicentric one, in that this new medium of exchange provided a common denominator for all commodities to be compared and exchanged. Money, Bohannan (1959) concluded, "is one of the shatteringly simplifying ideas of all time, and like any other new and compelling idea, it creates it own revolution."

Applying Bohannan's terminology, we may call the traditional Sumbanese economy multicentric, and given Versluy's evidence we can safely say that it consisted of several ranked spheres: the subsistence sphere, consisting mainly of foods (rice, corn, tubers, beans) that were transacted by barter and later by market exchanges; the prestige sphere, in this case livestock, and especially water buffalo, which served as a medium of exchange, a standard of value, and a means of payment; and the sphere containing goods of "unique value," by which Bohannan meant rights in human beings, in particular rights in marriageable women, but which for Sumba should be extended to heirloom valuables. The vast majority of exchanges were what Bohannan would call "conveyances" *within* the sphere; these were morally neutral, as in the exchange of buffalo for pigs

and cloth between wife-givers and wife-takers. But "conversions" between
the spheres could occur as well, as when an individual was forced by acute
hunger to exchange livestock for food.

On Sumba, however, the impact of money was not at all as significant
as it was among the Tiv. In the final report submitted by A. Couvreur,
Sumba's controller from 1911 to 1914, the colonial administrator who
presided over the first tax collection describes its effects (1914, 10):

> Small silver and copper coins were unknown a couple of years ago
> on Sumba. The Sumbanese knew only barter, and didn't need
> money, so merchants out of self-interest did not do much to intro-
> duce money. No specific measures were taken to introduce Dutch
> coins, but by introducing the tax system in 1911 this came of its
> own accord. . . . In 1911 the first tax collection was very difficult,
> because of the lack of coins and people's unfamiliarity with them.
> . . . By 1912 the situation had much improved, and nowadays pay-
> ment in kind in West Sumba is not found anymore.

Although it seems naive to say that the transition to at least partial use of
money "came of its own accord" when the government was in fact creating
a need for money with taxation, it is a fact that in just a few years (1911–
14), coins and change became widespread in West Sumba. In eastern
domains like Umbu Ratu Nggai, only the nobles interacted with merchants
and foreign persons, so they controlled the flow of cash and took on the
responsibility of paying taxes for their dependents. In western domains
like Kodi and Lamboya, more people were forced into interaction with
merchants and with the newly established markets. People grew accustomed to using money, the cent became a unit for things of small value,
and money came to serve as a medium of exchange for small trade.

Versluys (1941, 481) concluded his study by saying, contrary to Bohannan's predictions, that "the use of money did not have a revolution-
izing effect," except to stimulate retail trade, "for it created a unit for
things of little value, and also made the people aware of the opportunity
to sell or exchange small surpluses at markets." He added that other
changes—the effective establishment of the Dutch colonial government,
the settlement of Chinese merchants in certain regional centers, the arrival
of Protestant and Catholic missionaries—were much more important, and
had an "enormous impact," but there was an apparent continuity in the
traditional economy.

Since making this argument, Versluys has been joined by many other
recent commentators on such processes. Several have pointed out, for

example, that Bohannan did not give enough weight to the British outlawing of the favored form of marriage (patrilateral exchange), which challenged the authority of the elders and destroyed the impermeability of the highest sphere, that of the exchange of women (Sherman 1990, 294–95; Bloch and Parry 1989, 14). Thus it was not money in itself but a disruption of traditional exchange boundaries that had a "revolutionary" effect. The continuities that Versluys observed in Sumbanese exchange after the beginning of the colonial era (which I also observed some fifty years later) can be attributed in part to the preservation of the forms and categories of indigenous exchanges and also, I will argue, to an indigenous notion of value which Versluys hints at but did not fully discern. What is most important in his study, besides its documentation of internal exchange at a crucial point in history, is his observation that money was a unit of value *only for things of little value*, and all animals and objects of greater value were negotiated for in separate contexts. This principle holds true in present practice; the locus of greater exchange value, namely, lies elsewhere, in an investment of time rather than coins.

A View from the 1980s

Although the end of the colonial period, the Japanese occupation of 1942–45, and the creation of the independent state of Indonesia all had far-reaching effects on economic practices, at the time of my field research it was the convergences with Versluys's description of traditional exchange, not the departures, that were most striking. Throughout the 1980s, less than 10 percent of the population had any regular cash income, and it could be said that money still remains scarce and excluded from many transactions. It is not used for any large traditional exchanges (feasting, bridewealth, funerals, or land purchases); instead the favored model for all negotiations involving the transfer of substantial wealth is still taken from alliance, with the two transactors cast in the roles of wife-giver and wife-taker.

Taxes are no longer the most important occasion for which people need money. The increasing presence of both retail trade and government services has made the demand for cash greater and more various. People need small amounts of money to pay school fees and buy uniforms, since almost all Kodi children now go to elementary school for at least a few years. Money is also needed to pay for routine medical care; to buy shirts, plastic sandals, plates, and glasses at markets; and to pay for rides in a truck or minivan that links the region to Weetabula and Waikabubak. Large amounts of money are needed occasionally to leave the island for operations or to

Pigs with long tusks (at least ten years old) are the obligatory gift presented by the mother's brother at a marriage negotiation. 1984. Photograph by the author.

send a child to college on Java or Timor. So when I tried to follow Versluys's example and ask at tax collection time where the money had come from, people found the question somewhat quaint. They had enough money to pay their taxes, since they knew they would need money for that purpose and had been able to sell goods at the market to obtain it. But they did express anxiety about their ability to raise enough funds for educational and medical expenses. They also said, in a virtual chorus of unanimity: "It is not the need for money that is the heaviest burden; it is the requirements of traditional exchange."

To understand the processes of exchange and investment from the perspective of the actors involved, in 1988 I conducted a detailed survey of exchange activities (including those that involved substantial amounts of cash) among fifty-two households over the five years 1983–88, as well as collecting background information on important exchanges before that period. Since I lived in the area for thirty-seven months in the period 1979–88, I had attended many of the events I interviewed informants about, and had heard of others.

The interviews were conducted as long conversations held in a relatively private place, usually the informant's home. I had printed up a list of questions which I brought to show each head of household, but none of them filled out the form and few addressed it directly. Familiar with somewhat similar government surveys, most only glanced at it briefly. It described my purpose as understanding the forms of cooperation and obligation in the traditional economy (*ekonomi adat*) and offered them assurance that although I noted the names and categories of relationship for each exchange, the results of the survey would not reveal personal names or assets.[3] I also asked my informants to interpret the sense of the strategies used in the exchange process, to comment on whether they had "lost" or "won" in particular transactions, and to tell me when they thought notions of investment, interest, and return were useful in analyzing their activities. The questions on the form were in Indonesian (in which most informants had some basic literacy), but I summarized them in Kodi, and most of the interviews were conducted in Kodi, with lapses into Indonesian to permit comments in a more "distanced vocabulary." (I will return to the interesting question of differences in self-description and the representation of relationships in the two languages, since many informants made statements in both.)

A Slice of Time: Exchange in the Period 1983–88

The sample was not intended to be representative in a statistical sense, but more one in which a wide range of possibilities would be displayed. Because I conducted most of the interviews in Bondo Kodi, the district capital, I did not include the most isolated families, which in any event were often not extensively involved in ceremonial exchange. To get detailed histories of contributions at large-scale events, I interviewed a disproportionate number of prominent older persons, several of them very wealthy. This intentional bias weighed on the statistical data, but allowed me to make an analytical distinction between the different perspectives of households at all levels of wealth and achievement. "Simple folk" who could not afford to play prestige games made up about 40 percent of the sample, but in fact represent some 60 percent of the total population. Three of the households I interviewed are among the most active in

[3] Although I often prompted people with questions about whether they had contributed to a specific event, I did not reveal what other informants had told me in the course of cross-checking the responses I received. Most exchanges are public acts, conducted and acknowledged on the ritual stage, but some are more private and their negotiation can be a sensitive issue. The assurance of confidentiality vis-à-vis their neighbors was more important to most of my informants than the use of pseudonyms in publication.

feasting, but in addition they have extensive networks among "simpler" relatives; this fact made their comments particularly valuable.

I asked informants to tell me about their own exchange careers to the best of their recollection, and I would note down the livestock they had contributed and received under each event category (feast, funeral, bridewealth). Most informants initially adopted my groupings, and responded by listing the amounts they had contributed first to bridewealth, then to funerals, feasts, and so on. In the course of the interview, however, many slipped into a more chronological narrative, or one that showed a pattern of gifts and reciprocation between specific households ("I contributed a horse to his bridewealth, and when my father died he brought me a long-tusked pig"). Since these occasions moved across event categories, keeping careful track at the time of the interview often proved problematic; I therefore taped the conversations or noted them in longhand in a notebook, and later filled in my forms with the totals.

The households in my sample included members of twelve different patriclans, a total of 302 persons, or almost six persons per household on average. The most significant differences between households were related to their place in the domestic cycle, which temporalizes family relationships in relation to crucial exchange transactions. The largest households had been established some ten to twenty years earlier, and these tended to have over ten members. Newly married couples ("new" households) and those in which many children had already married out ("older" ones) were usually smaller. Twenty-one people included in the survey were "dependents": though "attached to" households, they were not part of them, falling rather into the category of servants or former slaves. These people do not have property of their own and do not participate in traditional exchange.

Of the households surveyed, virtually all were known to me over the previous decade, and in all cases I was able to recall having attended at least some exchange transactions in which they participated. Nineteen of the households had been established for less than a decade; usually, the head of such households was between twenty and forty years of age and had children still under ten. Ten households had been in existence between ten and twenty years, and the head of household was generally between thirty-five and fifty-five years old. Twenty-two households were older—that is, established for over twenty years—and two of these were headed by widows. All of the older households had some children who had already married. Finally, four single people were included—one widower and three who had never married but were self-supporting.

Table 3. Exchange Survey: Gifts Given, 1983–88

	Households Participating	Total Gifts Given	Average no. of Gifts Each Time	Five-year Average
Own brideprice	11	160	14.5	14.5
Relative's brideprice	34	148	1.2	4.3
Funerals	31	149	1.1	4.8
Feasts	26	100	1.1	3.8
Stone draggings	6	21	1	3.5
Matching partner	2	13	1.8	6.6

STATISTICAL DATA

Each exchange was recorded as a single transaction for the giver and a single transaction for the receiver; thus, separate data sets were compiled for animals or exchange valuables that came in and went out of the household.

Many small gifts are exchanged between kin and affines that are not subject to the rules of reciprocity but only to standards of politeness and consideration. The loan of sarungs, blankets, and mats, or gifts of coffee, sugar, and a chicken when guests are received are not part of the "traditional economy" and so were not included in the survey. In explaining the project to my informants, I asked them to remember only those things that were "of value" (*na pa wali;* Ind. *berharga*) and could create debts. In effect, this meant that people cited only large animals and gold valuables. As the parameters of the indigenous notion of value became clearer, I ascertained that it included buffalo and horses of all ages, but pigs only after they had begun to grow tusks. Younger pigs brought as contributions were counted as simple gifts of food, not as part of the exchange reckoning.

In compiling statistics, I tried to determine the frequency and directionality of prestigious gifts. I have thus counted them as single units, although each unit here could represent a horse, a buffalo, or a long-tusked pig, with cash equivalents ranging from 25,000 to 350,000 rupiah. The numbers in tables 3 and 4 do not necessarily reflect indexes of value, therefore, only of transactions. Other objects of some value, especially fine textiles, moreover, do not figure in these statistics; people told me they had to give cloth so often that they could not remember all the occasions, so strict enumeration became impossible. In traditional exchanges, the formal presentation of a long-tusked pig is always accompa-

Table 4. Exchange Survey: Gifts Received, 1983–88

	Households Participating	Total Gifts Received	Average no. of Gifts Each Time	Five-year Average
Own brideprice	14	191	7.1	7.1
Relative's brideprice	3	18	1	6
Funerals	10	95	1	9.5
Feasts	4	21	1	5.2
Stone draggings	3	16	1	5.3
Matching partner	4	16	1	2

nied by the gift of a man's cloth and a woman's sarung. My informants did, however, remember giving or receiving eleven gold *hamoli* pendants, which have a standardized equivalence in the exchange economy of a mature buffalo. Because they function as "substitutes for livestock" in bridewealth contributions, they are reckoned in the head count in this survey.

More livestock and valuables circulate in bridewealth than any other kind of exchange, although funerals come a close second. It is useful to break down the statistics according to event categories and to examine the rules and strategies used for each.

BRIDEWEALTH

The Kodi say that the wife-takers should bear the brunt of raising bridewealth, and clearly they do. Of the 308 head that people reported giving in bridewealth payments, only about 30 percent (92 head) came "from the family corral"; the rest had to come from gifts from clan mates or sisters' husbands, exchange partnerships, or cash purchase (table 3). Of the 148 head that were reported in the survey as contributions to another person's bridewealth, 103 (71 percent) came from persons in the category of *nobovinye*, or wife-taker; others came from married brothers, cousins, and schoolmates. In seven cases, gifts of livestock that were presented to the prospective groom's father reciprocated earlier gifts he had made. Livestock presented by nonrelatives required more immediate reciprocity, and indeed, half had been reciprocated within the span of five years.

Eleven households, all of them "new," were still paying substantial parts of their own bridewealth during the period of the survey. For the largest sums of bridewealth (fifty to a hundred head), even major contributions from the family corral required some outside purchase. One young man from a very prominent family (one of the sons of the former raja) who wanted to marry outside his district was asked to pay a bridewealth of one hundred head. Although he received eighteen head in contributions, he still had to buy twenty head with his own cash savings. One-fifth of the initial bridewealth payments enumerated in the survey required that some of the animals be bought with cash, but the others drew on extensive networks for this initial payment. In one case, a bridewealth of thirty head required only three animals from the family corral because of the great number of outside contributions.

Bridewealth was received by fourteen households during the period covered by the survey, at a bit more than seven head each, on average (table 4). The figure may seem small, considering that bridewealth sums in fact ranged from ten to one hundred head; it must be remembered however, that the actual number that come into the corral is considerably diminished by the need to redistribute animals received to those who helped on earlier occasions. In one case, for example, eighteen head were given immediately to others who were owed a swift return gift.

FUNERALS

At the news of a death, almost everyone who is related or even acquainted with the deceased will bring a gift of cloth to express sorrow. The heaviest burden of funeral gifts, however, is again on the wife-taker. The death of the wife's father (*ghera*) will require the best animal that he can find. Sons and brothers must also contribute substantially. In my survey, the ten households that had funerals during this period received a total of ninety-five head of livestock in contributions, or just under ten head apiece, on average. Significantly, the size of the funeral sacrifice is often less than the number of animals received—perhaps one or two large animals to the dozen or so that may be bestowed; in that sense, funerals "turn a profit" in the exchange system, bringing in more animals than are required to serve to guests during the funeral itself. The "profit," however, is consistent with the aim of these gifts, which is to replace life lost with new life and to compensate the grieving family for their loss. As Versluys noted earlier, the bereaved family should reciprocate funeral gifts, but if they encounter continuing hardship (especially if the family member lost had contributed to household expenses), these debts are most likely to be forgiven.

FEASTS

Funerals come unexpectedly, if inevitably. Feasts, by contrast, require the commitment of the group, and their occurrence is far from inevitable: no organized feasts take place without consensus. The larger the feast, the larger the number of people who must serve as sponsors. A single night of singing (*yaigho*) in a garden hamlet, for instance, will be put on by only the immediate members of the sponsoring house. They provide a pig for sacrifice the next morning, as well as two ritual specialists, a singer (*tou yaigho*) and a diviner (*tou parupu kaloro*), to pray on their behalf. These feasts are usually rites of placation (Kuipers 1990) to beg the spirits to forgive an infraction. If important ancestors are concerned, however, the singing ceremony must be conducted in the ancestral village. All the households descended from the ancestor should participate, each bringing pigs and chickens and witnessing the negotiations with the ancestor conducted by the singer and diviner. Other orators (*tou ta liyo*) may also join the nightlong dialogue with the singer. The words of the orators and diviner are taken up by the singer and set to the rhythm of the drum, so that they can travel up to the spirits (Hoskins 1988a, 1988b).

The largest feasts, called *woleko*, are held to celebrate the completion of a major project: the rebuilding of an ancestral house or a megalithic tomb, or the final stage in a sequence of feasts promised to the ancestors. They involve several days of singing and dancing and culminate on the last day with a buffalo sacrifice. A complex cast of priests is involved: one to scatter rice in offerings (*tou wiha*), one to circle the sacrificial animals (*tou kanikingo*), one to pronounce the invocations (*tou ka'okongo*), several to serve as orators, and one to sing (*tou lodo*). A *woleko* in a garden hamlet requires the participation of each household in residence; hence, the sacrificial count will range from five or six to thirty buffalo. A *woleko* in an ancestral village should draw together all the members of a single patriclan, which can be over a hundred households and thus may involve over a hundred buffalo.

The *woleko* is organized by a single man, called the "master of the horse, owner of the boat" (*mori njara, mangu tena*), who calls the others together and convinces them to accept his leadership. Ceremonial leadership is evaluated along a ladder of seven stages, marking the gradual progression of an important man toward the title of *rato*, or "great feast giver." The title belongs not to the living man but to the ancestor. It is attached to his first name in respectful reference to him by his descendants. (The Rato Nale is the only living man addressed as *rato*, and for a very different reason: because of his ritual office, he represents an ancestral presence that walks in the light of day. Other important priests may be addressed as *rato marapu*, "the lords of the spirits," or with the respectful term *kabani*, "honored men," but never as simply *rato*.)

To be recognized posthumously as a Great Man, the feast-giver must complete the following sequence of ceremonies: sponsor a singing ceremony in his own hamlet (*yaigho mori cana*); sponsor a singing ceremony in his ancestral village (*yaigho la parona*); rebuild his ancestral house (*dari uma*); drag a tombstone for a megalithic grave (*gharu watu*); sponsor a buffalo feast in the garden hamlet (*woleko mori cana*); sponsor a buffalo feast in the ancestral village (*woleko la parona*); and sponsor a two-day feast in the ancestral village (*woleko wongo weiyo*). Only four or five men alive at the time of my research had completed this full sequence. Although wealth is a prerequisite for the holding of many of these feasts, the ability to summon followers and secure their participation is even more important. The sponsor of a feast must be an impresario, a dynamic speaker and negotiator who can convince others to join his own pursuit of glory.

The frequency of feasting responds to two different pressures: pressures from spirits and ancestors, who require feasts to placate their anger and remove sources of misfortune, and pressures from ambitious individuals, who use the feasts as ladders to the achievement of renown (*ngara*). When people perceive that a feast is performed to alleviate suffering they may contribute willingly; if they believe it is done only for self-aggrandizement, they may be more reluctant, but can still be persuaded that the event is necessary to maintain a collective sense of honor and enhance the shared reputation of the ancestral village. The weeks and days preceding a feast are a time of extensive bartering and trading of smaller reproductive animals in order to procure the oldest long-horned buffalo in the region. Most often, the rule requiring consensus works to delay feasts; that is, one finds sponsors constantly pushing the members of their village to act, while most villagers prefer to wait for an opportunity to make a more impressive contribution.

Contributions to feasts vary widely. Some are reckoned according to the usual networks of kin and affines, with gifts being given in the expectation of a delayed reciprocity. Some may also involve outsiders, those not linked through blood or marriage, who will require a more immediate reciprocity for the presentation of prestige gifts. To assure a large number of mature buffalo for the meal, the sponsor may ask wealthy outsiders (including Chinese shopkeepers and Moslem horse traders) to bring long-horned buffalo to the feast. He will specify the size of his countergift in advance and present it immediately. This practice of immediate "matching" in value still follows the principle that exchanges must be in equivalents and not identities; thus, a large buffalo may be "matched" with a long-tusked pig, two cloths, and a fine horse. In an important contrast to other transactions, the obligation begins and ends at that event. Because the "match" is specified in advance, no "interest" is allowed to accrue that will "lie on the back" of the animals offered.

Exchanges that involve immediate reciprocity are still relatively rare in Kodi. I call them "matching partners" in the survey, and heard of them only in the context of large feasts. At the *woleko* in Wei Lyabba in 1985, for example, the sponsor asked four wealthy men to present him with animals, which they did, receiving instant reciprocation. I also witnessed and recorded matching transactions at a stone dragging and a garden feast. The emergence of this phenomenon in the last decade or so reflects two influences in particular. One is the relatively individualistic style of feasting that exists in neighboring districts, where not all members of a village or hamlet are expected to contribute to a ritual slaughter. The other is the rarity of mature buffalo, and the fact that many of them are owned by a few wealthy men. If strong affinal ties have not already been created to allow for the transfer of these animals through traditional exchange channels, the use of this new "outside channel," which compresses the time scale of reciprocity and makes the exchange "almost like a purchase," becomes necessary.

While funerals are part of the prestige economy, they do not "count" in the same way feasts do, either in the reckoning of temporal investment or in the determination of "big man"–style generosity. The visible, enduring signs of an impressive funeral (the buffalo horns and pig's tusks) are taken out of the dead man's house and given to his "village of origins," to pay them for ritual services rendered to remove the pollution of death. They do not serve as prestige counters, but as a final reckoning of debts.

Reflections and Evaluations

The effect of grouping exchange events into "contributions" and "receipts" stimulated many informants to figure out whether they seemed to be "ahead" in the exchange game over the past five years. Most claimed that they had been more generous than others had been with them. Of the fifty-two households surveyed, in fact, thirty-five had a plurality of outgoing gifts, while fourteen had a plurality of incoming gifts, with only three balancing out exactly. Significantly, of those who had received more than they gave, all but two were older households and they included the six wealthiest households that I interviewed. The two new heads of households that seemed to be "ahead" benefited from a temporary imbalance: one had just received contributions to a bridewealth but had not yet delivered the animals, while the other had received gifts for his father's funeral.

The perception that exchange obligations weigh heaviest on younger families seemed accurate, though in time these families, too, will be able to collect on the debts incurred. Because the most compelling reason to ask for assistance in the exchange system is the death of a close relative, older households are more likely to receive generous gifts. They are also more likely to have given gifts to others that require reciprocation, and of course only longer-established households will have daughters old enough to bring in bridewealth payments. The imbalance in gifts given and received may also be partly due to a reporting bias. The memory is always better at retaining losses than gains, both because they hurt more and because remembering them can work to one's advantage—that is, a gift or favor must be remembered to compel an act of reciprocation.

The interviews presented an occasion for many people to reflect on their own position within the exchange system, the rise and fall of family fortunes, and whether the balance of payments seemed fair or unfair. Most bitter were members of more recently established households, who felt that their way was barred from success because of the structure of exchange expectations. From these actors' perspective, strategies were possible only once certain earlier conditions had been fulfilled. Here is what one younger man had to say:

> I had a hard time raising bridewealth, bringing funeral contributions, keeping our name good. Everyone gives credit to a wealthy man, but no one is generous to a poor man. Generosity is always linked to the expected repayment. I paid one bridewealth, then my first wife got sick. I had her treated by local healers, I paid hospital bills, but she still died and I had to bury her. My children are still small and I want to marry again, but no one is helping me this time.

His feeling was that a pattern of misfortune had made him into a lost cause, before he even had a chance to show his capabilities.

Actors' impressions of their standing in the exchange system do not depend on a simplistic calculation of what has been given and received, however. A relatively young man who headed one of the "established" households noted cheerfully that in the past year he had brought many more pigs and buffalo to feasts than he received. He was optimistic about the future: "People know that I can play the exchange game. My name is good, my credit even better. My corral may be empty now, but the animals will come when I need them. When I visit people who received animals from me, they serve me with their best glasses, treating me as someone who will soon be receiving a reciprocal gift." His early generosity put him in a position to collect later on debts, and his confidence in the benefit of giving helped to buttress his social credit.

Biographical Time, Exchange, and Rival Scales of Value

In evaluating the different exchange profiles of these various households, we need to consider two other factors: first, the relation between the biographies of household members (what used to be called their place in a domestic cycle) and the age of its domestic animals, especially buffalo; and second, the way the traditional exchange system has been affected by the introduction of a market for the purchase of horses and buffalo with cash, as opposed to their acquisition through exchange. These factors allow us to "historicize" different forms of exchange by locating them within local or larger time scales and at the same time acknowledging the ties that exist between an indigenous historical consciousness and postcolonial entanglements.

Looking first at the linkage of human and animal ages, we should remember that for a Sumbanese man the negotiation of his own marriage obligations and the payment of bridewealth to his father-in-law summon resources and debts for his own newly formed household. A formal requirement of the bridewealth is that it begin with the presentation of a cow and her calf (*ihya bei mono ana*) to the bride's family, so that the new herd will be at least potentially reproductive.[4] The first buffalo cow that a young man acquires is called the *kapunge pote*, "the trunk of the herd," and is of great personal and even magical importance. It is often said of a wealthy man that his *kapunge pote* was a "sacred buffalo" (*karimbiyo marapu*) that was able to reproduce at supernatural rates and mystically attracted other animals to the herd. The first cow is usually inalienable: she cannot be sold (especially not for cash), and can only be sacrificed on an important ritual occasion—usually the first major feast that a man gives in his life—through a special dedication. Kodi folktales contain accounts of the curses of misfortune that have fallen on men who did not respect the special value of their "trunk cow" and carelessly agreed to exchange her or slaughter her.

Since most Sumbanese men marry between the ages of twenty and twenty-five (and seem to have done so also in the past; Versluys 1941,

---

[4]Other animals given in bridewealth may be either male or female, and there are no other restrictions concerning their size, age, or gender. The most impressive bridewealths contain a number of mature animals with long horns, but this is not a rule.

469), and the "trunk cow" is ideally a young, newly reproductive female, she will continue to bear calves until her master is in his forties. At the age of about fifty, those men who have been reasonably prosperous will begin to plan their own feasts. (Usually, the first such feast follows the death of one's father and is in part a reciprocation for contributions brought to his funeral.)[5] At about the same time, the "trunk cow" becomes barren, and thus suitable for sacrifice. If her owner plans to launch himself into a competitive cycle of feasting exchanges, he will have to have kept a number of her calves, which should by then have grown into mature bulls with horns of impressive length.

Because the bridewealth of a young man's sister forms the basis of his own exchange career, it is understandable that as they both grow older he has a continuing obligation to assist her and her family by contributing to ceremonial expenses. These contributions, though modest at first, will escalate as his fortunes rise.[6] Over the course of the domestic cycle, that is, we see a pattern of young households contributing smaller, immature animals, while older households supply larger, more mature ones. The reasonable expectations of this system become problematic when we consider the exchange needs that emerge with feasting, especially given the "sliding scale" by which buffalo are assigned value according to their horn size. Even a young man may need an older animal for an important ceremony, and he will pass on this request to his sister's husband. One young man told me:

> My brother-in-law's village was having a feast, so he asked me to bring a buffalo. It would be his first public sacrifice, with his whole family bringing animals for slaughter, so it had to be a mature bull with long horns. Where could I get such a bull? The oldest animal in my corral had horns only a wrist length long. For a month, I visited relatives to look. When I found a bull, I had to trade three smaller animals, one calf and two fertile cows. We brought the bull

[5] I was sometimes told that a man could not sponsor a large feast before the death of his father. I did, however, know of several people who did so, often because their fathers were already weak and bedridden, so I would suggest that the rule is intended simply to prevent competition between fathers and sons. It is true that the sons of an important feastgiver are honor-bound to support his efforts and not present feasts "for their own names" as long as he is actively engaged in the ceremonial arena.

[6] In families with many children, a brother and sister of close to the same age who marry at about the same time (the sister usually would marry between the ages of sixteen and twenty-one, thus a bit before her brother) may be specifically "paired" as exchange partners. While other family members also contribute, these "brothers and sisters who love each other" (*pa lawinye pa lamone pa manawaro wuna*) are especially active in mutual exchanges.

in a great procession. I danced at the gates, and everyone saw how big he was. My name has stayed good, but now we have nothing to exchange for school fees.

The trade of three healthy young animals for a skinny older bull was perplexing to me. "Why" I asked, "didn't you try to buy a bull from the livestock traders in the city? They might have given you a better price."

"What, them? They don't know value." Seeing my confused expression, he then repeated the same phrase in Indonesian, asserting that there were two kinds of value (*harga*), one defined by traditional custom (*harga adat*) and another corresponding to monetary value (*harga uang*). When an animal is bought for exchange, the price is specified in terms of other animals, the criterion being the age of the animal as measured by the tusks. When an animal is sold for export, "the price is only for the meat" (*harga daging*)—that is, it is set according to size and weight.

This man's shift into Indonesian from a conversation thus far carried on in Kodi signaled a change in perspective: he moved from a personal point of view to a more general description of the system in order to make it comprehensible to an outsider. The shift was necessary so that he could clarify the difference between the Kodi term *wali*, designating a "price" determined by negotiation and often comprising several different components (animals, cloth, etc.), and the Indonesian term *harga uang*, which denotes a monetary price set by external agents and complexly entangled with a wider market economy beyond the island of Sumba.

To make this distinction clear, I turn to the complex relation between human lives and animal lives, and how the passage of time is measured in horns—the "biological clocks" that animals wear over their ears. The next chapter explores how local constructs of value are formulated in opposition to much larger historical and economic forces, which define a very different form of value, one that contrasts and conflicts with a distinctively Kodi notion of time.

7

Time as Value
Taking the Bull by the Horns

The daily timepiece is the cattle clock, the round of pastoral tasks, and the
time of day and the passage of time through a day are to a Nuer primarily
the succession of these tasks and their relations to one another.

Edward Evans-Pritchard, *The Nuer*

If you want to see my life, the lives of my ancestors, the things that they
did, look at the row of horns in front of my house. The greatness of the past
can be measured there, the size of our feasts and spread of our name.

A Kodi comment

The visitor to any of the great feasting houses in Kodi is immediately
confronted with buffalo horns on display. Climbing from the ground level
to the first bamboo veranda, the horns serve as steps to the inner sanctum
of the cult house. From the open doorway, a "ladder" of horns is visible,
stacked vertically along the main house pillar up to the roof. Other horns
hang from the ceiling beams in the large interior area used to receive
guests and perform divinations, or serve as hooks on which to hang baskets
and cloth. The small rafters under the thatched roof have rows of pig's
jaws, each one marked by the curl of tusks from a sacrificed animal.

As the visitor is seated and served with betel and glasses of tea or coffee,
she may ask the history of these horns and tusks. The host will proudly
detail the origin of each group as his guest admires them: "These horns
on the pillar are from a feast we held three years ago, which five hundred
people attended. Twenty buffalo were killed, four of them from this house,
as well as fifteen pigs. The ones higher up were from the funeral of Wora
Rehi, an important man in Bondo Kodi who died fifteen years ago. His
mother was from this village, so we claimed the buffalo heads. The tusks
hanging near the sacred corner are from the feast held to consecrate this
house when it was rebuilt eight years ago."

Each sacrificial event is marked by preserving a remnant of the animal
killed. The buffalo horns and pig's tusks are hung in the same part of the
house where human scalps were once displayed, the skulls having been
hung to dry on the skull tree. The horns and tusks are not mere aids to

memory, ways of "visualizing history" so that it will be retained by the descendants of these ancestors. Nor are they simple trophies, ways of "counting coup" in a competitive game of sacrifice. Their significance in the sacrificial economy is more precise: they show the temporalization of exchange value. The worth of animals in the sacrificial economy is reckoned in relation to their *age*, the time spent raising them, and the "biographical" investment made by their owner. The horns represent a part of his own life, given an enduring material form and guarded as a family heirloom for generations to come.

The Kodinese give us clues to this process when they say that "the name of a man rides on the horns of his buffalo" or "his reputation is tied to the horn span." Although they recognize the connection between a man's biography and his store of horns, they cannot articulate the full system of rules and strategies that lead them to make these statements. This system emerges only in contrast to the very different assumptions that underlie the market economy, cash transactions, and standards of value, which tie time to money and not to value.

Horns, Tusks, and Value

In the last chapter, we saw that horn length is used to evaluate the age and worth of a buffalo offered for sacrifice at a feast. This worth, however, seemed disproportionate, both to the amount of meat on the animal and to the number of other young animals offered in exchange. The logic of "horn counting" must be explained in greater detail, for in fact it does represent a relatively precise measurement, not only of the age of the animal, but also of its value in terms of an investment in time.

In buffalo, horns begin to grow toward the end of the first year and continue at a fairly even rate for twenty or thirty years. The Kodi term for a yearling does not refer directly to age, but to the newly budding horns: it is "the budding of a bull" (*kamboka ghobo*) or, in ritual couplets, *hanjoko wu kawallu, hinjalu watu kamba*—"just a candlenut bump of horn, one node of cottonseed." A yearling is also referred to as *hinjalu mete mata*, "one node with black eyes," marking the darkness of eyes that grow paler with age.

Horn size is measured along the right arm. An outsider watching two men bartering the exchange of buffalo or discussing a feast slaughter might assume that they were talking about glove lengths instead of livestock, as their hands keep moving up and down their arms. The index finger is placed at various points between the fingertip and the armpit, usually preceded by an apology in Indonesian (*"permisi"*) for the indelicacy of pointing. Common measurements are at the finger joint, the base of the thumb, wrist, mid-forearm, elbow, mid-bicep, and the armpit. When a promised animal is finally presented, the estimated horn length may be verified by stretching the arm along the horns, fingertips resting at the skull and the tip of the horns determining the final measure.

The practice of using horns and tusks to indicate value of some sort is quite widespread. In other areas of Indonesia where buffalo sacrifice is highly developed, such as Toradja, the display of the horns is also commonplace (Volkman 1985). In the "pig-loving" areas of Melanesia, where prestige exchanges center on that animal, a similar cultural significance is given to pig's tusks. Special "tusker" boars are created by invulsing the upper canines and allowing the lower ones to grow unimpeded, so that the animal's tusks form a perfect circle (Jolly 1984).[1] Sumbanese perform a related operation on gelded buffalo (*mandopo*), whose horns subsequently make the most impressive house decorations. After gelding, a buffalo's horns grow so long they may threaten to pierce the skull; hence, the horns of a gelded yearling are heated and forcefully twisted away from the head to form a large arc like that of long-horned cattle. The Sumbanese, who find aesthetic pleasure in contemplating an impressive spread of horns, boast that after this operation some animals' horns grow all the way to the ground, forcing them to walk about with permanently bowed heads. Indeed, many older gelded animals cannot be taken to pasture and must be hand-fed with grass at the back of the house.

Gelded buffalo form a special category in Kodi sacrifices. Although the most prestigious gift is an older bull, the distinctive *mandopo* may be preferred when the donor wants his gift to be singular and unforgettable. In theory, a very long-horned buffalo can be reciprocated only by another *mandopo*. Horn length used as a criterion of value in buffalo is paralleled by tusk length used to determine the value of pigs.

[1] The particular value of the tusker is variable in Melanesia. In Malekula, Vanuatu, value "resides not so much in the flesh of the animal as in its tusks" as "most boars sacrificed are so old and scrawny as to be inedible" (Jolly 1984, 85). Once the tusks are separated from the animal, however, they lose their value. In South Pentecost, the tusks are kept as ritual mementos of the glory of past grade-taking rituals; and in the Massim area they circulate as kula valuables and are mystified as "snakes' teeth" (Jolly 1984). Although the tusks are believed to have magical and mystical powers, the animals that grow them are clearly incapacitated; the tusker becomes unable to scavenge on its own and must be hand-fed. In Malekula, long-tusked pigs are the prize possessions of men, while other pigs are tended by women.

A young man dances as he leads a long-horned buffalo, around twenty-five years old, onto the slaughter field at a large-scale feast. The gift of the buffalo fulfills an affinal obligation from a wife-taker. 1984. Photograph by the author.

From Livestock to Pigs:
Equivalences and Conversions

The small, dark, and somewhat swaybacked pigs raised on Kodi are part of a race that has been on the island for several hundred years. In the early part of the twentieth century, the Dutch introduced a race of fatter, white pigs, known as "foreign pigs" (*wawi jawa*), which now are interbred with indigenous ones. The females are raised as breed animals, while the males are destined for exchange and eventual sacrifice. Boars begin to produce tusks when they are a little over a year old, but these are not of impressive dimension until the animal is at least three or four years old. When the tusks reach the length of half a man's finger, the animal becomes appropriate for prestige exchanges. Until then, a pig's value is markedly less than that of a buffalo or horse, and it is assimilated with chickens in the category of "food animals." As one person put it, "Without tusks, a pig is just good to eat. But once the tusks have grown, he is also good to trade or to sacrifice."

The emergence of tusks also establishes a form of equivalence between calves and pigs that is important in determining the appropriate size of counterpayments. On ritual occasions where a wife-taker comes bringing a buffalo of six or seven years—that is, with horns just past the wrist— his gift should be matched by a long-tusked pig and two quality textiles, a man's loincloth and a woman's sarung. It is the *age* of the animals that forms the basis for the evaluation of comparable value.

The problem of value determination is complicated by the separation of pigs and buffalo according to gender categories. On Sumba, the routine care and feeding of livestock is entrusted to men, while that of pigs is entrusted to women. This practice follows an extremely widespread pattern, which brings together aspects of African cattle complexes and Melanesian pig complexes. In an article comparing patterns of inequality, political competition, and political subordination in Africa and the Pacific, Andrew Strathern (1972, 130–31) argued that key determining factors were the diverse demands of tending different animals and the sexual division of labor. Pigs, for example, are domesticated by small household units, not in large corporate corrals. Pigs are sources of food only after death, when they offer up their flesh, whereas most pastoralists also "eat their animals alive" by draining them of blood and milk. Pigs reproduce prolifically and quickly exhaust available resources; livestock, by contrast, are free to roam to greener pastures and so require a less regular cycle of slaughter.

The Sumbanese economy, however, combines pig and chicken keeping with stock raising in a way that assimilates both systems: all animals—pigs, chickens, buffalo, and horses—are owned on a household basis, even though the larger ones may be housed in a communal corral. The blood or milk from buffalo is not drunk, and in Kodi the animals are rarely used in agriculture because there are so few wet-rice fields. Livestock, rather, are raised for sacrifice and exchange. The hot, dry climate with its fresh sea breezes is particularly suited to promote the fertility of buffalo, which produce one calf a year in this region, but often only one every other year in wetter inland areas. This still cannot compare with pigs, which produce litters of five to six piglets. Even so, heat and periodic water shortages are harder on pigs than on buffalo. Pigs do not sweat, so they cannot reduce their body temperature without access to mud. A buffalo can survive the long march to a distant feast, but a pig, carried on a litter under a cloth banner, may die of heat prostration on the way. Cattle rustlers and disease have long endangered livestock, but unfavorable climatic conditions make the pig population as vulnerable to death and destruction as the buffalo herd.

Both pigs and buffalo are raised for exchange and increase in value as they grow older. Both are exchanged against more purely economic commodities and against the values of human life that we summarize under the notion of kinship. Both are prized for their "mediative capacities," in that they serve to mark and organize the relations between groups and between men and women. In ceremonial contexts, many of the cultural tensions inherent in the notions of male and female are represented by the buffalo and pig.

In bridewealth payments, funeral sacrifices, and feasting contributions, pigs and buffalo are matched against each other as complementary gifts. The symbolic femininity of the pig and the masculinity of the buffalo are balanced in a requirement that they offer equivalent, but not identical, values. The baseline determination of value comes from the age of the animals, as measured by the length of tusks and horns. Since buffalo can be considerably older than pigs, the gift of a pig is usually "completed" by the additional gift of one or two textiles.

Although it would be unthinkable to exchange a buffalo calf for a piglet, once the pig has grown tusks (and been fattened to impressive dimensions) it can be exchanged for large livestock. No exact equivalence in years is reckoned, but informants do cite the relative ages of animals when they compare them:

> I had been raising that pig since my first child was born. He is now nine. Someone offered me a calf for him. But the calf was just a

yearling. My pig had tusks as long as this extended finger. It was clear that it was worth more than a knuckle length [of buffalo horns]. I said no, it had to be a bull with horns as long as your hand. [How old is that?] It had to be an animal of equal value, at least seven years old. When they came back with a buffalo whose horns matched the side of my hand, I accepted, and gave them a cloth to seal the deal.

Bridewealth equivalents are always figured by the wife-givers, who reserve the right to judge the value of the livestock they receive from prospective wife-takers. The counterprestation for a bridewealth of ten "tails" is conventionally two pigs of equivalent value, one given live and one killed for the guests. The two pigs must have tusks that "match" the age of the buffalo received and are presented along with a pair of men's and women's textiles.

Equivalences can also involve several younger buffalo and horses given to secure a single large older animal appropriate for a feast:

My mother's brother sponsored a feast in Wei Lyabba. He asked me to bring him a buffalo, a good one with long horns. I had one cow in the corral, fat and fertile, and two of her calves, one with horns just budding, the other with about a knuckle or two of growth. I went to someone in my matriclan to barter. He let me buy his best bull, but I had to give all three younger animals, along with two horses, in order to get him. His horns were as long as a whole arm, all the way to the armpit.

[How old do you think he was?] He must have been eighteen or nineteen. He wasn't even slaughtered. My mother's brother got another large animal from his wife-giver, and he gave him as a counterprestation.

A calculus of total value was derived from the sum of the ages of the animals transacted for, including horses added to complete the deal.[2]

The complex combinations of different ages and sexes used in traditional exchange are negotiated in relation to the time invested in raising the animal. Before a pig has tusks it is not a prestige animal and can be given as a contribution tò the "vegetables" (*roghe*) served along with the

[2]Horses seem to have been used here to "fill in" as functional animals whose value is more stable, usually from Rp. 25.000 to Rp. 50.000, as long as the animal is healthy and ridable. The value of a horse is equivalent to a fine indigo dyed textile, and that of a colt somewhat less.

meal, but it is not appropriate for formal sacrifice. It can, however, be part of a combined equivalent offered in recompense for an older animal:

> My brother-in-law went to a feast and "borrowed" a pig to give to his wife's family there. We let him take it because he said it would be replaced in a few months, by the time we were harvesting rice. The pig was five years old, and its tusks had just appeared. When he came to help with the harvest, he had two piglets, but neither of them was much over a year old. "What are these worth?" I said to him; "neither of them could be taken anywhere!" We made him take them back. Later, he returned with a sow and a pig with budding tusks. We accepted them.

Young animals can be brought to simple ceremonies like village *yaighos*, where many pigs are killed for a shared meal, but they cannot be matched with buffalo and horses for larger feasts, bridewealth, or funeral exchanges.

The struggle to find an animal that can match others of considerable age often proves ruinous:

> We got the news that my father had died, and as his oldest son I had to bring a long-horned buffalo for the funeral feast. I wanted a bull, but no one would give one to me, not for anything. So I found a cow who had become sterile. She must have been twelve or thirteen. I gave them three animals from my own corral—one was a bull with wrist-length horns [about four years old], another one with thumb-length ones [about three], and finally a cow who must have been four or five and could still bear more young. That was how much I had to pay in order not to lose honor at my father's funeral.

Although this person's corral later became well filled by the contributions of others, the high social importance of the son's sacrifice made his immediate need intense and justified the losses he had to assume to pay this final act of respect to a deceased parent.

The use of an animal's age to determine its value is a principle of "temporal investment," but it is not a measure of labor as a Marxian model would suggest. Pigs and chickens require more attention per animal than do horses or buffalo because they must be fed carefully prepared meals of house scraps and cannot simply be taken out to pasture in large numbers or led docilely to the water. Since buffalo are tended in herds by young boys, the total number of man-hours devoted to each head of buffalo is certainly much less than the woman-hours invested in fattening a single pig. Does a cultural bias give greater importance to man-hours than woman-hours in reckoning labor costs? Perhaps, but pigs also require a certain amount of men's work in building pens and protecting crops. The key lies not in labor, but in temporal links and the social meaning of exchange intervals.

The great value of older animals is due to the way their lives are tied to their master's biography and come to serve as metonyms for his identity. Because a man begins to raise animals on his own as soon as he establishes his own household, his animals represent the temporal moment in which he achieved adulthood. One animal, perhaps a favorite calf, may at that point be specially dedicated to a ritual purpose that lies in the still-distant future—such as the dedication of a newly rebuilt lineage house, the funeral for the owner's father, or a feast in which the household head takes a new horse name, thus establishing his renown. As he raises the animal, it is identified with these plans and with the owner's own career in the ritual arena. The animal must be protected from disease and drought for its master to obtain social recognition. Sacrificial identification, in short, builds on a long association in which the life of the man and the life of his animal run parallel courses.

The argument I have made can be summarized in four related propositions: (1) The meaning of horn and tusk length is a measure of the animal's age, with the result that "prestige value" is in fact a code for "temporal value"; (2) the visual "record" of a feast displayed in the ancestral house in the form of horns and tusks indexes temporal investment; (3) temporal investment is measured along a man's own life span and has its origins in the idea of sacrificial identification between man and beast; (4) the respective ages of animals provide a standard for equivalence and exchangeability and can allow for conversions across species.

The Meat Market Versus the Exchange Market

The special characteristics of sacrificial animals bring us back to the second factor that was mentioned earlier (see chapter 6): the existence of an alternate market for livestock based on cash. Why couldn't the bereaved son have decided to purchase a long-horned bull with money? How are the rules for determining value different in feasting and in cash sales?

There are two parts to the value of an animal in the traditional economy. The first is its value alive, as part of a herd that can reproduce and increase in numbers. The second is its value in sacrifices, where it will provide both a measure of the sacrificer's prestige and a gift to the invisible ancestors who bring new resources into the hands of their descendants. Both of these values assume that an animal is never completely lost; it is simply moved to a place in another cycle of meaning. The sale of an animal to a meat merchant, however, does involve a loss. And that loss is justifiable in local terms only if what was acquired in compensation for the animal is of enduring value.

For several hundred years, Sumbanese have sold some of their livestock to merchants who shipped them to other islands. Payment for horses and buffalo was presented in an imperishable form: Dutch guilders and English pounds sterling were melted down to make gold jewelry; metal knives, swords, and gongs were stored for generations in cult houses. The development of a cash market for Kodi livestock did not come until the period of independence, when road improvements allowed merchants to transport animals from the more distant areas of the island to the port towns. The cash market is still irregular and unreliable, with merchants generally coming to buy before large Moslem feasts such as Hari Idul Fitri, when the demand for meat on Java goes up dramatically.

New market transactions have established a different standard of value, the "commercial" standard based on the amount of meat on the body. At the ports of Waikelo and Waingapu, buffalo are weighed on a scale, and their price is determined by a set per-kilo rate. For village purchases in Kodi, the animals cannot be weighed, but they are measured and estimates are made of the amount of meat on the body.

Livestock are sold only rarely in Kodi; in essence, they are a protected domain of stored value (Ferguson 1985) because of their importance to the community. Whenever an owner thinks of selling an animal, many people will try to discourage him from doing so. These people may have some claims on the animal because of earlier debts, or they may anticipate wanting to borrow the animal in the future. As a rule, livestock are sold only to cover major expenses on which there can be some group consensus: a life-saving operation, materials to build a stone house, or a son's college expenses.

Evidence from my survey of exchange activities suggests that fewer than a hundred animals are sold each year from the Kodi district, and most of these are horses or cattle. Official statistics for all of West Sumba record that 175 buffalo were exported in 1986, as against 1,396 horses and 615 cattle (Biro Statistik 1986, 89). Because exports are subject to regulation in the port city, these figures are probably fairly accurate.[3] Estimates of

---

[3] Official statistics for the livestock slaughtered in traditional feasting in 1985 are 200 buffalo, 12 cattle, and 132 pigs. These figures are gathered at the time the slaughter tax is collected and are acknowledged by all sources (including the livestock department employees) to involve gross underreporting. I was often told of animals hidden from government clerks and (perhaps more common) tacit

the number of buffalo slaughtered each year in traditional feasts usually amount to two or three times this figure. The small sample of fifty households in my exchange survey included three separate feasts at which over a hundred buffalo were killed (Balaghar in 1984, Wei Lyabba in 1985, and Parona Baroro in 1986), and twelve funerals involving the slaughter of an average of two and a half head.

There are, however, crucial symbolic differences between animals sold for export and those offered for sacrifice, which show how this system of cultural diacritics can work. The various considerations of these markets can be summarized as follows:

Meat market	*Exchange market*
Value = quantity of flesh on the body, measured by weight	Value = time invested in raising the animal, measured by length of horns and tusks
The body leaves the island and is lost, not part of any recycling from one generation to the next	The animal's soul is given to the ancestors, who store it in a corral so it can be reborn in future generations
Cash can be quickly collected, but it is not remembered "visually" or publicly exchanged	Value is not lost, but returned with interest through the system of credits and debts
Cattle sold as meat are not socially reinvested to fulfill other ceremonial needs	Cattle given away and even slaughtered remain part of the communal "bank"

Animals in the traditional exchange system are "reinvested" in two different ways. One occurs during the span of a human life, what I call biographical time, the other only in the longer-term exchanges of ancestors and descendants, that is, in intergenerational time. Debts are returned to individuals through the obligation to "replace the meat" distributed at a feast or to return another animal for one "loaned" in a time of need. The principle of delayed reciprocity requires an increase in the value of the gift consistent with the passage of years or months before it is repaid. A similar principle, transposed onto the relations between ancestors and descendants, operates in extending the process of reciprocity down through the generations: because the souls of animals offered to the *marapu* are believed to be recycled into the corral for their descendants, if previous

---

agreements between feastgivers and government clerks to note down only a portion of those actually slaughtered so that the feast would not appear to violate government restrictions on animal slaughter.

generations have been generous, the living can draw on their reserves of fertility and prosperity. These differences become clearer when we explore other contrasts between an exchange market where animals can be used in sacrifice and a meat market where they are mere commodities.

Sacrificial Economies and Commodity Economies

In commodity exchanges, people act as autonomous individuals and their association is mediated by things. The things change hands, payment is made, and the transaction is finished. In sacrifice, people are brought together through association with a mediating animal, and the destruction of the animal creates a bond between them and its recipients, the spirits or *marapu*. The return on sacrifice, as in most traditional exchange, is a delayed return. It may bring benefits to the sacrificer, or only to his descendants. The precise inversion of many of the characteristics of commodities in sacrifices suggests why these two models should produce such different standards of value.

Traditional exchanges between living people use biographical time as a measure of value. A buffalo is esteemed because of the years of his own life the owner has invested in raising it. When this animal is offered for sacrifice, therefore, the owner is giving up a section of his biography, which is presented to the *marapu* in the hopes of receiving still greater blessings from them. These blessings, however, may be delayed, appearing only in the next generation. Thus the biographical time that determines exchange values has to be supplemented by the intergenerational time of sacrifice.

The special temporality of sacrifice comes from its role in social reproduction. In sacrifice, ideas of cyclicity and reincarnation depend on a reciprocity that embraces both human beings and the ancestral spirits. They are the ones who consume the essence of sacrifices, who "eat time" or "eat memories" instead of consuming the flesh itself. Through the invocations of each animal, they first "eat its own history"—its connection to other persons and the exchange paths that led it to the sacrificial field. Their later gifts of fertility allow for the renewal of life and the continuation of new generations.

EYELASHES AND EXPORTS

A contrast in the treatment of animals sold in commercial transactions and animals sacrificed reveals how this principle of renewal works. Buffalo that die in the ancestral village travel to the great "corral of banyan wood" (*nggallu maliti, nggallu kadoki*) in the skies, where their souls await rebirth to the descendants of those who sacrificed them. They must die as complete animals so their souls will travel upward intact. Animals sold to the meat dealers who eventually ship them to other islands, however, have their eyelashes removed before they leave the village.

This apparently trivial plucking of lashes has considerable symbolic importance, for it removes the sign of a payment that is made in the expectation of a return. The term for eyelashes, *wulu mata*, is also used in Sumbanese languages to refer to the fringe of traditional textiles, and is a polite term for all kinds of ritual payments that compensate persons for performing as ceremonial mediators. Thus, the go-betweens in a marriage negotiation are paid in *wulu mata*, as are priests who perform at a feast or the messengers who help to work out a truce between feuding parties. Usually these payments consist of cloth, small sums of money, and betel nut. They are called "eyelashes" as a form of modest speech indicating that the debt owed to these intermediaries is greater than the compensation offered, but further benefits will be provided by the spirits in attendance. The "fringe," in other words, is only the visible payment; it stands for a much larger invisible payment that should follow.

The "fringe payment" of eyelashes is also what protects the source. Lashes are the furry shield of each *mata*, which has the double meaning of "eye" and "origin"; thus *wulu mata* refers also to compensations made to protect source villages and the source of fertility for each animal. The continuity of the ancestral village is protected by sacrifices to feed its ancestors. When an animal is sacrificed within the village, its eyelashes do not leave. Its head is given to the person who "owns" the sacrifice; it is then cooked in a special meal four days after the feast. Only after this meal has been prepared can the souls of the buffalo depart to the afterworld.

When livestock are sold for export their souls are not recycled to the ancestors to promote life in future generations. Plucking the eyelashes, then, is a way to hold on to a part of the animal's vitality, and particularly the animal's reproductive powers, even if its body is definitively sent away. Eyelashes, like horns, are vital excrescences which show that the animal is alive. Removing them and storing them in a coconut shell along with other ancestral treasures in the attic keeps a part of the animal in the village. The Kodi say that the eyelashes "keep the soul from leaving," even when the flesh is gone. Through prayers recited over the eyelashes, the *ndewa*, or ancestral essence, of the animals may be called back. Although the meat itself cannot be dedicated to the ancestors or consumed and distributed, one small aspect of the animal's vital essence is set aside, not lost to outside forces.

Plucking the eyelashes magically removes the reproductive capacity of the animal. Its physical body may leave the island, but its regenerative powers are supposed to stay there. Since exported livestock are destined for immediate slaughter, this magical procedure makes no difference to local traders. As one Moslem exporter said, "On Java, they don't pray over them, they just eat them. No one cares there about their eyelashes."

In the context of local Kodi exchanges, however, the presence of absence of eyelashes can be an important issue. If the horses or buffalo presented to pay bridewealth are not reproductively intact, the wife-givers will surely consider this a serious affront. The gift of livestock in marriage payments is meant to begin a herd and to circulate among family members to produce new animals. A buffalo or horse given without eyelashes is given in bad faith. Only its physical form is surrendered, but part of its essence remains behind, and the herd cannot prosper. Although I doubt that it occurs very often, I heard of one wife-giver who was suspicious of his affines and claimed they had given him a cow with no eyelashes. The cow, though still young, in fact was prematurely sterile: she had borne calves for her earlier masters but not for him. He told me that the appropriate retaliation would be to withhold his "blessings" (*wei myaringi*; lit., "cool waters") and so deny the new couple the possibility to bear children. The cow's barrenness would be reciprocated by his own daughter's barrenness, an inability to provide descendants to her new house and village. Once the wife-takers were advised of the wife-giver's suspicions, they tried to appease him in a special ceremony called *horongo bahi*, "extending the metal." Gold and an additional cow (complete with eyelashes) were presented to repair affinal relations and ask for fertility to be restored. Only after this second cow was with calf did the new bride come to conceive a child—at least as the story was reported.

Time, Exchange, and Traditional Economies

The ways time constitutes value in Sumbanese exchange shed light on a number of anthropological debates about exchange and temporality, ranging from earlier ideas of "dual economies" and ecological "rationality" to current efforts to articulate "moral spheres for exchange" (Appadurai 1986), "transaction orders" (Bloch and Parry 1989), and the "work of time" in exchange games (Bourdieu 1990, 98–108).

Theories of dual economies oppose a "traditional economy" ruled by religious, social, and symbolic concerns to a "modern" or "rational" economy that privileges the marketplace over all else. If the contrast between the meat market and the ceremonial exchange market in Kodi is interpreted in these terms, then the penetration of the commercial standard of value based on the amount of flesh on the animal's body must be seen to be gradually displacing the "traditional" emphasis on temporal investment.

There are, however, clear economic advantages to using time as a standard of value, and these have important social consequences that make the ceremonial exchange market as "rational" as the meat market. Emphasis on the age of the animals killed, rather than on size or quantity, serves to space out the performance of the largest feasts, to put a brake on ritual inflation, and to control the competitive spiral of rival feasts held by near status equals. Pressures from wealthy impresarios on their poorer dependents are kept within bounds by the temporal standard, and the wealthy man must reciprocate *with interest* whenever he does receive contributions from his exchange partners.

These social factors would satisfy theorists of a generally utilitarian orientation, since they show how many apparently misguided traditional practices are in fact reasonable choices given local circumstances and constraints. But although they show how the system of temporal investment works (and reply to the superficial criticism of government officials who see it as merely "wasteful"), they do not explain why it can come into existence or how these standards of value work.

The recent literature on cultural exchange situates these problems in terms of the relations of gifts and commodities and the transformative power of money. The meat market and the exchange market could be considered separate spheres of exchange; that is, although some goods (especially buffalo and horses) change hands in both markets, they do so according to different rules. They are separate "value classes," in Kopytoff's (1986) terminology, which only roughly fit the more classical opposition of "gift" and "commodity" (Gregory 1982). The difference in rules corresponds not to varying degrees of "penetration" by an external economic standard, but to different cultural values linked to temporal differences.

This idea of temporal differences has been used by some analysts to refer to universal characteristics of exchange systems, but I argue that it must be given a specific local interpretation. Bloch and Parry (1989, 24) argue that two transactional orders exist in all societies, one "concerned with the reproduction of the long-term social or cosmic order" and the other "short-term transactions concerned with the arena of individual competition" (Bloch and Parry 1989, 24). Their explanation of how money is either opposed to or integrated into the morality of exchange in a variety of societies hinges on this temporal distinction. Spheres of exchange are defined to protect the long-term goals of the social order from being overly affected by adjustments due to gains or losses in the short-term arena.

Individual acquisition, then, is "consigned to a separate sphere which is ideologically articulated with, and subordinated to, a sphere of activity concerned with the cycle of long-term reproduction" (Bloch and Parry 1989, 26).

The separation of transactional cycles is endangered if grasping individuals divert the resources of long-term cycles for short-term transactions. The sale of livestock for cash to merchants who plan to export the animals would fall into this category, since the animals are removed from the local sphere entirely and the cycle of intergenerational renewal is broken. One standard of value, which operates on the basis of quality, subjects, and superiority, is displaced by another where quantity, objects, and equivalence are primary (Gregory 1982). It would be wrong to attribute these differences simply to the presence of money itself. The difference comes from moral evaluations that contrast the exchange of inalienable objects between interdependent transactors (the "gift economy") to the exchange of alienable objects between independent transactors (commodity exchange).

Time constitutes value in the traditional exchange economy because it marks the bond between the subject and his possessions and makes each possession more valuable because of its identification with its owner. The logical culmination of this identification is the complete inalienability of heirloom wealth. Along the scale from heirlooms down to trivial commodities, value is reckoned according to the time invested in an item's acquisition. Assertions that certain heirloom goods were presented to the founding ancestors are ways of lifting these goods "out of time" and making them absolutely inalienable. Assertions that any kind of object is completely replaceable, that it has no individual history acquired over time, in contrast, devalue it to the category of the commodity.

Bloch and Parry see a utilitarian approach as appropriate to the short-term cycle, but use a "moral" economy approach for longer-term transactions. I find the opposition of short-term schemers and long-term communitarians unconvincing. Bourdieu has shown that time and the tempo of exchanges constitute the exchange system in its most significant dimension. The gamelike aspect of exchanges, he noted, must be played out over time: "To abolish the interval is to abolish the strategy" (1990, 106). He does not carry the point even further, however, to say that an accumulation of intervals (of strategic delays and lapses in time) eventually makes up a new form of "objectified" value. The timing of exchanges, which participants experience as irreversible but observers may collapse into reversible cycles, is in fact the raw material from which exchange value is constructed.

Biographical Time, Intergenerational Time, and Social Reproduction

Instead of being two separate but related transaction orders, I argue that short- and long-term exchanges occur in interlocking cycles that influence ideas of convertibility. An heirloom gold valuable should not, and cannot, be exchanged for cash. A handful of rupiah bills could never, and will never, be reckoned into ceremonial exchanges between affines. But all along the long ladder that stretches between them, we find a relatively precise and accurate measuring of units of time invested, as represented by horns and tusks hanging on the wall. Thus, through exchange, reciprocal payments, and sacrifice, a system of value is established that is distinct from the commercial values of cash and commodity exchange.

From an actor's perspective, time has strategic value in that it can be cumulatively invested in gifts, which gives a generous household an advantage when debts are finally collected. This notion is relevant to the familiar debate about the "interest" that is added over time to the value of a gift. This interest is not simply a mystical quality inhering in the object, or a utilitarian quality figured in the same way as bank interest. Calculated in reference to individuals, rather, it measures the social value of the temporal intervals between the moments of giving and receiving. Time is measured not in years or months, but as it has been inscribed on human biographies—that is, as a "personal investment" reckoned in terms of a biological clock. The most direct expression of this form of time appears in the bodies of the sacrificial substitutes for persons—their livestock, whose own clocks are suspended over their ears.

Biographical time measures the forms of reciprocity that can be paid back over an individual's lifetime. It is inscribed within an intergenerational cycle, where the benefits of individual pursuit of renown are passed on to one's descendants. The reproduction of the group is a long-term goal, but one not necessarily at odds with the strategic manipulations of individuals. The *marapu* bestow blessings of fertility and prosperity so that their own names will be repeated in invocations and their own renown will be carried forth in time. The cult of the ancestors is also, in this sense, concerned with the future—but only as long as obligations to the past are recognized and the heritage of forebears is acknowledged.

Feasting in the ancestral villages promotes the reproduction of the collectivity through the leadership of an individual sponsor. Prayers request the continued fertility of both people and animals, offering animals for sacrifice as metonyms of their masters, small pieces of the greater human community. The politics of value in this situation concern not the "universal" opposition of long-term and short-term interests, but *locally specific* constructions of value, measured in time and in the relation of animals to human lives.

Time as Value Versus Time as Money

E. P. Thompson's famous discussion "Time, Work-Discipline, and Industrial Capitalism" shows how the historical transition to industrial society in the West involved a restructuring of working habits accompanied by a new "time sense," which changed inward apprehensions as much as external activities (1967, 57). Time in a great many non-Western societies is not something that can be wasted, used up, or saved; nonetheless, it remains a crucial social resource that is deployed in very specific, if variable, ways. In the West, the technological conditioning of the "time sense" and the introduction of time measurement as a means of labor exploitation interrupted a previous work rhythm structured by task orientation and in which bouts of intense labor had alternated with idleness. Thompson (1967, 70) argues that the first notions of compensation for labor time appeared in strategies for paying harvesters, with a "share of the harvest" made proportional to time invested: "Attention to time in labor depends in large degree upon the need for the synchronization of labor."

We saw in part one how a concern with the synchronization of agricultural activities was expressed in the symbolic domination of the Rato Nale, who holds the highest ritual office in the region because of his control of time. Here, however, we see how the early Dutch observers who preached industry and offered a moral critique of idleness were blind to a native construction of time as a source of value because it worked on a larger time scale than they were accustomed to using. Labor hours were not counted in traditional Sumbanese society, and proportional payments were more often pegged to social relationships (and the expectation of reciprocal returns) than to time investments. But although minutes and hours did not constitute a "currency," and were allowed to be "passed" rather than "spent," years and generations were, as units of *longue durée*, tied to the notion of value in a relatively rigorous fashion. Time was not commodified; rather, it was presented as a characteristic of prestigious wealth objects and a measurable attribute of sacrificial animals.

The limited impact of money on the traditional economy and its relative marginalization or "estrangement" (Versluys 1941, 435), which continues into the present, should cause us to reflect on the great difference between the two statements "time is money" and "time is value." Money, in Sumba, has become a unit for measuring things of significant but not substantial value. The price stated in coins, for example, replaced the somewhat casual measuring of rice and corn staples in petty trade. Value, by contrast, is always connected not only to an investment in time but also to a personal tie, a bond that has lasted through the years. Value accrues as time passes; "money," though, must become "capital" to display the same characteristics.

It is dangerous to translate concepts of economic value too readily into categories such as Bourdieu's famous "symbolic capital," which only obscure their continuing economic character. When traditional valuables are hoarded because they are believed to magically "attract" other wealth, they are a form of "capital" based on indigenous expectations of repayment, and their value is no more "symbolic" than that of a bank's assets. Thus, I do not argue that time results in the accumulation of "symbolic capital," but that it provides a way of measuring and storing values which are "economic" at the same time that they are "symbolic." Symbolism is not capital. It does not follow the same rules of accumulation, scarcity, or debt, and although it can only be shared according to cultural rules, these rules are so various that the concept is hardly of much use to demarcate a relation between the symbolic and economic realms.

Thompson (1967, 95) suggests that in the West the growing popularity of the axiom "Time is money" signaled a "restless urgency, that desire to consume time purposively" which was a heritage of Puritanism and has made leisure problematic. He traces this change partly to the erection of barriers between "work" and "life," and this provides a clue to the difference we have also observed in Kodi. "Time as value" concerns the values of life, not narrowly those of work, and this is where it is so different from "time is money." Lived time consists of sustaining personal and social relations over the years and of enriching those relations with the exchange of goods and services. In a famous passage about the lack of an expression for "time" in the Nuer language, Evans-Pritchard (1940, 103) argued that the Nuer are "fortunate" because they do not have the same feeling of fighting against time or of having to coordinate activities with an abstract passage of time: their points of reference are the activities themselves. This "blessed ignorance" does not mean they are ignorant of the consequences of the passage of time. Among the Nuer, as in Kodi, it would seem to be more the case that time is valued for its long-term processes, for notions of growth and development, which cannot be encapsulated into small units such as hours and minutes, but need to be reckoned in years, generations, and epochs.

8

Contested Time

The Feast in Dream Village

> Among the first groups of beings with whom men must have made contact were the spirits of the dead and the gods. They are in fact the real owners of the world's wealth. With them it was particularly necessary to exchange and particularly dangerous not to.
>
> Marcel Mauss, *The Gift*

> The play of time transforms ritualized exchange into a confrontation of strategies.
>
> Pierre Bourdieu, *Outline of a Theory of Practice*

The perception of "time as value" is inscribed on individual biographies and life cycles, not reckoned with the mechanical units of clocks, schedules, or timetables. To understand how this works, we must move from the level of general formulations to personal experience. In the next two chapters, therefore, I turn to fine-grained descriptions of individual events, where the shape and meaning of exchange transactions can be appreciated in all their specificity. This chapter explores people's attitudes toward time in the short-term frame of a single feast, where the timing of ritual stages becomes the subject of intense debate. Chapter 9 examines a funeral and divination, which encapsulate the longer frames of the human lifetime and the transition to the afterlife.

Both events were documented not only with notebooks and tape recorders, but also with film. The movie camera has the unique capacity to stop time, freeze it, and preserve it, arresting a process and setting aside a visual and audio record of what transpired. Many of the people who appear in this footage had never seen a film before, and had certainly never seen themselves on the screen. They agreed enthusiastically to allow our small film crew (myself, a camera woman, and a sound person) to shoot these events because they wanted to preserve them in "images that could be brought to life again" (*nggambaro pa mopiro*). At the time, neither we nor they perceived that "bringing images to life again" could be profoundly disruptive of the ritual process, raising issues of sequence and authority that closely paralleled those debated within the feast itself.

Feasting constructs its own particular form of temporality, which relates human lives to longer cycles of renewal through ideas of debt and obligation. Ancestors are promised feasts if they pass on gifts of fertile crops, healthy children, and exchange magic to their descendants. If the feasts are not held, the continuity between the generations is interrupted and more elaborate rituals are required to reestablish harmony. The feast we attended at Mangganipi ("Dream Village") combined efforts to recover the power of an ancestor's dream of wealth with a rite to legitimate newcomers to the village and pass on leadership in the feasting arena. Its most explosive moment occurred when the host yielded to pressures to alter the temporal sequence of events in order to please outside guests. The head priest flew into a rage and made a dramatic statement that he was the guardian of the order, which had been mandated by the invisible audience of spirits and could not be changed to suit the visible audience of human beings. Through his outburst we gain an insight into why so many debates about protocol and procedure focus on the politics of time. When we returned to the same village two years later to show the footage, we also learned how the filmic images we had recorded could be given a new interpretation after the passage of time.

Feasting and the Politics of Time

The importance of temporal sequences—their order, directionality, and the coding of relations between the human and spirit worlds—must be treated within the wider syntagmatic structure of feasts. As chains of events, words following actions, and actions that are later reinterpreted as words, these sequences define an etiquette of precedence, deference, and respect that focuses on the significance of the control of ritual time. Since control of time measures power over invisible forces, existing sequences may be challenged by those who seek to take over control. Even when stages occur in a rigidly prescribed order, their duration, pacing, and execution can be subject to strategic manipulations.

Ordered sequences, intervals, and chronological markers are central to the Kodi concept of ritual; indeed, it could be argued that control of time is *the* defining feature of ritual, here as in many other societies (Leach 1961). The Kodi equivalent of our term *rite*, used to designate a range of events from stone dragging and house building to feasting, is *katadi marapu*, translated as "the sequences required for the *marapu*" or "the stages relating to the *marapu*." It refers to the categories of action having to do with the sacred domain of invisible powers, and specifies that the *form* of these actions is prescribed and ordered in time. Since *katadi* carries

The head priest, Piro Pawali, invites the spirits of the dead to attend the feast in Mangganipi, while the host and other priests display their fierceness and determination in a war dance. 1986. Photograph by Laura Whitney.

with it a sense of ranked succession (the "stages" are usually enumerated from the simplest to the most complex), it involves a hierarchical element. Kodi rites are not simply idiosyncratic responses to misfortune, but part of sequences that have a cumulative weight and may extend achievements and obligations over several generations.

For a *woleko* feast in a garden hamlet, four "stages of the *marapu*" must be followed. On the first day, the spirits are invited (*palaru marapu*) and welcomed into the central circle of thatched houses. The next evening (*raka malo*), the history of misfortunes the village has suffered is recited, and angry spirits are begged to show mercy in exchange for modest offerings of "rice to eat and water to drink." On the third day (*raka lodo*), the final invocations are pronounced and buffalo are sacrificed. Then, four days later, a closing ceremony is held to send off the buffalo souls to the upperworld, bearing messages from the human community. Priests are hired by the host to investigate categories and hierarchies in the spirit world, mark off sacred spaces, and establish the rules and boundaries required to fulfill an obligation to the ancestors.

Disturbances of these sequences are also disturbances of cosmological order, and their consequences are serious. The challenge to the intervals established at the feast in Mangganipi shows how the "play of time" is implicated in local political struggles to define ritual authority.

Land Rights and a Dream of Wealth

Mangganipi, a name having the literal meaning of "dream," is an area inhabited by some three thousand people that has been designated a *desa*, or administrative ward, by local government officials. The feast that we describe occurred in the hamlet of Wyegha, one of the largest settlements in the area, but it concerned rights to land and fertility that go back to the time of Maha Laghora, the first ancestor to settle the area. Dreams for the Sumbanese are occasions to receive communications from the spirit world and are taken very seriously. Through dreams the spirit of a dead parent or ancestor may make a request to a living descendant, disclose special kinds of magical knowledge, or pass on skills in oratory, healing, and the acquisition of wealth.

Maha Laghora dreamed that he had an encounter with two wild spirits who lived in the forest that once covered the region: a small sparrow (*kogha*) and a long thin snake (*hugha*). As in all parts of Sumba (Adams 1979; G. Forth 1981), an encounter with a wild spirit signals access to a dangerous and illicit source of wealth and power. The wild spirit takes the form of a seductive woman, asking for gifts and sexual favors in return for the magical powers she controls. Maha Laghora established a contract with the wild snake and bird, offering them pigs and chickens at a secret location in the wild. In return he received the gift of "exchange magic" (*mangu marapu*—the power to ask for wealth and receive it on credit). Whenever he wanted to hold a feast, he could command others to come bringing gifts of pigs and buffalo that would be sacrificed in his name.

Maha Laghora lived around the turn of the century, in the period before the Dutch gained control of Sumba in 1914. At the time of my first field research in 1979 his son, Rehi Canggu Bola, was a respected elder living in the nearby settlement of Homba Karipit. He continued to meet the wild spirits that had helped his father, but he was not strong enough to resist their allure. Rehi Canggu Bola was seduced by the wild spirit woman he saw and entered into a "spirit marriage" (*ole marapu*) with the *kogha* bird. She put many restrictions on his behavior. For example, he had to live in a simple thatch-roofed house; when he tried to build a wooden house with a corrugated iron roof, it was destroyed by winds. She also forbade him from sponsoring any feasts under his own name; his sons could do so, but not him.

Throughout his life, Rehi Canggu Bola had liaisons with women who resembled the spirit apparition he saw in the forest, but he took only one official wife. Each of his mistresses (*ole ndaha*) had to be approved by his "spirit wife" (*ariwyei marapu*). She was also jealous of the ritual attention he gave to Inya Nale, the goddess of the new year. The wild spirit required that he sacrifice a small pig to her each year during the sea worm festivities, scattering betel nut in the forest (to parallel that scattered on the tombs of his ancestors) and roasting a chicken for her when they returned to the gardens. Whenever he was late or negligent in fulfilling her needs, the spirit wife made her human consort suffer a series of small illnesses. Rehi Canggu Bola had three sons, all of them wealthy and influential: one became head of the administrative ward (*kepala desa*), another ran a trade goods shop, a third had substantial herds of livestock. Yet it was always uncertain whether any of them had inherited his special relationship with the wild spirit.[1]

Four years after Rehi Canggu Bola's death his sons sponsored the feast I attended, in conjunction with another faction in the village. Members of three houses that had married into the village and built gardens there wanted to use this ritual effort to renew the fertility of the land and legitimate their claims of residence and group membership in the garden community. Although temporary rights to make a garden of rice or corn ("usufruct") are extended to sons-in-law after marriage, they do not acquire permanent rights until they have contributed to major feasts, receiving guests and offering them sacrificed pigs and buffalo. They may not plant long-term crops such as coconuts, betel palms, cloves, or fruit trees; rather, their status is always a bit like that of illegitimate children, "sitting on the edge of the veranda" (*tou la hupu katonga*) and not yet allowed into the central sacred portions of the house.

When the fathers of Ndengi Yingo and Pati Njahamene moved to Wyegha as young bridegrooms, they were given land as "the pig that will not get sick, the cloth that will not tear" (*wawi nja kapore, kamba nja madiryako*)—that is, as a substitute for the perishable gifts of pigs and cloth usually given by wife-givers. Muda Muda's feast to renew the power of Maha Laghora's dream provided an occasion for them to present the products of their labors (pigs and buffalo, rice and corn) and ask to be accepted as permanent inhabitants of this interior valley. Each wanted to offer a buffalo for sacrifice to the "Lord of the Land" (*Mori Cana*), the

---

[1] The spirit of wealth is not automatically passed down the patriline: each descendant must prove himself worthy of it and show the strength of spirit to control its demands. The wild spirit's intimate relationship with a human friend is described as "[close as] the two pockets of a betel pouch, [tense as] two feet on a climbing rope" (*ndepeto kaleku, hangato kalembe*)—a dangerous combination of intimacy and possibility of betrayal. For the person strong enough to control these magical powers, such a spirit can be a source of great wealth. But for someone who is not compatible (whose "body hair does not suit it"), such contact leads to exhaustion, emaciation, and premature death.

local spirit who watches over each garden settlement. If this sacrifice was accepted by the spirit, they would obtain equal standing with the founders of the settlement and equal inheritance rights.[2]

OPENING CEREMONIES: INVITING THE SPIRITS (*PALARU MARAPU*)

The priests who officiated at this garden feast included two prominent ritual specialists called in from the outside—the head priest, Piro Pawali, and the singer, Ra Kamburu ("Ra the Blind One"). An outside mediator is generally believed to be more effective in addressing the invisible audience of *marapu*, but since he knows little about the local history of misfortune, he must be guided by an orator and diviner who are familiar with the host and his family. The head orator and diviner at this feast, therefore, were both residents of the garden settlement; in addition, they were related as father and son. The son was training to be the eventual successor to his father and had to officiate at a feast on his home territory before he could perform in other settlements.

The rites began with a ritual demarcation of sacred space. The drum was placed in front of the tree planted in the center of the village square, representing the guardian spirit or Lord of the Land, who watches over communities in the gardens and reports back to the higher-ranking spirits in the ancestral village. The head priest and orator took eight large strides toward the drum, thereby defining the axis that would operate throughout the feast: a spatial opposition between the trunk of ancestral protection and the invasion of outside human voices and actors who assault it.

The spatial symbolism of the diagonal axis, traced first in one direction by the priests' steps and later in the other direction by their arrangement of the horns of sacrificed animals, lies in the meeting of different temporal forces. The priests approach the tree altar and recite prayers that reiterate the authority of the founder and the importance of stability: the garden altar must "stand firmly and sit soundly" (*ndende ndicako, londo mondongo*) at its present location, offering proof of the first rights to land established by Maha Laghora. The fierce war dances of young men who charge into the village square later appear as violent attacks on this authority, but the dancers will be finally incorporated into the traditional

---

[2]Of the ten houses standing in Wyegha, four were affiliated with the clan of Wei Yengo (including the house of Muda Muda, the host and sponsor), two were part of Bahewa (including the cosponsor's house across the central dancing ground), one was part of Malandi (the home of Ndengi Yingo and Radu Yingo, the father and son priests) and three were associated with Kere Homba (and its subdivision Hambali Atur). The names of the ancestral founders of each of these clans were recited in prayers to the *marapu* asking for their collective blessings.

land tenure system once "blood has been spilled and rice has been offered" in the feast. The founding group retains its ritual superiority even after others are granted full cultivation rights; the oldest house thus continues to receive the first fruits of each harvest at its altar.

Offerings of betel nut and fresh water were made to the drum before each sequence of ritual action. Sitting at the topside of the axis, the drum served as the crucial nonhuman intermediary as it was sent on a journey up through the seven layers of the heavens and six layers of earth (*pitu ndani cana, nomo ndani awango*) to the upperworld on the eighth level to ask for blessings (Hoskins 1988a). The eight paces taken by the priests counted the stages of their own earthly journey (in words and music), to be carried farther along an invisible vertical axis by the drum. Seven bundles of *sirih* leaves, one for each level of heaven, and four piles of betel nut were placed on top of the drum to open the four gateways into the spirit village. Then the drum was told to travel "like the butterfly sent off flying, like the bird sent off singing" (*kapudu pa pa lerango, kahilye pa ha puningo*) to its distant destination.

Invocations to the spirits began with the call to "listen with the ears, gaze with the eyes," as a small procession formed, beating drums and gongs to circle the settlement, traveling counterclockwise first to the eastern "upper gate" (the pathway back to the ancestral village) and then to the western "lower gate" (the pathway out to the fields and sea). The tracing of a circle suggested a protective metaphor of closure, in which the invisible powers were drawn in and centered on the altar tree and stones.

Dancing was initiated to "cleanse the central plaza" (*homba nataro*), and the singer began to chant the history of misfortune in the hamlet. In August 1964, a fire had destroyed all the houses and gardens, and the next year there was a horrible famine because all the rice and corn had been consumed by the flames. In 1986, a singing ceremony had been held to call back the souls of the houses of the settlement, but the curse would not be lifted until this promised feast was completed. The orators burst in with new contributions, completing the singer's story and adding more details so that the whole area could be purified of this humiliation, "washing off its body, rinsing its hair with coconut cream" (*pa ihyo ihi, kalapa longge*).

Dancers must be members of the houses sponsoring the feast. Outsiders are welcomed as spectators, but only those who contribute buffalo to the sacrifice can perform in elaborate traditional costume. Headcloths made of traditional barkcloth or store-bought fabric, usually orange or red (the colors associated with the Kodi region), are worn by both men and women. The men's cloth is tied in two peaks resembling horns. The women's is pleated at the center to make a flouncing crest, like that of a cockatoo. The dancers' movement in unison represents and enjoins a spirit of harmony and accord in which opposing forces are brought together and balanced in pursuit of a common goal, as expressed in the following verse:

The shining of the cockatoo's crest	Rere moto kaka
In the shade of the citrus tree	Ela maghu munde
The fan of the rooster's feathers	Bareyo wulu ghalio
On the stone foundations	Ela pombo watu
So the words will beat to the same beat	Tana paneghe hama tuku
So the speech will row to the same rhythm	Tana patera mera bohe

The drums and gongs continued to beat without interruption all night long, as human feet shuffled about on the dance ground and singers and orators exchanged verses of prayers. In the early hours of the dawn, all participants retired to sleep on the wide verandas, resting until the ceremonies began again that night.

EVENING OFFERINGS (*RAKA MALO*): REMEMBERING TIME PAST

The invocations spoken on the second night commanded the widest audience of human spectators and invisible spirits. A line of priests formed facing the garden altar, with the head priest in the center holding the divination spear. To his right was the feast's sponsor, to his left the co-sponsor, with the main orator at the right end of the line and the diviner at the left. Holding the spear high, the head priest began with a strong exhortation of unity, calling together "all the piglets of one sow, all the monkeys with one grandparent" to unite as descendants of a common ancestor. He reminded them of the many years that had passed since the feast was planned:

Remember the bark of the areca palm	Tana ape ba pa bandalo
Aged for the spirits	A kyomboko marapu
The tobacco has grown old	A mbaku la mandeiyo
The areca nuts have turned golden	Labba pa pa rara
The *sirih* leaves have matured	Rou uta pa ha madu
We are not simply amusing ourselves	Njama ghanggu lelu
We are not dancing out of joy	Njama mangguna ate
It is only because of all those who lay down and died	Di pimoka a danga mate la ndoba

Who passed away and disappeared	A heda la mbunga
That we lift our buttocks to move	Pa kede waingo kere
That we push our feet to step	Pa pangga waingo witti
Combing out our hair	Horo waingo longgena
Washing off our faces	Mbaha waingo matana
To bring our message to the spirits of our ancestors and forefathers	Tana dukingo a liyo ela ndewa ambu, ndewa nuhi

The years invested in planning the feast, aging the tobacco and drying the areca, were invoked to explain that this feast was no mere occasion of merrymaking, but the fulfillment of an ancestral promise. The long period of preparation demonstrated the collective commitment to its performance, shared by all the members of the hamlet.

His words were followed by many hours of dancing, which, after midnight, became raucous and uncontrollable. A few male dancers began to tremble violently, reeling out of formation and veering dangerously close to the spectators along the sidelines. One man fell into uncontrolled spasms, shaking his spear and shield in a threatening fashion at onlookers. A woman screamed, and others came in to restrain him and lead him away. He said that he had grown afraid, feeling "the breath of his ancestors" in the dark shadows of the crowd. The invisible spirits invited to attend a feast in fact do heighten dramatic tensions—hence the stringent requirements of ritual appropriateness. Participants are supposed to mime violent confrontations, rather than actually strike anyone. They do not lose control unless they disassociate and fall into trance. In this case, the physical conflict was immediately suppressed, but it magnified the sense of foreboding and spiritual uncertainty that prevailed at this stage of the proceedings.

Order was restored by the singer and orators, who conducted a dialogue of song and speech in which the story of their misfortunes was compiled. One speaker initiated the sequence, and was answered by another speaker, often his senior, who verified what he said and expanded on it. The singer then composed a consensus version of words taken from both speakers set to the rhythm of the drums and gongs to travel up to the upperworld:

So they will go up through	No bana na tongerongo
The seven levels of the heavens	Ha pitu ndani awango
And the six levels of the earth	Mono ha nomo ndani cana
Piercing all the way to the	No bana kobekongo
Home of Byokokoro guardian of the dam	Pandou Byokokoro kori lyoko

And Manjalur standing silently beside	Mono Manjalur nduka ndende
Where roofs are thatched with feathers	Na kawendengo wulu manu
Where racks are hung with pig's tusks	Na kandilengo ule wawi
And the smoke swirls darkly	Ola ngawuho kawendo
On the veranda darkened by fumes	Ola nggiringo katonga
Whose fire logs are pork fat	Na kahupungo lala wawi
Whose hearthstones are human heads	Na talurongo kataku toyo

These images of opulence and abundance combine deception and wish fulfillment. By praising the wealth of the invisible world, the orators and singer hope to convince the spirits not to make further demands on the living for sacrifices. The rhetoric of sumptuous consumption in the upperworld is opposed by the rhetoric of poverty and hardship used to speak of the living, for the object of creating these tensions and differences is to push the invisible ones to give more to their descendants and worshippers.

The head orator (*tou ka'okongo*) established the final list of *marapu* who would receive sacrifices the next day. His words were carried by the drum to the upperworld in the early hours of the dawn. As soon as the morning star appeared in the sky, a young calf was killed and its liver examined to see if the message had arrived safely. The signs were positive, so the priests could step down, curling up on the veranda to sleep for a few hours before the larger sacrifices of the next day.

It was as they wakened from this morning rest that the explosion between Piro Pawali, the head priest, and the host and singer occurred.

THE QUARREL ON THE FEAST DAY:
TIME QUESTIONED AND INTERVALS DEFIED

Certain important and wealthy guests were late in arriving on the third day, some of them still desperately trying to assemble impressive animals to contribute to the sacrifice, others attending Mass at the Catholic mission five miles away. The priests had finished their second night of oratory, establishing the agenda of misfortunes, and of the angry spirits who had caused them, and ranking them hierarchically to establish the order of sacrifices. All that remained before the sacrifices could begin was the ritual payment of the priests: token gifts of betel nut, cloth, a bush knife, and a small amount of cash to show that their exposition of the causes of the feast was complete.

The host did not want to proceed until he was sure that his guests, and the animals they would bring, were on their way. When messengers arrived to say that more time was needed, he tried to slow down the sequence of events. Pigs, speared that morning to feed the arriving guests, were being carved and cooked, their livers carried to the priests to make certain they contained no negative auguries. Although the head priest had asked for the mat to be set up for the final payment, the host slipped beside the gong stand to ask the singer to continue the relaxed singing and dancing of the early morning sequence for a bit longer.

Once the head priest heard about this request, he became furious. A roar of disapproval and rage echoed across the ceremonial field as he stood to protest: "How dare you do this to me?" he shouted. "You are trying to push me aside! *I* am the one to set the ritual order! *I* am the one who talks to the spirits and controls the timing!" He indignantly started to toss off the cloth he had been given when asked to serve as head priest. He protested that he had just spent the whole night directing oratory and singing, risking his own life, since an error in procedure is punishable with illness or death. Exhausted by his labors, he refused to surrender control or give in to shifts made to accommodate outside guests, especially Christian ones.

His thunderous outburst was ultimately successful: the host and singer, through their intermediaries, assured him they would proceed with the payment. Both of them knew that once it had been made there could be no more singing or dancing until the final invocations and dedication of the sacrificial animals. The head priest was in a position to enforce the temporal ordering he preferred: as the main intermediary with the invisible spirits, he set the stages that had to be followed. Refusing to bend to the host's concern to entertain his guests and soften the delay, he maintained a sharp separation between the rules set by the invisible ones and the social requirements of receiving human spectators.

In the midst of his rage, the head priest explained his reasons for insisting on the integrity of the sequence. The payment closes off the portion of the ceremony in which priests address the invisible ones to determine the reasons for their anger. Once it has been made, the priests' burden is lessened, and the dancing and dedication of the animals can proceed with little threat to their well-being. Before that moment, however, any ritual errors or variation in timing would be blamed on the priests as human intermediaries, and it would be the priest himself, instead of the animal victim, who would feel the full force of the spirits' disapproval.

Once he had thrashed out his differences with the host in such spectacular fashion, the priest sat down on the veranda and draped himself again in the folds of his ceremonial cloth. He had augmented his traditional costume—headcloth, indigo loin and shoulder pieces, and a bushknife at the waist—with a few fanciful Western garments. Now, wishing to show his full disdain for the insult to his authority, he took out his prize possession: a pair of thick dark glasses, which glowered with particular malevolence above a shiny plastic flight jacket. Hiding his rage behind this mask of modern cool, he retreated into silence on the sidelines.

The host's request had been made without thinking of the dialogue with invisible powers in which the priests were still suspended. He acted, rather, in consideration of the visible guests—his relatives, exchange partners, and superiors in the government—who were spectators at a social occasion. The clash as the priest saw it opposed the *marapu* to the human guests, the invisible audience to the visible one in the ritual performance; the timing of the events was the most important strategic resource that priests through their role as mediators were able to control.[3]

[3] The questioning of who decided the order and intervals of stages of the ritual was part of a larger questioning of the social and sacred dimensions of Kodi feasting, including who has the authority to decide how feasts should be run. My own presence as an ethnographer and filmmaker was one bone of contention in this process. Although I had visited Wyegha the day before the feast to ask the permission of the sponsor and his family to film the event, and had informed government authorities in Jakarta, the provincial capital of Waikabubak, and the district captial of Bondokodi, the head of the ward had not been at home when we passed on the way to the feast. When he heard that I and two others were already there with all our equipment, the ward head fell into a rage. "Don't you realize that I am the head of the government here?" he exclaimed. "Suharto is the head in Jakarta, but I am the Suharto of Mangganipi." He said if he had known we were taking film equipment into the village, he would have sent his own guards to watch over it and assure that it was not stolen. (Of course, he did not in fact do so, even after having staged this angry scene.)

An overheard exchange with the head priest revealed their differing attitudes. The ward head said to the priest: "They tried to steal your soul, old man. They hadn't reported to me yet." The older priest, who had been listening to his rage with some amusement, replied: "Nobody steals my soul because of you, younger brother. I report directly to the *marapu*, and we told them in our first prayers that we were being watched by the ducks from over the land, the geese from across the seas [*ndeha bali cana, bandu bali lyoro*—the couplet name for people from outside the island]." While the priest was perhaps equally suspicious of outsiders, he did not feel that he had to report to government authorities. His concern was the order of the spirit world. The interpretation he presented at this early encounter was later played out in the more public scene he staged to protest the host's waiting for human guests.

The head of Mangganipi was furious that he had been bypassed in the government hierarchy of authority and did not accept the invitation from the feast's sponsor as adequate recompense. The head priest was angry that his jurisdiction over ritual intervals and the timing of the feast was upset by the host's concern with pleasing powerful relatives (like the ward head) and government officials. Some of the priest's insistence regarding the sacred dimension was also a strategy for gaining attention from his human audience. But he did so with a purpose: to remind them that this ceremony had a fixed ritual sequence with invariant procedures; it was not simply an occasion for gathering people together to slaughter

After the head priest's outburst, the host and singer agreed to go ahead with the ritual payment of the priests. A pandanus mat was opened up in front of the rock and tree altar, the drum was placed at one end, and plates of betel nut were collected from each of the sponsoring houses, along with small amounts of money. The singer received several meters of blue cloth and a bush knife, the head priest and orators each got modest cash payments (equivalent to about $10), and offerings of betel nut and slivers of silver wrapped in *sirih* leaves were made to the spirit of the drum.

THE BUFFALO SACRIFICE

After the payment, several hours passed before the first processions of guests began to arrive. When messengers sent word that they were on their way, drums and gongs were beaten in the central field, and spectators gathered along the sidelines near the entrances to the settlement. A parade of male and female dancers, pigs carried on litters, and buffalo, their horns draped with orange cloth, marched into the main arena, with banners of fine textiles hung from poles above them. At the gates of the settlement, a dramatic confrontation occurred: the guests stamped their feet and shook their spears in a mimed attack, while their hosts rushed to greet them with equally vigorous dancing and waving of swords and spears. The "heat" of this meeting was then "cooled" with a gift of cloth, presented as the "shelter from the sun, protection from the rain" (*kada ngindi lyodo, kaluri tipu ura*). Betel nut, water, and cooked food followed, part of a sequence of gifts given by the hosts to subdue their guests, demonstrating the effectiveness of exchange to mediate conflict and provide social recognition for the sponsors.

Receiving guests, gossiping with them, and feeding each one a plate of rice and pork took several hours, and the final invocations and sacrifices did not get under way until about four in the afternoon. The head priest, rather exhausted after his morning rampage, stood again in the ceremonial formation, holding a spear and surrounded by his assistants and the sponsors. In a feeble voice, he called down all the spirits invited to share "rice to eat and water to drink" with the human guests, begging them humbly not to be disappointed in the meagerness of the fare offered to them.

Another confrontation occurred on the slaughter field, this time between the houses that had cooperated to host the feast. The sponsor led out his own buffalo to receive the consecratory offering of a raw egg (thrown onto its forehead at the spot where the life force [*hamaghu*] is

---

animals and share meat. The forcefulness of his insistence emphasized his role as mediator between *marapu* and people and as guardian of temporal intervals.

attached); meanwhile, though, two other buffalo were surreptitiously led out from the corrals of his neighbors and similarly consecrated. This caused immediate confusion, since the egg is traditionally given only to the sponsor's buffalo, the "highest nose" (*iru deta*), who is sent as a messenger to the Lord of the Land, guardian of the hamlet.

One visitor, a priest from Watu Pakadu, objected when he saw two other buffalo being led into the arena before the sponsor's buffalo had been dispatched. "What are these other buffalo doing here?" he asked crossly. "Leave space for the highest nose to go first!"

Ndengi Yingo, the orator from the Malandi faction within the settlement, answered him sharply: "Each clan is killing its own buffalo for the Lord of the Land." He glanced quickly toward the sponsor for confirmation. The latter nodded; the solution had been agreed on to resolve questions of land tenure in the settlement and grant permanent status to a sponsor's wife-takers. But the visitor stormed out, saying, "None of these sequences is being respected here."

Immediately after the sacrificer's knife had cut the carotid of the sponsor's buffalo (representing the descendants of Wei Yengo), the large one to his right, brought by the Malandi faction, was struck, and then the buffalo of the clan of the cosponsor, Bahewa. Each died relatively quickly, an auspicious sign that the Lord of the Land accepted this triple slaughter and would not resist further efforts by members of the latecomer clans to gain full ceremonial and proprietary rights over the land.

Twenty-one more buffalo were slaughtered in the next hour, in an increasingly elaborate, gory, and violent display of human power over animals. A second big buffalo from Bahewa was the one killed to "close the gate" (*ghobo todi binye*) and end the sacrificial sequences. The last animals killed resisted most intensely, stabbing the ground with their horns, bolting halfway out of the central arena, spraying onlookers with blood. But finally all were brought under control, and after examining the livers with some care the ritual specialists pronounced it a successful slaughter: the Lord of the Land had accepted the offerings, although a few ancestors in the cosponsor's group were reluctant to agree to the merger.

Members of the sponsoring houses dragged the carcasses from the central arena, butchering the meat so it could be distributed. Coconut fronds were arranged to form a smooth green surface to catch the blood, and shares of the finest sections (the hind quarters and sides) were cut to present to the priests. Government officials and prestigious guests received the second shares, then a complex reckoning began of all the people in attendance and the relative "meat debts" that were owed to each. A man who contributed a live buffalo or pig had to receive a large portion of meat, but the share might be even larger than he deserved if the host anticipated having to count on his generosity again. From the size of the meat shares handed out, the social "credit rating" of each participant at the feast could be assessed. The soft, bleeding bundle of accumulated prestige was carried home by each participant to show how his fellows had ranked him.

The head priest, Piro Pawali, watched the meat distribution from a distance, occasionally wandering through the field to make sure the choicest cuts were being set aside for him. He still seemed disgruntled, but he would be able to redistribute a generous share of raw meat to his family when he returned. Placing the dark sunglasses on his nose again and gazing out mysteriously at those who still hurried to finish their work of carving up the bodies before darkness fell, he again withdrew. He in fact refused to attend the final ceremony four days later to send off the buffalo souls to the upperworld, pleading illness and injury. Some speculated that it was his pride that had suffered the greatest injury.

Sequences and Simultaneity: Prayer Versus Sacrifice

Much of the tension and disagreement in this feast came from the head priest's emphasis on sequence (expressing notions of rank, precedence, and genealogy), which was opposed by other participants' stress on simultaneity. The alternation throughout the ceremony of oratory and dancing underscored this contrast, at times bringing forth a recitation of a chain of ancestors, events, and places, at others blending them together in assertions of everyone "beating to the same beat, rowing to the same rhythm."

The most important dramatic focus came in the delicate resolution of the buffalo sacrifice. The sponsor's house was from Wei Yengo, the founding clan of the settlement, the only one with established rights to sacrifice to the Lord of the Land at the tree altar. The head priest's verbal consecration mentioned the Lord of the Land once, dedicating the first sacrifice to him with conventional entreaties that he receive the offering, meager as it was, because the villagers were still poor. The political maneuvering to offer three animals instead of one was not hinted at in the oral rites.

When three buffalo were led into the central arena, a visual statement of simultaneity was being made: members of the clans of Malandi and Bahewa were asserting that they had cooperated fully in sponsoring the feast, so they should also receive ritual recognition and the right to offer sacrifices to the garden deity. The assertion was made in acts, rather than words, so that once the buffalo blood had been spilled and the animals' livers examined, the guardian spirit himself could be said to have given his consent. Through this simultaneous offering, claims were made to a more permanent relationship to the land, with the other coresident clans trying to establish their own legitimacy and authority to sponsor future feasts. By not so much stating their equality with Wei Yengo as displaying it, they attempted to circumvent complicated hierarchies of temporal precedence and present a request in flesh and blood (in the most literal sense of a sacrificial gift) instead of metaphoric speech.

This apparently audacious act succeeded only because the sponsor had already agreed to it and was willing to surrender much of his leadership to the other residents of the hamlet who helped him fulfill an obligation to his dead father. Animals cannot, however, be sacrificed simultaneously. Even when the arena is crowded with wounded and dying beasts, they are brought there in a strict order, and this same order will be followed in arranging the horns for display on the spirit ladder and mounting them inside the cult house. In the end, then, an assertion of simultaneity had to defer to an acceptance of precedence, though the common dedication to the hamlet spirit deity assured that the most important intentions of the cosponsoring clans were realized.

The sequential and simultaneous dimensions of feasting coexist with a hierarchical dimension, which encompasses variation between one performance and another into a structure of relative invariance. The head priest insisted on, and was granted, control of the crucial sacred stages: the oratory at early dawn when the message sent by human speakers reaches the upperworld, and the reading of the response of the spirits in the bodies of sacrificial animals. He chose to exercise his authority to keep these acts uncontaminated by the political compromises of shifting land rights and exchange obligations. While his fiery display of temper forestalled a modification of temporal sequences for the benefit of absent guests, he nevertheless agreed to allow the first sacrifice to proceed in a rather unconventional manner. Adjustments to fit contingent circumstances were possible once adherence to the wider sequence was clear.

The head priest permitted the feast to finish after his sense of outrage had cooled, but he would not lend his authority to oversee the closing ceremonies. At this stage, the father and son orators from Malandi, insiders who had legitimated their land claims on the sacrificial field, stepped in to recapture the integrity of the temporal sequences and establish closure by assuring the safe departure of the souls of sacrificed buffalo. Rules of sequencing and precedence were meticulously observed, eclipsing the earlier dispute by assertions of a shared consensus that had already achieved the approval of the spiritual Lord of the Land.

Regaining Time in the Upperworld:
Sending Off the Animal Souls

The closing ceremonies are conducted to remove impurities from the field of slaughter and guide the souls of the pigs and buffalo sacrificed to the upperworld. As with a human death, the transition from the world of the living is not an abrupt one but a gradual detachment. For four days after the slaughter, the souls of the dead animals remain inside the village; they must then be reminded of why they have died and led carefully out the gate to take their message to the upperworld. Since Piro Pawali refused to attend this ceremony, his place as head priest and leader of invocations was taken by Ndengi Yingo. Members of the fifteen houses who participated in the feast gathered with the priests for this relatively intimate rite assuring the animal souls of a safe passage.

Buffalo horns were carefully mounted, in the order in which they had been sacrificed, on a pole erected beside the garden altar: the sponsor's buffalo, or "highest nose," was at the top, the others below, and pig's jawbones and tusks were hung horizontally on a bar across the middle. The younger diviner started the evening oratory, reminding everyone of the stages leading up to this final one:

Some time ago	Hei wa nene
We planted the gong stand	A wolo bandikya kadanga langa tala
Offering [meat] scorched and roasted	Mono ngara ha tunu ha manaho
Some time ago	Hei wa nene
We erected the post for the drum	A rawi bandikya katuku ndende bendu
Distributing tobacco and areca nut	Mono ngara ha mbaku ha labba
The horns of the buffalo	Ha kadu kari
Wait yawning by the gates	Na pondako hangango
The jaws of the pigs	Ha nengo wawi
Pull impatiently on loincloths	Na kalambo habba huala
They haven't yet reached the corral	Njana toma pango a nggallu maliti
They haven't yet entered the fence	Njana duki pyango a nggallu kadoki
Erected by our Mother Binder and Father Creator	Hola wolo inya, hole dari byapa

His father followed, carefully going over the reasons for the feast and asking the animal souls to travel to the heavenly corral with the message of poverty and suffering tightly secured to their heads:

Bind it like barkcloth to your horns	Pa kapotongo la talo kadu
Secure it soundly on the forehead	Pa kalepango la talo togho
Don't let it slip from the waistband	Ambu waingo pa taloki lali biluna
Don't let it fall from the armpit	Ambu waingo pa bughe wei halilina
Place it at the horse's withers	Tana tahi la kadenga ndara na
Hold it in the back of the canoe	Tana tahi la kamudi cena na
Carry it like stones on the shoulder	Pa pa holongo rabba watu
Lift it like land on the neck	Pa pa lembango lemba tanango

When the morning star appeared, a crashing noise was heard, and the "tree" of horns and jawbones trembled with the impact. This was interpreted as a sign that the message had arrived safely and the soul of the burned village had returned to earth. Leaves that had been scattered on the slaughter ground, soaked with blood, chyme, and excrement, were swept into the center of the village and burned.

The horns of the sacrificed buffalo were removed from the tree and arranged on the ground, repeating the order of sacrifice along the axis moving from the garden altar to the base of the field and forming a horizontal "ladder" to replace the vertical one just dismantled. "Our words travel up along the tree of horns to the spirits," the diviner explained, "but the buffalo souls themselves must walk along the land to the village of the dead [*parona marapu*], where we will eventually travel to meet them ourselves."

Fifteen plates of cooked rice and betel nut were placed in front of the line of horns, one for each house, and offerings of rice, betel, and slivers of silver wrapped in *sirih* were made to the drum, gongs, and gong stand. The drums were lifted up and carried out of the village in a procession that reversed the steps followed in the opening ceremonies: they left by the western gate and circled clockwise to the east, resealing the boundaries of the human settlement. Outside the village, a small sacrifice of water, a few balls of cooked rice, and a broken egg was left for the spirits of the wild, to bid them farewell after attending the feast.

The procession returned to the village to the beat of the drums and gongs, this time entering from the east, and sat down on mats in front of the Lord of the Land. The priests and sponsors ate the tongues, lips, and brains of the buffalo. Since their message had arrived safely, the animals were no longer needed as intermediaries; now their vocal organs could be reabsorbed by the human spokesmen. Discussion then turned to the future, and the cosponsor repeated his intention to carry out another feast in two years if prosperity continued and the harvests were good.

Redundancy, Rhetoric, and Innovation

In describing the sequences of this garden feast, I quoted only short passages for reasons of clarity and brevity. An important characteristic of ritual sequences, however, is the high degree of redundancy within and between the four stages of oratory and sacrifice. The "ritual agenda" given on the first day when the spirits are invited is repeated, with only minor variations, on the second and third days, and again at the closing ceremonies.

Each night of oratory opens with a general call to attention and an invocation of the spirits most directly concerned. The local Lord of the Land (*Mori Cana*) must be invoked first, followed by the ancestors of the various clans whose descendants are concerned. As the reasons for the feast are given, the findings of the divination are reiterated, and orators from both within and outside the sponsoring houses summarize the ritual agenda from their own perspective. The many repetitions create a contrastive background against which apparently minor variations become significant. The order in which afflicting spirits are cited constructs a hierarchy of the misfortunes suffered, a hierarchy later mimicked in the order of sacrifices.

A great deal of oratorical energy is spent on exhortations of unity in a deliberate effort to cover over differences between speakers. The alteration of oratory with song diffuses differences that may retrospectively be treated as incidental or unimportant. A rhythmic interlude generated by the small orchestra of drums and gongs follows each speech, giving the singer a few moments to compose a compromise version for the listening spirits. His task is formally defined as repeating the words of the orators, setting them in shorter lines so that they can be sung. Since he can repeat only a selection of what has been said, he must make choices. The singer must be a diplomat, reconciling competing versions through omission and tactful ellipses, struggling to satisfy the listening orators that he has not ignored their contributions.

At Wyegha, the singer walked a difficult line separating the sponsor of the feast, who used the head priest's oratory to present the reasons for the feast in view of his own genealogical duties, and the orators, more recent residents who wanted the history of their own moves and gardens to be heard in the invocations. Although the singer repeated the couplet names of their clans, he did not present their litany of hardships to the Lord of the Land for resolution. This unusual approach foreshadowed the joint sacrifice to the Lord of the Land, with the sponsor's buffalo being slaughtered first, followed immediately by the other two.

Repetitions may mask complex accommodations and adjustments. Each of the ritual specialists participating was aware that at least the illusion of unity had to be maintained, despite tensions among various parties, to assure persuasive symbolic power. Their commitment to keeping up a front of consensus meant that outbursts like Piro Pawali's occurred "off-stage," in direct negotiations with each other or the host, but not in speaking to the spirits or the wider human audience.

Redundancy can serve both as a mask and as a magnifier. For laymen, spectators with no direct interest in the content of the oratory and little knowledge of the events recounted, the repetition of each sequence of oratory in song is simply part of the rhythm of the feast. For the insider—the other orators, members of the sponsoring house, or rival parties—repetitions with slight changes focus attention on points of contention, with restatements required until an acceptable compromise is reached. The lengthiest discussions (all highly formalized and indirect) are not empty rhetoric: the issue at stake may be only alluded to in ritual speech, but it is of crucial importance to those concerned.

Reflections After the Fact: Comments on the Film

Two years after these events, we returned to the Mangganipi area to show the edited version of this feast on film and interview participants and spectators once again. Great interest was shown in all the stages, but particularly those involving Piro Pawali because he had died just a week before our arrival. When noisy children obscured part of his oratory, they were severely admonished: "Don't you realize who is talking now? This man has just died. Be silent for the dead!"

People who watched the film were disconcerted by seeing Piro Pawali's face so soon after his death. Some laughed nervously, others sat in stunned silence. The reasons for this reaction surfaced when we talked to participants after the screening. "It is good that you came to bring his image back to life at this time," the feast's host told us. "Now we understand better what he was fighting against," Ndengi Yingo said. "We have seen the consequences." He went on to explain that the undermining of ritual sequences and priestly authority that Piro Pawali had raged about in 1986 must eventually have been responsible for his illness and death. "People do not have enough respect for the *marapu* now, especially the younger generation. He shows us how dangerous that is, and now that he has joined the *marapu*, he will be certain to make the rest of us feel it as well." The film was held up as a moral lesson to show young people the dangers of disturbing ritual time.

The diverse responses among spectators at the screening revealed how hotly contested these points still were. When some young boys giggled at the most fiery outburst, others turned to quiet them with great rage. The visual record of a clash of strong personalities was used to debate whether the priest had suffered because he was fighting the right cause or defending the wrong one. A prominent Catholic noted that "all the old priests are dying now," but commented approvingly on the old man's show of spirit and vigor in these exchanges.

The mood was one of mourning for an accomplished older man, whose skill in speaking and splendid performances would be greatly missed. "Even if we do not pray to the *marapu*, we worry that the feasts are not held properly anymore," one young educated man added. "We will try to learn from his words, which you have brought back from the tomb to allow us to hear."

When All Is Said and Done: Visual and Verbal Elements

The repetition of couplet sequences, place names, the names of spirits, and stages of preparation is paralleled by similar repetitions in other sensory modes: dances that are reenacted on the ceremonial field, always by the same group of women; musical refrains that follow the oratory and gather it up into song. The "message" expressed in these nonverbal channels is a simpler one than the subtle and nuanced manipulations of verbal images. Unity is asserted and acted out in an effort at persuasion and common movement, which usually wins over divisiveness and brings the participants back to their central concern: the fulfillment of ceremonial obligation.

The Kodi distinguish the verbal statements made by priests, which are the "trunk" or "core" (*pungena*) of the rite's meaning, from the visual display (the "song and dance," *ore mono nenggo*, although the term's reference includes also gesture, exchange prestations, and sacrifice). The formal goals of the rite are achieved when the drum-messenger returns with a positive response from the upperworld. The human community may be more concerned with the visual show, especially with political struggles over the order of sacrifice and division of meat, as were so important in this example.

The communicative structure of Kodi feasts creates a division of verbal and visual modes that allows strict verbal sequences to coexist with complicated strategies associated with the timing and arrangement of prestige displays. Much of the indirectness of formal speech operates as a face-saving device, allowing requests to be negotiated without direct confrontations or refusals. Whenever the spirits are addressed, a humble language is used that underplays the display element of prestige feasts and presents them as motivated only by hardship. Using Stanley Tambiah's (1979) vocabulary, the Kodi use of visual elements is *indexical*, in that it serves to validate the rank and prestige of the actors, while the use of verbal elements is *explanatory*, for it relates the ceremony to the wider belief system and a whole web of other meanings. The formal goals of feasts are to explain human misfortune and effect a reconciliation with the spirits involved. Informal goals of the staging and scale of ritual performances, however, may embrace other concerns. By establishing permanent rights to the land at Wyegha, the cosponsors of the feast were also laying the groundwork to sponsor new feasts and thus enhance their own status and renown.

The double-layered quality of Kodi ritual communication is related to its temporality, involving as it does a contrast between short-term and long-term goals. The immediate goal of the Wyegha feast was to open the way to Pati Njahamene and his family to lead at future events. The longer-term goal, which was linked to the first, was to restore the dream of wealth and fertility of Maha Laghora, and to use the fruits of future harvests to expand the community and its ceremonial activities.

The verbal and visual aspects of ritual performance have surfaced in debates about "structuralist" or "dramatistic" approaches to ritual analysis. James Fox's (1979a, 147) articulation of this difference reminds us of its semiotic base:

> The two approaches in anthropology that have recently developed to deal with the varying forms of symbolic behavior tend to rely on the analysis of different sign systems. The structural approach, dominated by linguistic analogies, focuses on the logical combinations and cognitive manipulation of definably discrete units; the "dramatistic" approach examines the sequencing of human actions, physical gesture and the theatric display of objects, all endowed with emotional as well as intellectual significance. . . . The choice of one of these approaches reflects more than the personal preferences of individual investigators. . . . It reflects the different modalities of the rituals in different cultures.

Rituals that emphasize "acts of oration," which keep local tradition alive in oral memory, predominate in some areas of Eastern Indonesia, like Roti, where widespread conversions have discouraged ritual performances. On Savu, by contrast, rites emphasize "acts of ostention"—dramatic displays of force or unity that are often carried out wordlessly (Fox 1979a, 148–50).

Kodi feasts combine both elements. The formal sequence is primarily a ritual of oration, while private strategies are more often expressed in acts of display or outrage, which occur—like the priest's outburst and the simultaneous buffalo sacrifice—off the official "stage." To a certain extent, the two modalities serve different ends. Whereas the verbal portion of each rite stresses unity, humility, and self-deprecation, the visual portion is a forum for competitive, often splendid displays of self-aggrandizement. The two messages may seem contradictory, but the apparent contradiction is softened by the fact that they are often directed to different audiences: the listening spirits are addressed with words, while the watching human spectators are impressed with actions. Because the words are at least formally more important than the actions, the hierarchy of messages avoids confusion at any given level. As we shall see in the next chapter, a strict division between rites conducted in speech and those performed in actions is also characteristic of death rituals, though here the separation is linked to separate exchange paths.

9

Death and the End of Time

Final Exchanges

This is the day that the hands separate
And the feet step apart
One of us going off to dig the gardens and weed the grass
The other to rest in the tombs in a row, the graves in a line

From a Kodi death song

Death represents the end of one strand of time, the time that an individual spends on this earth, and the adjustment of several other strands, which have become entangled in the time span of personal biography. A funeral provides a final accounting of temporal relationships and a reckoning of exchange obligations. It is the occasion on which the different temporal values of affinal and agnatic ties are made visible. Affinal ties stretch horizontally through Kodi society, binding a man to his wife-givers and his mother's village of birth. The affines are the "givers of life" and remain able to bestow health, fertility, and descendants on their wife-takers. At death, conflicts with them must be resolved so the pollution of the corpse can be removed from the village and the soul can be reclaimed by the patriline. Agnatic ties, in contrast, are traced vertically, up and down the time line of descent. They endure even after the dissolution of the physical body and may be expressed as promises or infractions from the past carried forward onto future generations.

Death rites require a final separation of affinal and agnatic ties, as the deceased is separated from the living and incorporated into the community of the *marapu*. At the funeral, the authority of the dead person is reclaimed and redistributed by his or her descendants. Silent exchanges with affines and extended verbal negotiations with agnates mark the contrast in temporal modes: the ties of affinity are vital but perishable, while those of agnation are frozen but enduring. A married woman's funeral is held in her husband's village, the final act in the exchange drama that brought her there. A man's funeral is held in his own ancestral home and can reach far into his past. As the dead man takes leave of his family and their affairs are put in order, his descendants must journey back through the generations to understand the reasons for his death. The mystery is probed, suspects are interrogated, and when the angry spirits are found they are placated with gifts and promises. The living bargain with their own ancestors for a bit more time to fulfill their obligations, asking for the blessings of health and long life to hold the promised rituals. Their solutions are personal, not philosophical, but they reveal the private strategies that unravel around predetermined sequences. The predetermined sequence of a funeral must encompass the idiosyncrasies of an individual biography. In studying a single funeral, we see how at times these sequences may themselves be changed, or reabsorbed, into longer-term phases of the life cycles of houses, villages, and clans.

The process begins with the separation of death and the efforts to interpret its meaning for the living.

Mortality as a Break in Time

The news of Ra Honggoro's death broke just as the mounted ritualized combat of the *pasola* finished. Throngs of elaborately costumed riders, their heads bound with red and orange cloth, their horses decorated with bells and streamers, rode back from the grassy field near the beach along the line of ancestral villages. As they passed in front of Malandi, the taunts of greeting and shouted replies mixed with wails of mourning, and even casual passersby realized what the news must be.

Ra Honggoro was a wealthy and prominent man, who had already dragged a large megalith for his own grave and placed it along the path that the riders and spectators would follow as they returned from the *pasola*. Three years before, he had sponsored a large feast to consecrate the stone, and hundreds of pigs and several dozen buffalo were sacrificed. In recent months, realizing his illness was serious, he had left behind his garden hamlet and the wide pasturelands where his herd of over a hundred animals grazed to return to Malandi. Moving into the lineage house he had built at another feast some eight years before, he lived close to the graves of his own father and grandfather with his second wife and the three youngest of eleven children. When relatives came to scatter betel on the tombs of their ancestors, he was already too weak to get up to receive them, and the chickens roasted in the morning to read the portents of the new year bore red flecks of danger on their entrails.

He had been a vigorous, powerfully built man who did not surrender easily to fatigue or adversity. When he sponsored his first major feast in the gardens, he had chosen a name for his horse and dog that epitomized the destiny he wanted to fulfill:[1] His horse was Ndara Njamagha'a, "the horse that is never satisified," and his dog Bangga Njamanukona, "the dog that shows no reluctance." He saw himself as a fighter, a man who had built up his own fortune and pursued his goals with energy and persistence. The tenacity with which he amassed his wealth had lasted through several major illnesses. But finally, at the age of about fifty, he succumbed to gout and kidney failure, just as others were celebrating the rite of regional renewal.

His widow and daughters were the first to shed tears over his body and stroke it with their hands. The dirges they sang were full of bitter accusations, for Ra Honggoro's death betrayed the very qualities he had identified as his own. "How could you leave us like this, father," wailed his oldest daughter, "you as proud as a noble parrot, you as strong as the lordly cockatoo? How could you go off on your own journey when we are left alone without you?" "What made you slip this time, what caused you to fall into the trap?" his widow wailed, "when so many times you came back to us, when so often your strength returned?"

Women monopolized the early stages of mourning, clustering around the corpse as it lay on the front veranda, at the point marked for transitions inside and outside the house. They reproached the dead man, accusing him of callousness, of a selfish separation from those who loved him, of disregarding their needs and their dependency on him. Through "the flowing of mucus and the shedding of tears," the living exorcise their feelings of loneliness and betrayal, performing a public drama of hysterical grief and sorrow.

The elaborate display of emotion was directed more to the human audience of funeral guests than to the invisible one of the spirits. The dead man himself never hears these reproaches; his soul sits with the family on the veranda and shares its meals, but remains unconscious until four days after he has been buried. Only then are the lines of communication between the dead and the living reopened, but on different terms, for now the unconscious ghost wakes to discover he has been remade as an ancestor.

---

[1] All prominent Kodi men (as well as some women) have horse and dog names, which can be used in polite speech to signify their renown. Some of these names are inherited, usually from a famous grandfather. Others can be chosen by the individual in question to stress a part of his own biography—his achievements or hardships encountered. Hoskins 1989a discusses the horse and dog names of one prominent Sumbanese man and several of his wives.

Ra Honggoro's body is attended by his mother, seated in the upper left of the picture, with her hair loosened in mourning, while his widow and daughters, to the right, caress the shroud and sing of their anger and despair. 1988. Photograph by Laura Whitney.

Visible and Invisible Participants

The movement a person makes from sharing the lives of the living to becoming part of the invisible community of the *marapu* defines the particular intimacy and ambivalence that characterizes relations with spirits of the dead. Other invisible beings—the *marapu* who guard the house and village; the spirits of wealth objects, fertility, or garden crops—are addressed and propitiated in Kodi rites, but they have never "crossed over" from the human side and do not have human shapes, personalities, or characteristics. The spirits of the dead, however, retain many human attributes and are nostalgic and jealous of the time when they lived among their descendants. They constantly strive to converse with the living, to reestablish a casual give-and-take in conversation, to return to the reciprocity and equality they enjoyed in their lifetimes. Communications with the dead oscillate between efforts to achieve contact on the basis of common experience and substance, on the one hand, and efforts to keep them at a distance, on the other. The residues of personal memory are plumbed and exhausted in the work of mourning, to achieve a new control over communication with the dead, channeling it away from personal contact into the formal interchange of blessings and obedience to ancestral law. The envy and resentment the dead feel because of their exile from the world of the living has to be transformed into passive resignation, a willingness to serve as an arbiter of tradition rather than a personal advocate.

The spirits of the dead suffer feelings of estrangement, a yearning for renewed closeness with their families. When they try to move closer, the rituals of death send them away: The dead person is moved from the category of one who speaks as a kinsman, a person with individual attachments and loyalties, to one who acts as an ancestor, the detached voice of collective law, who protects and sustains his descendants with impartial wisdom.

Ra Honggoro's funeral displayed the two processes that operate to turn the conversation mode (appropriate to relations with the living) into a mode of ritual exchange (appropriate to relations between the living and dead). The first process, entrusted to affines (relatives from the dead man's village of origin), concentrated on *separating* the physical substances of the living and dead, by removing the pollution of death that had settled on the house where the corpse lay in state. The second, entrusted to his agnates, was achieved through sacrifices, oratory, and divination. It brought about the *transformation* of the dead person into a *marapu*, by summoning the invisible community of ancestral spirits and discovering the cause of his death.

Both processes are concerned with exorcising dangers associated with death, but whereas the first deals with dangers arising from earlier closeness and identification with the dead man, the second identifies the dead man in a collective, legal sense as a member of a specific lineage and the inheritor of debts and obligations. The pollution removed by the affines is the pollution generated by the conflicting web of affinal relations, which bound Ra Honggoro to Bondo Maliti, the village of his mother's birth and the "source of his own life" in Kodi exchange theory. Death and funeral exchanges are the last act in a long affinal drama begun when his mother first married into Malandi. Livestock and gold were presented to her parents to secure the right to claim children as members of the Malandi ancestral community. The wife-givers communicated their assent at that time with gifts of pigs and cloth. Half a century later, they now come to receive the heads of sacrificial animals, the final gift that marks the end of the cycle. Once this last debt has been paid, they renounce any further claims on the soul of the dead man, and he can be fully integrated into the village of his patrilineal ancestors.

The two parts of the process thus end the obligations of affinity even as they reassert the enduring ties of agnation, reconstituting the dead person as an ancestor. The living are bound by many complex and ambiguous exchange ties. In the ceremonies of death, some of these binding ties are loosened, while the force of others is made more salient. As the corpse itself decomposes for the three or four days that it lies on the veranda, the person, too, is decomposed into different kinds of constitutive relationships. Some are sloughed off as the flesh separates from the bones; others are preserved as enduring and permanent parts of his name and reputation.

Affinity and agnation are contrasted as vitality and immortality, perishable and imperishable, silence and speech. Wife-givers present gifts of cooked meat, cloth, and rice in the inarticulate expression of grief, shared substance, and loss. Lineage descendants and wife-takers bring live animals, gold, and money, gifts to help in reconstituting the house and its members. Once the exchanges are completed, the affines return home, but the agnates remain gathered in the house to investigate the causes of the person's death. The divination is framed as an interrogation of the past. Several generations of family history are combed through as the participants search for sources of disagreement or neglect of ceremonial obligations, discovering points of weakness within the lineage. Working at first from ignorance, gradually supplemented by testimony from the audience of family and relatives, the diviner spins elaborate verbal nets of possibility and speculation, hoping to catch the killer in these nets and confirm the result with spear and chicken divination.

Affinal exchanges involving food and the personal effects of the dead disarticulate and dissolve the dead man's earlier unity, his physical body, into separate parts. Agnatic negotiations with the spirits, in contrast, articulate and construct a shared version of collective history. This interpretation, distilled from memories scattered through many individual minds, is then linked to a future plan of action. Death is the end of one kind of time, that of a person's vital involvement in ongoing exchange, but the beginning of another, that embracing the collective traditions of the lineage. The diviner and his audience gradually shift from speaking to a husband, father, or brother and begin a ritually mediated interchange with a *marapu*. The personal life history is revised to become part of the *li marapu*, the ancestral invocation that binds the collectivity to its past.

Making Peace with the Wife-Givers

The death of an important man immediately mobilizes his network of affinal relatives as messengers are sent out to announce the event to all those who must bring contributions to the funeral. In the case of Ra

Honggoro, his wife and mother quickly began to bathe the body, binding his knees close against the torso, folding the hands on the chest, and resting him on the right side as a sign that his death was a peaceful one. At the same time, his sons and brothers rode off to summon parties of mourners, who converged on Malandi bearing fine textiles for the many-layered shroud. All those who had given wives to Malandi brought pigs, for a total of twelve; those who had taken wives brought six horses and five buffalo.

Drums and gongs were beaten continuously in front of the house of mourning. Each approaching party was greeted by male and female dancers—the men charging toward them with spears, then retreating after a brief display of anger, the women fluttering their arms gently and beating the ground rhythmically with their feet. The greatest anticipation, mixed somewhat with dread, concerned the arrival of Rangga Raya, Ra Honggoro's brother-in-law, who had also for the last three years been his sworn enemy.

The trouble between the two men stemmed from differences in exchange expectations. Ra Honggoro had twice paid bridewealth to Rangga Raya: some thirty-five years earlier for his first wife, Pati Kyaka, who died after bearing him five children; and again ten years ago for her younger sister, Gheru Winye, the mother of six more. Their brother had insisted on repeating the alliance by replacing one sister with another because he did not want a strange woman to raise his nephews and nieces. As a wife-giver twice over, Rangga Raya was expected to be generous with his sisters' children. Nevertheless, when Ra Honggoro's eldest son, Tonggo Radu, wanted contributions to his own bridewealth, his mother's brother said he had nothing to spare. Angry, the boy went secretly to his corral and took a large buffalo without permission. He called it borrowing; Rangga Raya called it stealing. The case was resolved through traditional litigation, and Ra Honggoro agreed to pay a fine of ten buffalo, only five of which had been presented by the time of his death. The two had not spoken or visited each other since these events.

Funerals are occasions for burying resentments and certain debts as well as collecting on others. After years of furious rhetoric, Rangga Raya came back into Malandi leading not simply the large pig expected of an important wife-giver, but also a buffalo bull. The bull was offered as a *wawi njende*, something "to stand for a pig," and, in fact, also for much more, because this disproportionately large gift was presented as the "branch of white millet, the strands of yellow beans" (*kalangga langa kaka, kategho kembe rara*)—a peace offering extended to end the dispute.

As soon as his party was seen on the road, the drums beat faster and

people thronged near the entrance to watch an emotional scene of reconciliation. Rangga Raya walked up into the house of mourning holding a
fine man's cloth, which he placed on his brother-in-law's body, sobbing
profusely. Then he turned to embrace the widow, his younger sister, and
finally even Tonggo Radu, the accused thief. He stood beside the body on
the front veranda and made a tearful plea for forgiveness to all present:

We hadn't yet sheathed the knife because of our quarrel earlier	Nja pango mija la maloho oronaka ha mera ngandu atu
We hadn't yet cut the rope of our resentment	Nja pango ropo la kalembe oronaka ha mbutu ate
So we didn't drink water together	Mono inde pa inundi weiyo
So we didn't eat rice together	Mono inde pa mundi ngagha
But now let it all go	Henene tanaka
Under the cool shady leaves	Laiyo ela ndimu ndaha rouna
Beside the fruit of the ironwood tree	Laiyo ela komi njaha wuna

In banishing the reasons for the quarrel, he reopened the path of visits,
credits, and loans between affines.

The reconciliation was necessary not only for social reasons but also
for a ritual one. Because the grave of Pati Kyaka had to be opened in order
to place her husband beside her, an additional sacrifice was required to
serve as "hot water" (*wei mbyanoho*), a libation poured on her grave to
allow it to be opened and refilled. Rangga Raya was the only one who
could remove the pollution of death from this opened grave by receiving
the head of the sacrificial buffalo. Without his participation, the ghost of
his sister could not travel with her husband to the afterworld, but instead
would remain restless and likely to trouble both households.

Returning Life to the Origin Village

Ra Honggoro's own life was owed to the village of his mother's birth,
Bondo Maliti, which had served as the "steps and doorway" (*lete binye*)
through which she traveled to come to Malandi to marry his father. While
relations with his wife-givers had been intense and conflict-ridden, the
ties to Bondo Maliti were "cool"—without struggle, but also without much
contact over the past fifty years. Still, those villagers remained the only
ones who could reclaim his most personal possessions (his betel pouch, his
plate, and his drinking gourd), place his body in the grave, and take the
life of his favorite riding horse.

The Bondo Maliti contingent did not arrive until the third day after his death. They had wanted to delay their entrance until they had been joined by family members who lived in the eastern part of the island, but were finally persuaded to come by Ra Honggoro's sons, who feared the body would not last another day in the intense heat. About fifteen people from Bondo Maliti marched in with a long-tusked pig on a litter covered by a fine cloth, led by Ra Honggoro's cross-cousin and the present headman of the township. Each person brought a fine textile to place on the corpse, along with tears and laments. Another man's cloth was draped over the neck of the Horse That Is Never Satisfied, which was tied under the house just below his master's body so that Ra Honggoro's soul could ride on his own horse in the procession to the tomb.

After they had been seated in the house and served a meal, preparations were made to move the body. Some younger members of the Bondo Maliti contingent were sent to open up the stone tomb and wrap the bones of Pati Kyaka in new sarungs to prepare her to receive her husband. Ra Honggoro's eldest son stepped up to mount his father's horse, leading the procession from the ancestral village to the tomb. His brothers and agnates went into the house to lift up the body and carry it, bound in a shroud of many layers of textiles, to its final resting place.

The moment the corpse was moved from the house provoked a great display of emotion from the women who had been guarding it and singing to it for the past three days. As other arms started to lift it up, they resisted violently, wailing and shrieking, desperately caressing the bundle of cloth one last time before it left. The men at this time were grim and determined, showing little feeling as they lifted the bundle onto their shoulders and walked after the horse out the village gates and toward the stone grave, followed by several hundred distraught mourners.

Members of the origin village received the body at the tomb, placing it inside the chamber along with many other textiles and gold omega-shaped ear pendants (*hamoli ryara*). The gold was given as "tears from the house" so that other *marapu* in the land of the dead would know that he was an important person. As Ra Honggoro was arranged in the grave, the Horse That Is Never Satisfied galloped four times around the tomb; the steed was then led to the representative of the deceased's mother's brother's house. Holding on to the bridle, the mother's brother struck at the neck three times with a bush knife, thus displaying his right to take the horse's life, but then choosing to spare it.[2] A younger man in the party mounted

[2] The sacrifice of the dead man's horse is a convention of Sumbanese funerals that is nowadays only rarely observed. In the past, it is said that the horse was always killed to accompany his master on a voyage to the afterworld. At royal funerals in East Sumba, this is still often done, but increasingly the people of Kodi and

the horse and rode it triumphantly up and down the field before the gathered spectators.

As groups of sobbing women headed back to Malandi the horse was ridden to Bondo Maliti where a special ceremony was performed to bring its soul back from the journey into death. Water from a sacred source was placed in a wooden plate and circled over the horse's head four times to the left, then a *kambukelo* leaf was used to sprinkle several drops on the horse's forehead. This rite was designed to separate Ra Honggoro's soul from the horse and end his attachment to it, so he would not be jealous of its new master and cause the horse to sicken, fall, or be stolen. The circling was then repeated to the right, to fix the *hamaghu* or life force at the forelock. Members of the mother's brother's contingent now returned to Malandi to receive a ritual payment of a bush knife and spear (*kioto bilu, nambu mbani*), presented on a plate with betel and a small amount of money, in payment for serving as the "counterpart to bury the dead" (*nggaba pa tanongo*).

The funeral sacrifice (*kaparaho*) must be performed in front of the dead man's house by members of his origin village or their representatives. Ra Honggoro's mother's brother from Bondo Maliti struck three times at the neck of the first sacrificial bull, then handed the bush knife over to another wife-giver to finish the slaughter. Government regulation limited the total to five large animals: three bulls and two large cows past reproductive age. The animals' livers were inspected to confirm that Ra Honggoro's soul had left on its journey to the afterworld, and their bodies were cut in half latitudinally, separating the head and front legs from the rear quarters.

This division of sacrificial meat is done only at funerals; it represents the separation of the dead man's body into the maternal contribution (the "life" received from affines), which must be returned to the origin village, and the paternal contribution, which remains in his village and is divided among the guests. The front part of the buffalo's body is strongly tabooed for all agnates of the deceased—not just members of his house, but everyone in his ancestral village. Any agnate who took a bite of this meat would be "eating his own brother," consuming flesh that was part of his own substance, and certain to die from the poison of self-cannibalism.

The heads and front sections of the buffalo were presented to the people of Bondo Maliti, but they asked that a pig also be killed and divided

---

other districts in the west may choose to surrender the horse to the mother's brother alive. In the present case, the people of Bondo Maliti who received the horse said they spared its life "so that its master's name would not be forgotten and would be repeated by anyone who saw his horse." Even after its purification, a named horse cannot return to its master's house or village under any circumstances.

horizontally to accompany the spear and knife that they used to open up the dead man's tomb. No pig was available, so a young colt was presented to replace the pig and "lighten the burden" of those who had to return home carrying the pollution of death. The mother's brother's contingent came back with five half-carcasses; the meat from the body was divided among all the members of Bondo Maliti, but that of the heads was set aside, dried, and salted for a special rite to be held four days later.

The Final Time of Separation

As the guests returned home with their bloody burdens, the village of Malandi ceased activity for several days. Only close family members remained in the house of mourning, where the soul of the dead man lingered, still unconscious of the fact of his death. The spot where his corpse had lain in state was guarded by an older female mourner (*tou kalalu*), in this case his mother, who followed a series of taboos that identified her with the corpse.[3] From the time of his death, she remained confined within the house, her hair loose and disheveled, unable to bathe or go out in the sunlight—in fact, almost completely immobile. She was also forbidden to hold on to burning logs or a knife, or to come in contact with anything hot or sharp. She took the place, in effect, of Ra Honggoro's own consciousness: her release from these restrictions would not come until he became aware of his fate, turning into an ancestor instead of a human being.

For four nights after the burial, Ra Honggoro continued to receive a serving of food at each family meal. His plate and cup remained at their usual places, and family members spoke to him casually, as his ghost was believed to stay among the living until the final rite. On the evening of

[3] The mourner is the most senior person among those women who have married into the house. Thus, the role can be filled by a man's mother, widow, brother's wife, or daughter-in-law, but may in no case be taken by a daughter, sister, or grandchild. A woman may be mourned by her mother, married sisters or daughters, and daughter-in-law, but not by an unmarried daughter, sister, or grandchild. No woman can mourn someone still in the same agnatic group as the one into which she was born. The mourner's main qualification is the previous experience of being transferred: like the dead soul, she has also undergone a transition from one world (the house into which she was born) to another (her husband's house, where she was moved at marriage). Both immersion in death and purification from its pollution are associated with the affinal relationship, a formulation often noted in Eastern Indonesia (Traube 1981; G. Forth 1981). The specific symbolic links that cause the Kodi to argue that "dead souls are like brides" are further explored in Hoskins 1987.

the fourth day, a small bamboo platform was erected in the bush just outside the village, and the "counterparts to bury the dead" from Bondo Maliti came back to Malandi to weave small baskets of coconut leaves and rice (*kahumbu*) for the last meal fed to the soul of the dead man. The four first baskets made, marked with a long leaf-stem, were the sacred ones reserved for Ra Honggoro's ghost. They had to be boiled in absolute silence in the wee hours of the night. Others, distributed to kinsmen and affines, were boiled afterward and hung in the right front corner of the house.

At dawn, the widow and her children took the rice baskets, two pouches of rice, four ears of corn, and a bit of mashed banana to the platform outside the village. Two daughters waited to keep watch until a bird came to come nibble at them, a signal that the dead man's soul was ready to be sent away.

Ra Honggoro's soul realized he was dead at that moment. His daughters said they walked quietly back beside his stone tomb and overheard sobs, very faintly, from within the tomb: "We knew that father was singing his own funeral dirge." They bore the news to Malandi, and all the houses in the ancestral village began to bring contributions of rice and other food-stuffs for his final meal. Funeral gifts were redistributed to reciprocate those individuals who had been generous to the house of the dead man: textiles were given to those who brought horses or buffalo, and livestock were given to two of the wife-givers, who brought impressive pigs.

A pig was speared and divided latitudinally to receive the guests: the front part went to the "counterparts to bury the dead," the rear to the other guests and members of Ra Honggoro's own clan. Two plates, one sacred and one profane (*tobo hari, tobo kaba*), were brought down to the lower veranda and offered to the mother's brother, along with the dead man's own plate, glass, spoon, and drinking gourd and the cooking vessel used to boil rice baskets for the final meal. A chicken was sacrificed to check that his soul was ready to leave. No food was served to him on the plate this time. Instead, shares of rice, chicken, and pork were placed on a *kambukelo* leaf (the same kind used for the blessing of the sacrificial horse), the marker of a transaction conducted with him no longer as a member of his house and village but as part of the invisible community of the *marapu*.

Silently, the mother's brother beckoned to the female mourner to come down out of the house and seat herself before him on the veranda. She came down, first covering her head with a folded textile to shield it from the sun's rays. He dipped the *kambukelo* leaf in the water used to separate off the dead soul and dabbed a bit of it on her forehead, calling back her own soul from its long journey into the land of the dead. He pushed the textile off her head and gathered her long, unruly locks in his hands, helping her to bind them again in a knot and prepare for her ritual bath.

Shares of cooked food, raw pork, and cloth were then distributed among the guests, wife-givers, and wife-takers, who returned home with sections of the appropriate half of the sacrificed pig. The "counterparts to bury the dead" brought the dead man's plate, glass, cooking vessel, and spoon back to his origin village, where they were cast off to the west to follow him into the afterworld. Then a special meal was prepared of the tongues and the meat taken from the buffalo heads, which was eaten by those who had removed the pollution of death. From then on, Malandi and Bondo Maliti could continue to "give and take back the life" that was transferred through marriage alliances. This funeral marked the end of one series of affinal obligations, but it also reopened the path for new exchanges; because the proper sequences had been followed, the way was not blocked by the personal resentments of a still-too-human ghost.

The Meaning of Final Exchanges

Affinal exchanges are conducted almost as a pantomime: with few words, a transfer of substances and perishables is carried out to neutralize the dangerous contamination that the living experience in proximity to the dead. Women mediate between the living and the dead; their identification with the dead reveals a "feminization" of the dead soul itself, made passive and compliant for its transfer to the afterworld (Hoskins 1987a). In the words of the funeral dirges, women mourn their dead by recalling the feelings of detachment and separation that they experienced as brides, transferred to another house and village. The funeral is the time when obligations to maternal relatives must be remembered, because only members of the origin village can remove the pollution of death and cleanse the house of the filth that collects around the rotting body.

Ra Honggoro's funeral did, however, reveal many of the tensions and conflicts that can arise among affines as exchange obligations become the subject of disputes and litigation. The dissolution of affinity divides the dead person into that portion which was contributed by his mother's blood and the protective power of her relatives, and the portion that will remain within the patriline, elevated to the status of an ancestor. And after the silent transactions of the initial funeral, this second stage requires an extended verbal interrogation.

The Divination: A Journey into the Past

A funeral divination has much of the suspense of a detective story, as a whole array of spirit "suspects" are summoned down to the mat where rice is scattered, then sequentially interrogated as to their possible motives for withdrawing protection from the dead man. The real killer might be an ancestor, a guardian deity of the village or garden hamlet, or a wild spirit-companion who has been inadequately compensated for her gifts of wealth.

A week after Ra Honggoro's funeral, two diviners came to the house of mourning to begin a several-hour-long investigation of the causes of his death. The older one, Rangga Pinja, was a blind orator from a neighboring village who scattered rice and spoke the invocations to each of the spirit suspects. His younger assistant, Rendi Banda Lora, held the divination spear outstretched in his arms—the handle grasped by the left hand, the right arm traveling the length of the spear with the right thumb extended beyond the point. As the diviner presented questions to the *marapu*, his assistant lunged toward the wall of the sacred right front corner (*mata marapu*) where the spirits were believed to come down. When his thumb touched the wall, the spirit's answer was positive, and he murmured his assent; when it fell short, the answer was negative, and he called back "Aree!" to his companion, a signal that the interrogation must continue.

The first spirit summoned was the spirit of the divination spear—*mone haghu, mone urato* ("the Savunese man, the divining man"), a magical object imported to Sumba from the small island of Savu and used as an intermediary to contact the other *marapu*. The spear probes the anger of the invisible ones, its sharpened tip cutting through their reluctance to reveal the truth or falsity of the diviner's speculative scenarios. As soon as the spear holder had confirmed that the spear's invisible spirit was present, the diviner began to "bring down the monkeys"—that is, to call on all the *marapu* who may have had reason to be upset:

From your throats and your livers	Wali kyoko wali y'ate
From your backs and your bellies	Wali kabendo wali kyambu
We bring you our language and speech	Mai dukinggumi paneghe patera
To ask you about a person	Tana pa kalirongo a toyo
Who was entered by death	Na tamaka a mate
Whose disappearance arrived	Na dukingo a heda

What was the anger and the resentment	Ngge nikya a mbani a mbuha
Which caused his death?	Na pa orongo a mate?
Was there something skipped like a forgotten piece of thatch?	Ba nei jo kingo a katadi hambule la rapito ngingo doyo?
Was there something missed like a bamboo slat out of place?	Ba nei jo kingo pa letengo la boki onggolo doyo?

Metaphors for the vulnerability of the person use the idiom of the vulnerability of the house, which was so weakened by the intrusion of death that the final divination is described as a rite "to mend the walls and close the gap in the bamboo slats" (*wolo handa, todi byoki*) where danger first came in.

The diviner's search moved through space, from the house and ancestral village where the funeral was held, to the various smaller settlements where the people of Malandi cultivated their gardens and the pasturelands for Ra Honggoro's extensive herds and unfinished stone house. Early hints suggested that the scene of the crime lay in distant garden lands, where one of Ra Honggoro's direct predecessors had made a promise to the *marapu* which was not fulfilled. A positive response was obtained for this first, exploratory suggestion of the reasons for his death:

Great was the wrongdoing of Raya	Bokolo pa ngandi Ryaya
That he didn't heed the speech of the souls of grandparents and ancestors	Nja la tanihyada ha paneghe ndewa ambu, ndewa nuhi
Short was the life of Raya	Pandako pa deke Raya
That he didn't set aside the words of souls of mothers and fathers	Nja awa ta bandalango liyo ndewa inya, ndewa bapa

The questioning now returned to the genealogical line, since the spirits of Ra Honggoro's father, Tonggo Radu, and grandfather, Maha Rehi, seemed most directly involved. Both, however, refused to come down when summoned. The diviner protested this recalcitrance by reporting it to the higher deities:

Stepping with their feet	Pangga ha witti
They wouldn't step with their feet	Nja pangga ha witti
So a dam came to block our speech	Pa kawata kori lyoko a paneghe
Raising their buttocks	Kede ha kere
They wouldn't raise their buttocks	Njaha kede ha kere

The flow of water stopped for our words	Pa hanamba nimbia weiyo a patera
They won't cross their legs on the mat	Njana mbara mbica witti la nopo
They won't fold their hands by the rice	Njana hangga hara limya la wiha

Exasperated that his spirit intermediaries did not produce the needed witnesses, the diviner himself stepped back and allowed his assistant to begin a new series of questions, insisting again on the distress of the living and their need to establish an answer.

The younger man threw himself into the fray with great speed and vigor, invoking the deities that oversee divination within the house and can constrain reluctant ancestors to appear:

The loincloth must be unfolded, I say	Pa kawakaho kalambo wenggu
The basket must be opened, I say	Pa bunggero kapepe wenggu
I speak from the trunk of mother	Yayo wali pola inya da
No more chasing lost horses	Tana ambu kandaba ndara mbunga
I speak from the building of father	Yayo wali dari bapa
No more straining the throat in vain	Tana ambu koko wei kaweda
Something made the throat close in anger	Nengyo diyo pa wolo hudu koko
Something made the liver tight with rage	Nengyo diyo pa rawi reka ate
A reason the pig fell in the hunter's net	Uru pa nengyo pokato wawi kalola
A reason the horse tripped on the reins	Uru pa nengyo ndara nduka nambi

Finally he succeeded in contacting the spirits of two resentful ancestors who agreed to come down to answer the questions of the older diviner. He then stepped back and allowed his superior to continue the questioning.

Rangga Pinja established that the trouble came from Lolo Peka, Ra Honggoro's pasturelands in the distant region of Balaghar, where he had made a pact with a wild spirit that was not fulfilled. Once he verified the role of the wild spirit (the one "close as the pouches of a betel bag, the folds of the waist cloth," *ndepeto kaleku, hanguto kalambo*), he broke out of the ritualized dialogue with the spirits to ask his human audience to supply some of the missing details. "Who was this secret spirit-wife of Ra Honggoro's?" he asked them. "Has anyone seen her? Is she the same as his grandfather's secret consort?"

Relatives from the pasturelands in Balaghar remembered that they had heard stories of a tall beauty from the sea who had formed a pact with one of Ra Honggoro's ancestors. Others said they had seen her from a distance near his buffalo, or wandering off into the forest with him. She could take the form of a megapode, a wild forest hen with long legs who lays very large eggs. The megapode is a prodigal of fertility and productivity, but she is a bad mother: she builds elaborate mud nests for her eggs, regulating the temperature for incubation by means of elaborate tunnels, but then leaves her young to hatch on their own. Megapode fledglings are born as orphans, deserted by their mother, and forced to make their lives on their own.

The megapode bird represents reproduction without nurturance, fertility without feeling, and is associated with the rapid growth of wealth and descendants but improper care. In the same way, a wild spirit-wife may give riches, but in return she saps the life of her human consorts, or demands sacrifices of them and their children. Ra Honggoro had earlier promised to offer a long-tusked pig and a buffalo with elbow-length horns to the wild spirit when he gave a feast in the gardens, a vow he had neglected to carry out. As a consequence, his spirit consort began to weaken him until he agreed to comply with her wishes.

She broke apart the bridge leading over the river	Na mbata nikya a lara lende loko
She extinguished the flames of the torch by the tides	Na mbada nikya a api hulu mara

She shortened his life using the same magical power that had earlier increased the fertility of his herds and added to the splendor of his feasts. Through the image of the neglected wild bird-woman, Ra Honggoro was presented as a victim of his own careless pride.

The divination revealed, however, that the wild spirit did not do her work alone. She had accomplices among the guardian spirits of the hamlet, who also felt that a debt to them had not been repaid. To probe the reasons for this discontent, Rangga Pinja once again opened up the floor to the human audience, who told him stories of illnesses and deaths in the garden hamlets that they suspected were part of the same complex of guilt.

Because no one knew why the spirits wanted them to feel guilty, the diviner asked for two chickens to use in intermediate offerings. The first was dedicated to the spirit of the divination spear, to confirm that they were still moving in the right direction ("toward the tail of the bay horse, toward the base of the knife's sheath"). The second was dedicated to the

Lord of the Land, the angry garden spirit, who was promised a sacrifice for renewed fertility once the mystery of the death was solved.

The signs in the chickens' entrails were positive, so the questioning continued. The diviner traced the locus of discontent to the settlement at Homba Rica, where the problem seemed to concern rice spirits that had been displaced without ever having been properly restored. "Did rice fields burn in this area? Were there ceremonies to call back their souls?" he asked his audience.

Yes, he was told, paddy had once burned on the stalk—some fifty years ago—and the souls had been called back by Maha Rehi, Ra Honggoro's grandfather. But one old man remembered that once the spirits had been called back, the villagers should have held a singing ceremony (*yaigho*) before planting to bring the lost rice souls inside the gates of the hamlet— and that ceremony had never taken place. The burnt rice was left outside, unable to enter the hamlet and growing increasingly impatient.

As soon as this negligence was established, Rangga Pinja called on all those present to commit themselves to holding the long-delayed ceremony. They agreed to try to hold it within a year, a promise the diviner repeated to the angry spirit:

This is why monkeys fell in the dark	Mono a pena ba koki mandi myete
Cockatoos flew in disarray	Kaka walla nggole
The trunk of the horse post	Oro kapunge pola ndara
Traveled on the road of our words	Helu wallu lara a paneghe ma
The great source of water	Oro mata wei kalada
Sailed on the current of our speech	Tana tena wallu teko a patera ma
So I say to you now	Mono ba hei wyali ba henene
When the waters start to flow anew	Ba helu kendu a weiyo
Go to wait at the edge of the planting post	Tana kadanga waingo rema ela tilu wu patuku
For the rice of the sea worms	A ngagha nale
When the rains begin to fall	Ba helu mburu a ura
Be patient by the seed platform	Kamodo waingo mangga ela londo wu pawini
For the rice of prohibitions	A ngagha padu
Brought to the garden hamlet	Tana tama waingo witti ela bondo lihu
At the feet of Mother of the Land	Tane waindi witti a inya mangu tana
Carried to the corn granary	Tana duki waingo limya ela kalimbyatu

In the hands of Father of the Rivers	Ghughu waingo limya ela bapa mangu loko

Once the rainy season began, he affirmed, the proper sacrifices would be carried out to bring the lost rice souls back into the hamlet and formally place them under the guardianship of the Lord of the Land.

Rangga Pinja rested after finally getting to the core of the *marapu's* distress ("the trunk of the horse post, the great source of water"). His assistant continued the interrogation, asking if there was any other unfinished business in Lolo Peka, Ra Honggoro's pasturelands. The spear indicated that something remained which could threaten the health of the livestock:

There is leftover speech	Nengyo oro paneghe
Where you built the hen's perch	Ela pandou pa woloni keka manu
There are traces of words	Nengyo oro patera
Where you made the pig's trough	Ela pandou pa rawini rabba wawi
Making the tails entangled	Ba wolongoka kiku na pa tane
Making the snouts bite	Rawingoka ngora na pa katti
Slipping into the hunter's net	Pa nobongo waingo a duki rembio wawa
Struck as they cross the forest	Pa ghena waingo pagheghu la kandaghu

The local spirits, it seemed, were upset because when preparations were made to build the stone house, a feast should have been held to announce these intentions to the *marapu* of the region. In the rush of assembling all the necessary materials, however, this stage had been omitted; those involved did not even sacrifice a chicken in the house to tell their own ancestors. The diviner recommended an immediate apology, with the modest sacrifice of a small pig to persuade the local spirits to wait until the stone house was finished to receive their full share.

The last offense discovered was a minor one: the Elder Spirit of the clan was annoyed because people had planted tobacco beside one of the houses in the ancestral village. This violated the division of space between the productive centers in the gardens and the centers of worship in the ancestral villages, the "land of sea worms and prohibitions" (*tana nale, tana padu*). A chicken was offered to ask forgiveness ("stroke the liver, caress the belly," *ami y'ate, ghoha kambu*) and assure the Elder Spirit it would not happen again.

Closing Off the Opening Between Past and Present

At last, the investigation of all the causes, great and small, of the discontent of the *marapu* was finished, and the diviner made his concluding statement. He began by reminding his listeners of the problems he had *not* found: Ra Honggoro had not been poisoned, there was no sign of witchcraft, and there was no need for a vengeance killing. The neglected feasts that they had learned of could be reasonably carried out in the next few years, as long as the ancestors agreed to accept the terms offered and not pass on resentments to future generations. The human and spirit worlds must remain separate, and these promises would provide occasions for them to reunite briefly. This funeral, though, must conclude with the reestablishment of distance.

The *marapu* were entreated not to take any more victims from the house, which death had emptied of all valuables. With Ra Honggoro's death, no worthy descendants remained to carry on the tradition:

No one here speaks as a great man	Njaingo na paneghe bei kabani
Among the fruits of the yellow tree	Ela wu malandi ryara
No one talks like a great woman	Njaingo na patera bei minye
With the juice of the *malere* vine	Ela wai malere lolo
No roosters are left to crow	Njaingo manu kuku
No dogs are left to bark	Njaingo bangga oha
Only snails with no throats	Di pimikya ha buku nja pa koko
Only spiders with no livers	Di kanehengoka ha nggengge nja pa ate
We are all alone and lonely	Kanehengo mono kariyo

A special plea to the Great Spirit at the house pillar, protector of the inhabitants of the house, raised the threat of total devastation:

Mother at the edge of the corner	Inya na londo ela tundu wu kabihu
Father at the top of the roofbeam	Bapa na ndende ela tane wu karangga
If you break the bracelet	Ba na ndelako kalele
Who will fetch you water	Nggarani na woni weiyo
If they are all gone and silent?	Na kanagha ka dana?
If you snap the rope	Ba na nggonggolo kaloro
Who will serve you rice	Nggarani na woni ngagha
If they are all wiped out?	Na kanguhu ngoka dana?
There will be no one left	Njaingo dangu wemu we damu
To bind the tall enclosures	Ba wolongo kanduru pa madeta

There will be no one there	Njaingo dangu wemu we damu
To repair the many corrals	Ba rawingo nggallu pa madanga
Here on the wide stone platform	Yila kambattu mbeleko
Here in the ancestral village	Yila parona bokolo

This pathetic portrait of the family's decimation by death and disease, leaving it so weakened that even the simplest ritual tasks could no longer be carried out, was intended to convince the *marapu* that they really must leave their living descendants alone. "Now is the time to close the floorboards, to mend the walls," the diviner repeated in the last verses he spoke. "Let the hands separate, let the feet step apart."

These words were accompanied by actions to confirm the divination and commit participants to the promised schedule of ceremonies. A pig was speared to appease the angry spirit-wife who had provided such wealth:

You who hold the buffalo's rope	Yo na ketengo a kaloro karimbyoyo
Close as pockets of a betel pouch	A ndepeto kaleku
You who guard the horse corral	Yo na daghango a nggallu ndara
Tight as the folds of a loincloth	A hangato kalambo
Who snapped open the yellow fruit	A mai mbiki nggama wuyo rara
And chewed the green leaves with us	A mai routta nggama rou moro
Since that meeting at the spring	Ba na mata wei pa toboko
Since the encounter at the vines	Ba lolo ghai pa rangga
Soften up your throat	Ropo moka a koko mu
Stretch out your liver	Mbomo moka a ate mu

The earlier intimacy of Ra Honggoro's rendezvous with the wild bird-woman of the forest was evoked here to suggest establishing a new sacrificial relationship with his descendants, who hoped that by honoring his earlier commitments they too could enjoy the prodigious reproduction of his herds of buffalo and horses. The capriciousness of wild spirits is notorious, however, so there was no certainty that she "would like the smell of their bodies" and accept the same intimacy with other members of the family.

Two chickens were killed to repeat promises to hold feasts: one for the rice spirits in Homba Rica, the other for the promised ceremony near the buffalo corral. The next three sacrifices were addressed directly to the spirit of Ra Honggoro. The diviner called him to come down as a kinsman and then tried to convince him to leave as a *marapu*:

Hear this now, cross-cousin!

This day our hands must separate

Our feet must step apart

Do not come to the garden hamlet

Do not weed the grass, dig the land

We are just playing with baubles

We amuse ourselves with trifles

I must tell you cross-cousin

We separate completely on this day

So you can go to the spirit mother, spirit father

Arriving at the ancestral village, wide stone foundations

Here you must leave behind your brothers, your children, your wife, your grandchildren

All these—including your daughters and their families

So the separation will be complete

The chicken will mark the boundary

Between the paths of our feet

Rongo baka hena, anguleba!

Yila lodona limya hilu hegha njandi

Witti ndimu deke njandi

Ambu ngandi ela bondo lihu, kalimbyatu

Ambu ndihi ela batu rumba, dari cana

Ta mangguna waingo hario

Ta manghana waingo lelu

Yo dougha taki anguleba ba henene

Tana ta hegha baka yila lodona

Tana duki wabinikya ela inya marapu, bapa marapu

Tana toma wabinikya ela parona bokolo, watu mbelako

Hengyo iyi mandala gha ena ha dungo kambunamu, ha anamu, ha ariwyeimu, ha ambumu

Ngara iyiya, mono ena a nobo vinye

Tana heka a hambolo

Hengyo a manu na hiri a lara

Na ndiki ha witti

The mixture of language in this text between casual forms taken from intimate conversation ("I must tell you now, cross-cousin . . .") and formal oratory displays the ambivalence of the ritual moment: the diviner reminds Ra Honggoro of ties of blood and friendship between them, but then asks him to go away, to accept the invisible spirits of his ancestors as substitutes for his living family. The deceased no longer needs to join his family in the fields or share their concerns, which appear as mere "trifles and baubles," of no more consequence. The prayer began informally, gradually increasing in formality and ritual distance as the listener moved into the category of a *marapu*.

An egg was offered to cleanse the members of the household, "bathing their bodies and rinsing their hair with coconut" after the rituals of death. The egg was addressed as a *bei wyoto*, a female beast past reproductive age, whose now-sterile womb could no longer produce new life. The egg offering stood for the end of a process, the mourning and the taboos of the *tou kalalu*.

The last sacrifice was of a small chick to seal off the house, "closing the gaps in the floorboards, so feet could not fall through, mending the holes in the walls, so hands could not slip out." Ra Honggoro was called down for the last time as a kinsman, then sent away with a series of lines reflecting on the inevitability of human mortality:

Once again I say to you, cross-cousin	Hena wali baka anguleba nggu
We all die like Mbyora at the banyan tree	Ba mate nggama Mbyora la maliti
There is no stopping the flow of the waters of Langgaro	Nja pa weinggelango a wete wei lyanggaro
We all pass away like Pyoke at the *waringin* trunk	Ba heda nggama Pyoke la kadoki
There is no damming the current of the tobacco river	Nja pa hundaronka liku loko mbaku
We only stop to rest as we stand	Ghica piyo li hengahu ndende mema
Here on this earth	Dani yila panu tana
We only pause to sit for a while	Ghica piyo li lyondo eringo mema
Here in the shade of the tree	Dani yila maghu ghaiyo
The tide goes down at dusk	La lena ndiku myara
The river sinks to meet the sea	La nggaba kindiki lyoko
And what are we to do?	Mono a pemuni dana?
The knife has already cut his death	A kiri kioto ndouka nggaka a mate
The paddy threshed for his passing	A pare ndouka ndali nggaka a mbunga

The metaphor of a final crossing over the river of death consigns Ra Honggoro to join Mbora Poke, the Kodi ancestor whose death also marked the origin of night and day. His widow then repeated similar verses of fatalistic resignation as she placed an offering of betel nut on his tomb. The ghost of Ra Honggoro accepted this last gift, showing that he accepted the irrevocability of death and released the living, so death would not return to their house.

Silence and Speech, Affines and Agnates

The process by which Ra Honggoro was moved from the category of kinsman into that of ancestor raises several important questions about the temporal relation of the visible and invisible worlds and the possibilities for communication between them.

The divination was not a simple "who done it," but an investigation of social tensions and collective history that encompassed much more than the details of Ra Honggoro's own life. For this reason, the "murder mystery" that began the investigation revealed not only a plethora of suspects but also a plurality of killers. Every death is overdetermined: there are

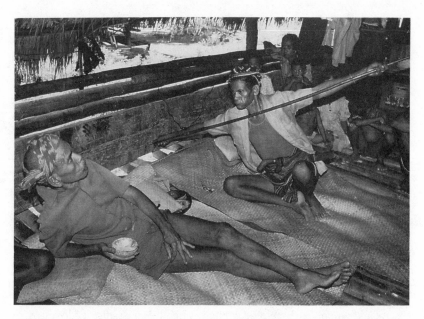

The divination to determine the reason for Ra Honggoro's death is staged as a dialogue between an orator, who questions suspect spirits, and a diviner, who lunges with a sacred spear to indicate positive or negative responses. 1988. Photograph by Laura Whitney.

many more reasons for the *marapu*'s anger than there are victims. The funeral of an important man is an occasion for reassessing the strengths of the group and reformulating hierarchical relations. During a funeral, implicit and explicit ideas of succession are sorted out in terms of seniority and precedence, and the social relations of affinity and agnation are separated.

The problem of the divination is much broader than simply finding a guilty spirit party. The important question is "Who is responsible to fulfill promises to the ancestors?" Death threatens the integrity of the group not only because it has diminished its members, but also because it signals transgressions or obligations that could claim more victims. The problem posed by death is how to turn a negative and fearful reaction into a positive value. All of the weaker connections between individual members and between ancestors and their descendants must be investigated, and these weaknesses must be bared at a conscious level for the group so that they can be resolved together.

There are two dialogues at each divination: one occurs in a parenthesis between the diviner and the human audience (supplying the diviners with clues to pursue); the other is the "official" dialogue in ritual language between the spirits and human beings. The diviner is an outsider who is able to mediate between both groups: "his spear cuts both ways," as it is said. Confronted with the finality of death, the living are less able to dissimulate real tensions and disagreements; the spirits, then, can be compelled to provoke a true account of their anger.

The transformations attempted by ritual contrast the largely silent exchanges between affines to the intensely verbal investigation of the causes of death by the agnates. The affinal exchanges end a relationship in pantomime fashion, releasing them from all obligations, while the agnatic rites bind descendants through words and sacrifices to new promises.

The division of the funeral sacrifice into two halves, one given to the village of origin and the other to the agnatic descendants, symbolizes the division of the person into two components. Whereas the contribution of "life," given by the mother and lost at death, must be "returned," the contribution of lineage identity, coming from the father, is more enduring. It is reconstituted in the final rite, which frees the deceased of ephemeral ties and transforms him into a *marapu*.

As a kinsman, each man or woman is tied by contradictory loyalties to a village of birth and one of descent. The maternal line provides the "visible" attributes of physical resemblance, bodily substance, and vulnerability to disease. The ghost may still be torn by desires to respond to these earthly bonds and appetites. To become a *marapu*, the dead soul must be cleansed of its affinal residues and unambiguously affiliated with the agnatic descent line, with its invisible order based on ritual precedent and obligation. The "problem of responsibility" brought to the forefront at the divination can be answered only by the agnates. Death marks the dissolution of affinity at the same time that it lays the stage for the creation of new exchange relationships.

The argument I present for the dissolution of affinity through sacrifice and exchange may appear a strange one for a part of the world famous for the enduring and even eternal character of its affinal paths. In other parts of the island, where prescriptive marriage with the mother's brother's daughter supports cycles of generalized exchange among affines who remain in the same relation over several generations, things proceed differently (G. Forth 1981). Perhaps because they are aware of their neighbors' customs, the Kodi attitude is somewhat ambivalent. Affinal relations are seen as a source of vitality and blessings, the "cool and refreshing waters" that allow descent groups to reproduce and thrive. They are terminated at funerals *so that* they can later be revived. To use the botanic metaphor favored for the health and well-being of the lineage, the dead branches are pruned off to make room for fresh growth. If these final payments were not made, resentments between the two villages would develop because of the unhappy state of the half-processed ghost. Since repeated alliances along an established path are highly valued, though not obligatory, generous gifts to the "counterparts to bury the dead" can influence their willingness to receive new proposals and hence to continue the relationship through time.

Alliance has great strategic value in a society such as Kodi, where there is much room for both parties either to pull out of an earlier relationship or to choose to renew it, though under somewhat different terms. The political dimension of mortuary payments is reflected in their size, timing, and distribution (and the strategic decision to include certain people in the ritual categories of affines and life-givers). Ra Honggoro's funeral became an occasion for mending one alliance tie, that to Rangga Raya, the brother of both his wives, at the same time that it ended another, the bonds to his mother's village of Bondo Maliti. The unity of the agnates was affirmed by their ability to negotiate with both other parties and, finally, to reach an accord among themselves.

Epilogue: Changing the Ties to the Past

The drama of collective guilt and debts has recently been called into question by a competing, more individualistic creed introduced by the Christian church. Ra Honggoro's widow was upset at the results of the divination and attracted to the idea of individual salvation achieved through faith and pious actions. Four months after her husband's funeral, she joined the Sumbanese Protestant church. She explained her decision thus:

> The problem with these traditional rituals is that so many people now do not carry them out. My husband would not convert because he owed it to his ancestors and his family to lead them in these rites. He fulfilled his promises to the *marapu*, but died because others before him did not. After the funeral, I wanted to get off the ladder of these ancestral obligations. Evangelists came to my house and said that the Christian God was merciful. He asks only a small ceremony of prayers, not such large feasts. He is not as demanding as the *marapu*, or as strict.

Her decision was not unique: four thousand people converted in Kodi during a large Evangelical campaign that ended at Christmas 1987. Shortly after Ra Honggoro was transformed into an ancestor in the traditional way, his own kin defected, leaving behind the ancestral cult. He thus joined the side of the authorities, those respected and worshipped if kept at a distance from the living, just as they were losing much of their authority—a tragic irony that was not lost on local observers.

Much debate about conversion and obligations to the *marapu* hinges not on problems of belief but on ideas of debt, responsibility, and the causes of suffering. People contract a series of obligations with invisible spirits at ritual events; for them, conversion is a way of moving into another system of obligations where the rules are easier.

Death ceremonies provide the focus for many of these debates, partly because evangelists have put pressure on many younger converts to bring their parents into the church before they die, and partly because funeral rites fix the dead person within a henceforth irrevocable status—as either ancestor or unprocessed ghost, traditionalist or Christian convert. Sacrifices and the division of buffalo dedicated to the dead person are performed in the same fashion for Christian converts as for pagans. While the church does not accept the interpretation that the liver is a message-bearer from the dead, it does not object to the silent drama of exchanges between affines and agnates, where the "gift of life" is returned to its origins. What they forbid is only the second half of the ceremony: the investigation of the causes of death through divination and the transformation of the personal soul into an ancestor. Native church leaders see the dissolution of bonds of affinity and their replacement by agnatic ones not as a distinctly "pagan" rite, but as a necessary step in the traditional exchange system. Creating new ancestors, by contrast, reproduces *marapu* beliefs in generations to come and is forbidden. The lines of communication with past generations must also be severed, so the church censors any direct speaking to the ancestors.

The wordlessness of affinal exchanges permits them to be classified as property transactions rather than as ritual acts. Only when the ghost is fed his last meal on the *kambukelo* leaf does the rite gain the label of "pagan." Christians may remove the pollution of death from their wife-takers by receiving the heads of sacrificial animals, but they may not prepare food for the ghost. The compromises involved in negotiating pagan *and* Christian participation inflect the temporal values of funerals by asserting that ephemeral affinal exchanges can continue, but the agnatic cult of the ancestors must come to an end. As we shall see in part three, time is one of the main battlefields on which the wars of conversion and its interpretation are fought, and it is as guardians of the past that leaders of the traditional ritual community now struggle to carry their practices into the future.

Local Time and the Encounter with "History"

10

A New Order of Time

Church and State

The house they enter on the seventh day
Weans them from the breast of the mother *marapu*
The office they go to on the other days
Pushes them from the lap of the father *marapu*

> From a song of protest
> by pagan Kodi villagers

In the last three decades, a new order of time has made itself felt on the island of Sumba. Control by the Netherlands East Indies did not become a reality until the twentieth century, and the spread of education, the market economy, and political surveillance was constrained during the colonial period. The horizontal expansion of the Dutch empire stopped when the eastern islands were brought under effective political control, but the vertical penetration of the state and its calendars, schedules, and history into the more isolated areas became complete only after control passed into Indonesian hands.

The period since 1950 is designated in Kodi traditional couplets as the time of the "land of independence, the stones of electoral campaigns" (*tana merdeka, watu kampanye*). Awareness of a new and different temporality during this period grew thanks to dramatic increases in the building of schools, the establishment of literacy programs for both adults and children, and an expanding bureaucracy that recruited many local people as civil servants. The articulation of the goals of the state as a state—that is, as an institution that imposes a particular organizational structure on its citizenry—is characteristic of Suharto's "New Order" and the ideological agenda of Golkar, the ruling party (Anderson 1990, 94–95, 117). The participatory, cultural "imagined community" of the nation was married to an older, corporate structure of the state, first formed during the period of the Dutch colonial administration. The period immediately following independence (1950–66) was concerned primarily with the idea of the nation, and efforts focused on fulfilling Sukarno's vision of a new revolutionary coalition; the period since 1966, however, has seen an increasing emphasis on administrative coherence and discipline, with much deeper consequences for local notions of autonomy, cultural diversity, and temporality.

New definitions of cultural citizenship within the nation have tied the increasing penetration of the state to evangelical activity. Conversion to a world religion (here, Protestantism or Catholicism) has become a prerequisite for participation in the wider world of government, schools, and trade. Although the history of missionary efforts on the island began in the nineteenth century with an ill-fated Catholic outpost, their success came largely after other important social changes took place which made the new faith attractive.

The triumph of Christianity in Kodi is in fact linked, I argue, to the appeal of a progressive model of time, a view of "history" as a global and linear framework for comprehending the evolution of man and society. Instead of defining themselves in relation to a distant past of origins, and a cumulative accumulation of traditional value, Kodinese started to frame their actions and expectations in terms of a model of future progress and achievement. This change is ultimately what explains the new success of conversion campaigns and the waning influence of the traditional calendar.

Entering the "Bitter House": Stages of a Dialogue

Christian missionaries first came to Sumba from Germany and Holland with the hope of bringing isolated pagan peoples into the wider community of the Catholic or Protestant church. They began a dialogue with the Sumbanese that initially paralleled other exchanges with significant outside interlocutors—the sultanates of Sumbawa, Flores, and Java and Dutch colonial officials. An important difference soon emerged: the missionaries wanted something more than accommodation to their power through the payment of taxes, the observance of regulations, and the acceptance of an overarching power. They sought conversion, a change in internal attitudes and convictions. "We came to bring them a totally new understanding of the spiritual world and a new way of acting toward it," explained a former minister. But few people in Kodi were convinced of these "new understandings" until other changes gave them relevance. Telling them of an omnipotent God, inescapable sin, and the promise of redemption did not make sense until the experience of secular power and material inequalities brought such notions home.

When the dialogue began, each side saw the encounter in fundamentally different ways. The Christian and Catholic missionaries believed that they were negotiating a meeting of two competing sets of gods. This

Ra Honggoro's tomb is painted to highlight images recalling his named horse and dog, at the same time that his widow and most of his descendants have left the *marapu* cult to convert to Christianity. 1988. Photograph by Laura Whitney.

perception is reflected in the title of a book, *Marapu und Karitu*, written by German Catholic missionaries about their experiences and describing mission activities as the meeting of local deities (*marapu*) and Christ (pronounced *karitu* in the Sumbanese fashion). A response to directives issued by the national government, evangelization went hand in hand with development, so "teaching them about Christ was also teaching them about the modern world." The "understanding" the missionaries brought was an expanded world vision in which lineage ancestors and spirits of named locales in Kodi would begin to seem parochial.

From a Kodi perspective, the theology of the first missionaries was a mystery, and what could be identified and used to define them was not a difference in ideas but a difference in practices. Members of the new faith were called "people who go into their cult house on the seventh day [Sunday]" (*tou tama uma lodo padu*) and observe prohibitions on noise-making and sacrifices on a weekly cycle. It was the *ritual temporality* of the first Christians—the way they demarcated sacred time—that set them apart from their fellows. Given the centrality of the regulation of time in the Kodi traditional system, this perception is not surprising.

The contrast in temporality marked the first stage of a process of conceptual reorientation, which shifted the notion of "religion" from one defined in terms of practices to one articulated as a system of beliefs. Indigenous worship of *marapu* was defined through traditional practices and rules of ritual procedure; only later did it become more self-conscious and concerned with doctrine. The terms of the dialogue changed in three separate historical moments: during the initial evangelical activity (late nineteenth century and beginning of the twentieth), during a period of retrenchment and controversy in the newly formed churches in the 1950s, and when new debates cropped up in the 1980s.

The first dialogue, carried on during the period of the first conversions, focused on contrasts in ritual practice and the slow discovery of what actions were considered "un-Christian" by the Dutch and German missionaries. When control of the Sumbanese Protestant church passed into local hands, the problem of what was "un-Christian" was rephrased in definitional debates about the meanings of "paganism," "custom," and "culture."

The second dialogue, which began after independence, was formulated in response to a notion of religion presented by the Indonesian state. Religious tolerance under the principles of Panca Sila ideology was applied only to those systems that qualified as *agama*. In effect, this meant monotheistic world traditions that could document their practices with reference to an authoritative text. Embodied in the Sanskrit word was the idea of a rich and foreign civilization with a tradition of learning and sophistication associated first with Hinduism, then with Islam and Christianity. Islam was in fact the clearest model, but Indonesia's early leaders, fearing the political power of Islamic fundamentalism, chose to specify religion as a "belief in one God" (Ind. *bertuhan*), thus skillfully allowing for religious diversity in a nation whose population was predominantly Moslem. The minority religions of small pagan populations were excluded from this category:

> Implicit in the concept of *agama* are notions of progress, modernization, and adherence to nationalist goals. Populations regarded as ignorant, backward, or indifferent to the nationalist vision are people who de facto lack a religion. *Agama* is the dividing line that sets off the mass of peasants and urban dwellers, on the one side, from small traditional communities (weakly integrated into the national economic and political system), on the other.
>
> (Atkinson 1987, 177)

On Sumba, the size and relative isolation of a large pagan population softened the initial impact of government policies to encourage conversion among those who "did not yet have a religion" (Ind. *belum beragama*). Sumbanese did, however, think about the new category of "religion" and reexamine earlier practices, applying new notions of moral discipline, community values, and the ethical distinction between good and evil. Many wondered whether the presence of a Creator figure qualified their belief system as monotheistic and began to search for the "underlying principles" of the metaphoric imagery of ritual language. The rhetoric of nation building and New Order pressures for ideological uniformity put some pagans at risk. As peoples who appeared to reject the authority of both church and state, some were suspected of having communist leanings. In order to defend their ancestral system and to understand it better, a number of Kodi tried to articulate its tenets in terms of the new vocabulary of doctrine and precept, creating written accounts of dogmas to constitute a parallel system on the model of, but in contrast to, the Christian Bible.

These new forms of reflexivity and self-awareness resulted in both an increase in conversions and a retrenchment of traditionalists. It transformed the nature of indigenous conceptual systems even in the absence of a shift to an alien faith, since it permitted Sumbanese thinkers to build a new world of relationships between ideas and actions within the old house of ancestral custom.

The third dialogue, that of the 1980s involving a reevaluation of church policy, was a response to continuing religious conservatism. Local leaders of the Protestant and Catholic communities wondered why they remained minorities in a society that in 1980 was still officially 80 percent pagan. New accommodations were made to allow for a return to the church after committing sins such as polygamy or sacrificing to the *marapu*. At the same time, word spread that the special "sixth column" on government census cards would no longer be an option in the 1990 census. Thus far, in addition to the five officially recognized religions of Islam, Protestantism, Catholicism, Hinduism, and Buddhism, local clerks had included a slot for *agama marapu*. Now, under increasing pressure to modernize, this would no longer be the case: an affiliation with a world religion, perhaps nominal at first, had become a requirement of full citizenship in the modern state. Church leaders were virtually assured a victory of numbers, but their prospective members insisted on a compensatory victory of content: they would convert, but only if conversion were redefined in a way that made the new faith more their own, a Kodi cocreation and not merely a foreign imposition. These incorporations of external authority into local social forms follow a pattern established in the distant past.

Finding "Religion" in the Indigenous System

The first task the foreign missionaries faced was to isolate the "religious" as a discrete category of experience from the wide range of loosely differentiated ritual, political, and economic practices of traditional society. At the beginning of this century, namely, the code of ceremonial etiquette and rules for interactions with the *marapu* also served to regulate marriage choices, the division of land, administrative prerogatives, and the exchange of livestock and cloth. Whenever a woman changed hands, whenever a promise was made, whenever a community shifted its residence, the ancestral spirits had to be informed and small offerings had to be made to them. They were the invisible witnesses of all important transactions, and they could hold the partners to their commitment by poisoning the very meat dedicated to them if such commitments were undertaken insincerely. The different domains of social life were so bound together that failure to follow the proper procedures in one—the performance of a burial rite, say—would have repercussions in another—failure of the crops, illness in the house, or destruction by fire or lightning. There was no separate "secular" realm where transactions could be carried out without summoning the ancestral spirits. Missionaries themselves constructed this division and so, unwittingly, became agents of secularization.

The relationship between the human community and the invisible world of the *marapu* was one of complementarity and balance. Exchanges with spirit entities were made in order to receive tangible rewards and to satisfy cultural ideas of completeness. In the dualistic terms familiar to peoples of the eastern end of the archipelago, this was the principle of *pa panggapango*, the idea that things were "paired" and had a "twofold" nature—meaning that the opposition of inside and outside, male and female, cultural order and natural vitality, was inherent to any dynamic process. The oppositions were always shifting and unresolved; often they were not totally discrete categories but parts of a single whole. Major deities, addressed with a double name such as "Elder Mother, Ancient Father" or "Mother of the Land, Father of the Rivers," epitomized the synthesis of male and female and were portrayed as protective parents who defended and nourished their living offspring. The high degree of integration between elements in the system reinforced the dependency of each sphere on another and made religion difficult to isolate from the social and spatial totality of life.

Rules and procedures for ritual practice were clearly articulated, but abstract ideas about the structure of the cosmos and its attributes were hard to find. The Kodi describe the universe as made up of six levels of land and seven levels of sky (*nomo ndani cana, pitu ndani awango*), but the spirits are not arranged on separate levels of this structure. The "highest deities," those who lived in the sky, were higher in altitude but not necessarily in status than those who lived in the ground. Relations of hierarchy and deference were expressed in an etiquette of address for speaking to the spirits. Only the less important spirits of the margin and periphery could be called on directly, while all of the higher deities had to be approached through spirit deputies and intermediaries, in a complex chain of communication that eventually led back to the Creator.

Foreign missionaries were intrigued by the fact that the Sumbanese did acknowledge a single maker and sustainer of human life. Yet they were somewhat puzzled by the fact that "the one who made us and formed us" (*amawolo amarawi*) was portrayed in Kodi as both male and female, a mother who bound the hair at the forelock and a father who smelted the skull at the crown (*inya wolo hungga, bapa rawi lindu*). Far from being an omnipotent and punitive God, whose divine justice was felt in the world, this Creator figure was rather distant from the lives of human beings. Referred to as the "one whose namesake cannot be mentioned, whose name cannot be pronounced" (*nja pa taki camo, nja pa numa ngara*), she/he could not be addressed directly in prayer; rather, a whole chain of intermediaries was needed to send a message. Minor entreaties and pleas had to be brought first to the local guardians of the garden hamlet, then to the ancestors of the clan village, and finally, carried by sacrificial animals, they reached the upperworld.

Both a cosmology and a theodicy seemed to be absent. Despite elaborate narratives about the voyages of the ancestors or the history of a particular sacred object, the Kodi had no detailed vision of life in the upperworld or the origins of deities and spirits. When asked about such issues, most Kodi simply confessed that they did not know. A particular, partisan version of the past was passed down a descent line or transmitted along with certain valuables, but no more all-encompassing questions were asked. Familiar themes in Western religious discourse, such as the ultimate destination of the soul, the origin of the human race, and the underlying reasons for suffering (beyond case-by-case instances of a given spirit's anger) were also largely ignored in the otherwise rich body of oral traditions. Explanations were undertaken piecemeal in terms of the context at hand, instead of being formulated in the abstract language of religious doctrine or dogma. A primary concern was for ritual correctness rather than cosmological speculation. The proper procedures for making an offering, reciting a prayer, conducting a feast, or erecting a gravestone were the focus of discussion and debate, but there was little need to reflect on how they fit into a wider model of understanding.

Ritual specialists who performed divinations, songs, and oratory saw their task as repeating the "words of the ancestors," preserved in the paired couplets of traditional verse, not as devising their own interpretations. Even the oldest and most respected priests would assert that they were only "repeating the words of the forefathers, stretching out the speech of the ancestors." Their role was not to assert or describe the order of the universe but simply to reenact the cosmic system in ritual procedures where the truth of the sacred mysteries would become evident: "We are just the lips told to pronounce, we are only the mouths told to speak."

This attitude of humility and self-deprecation before the unknowable meant that spokesmen for the traditional system retreated into disclaimers whenever their system of worship was challenged. It would be culturally inappropriate to claim a full understanding of the workings of the *marapu*, so all they could do was stubbornly insist that a logic informed the rites dedicated to the ancestral deities but it lay beyond their grasp. No single practitioner was qualified to serve as a prophet of tradition, and doctrines were not formally articulated as in the Christian church.

Early Evangelization

The period of early evangelization in Kodi was marked by three stages: first, a great curiosity and eagerness to receive the blessings of the foreign god; second, a growing awareness of difference and the gradual development of an idea of tolerance, when the new faith was allowed to operate in the separate sphere of government service; and third, a definition of the Christian and traditional systems in terms of a contrast in ritual practice, particularly with regard to the timing of worship and periods of prohibitions. These three stages formed the necessary preamble to the final period, when the dialogue between the Christian church and the indigenous system assumed greater importance and when we can discern the beginnings of a shift from a contrast in terms of practices to a contrast in terms of belief.

Christianity came to Kodi with two different faces: that of the stern, Calvinist creed of the Dutch Reformed Church (Zending der Gereformeerde Kerken) and that of the more elaborately ritualized Catholic mission, made up primarily of German and Dutch priests of the Societas Verbi Divini. The Catholics built the first permanent structures in West Sumba when they established a Jesuit mission in 1889 at Pakamandara, in the domain of Laura—a site chosen because of its proximity to the northern port of Wai Kalo and the availability of fine limestone for building. Upon arrival, the two German priests in charge, together with their staff of seven young men from Flores, placed themselves under the protection of the ruler of Laura, who had once visited Java and was willing to welcome them (Haripranata 1984, 121). The ruler was asked to explain the benefits of baptism to his people, and within a short while hundreds of people showed up to be baptized. The priests immediately christened 610 young children, but told adults they should wait to receive religious instruction before entering the church. One of the two priests, Father Schweiz, reported that the sacrament of baptism was enthusiastically received by the parents, "who held their children in front of us with such happy faces, as if they were about to be given gold valuables and fine jewels" (Haripranata 1984, 123). People were also eager for their children to attend school, and soon twenty-seven students from prominent families were allowed to begin their studies.

In 1891, Father Schweiz surveyed the area and reported: "I went on a trip into the interior, traveling to the domain of Kodi, about a day's ride by horse to the west of Laura. Kodi is a very beautiful and fertile land, with a large population. I hope that many of them will want to join the church, since they received me well. I asked that the sons of noble families be sent to our school, but who knows if they will comply with this request" (Haripranata 1984, 131).[1] His optimism did not endure, however. Ten

---

[1] There were no Kodi students at this first school, but the earliest converts did have an impact on the region. Seven schoolboys were baptized after having received

years after it was established, the mission fell prey to horse thieves, arson, and petty larceny. Conditions were considered too difficult to send nuns or supplies on a regular basis, and finally the political instability in the area caused church authorities to close down the mission. Very few adults had been baptized, and school administrators noted that as soon as boys reached adolescence they were taken back by their families, leaving no mature converts to build the Catholic community (Haripranata 1984, 172–73). In 1898, the mission in Laura was disbanded and its staff left the island.

In 1907, D. K. Wielenga, a Protestant missionary who had been working in East Sumba for three years, traveled to West Sumba and decided to use the abandoned buildings at Pakamandara for his own evangelical activities. He opened up a Protestant school, bringing Christian Indonesians from other islands (Roti, Savu, or Ambon) as teachers to educate the sons of local rulers and noblemen. Consistent with Dutch colonial policy at the time, the school was established to train future administrators, and admission was contingent on a hereditary claim to rank. Soon the Dutch Reformed Church built other elementary schools in neighboring districts. By 1913 there were seventy Protestant village schools and four secondary schools, as well as a "theological seminary" near the original mission station in Karuni, where promising students could continue their studies.

Competition between the two churches developed as soon as members of the Societas Verbi Divini asked to return to the earlier mission site. The Dutch controller Couvreur advised against the move, saying the presence of two foreign faiths would simply confuse the local population, making it more difficult to convert them (Haripranata 1984, 205). Invoking the 1913 "Flores-Sumba Contract," he reminded Catholic authorities of an earlier agreement by which the colonial government gave Flores to the Catholic church and Sumba to the Protestants (Luckas n.d., 18). The Catholics, however, having already established themselves soundly on Flores, now pleaded that their history of mission activity on Sumba was as long as that of the Protestant Reformed church and that they should be able to serve those converts left behind upon the Jesuits' departure. In 1929, the government finally relented, permitting the establishment of

---

religious teachings; one of them was the son of Umbu Kondi, the ruler of Laura, and another was Yoseph Malo, the future raja of Rara. Both later took Kodi wives, so the first ties to the region were forged through alliance. Polygamy, although condemned by the church, was what assured its expansion, since the marriages of important men later produced many new members of the Catholic community. Reineir Theedens, a Eurasian who came with the missionaries from Flores, remained on Sumba as a teacher and also took several Kodi wives.

Catholic schools and hospitals on the island but maintaining the policy that only the Protestants would receive government subsidies and the official stamp of approval, since they were seen as operating within the parameters of a privileged relation to the state (Webb 1986, 51; Van den End 1987, 43–44).

By that time, an alternative pattern of evangelization had been established by the Dutch Reformed Church. Recognizing that many Sumbanese wanted to gain literacy and knowledge about the world, though not necessarily to become Christians, the Protestants organized their church using an extensive network of native evangelists (*guru injil*), at first from other islands but soon largely Sumbanese, who carried the Malay Bible into distant regions. The evangelists were given literacy training, a small salary, and a prestigious link to the authority of the church. Their duties were to lead prayer and translate sections from Malay into the vernacular.

The Dutch Reformed Church placed great importance on language as a medium of conversion. The missionary-linguist Louis Onvlee published translations of the New Testament in Kambera and Weyewa, the two largest Sumbanese languages. But no foreign missionary, Protestant or Catholic, ever achieved proficiency in the Kodi language. Evangelists thus had much greater influence and autonomy in Kodi than in many other areas, and they enjoyed considerable freedom to reinterpret the foreign message in Kodi terms—a point of attraction for many. The first Christian convert in Kodi Bokol was Yohannes Loghe Mete of Kory, a tall, distinguished older man who was still alive when I first came to Sumba. He was baptized in 1919, after having completed his studies at a Christian elementary school at the age of fifteen or sixteen. He was attracted to the church as a doorway to apprehend a much wider world:

> At first we cannot really say that we were called by Jesus or by God, because we didn't really know what those things meant. I had gone to school to learn to read, to find out about how things were in countries across the seas. I became a Christian because my teachers needed help to translate hymns into Kodi and to explain the Bible stories to people here. They were very strict with all of us. I couldn't eat the meat at traditional feasts because it had been dedicated to the *marapu*. I had to tell people that polygamy was a sin. I worked as a village evangelist, going from one house to another to read the Gospels. People asked me if I wasn't afraid of the white foreigners, but I said no, I'm not afraid, they are the ones who can show us the path to move forward.

By the 1930s, two Kodi ministers had been ordained: Pendita Ndoda, a descendant of Rato Mangilo in Tossi, and Pendita Kaha, a member of the village of Kaha Deta, Balaghar, guardian of the rites of bitter and bland in that area. Both had genealogical claims to positions of spiritual leadership but chose to throw in their lot with the new faith instead.

Two things marked the new Christian community: the respect accorded to the written word, which was treated as sacred, and the requirement to attend church services on Sundays. Literacy came to be seen as an attribute of Christianity, so conversion was expected of anyone who continued his studies to the secondary level or beyond. Those who remained in the villages and did not aspire to government service felt no call to convert. One old woman told me that she wanted her children and grandchildren to go to school and enter the church, but such a course was not appropriate for her: "If I held the Christian Bible in my hand, I would not be able to read it. I cannot even understand the Malay prayers. So what use does it have for me?" Mastery of Malay and reading skills were seen as prerequisites for ritual correctness in the new Christian system.

The church took the name of the new unit of temporality that it introduced: the week. The "house that one enters on the seventh day" (*uma pa tama lodo pitu*) was associated with a series of religious prohibitions that seemed to parallel the prohibitions of the "bitter months" in the Sumbanese calendar: it was not proper to sing or dance on Sundays, frivolous activities and feasting were frowned upon, and the violation of these taboos was shrouded with threats of supernatural sanctions. Just as calling young rice seedlings and immature corn ears "bitter" was a way of setting them apart and designating them as inedible until the proper ceremony had been performed, in a similar fashion the Christian church regularly set apart a day for worship, and the interval between these worship days was also the unit used for reckoning market days and government-announced events. So the church became "the house of the bitter day" or simply "the bitter house" (*uma padu*).

This label did not in itself indicate hostility or suspicion of the church; it simply acknowledged a different demarcation of sacred time. The Christian church was assumed to parallel the indigenous system in expressing its truths and mysteries indirectly, through a series of procedures that gave followers methods for communicating with and appeasing the higher powers. The two were presented as alternate versions of the same sort of conceptual system—an approach consistent with Kodi understandings of the cultural variation that existed between different districts of the island.

In the 1930s, the Catholic church returned to rebuild the mission in Laura. All of the nine hundred children who had been baptized by the nineteenth-century Jesuits had returned to their traditional system of spirit worship, and many were now polygamously married. They could be traced only by the names they had been given on the basis of their day of baptism. On a Monday in 1889, for example, Father Schweiz had christened twenty boys as Ignatius, on Tuesday he called thirty girls Maria, and on Wednesday he called thirty others Theresia and Franziskus (May, Mispagel, and Pfister 1982, 23). The coming of the foreign faith to Sumba was presented as a new temporal cycle, a round not only of Sundays but also of saints and children named after the saints. In Sumbanese languages, the days of the week are now designated with numbers (Monday is *lodo ihya*, "day one"; Tuesday, *lodo duyo*, "day two"). Giving a personal name ("Domingus") to a day of the week (Ind. *hari minggu*) only perpetuated the idea that children in Western countries were named after the days of the week. Indeed, the saints' calendar does locate names on a time line, and this time line is then linked to celebrations of saints' days and religious festivities, so their view was not entirely false.

The Catholic church came to be designated quite often as simply "the mission" (*missi*). To recruit the early lapsed "Catholics" back into the church, a new temporal cycle of celebrations was established, and everyone was invited to attend. Huge festivities at Christmas and Easter, accompanied by traditional singing and dancing, became a hallmark of the Catholic mission. Collective ritual and dramatic spectacles attracted an audience, but these "entertainments" did not immediately effect conversion. A more powerful attraction came from the extension of social services—hospitals and schools—built by the mission with generous funds from Germany. Gifted Catholic students obtained scholarships, first to finish high school, then to study overseas, often with the express hope that a few of them would discover a vocation in the priesthood.[2] By 1936, two large hospitals had been built, one in Weetabula, Laura, and the second in Kodi, in a garden hamlet called Homba Karipit. In 1980, eleven Catholic schools were in existence, including a secondary school in Homba Karipit, and over thirty Protestant ones.

The several hundred employees of the schools and clinics were not formally required to convert, but most of them did, partly out of gratitude for the help they had received. "The mission is a good older brother," one convert explained to me; "my family could never have helped me so much

[2] Three Sumbanese priests have been ordained, but only one, Father Romi Linus Tiala, was alive at the time of my fieldwork. Two others, one of them a Kodi youth from the village of Mete, died shortly after taking their vows. Some twenty Sumbanese students have attended the Catholic seminary school in Flores, but most of them returned to their homeland to marry. The Catholic leadership recognized that their major problem in recruiting new priests was the rule of chastity.

to get into a job where I would wear the long pants of a civil servant." As a result, Catholics, who made up 6 percent of the population in 1980, were largely concentrated in pockets close to the mission itself. Those who lived at a greater distance had generally received their education under the auspices of the Catholic church and sent their children to board at the mission so that they could meet suitable candidates for marriage.

The First Dialogue with the Church

The first period of dialogue with the Christian church, in both its Protestant and Catholic manifestations, was marked by the gradual emergence of points of difference, points of conflict, and points of convergence vis-à-vis the indigenous system. As Christian concepts of true "religion" became more salient, local traditionalists began to speak to these concerns in their own formulations of *marapu* practice. Joining the Christian community or remaining outside it were alternative social strategies that defined one's relation to the powerful forces whose authority was represented by the church. The "bitter house" belonged to the "stranger mother and foreign father" (*inya dawa, bapa ndimya*) who commanded from across the seas and told its followers how to act. Leaders of the local population differed on whether the new faith and the older system were basically complementary or antithetical.

The question was first articulated with regard to the definition of church membership. The church was the first voluntary organization that most people had ever encountered, and so there was initial ambiguity about whether baptism was enough to define a Christian, or whether compliance with the rules and regular participation in church ritual was necessary as well. Since many of the first converts were schoolchildren, baptism was often misrepresented as a prerequisite for school attendance. Indeed, few people joined the church unless they had already made a commitment to schooling, government service, and relations with the outside world.

The key symbols of the Christian world were the book and pen, instruments to record messages and communicate them to people far away. The Christian Bible could be carried far from home, and the Christian God could be prayed to for protection even when it was not possible to visit the traditional village altars of rock and tree. Worshippers of the local spirits had to return each year to the site of ancestral stone graves, bringing the first fruits of the harvest and new entreaties for continued health and prosperity. They could ask a spirit companion to accompany them in a particular journey, but they could not bring the full protection of their forefathers to Java for schooling, medical care, or trade. Christians, by contrast, carried their altar with them, so to speak, in the Malay Bible, using it to enter another world, which ordered its worship schedule around the church gatherings on the seventh day.

Many traditional villagers who were not hostile to the church saw their own practices of spirit worship as operating in a socially and geographically separate sphere from that of the Dutch ministers. The Christian church extended the circle of ritually mediated interactions beyond the island to a wider world. In traditional practice, Kodinese who traveled outside their traditional domain made token invocations to the deities of the regions into which they ventured. In their first experiences of Dutch schools, hospitals, and local administration, many Kodi converts followed the same pattern: while the *marapu kodi* were worshipped in the ancestral village, the *marapu dawa* ("foreign gods") were invoked on the foreign terrain of government offices.

Christianity and the Critique of Colonialism

In 1942, the Japanese army occupied Sumba and deported all Dutch ministers and their families to internment camps. Religious teaching was forbidden in schools (even those run by the Protestant and Catholic churches), and religious meetings were banned, with Sunday becoming an ordinary workday. Many village evangelists and early converts were suspected of being Dutch sympathizers. One Protestant church leader, Pendita H. Mbai, was arrested and apparently executed in 1944 (Webb 1986, 95). The churches once linked to the apparently omnipotent Netherlands East Indies and prestigious European culture suffered a heavy blow.

In 1945, the Zending staff returned to their congregations on Sumba, but the growing struggle for independence aroused a new cynicism concerning Dutch power and Dutch teachings. A derisive little verse in Malay reflected these feelings:

The Dutch have the Bible	Belanda punya Bijbel
We have the land	Kita punya tanah
[But if] we stick to the Bible	Kita pegang Bijbel
The Dutch will stick to the land	Belanda pegang tanah[3]

In other words, conversion represented a capitulation to Dutch authority,

[3] Webb (1986, 121) quotes this verse, which he apparently heard from Peter Luijendijk, a Zending minister stationed in Anakalang. He also cites a commentary from the Sumbanese Pendita M. Ratoebandfoe.

and so long as the Sumbanese embraced their colonial masters' faith the Dutch would continue to exert their dominance over colonial subjects.

In 1946, Sumbanese converts left the Dutch Calvinist mission to form the Independent Church of Sumba (Gereja Kristen Sumba). They sought financial assistance from America and Australia rather than Holland, rebuking certain Dutch ministers for showing a "colonial mentality" toward native-born preachers (Webb 1986, 121). The leadership of the new church held its first synod at Payeti, Waingapu, opening the floor to a series of discussions about how to give the new faith a more Sumbanese flavor to speed up the conversion of the village population. Christian leaders thus allied themselves with the nationalist struggle for independence, thereby assuring the Independent Church of Sumba an important role in the government of the newly formed Indonesian state.

Beginnings of Conflict Between the Church and Local Practice

Conflict emerged in the restructured Independent church when the church leadership moved to expand its authority over the lives of its converts— this in a political climate already strongly influenced by Sukarno's vision of national culture and intense ideological debate at the state level. The specific point of contention was burial of the dead and, tied to that, the destination of the soul after death. For Christians, death was an immediate point of transition, the instant when an individual's soul was united with God and severed from the living. For Sumbanese, however, the dead continue to be enmeshed in social relations, growing in a sense even more powerful after death than before because of their ability to enforce supernatural sanctions and make demands on their descendants.

The church initially tolerated burials in the ancestral villages but discouraged communication with the dead through divination. Since dead parents and grandparents seemed to use the diviners only to demand new stone graves and the fulfillment of past ceremonial obligations, their requests were in direct violation of Christian practice. Once a temporary church structure had been erected in the district capital of Bondo Kodi, some land was set aside to serve as the consecrated burial ground for converts. Schoolchildren were among the first to be buried there, as well as some older people who chose the site (according to local gossip) in order to avoid the high costs of sponsoring a stone-dragging ceremony to erect a megalithic tomb in their own village. Yet as the number of bodies resting beside the small Protestant church grew, traditional diviners began to receive messages that some of the souls of the dead were unhappy there.

In the early 1950s, those dead souls whose family members had erected impressive stone graves now asked to be transferred to those socially more prestigious structures. Recurrent illnesses and hardships were explained by local ritual practitioners as resulting from the failure to bury the dead in the appropriate traditional manner. Soon the whole lineage and extended kin network began to mobilize for the transfer. Not only the bones of those buried on consecrated Christian ground would be moved, but also those of many younger wives, children, or poor relatives who had received initial burial in the garden hamlets before stone graves were ready for them. Many Sumbanese, it seemed, saw a Christian grave as only a temporary resting place before an appropriate ancestral site was ready.

To the church leadership, such a move was unacceptable. They claimed persons committed to Christianity were being "stolen back" into paganism after their deaths. The church also refused to accept the evidence of traditional divination, in which the spirits concerned were questioned through the medium of a sacred spear and made to reply at the base of the central house pillar. Communications from the invisible world were listened to more attentively by local government officials, who sought to avoid conflict by proposing a new use for the disputed land. They suggested erecting a government office and desacralizing the whole area.

The church firmly refused this plan. In 1952, after a long and tumultuous debate about the value of the church versus the importance of traditional obligations, a whole group of early converts seceded from the Christian community. Repudiating church rules, they insisted on returning the bones of their kinsmen to the ancestral village. The church leadership immediately banned them from attending further services and labeled them apostates, betrayers of the true faith (Ind. *murtad*). The division established at this time between those who had chosen the church and those who rejected it was to become very influential in molding the shifting concepts of church membership: did simple adherence to a series of practices (such as attendance at services or reading from the Bible) suffice, or was a strong commitment to the ideas and principles underlying the belief system necessary? Through conflicts over such issues as burial, marriage, and feasting, differences in doctrine and wider interpretations of the universe began to emerge.

Other discrepancies between church teaching and traditional practice were less dramatic. Polygamy was the most common reason for someone to be suspended from church membership and forbidden from taking communion. The strategy of early evangelization had been to focus on local leaders and important families, encouraging them to draw in their friends and relatives for large group baptisms. Polygamy, although practiced by only 10 to 15 percent of Kodi men, was the mark of a prominent social figure. As a consequence, the rate of polygamy after a generation or so of Protestant evangelizing was actually higher among baptized Christians than among the unconverted. The church, while continuing to condemn the practice, allowed the guilty husbands to continue to attend Sunday worship services but not to take communion. Their many wives and children, however, were still welcomed to drink the blood and eat the body of Christ.

When the Catholic mission was established in Homba Karipit in the 1930s, the German priests were stricter than the Dutch ministers had been, barring both men and women from the communion table if they were polygamously married. In the 1980s, a reevaluation of such rules by both churches allowed for a final forgiving of the "sin of love" (Ind. *dosa cinta*) for those older men, perhaps close to death, who agree not to marry again. Many prominent elders were brought into the Christian community by this leniency, but it understandably weakened the battle against polygamy. Virtually all men who took extra wives now hope to be forgiven before they die.

Participation at feasts, curing ceremonies, and divinations, though initially condemned by the leadership of both churches, was later accommodated under the rubric of family and community obligations. The early Dutch missionaries, to discourage attendance at feasts with a religious purpose, forbade their converts from eating meat dedicated to the *marapu* spirits. But in fact, almost no ritual killing of pigs and buffalo—such as for marriages, funerals, and naming ceremonies—occurred without the protection of the *marapu* being invoked. Christian converts, many of them important people who relished the honors conferred on them by active participation in the ceremonial system, objected that the church was in effect prohibiting them from eating any meat at all. Within a few years, this restriction was revised to a rule that prayers of consecration could not be pronounced by anyone who called himself a Christian. The rule was absurdly easy to follow, since almost all ceremonial ritual speech was recited by traditional specialists: the emphasis on message bearers and mediated communication with the spirits in the indigenous system meant that no man was allowed to be priest in his own house.

The last regulation also raised the question of what criteria distinguished a Christian ceremony from a *marapu* rite, particularly in light of the increasingly common practice of holding family rituals that included elements of both systems: a Bible reading and Christian blessing in Malay, followed by an invocation in Kodi ritual language by a traditional elder. A compromise was reached by dedicating one share of the sacrificial feast to the *marapu* and another to the Christian God, then dividing it among the guests according to their religious preference. When policemen or government soldiers from other islands were present, Islamic prayers and sacrifices were also included. The local church leadership finally concluded that it was best to tolerate such "feasts of syncretism"; after all, they provided a forum for people of different persuasions to hear the Christian message and benefit from it.

Christian prayer meetings (Ind. *pembacaan*) and "thanksgiving cele-brations" (Ind. *pengucapan syukur*) were often performed on the same occasions that traditionally had required the mediation of *marapu* spirits: at times of illness, transition (marriage, a shift in residence, or adoption of new lineage members), or hardship (after a fire, lightning bolt, or crop failure). As responses to a need for spiritual counsel and assistance, they followed the same pattern as nightlong *marapu* ceremonies: first the reasons for the gathering were explained, followed by the dedication of the animals to be slaughtered and the distribution and consumption of food. The most marked differences were in the languages used—biblical Malay versus traditional ritual speech—and the replacement of the sacred authority of the central house post with the portable gospel. There was also an important shift in the kinds of knowledge obtained from such encounters: whereas in traditional divination rites questions could be asked directly of the house post, with yes or no answers provided by whether the diviner's thumb reached its mark at the tip of the spear, the answers provided by the Bible were most enigmatic.

One informant told me that the major difference between Christian and *marapu* beliefs was that the *marapu* divination provided a much more specific explanation of human suffering and misfortune. Although Chris-tian preachers, too, interpreted illness and calamities as signs of divine displeasure, they could not pinpoint either the precise cause or the proper procedures to appease the high God. Speculation could run wild as to the cause of the affliction, and there was no way for the human community to know if the ritual compensation offered was adequate. *Marapu* divi-nations, by contrast, allowed the victim to identify the angry spirits by name, to ascertain the precise chain of events that led to the misfortune, and to mediate the problem in ritual fashion.

Local religious teachers presented this moral and philosophical uncer-tainty as the consequences of original sin; humans had an obligation to repent and suffer, even without full knowledge of the reasons for this suffering, because of a burden of wrongdoing inherited from the ancestors. Since Dutch missionaries had internalized the notion of intrinsic human depravity and the resulting guilt, they constantly prayed for strength over weakness, forgiveness for their bodily urges, and acceptance of their uncertain fate. When uttered by native-born religious teachers, these messages took on a somewhat different hue. In traditional Sumbanese understandings, the living are always laden down with obligations to perform ceremonies and arrange burials because of their duties to preceding generations; the idea of original sin was therefore interpreted as unfulfilled obligation to make it sound more compelling and convincing. The biblical story of Adam and Eve was recast in a Kodi idiom by village preachers, who spoke of the sin of "eating wrongly" in the Garden of Eden. A common consequence was the local perception that the sins of Adam and Eve lay not in eating the forbidden fruit of wisdom, but in failing to perform the necessary rites to "cool down" the land on which the apple tree stood, which would bring its fruit within the circle of ancestral protection so it could be eaten. The sons of Adam were condemned to suffer, in other words, not because of a thirst for knowledge, but because of disrespect for ritual boundaries and the category of bitter foods.

The distinction that the Kodi themselves make between the spirits associated with the inner, social world of ancestral authority and cultural control and the outer nature spirits of the wild was likewise reinterpreted in Christian terms. Early religious teachers, trying to convince the people to stop worshipping the invisible spirit powers, translated the local term *marapu* as *setan*. Although missionaries understood that *marapu* was in fact a very complex and multivalent term (Lambooy 1937), this gloss was the one most frequently used in village evangelizing, sometimes modified by the adjective *kapir*, "pagan." It identified all the members of the complex cosmological structure of Kodi with those malicious, capricious spirits at the periphery, similar to the Moslem *jinn*. When spokesmen for the traditional system protested that spirit beliefs provided a bulwark for community discipline and personal morality, some members of the church leadership began to distinguish between the "good *marapu*," which they identified as the ancestors, and the "bad *marapu*" or *setan*, who were the autochthonous inhabitants of the forests and fields, seashore and ocean. The spirits of natural surroundings were seen as innately evil; those of the established village centers were presented as good. This application of a moralistic, ethical creed to an opposition that was rooted in complementary principles of control versus vitality proved difficult to uphold. Death and suffering, after all, were more often attributed to sanctions imposed by the ancestors than to the nefarious activities of the wild spirits. Likewise, the *setan* of the forests and fields could appear as companions on long journeys through wild lands, who provided medicines and magical powers in return for small sacrifices.

The critical Christian interpretation of *marapu* beliefs stigmatized the worship of a certain class of spirits—significantly, that class of spirits most often addressed in a private, individualistic context. Hence it allowed the church to take a relatively tolerant attitude toward those large-scale rituals that would tend to come to the attention of its leadership and condemn only smaller-scale interactions, which were harder to observe. Clearly, this was a policy of "turning a blind eye" in some directions in order to maintain the momentum of conversion on other fronts.

Christian prayers were often granted a magical efficacy similar to that of the ritual language associated with ancestral centers. They were used to ward off wild spirits and extend the protection of the social community to newly planted crops. The church thus played a parallel ritual role in "cooling the land," bringing it into the realm of cultural control. To the extent that church leaders were aware that they were borrowing the local idiom, they tried to identify the Christian message with the nurturing, protective care of the Great Mothers and Great Fathers of the ancestral centers, in opposition to the more volatile spirits of the outside. The blessings of ancestors was expressed in the metaphors of Sumbanese ritual speech as the flow of cooling waters. For this reason, Onvlee, the Dutch linguist who translated the gospel into the West Sumbanese language of Weyewa, called it *li'li amaraingininga*, the "cooling or salutary words."

Translating Sumbanese religious concepts was a challenging task because of the very different semantic weights assigned to words in the two systems. Writing about his difficulties in finding an appropriate gloss for the Christian concept of "the holy," Onvlee (1938) provides some insight into the thinking of the early Protestant leaders. Initially, he thought that "holiness" could be invoked with metaphorical representations of fertility, prosperity, and well-being, the "cool waters" that are beseeched in traditional prayers to cure fevers. But it was soon clear that "holiness" could just as easily be identified with the opposing pole: those "hot," spiritually charged objects in which divine power was supposed to dwell—sacred houses, village altars, or the divination pillar. The Sumbanese ritual oscillation between hot and cold, bitter and bland, is part of a cyclical movement of spiritual energies that simply does not fit well into Christian theology. It assumes that the bitter, hot, or prohibited nature of certain things is merely a transitory stage through which they must pass before they are brought inside the circle of ancestral control where these energies are harnessed to social tasks.

Onvlee's discussion of the possibilities he considered supports an interpretation of the early dialogue between the church and local spirit worshippers as one phrased in terms of practices rather than beliefs, and one that privileged one temporality over another. His search for a parallel to the Christian concept of "holy" also led to terms that convey a sense of social distance from everyday life. The East Sumbanese term *maliling*, for instance, refers to the stipulations of respect and avoidance that must be observed between specific kin categories, such as father-in-law and daughter-in-law. However, in suggesting that the church could be described as a *uma maliling*, or "respected, separate house," he was unwittingly associating it with prohibitions and restrictions that made it suitable only for slaves. Many of the most sacred objects of the lineage are stored in the *uma maliling*: spirit drums, gold crests, heirloom water urns, and magical weapons obtained from overseas trade. These objects are seen as charged with so much spiritual energy that ordinary men are afraid to handle them. Taboos against defecating, swearing, or spitting in their presence mean that most people will not risk even living near to such objects. Only slaves are expendable enough to guard this sacred patrimony. Needless to say, it would hardly help the cause of village evangelization to define the church as a building so sacred that people would fear to gather inside it. The West Sumbanese term *uma padu*, the "bitter house" or "house of the seventh day," had something of the same sense but temporalized the associated prohibitions. Once a week, church members had to be set aside and appear as a community, but after this brief separation they could take part in daily life; the house of worship, in short, was not permanently dangerous. Onvlee's discussion underlines the irony that he himself observed in the process of translation: any word that seemed, in local terms, to define the Christian ritual center as important and sacred also set it apart from ordinary life and limited the number of converts who dared to cross its threshold.

Evangelization and Development: New Routines and Disciplines

After 1966, the New Order government asked foreign missionaries to devote most of their energies to "development," the main national priority. While evangelization could continue (and was encouraged, since the "Islam politics" of the new Indonesian regime was also fearful of Moslem fundamentalism), the emphasis was now on improving the standard of living of local peoples.

In the 1970s and 1980s, the Protestant and Catholic churches were already quite distinct in Kodi perceptions. The Gereja Kristen Sumba was an independent organization, staffed entirely by native ministers, and received no more funding from the Dutch Reformed Church. Its ministers became increasingly involved in politics, with two of them holding positions as elected representatives to the National Assembly (Dewan Perwakilan Rakyat) and all called upon to assume a role in Golkar election campaigns. The Catholic leadership, still primarily German priests, were forbidden from political activity, but concentrated instead on building projects.

In Kodi, the most important of these projects were digging wells and providing pumps to make fresh water available to the population. In early 1980, the small river that ran through Kory, the largest and most densely populated administrative ward (desa), went dry. The Catholic church built a large cement cistern to store rainwater, which it supplemented with clear water from an underground water source. In Bukambero, a solar-powered project at Payeti pumped an even larger cistern full of clean, fresh water, which villagers carried to their homes in buckets hung on the ends of long bamboo poles.

Water was a symbolically charged resource in an area where control of the rains and the seasons was once the supreme office. To get access to the underground rivers that they tapped, mission officials had to use a sacred source, which had lain untouched for generations. Special marapu ceremonies were held, and buffalo sacrifices were performed to make the area "bland" (pakabaya), compensating local wild spirits so they would allow the nearby inhabitants to drink this water. In agreeing to perform these sacrifices, the mission tacitly accepted the authority of local priests who stated their necessity. But the priests also showed that new technology and labor could provide people with a critical resource, one that they could not obtain by simple prayers and offerings to their ancestors. The wells and pumps made a deep impression on the population of the wards nearest them, now almost half Catholic.

The Catholic mission's concern with hierarchy and decorum gave it a different character from that of the Protestants, with their stress on village evangelization. Practical skills were taught in Catholic schools as well as basic literacy. Boys received lessons in carpentry and masonry, and their labor was used to build new cathedrals at each mission. Girls learned cooking, sewing, and household hygiene. At the Homba Karipit mission, students lived in a dormitory, where they learned to set their routines by the clock, responding to bells that both announced the passage of each hour and corresponded to duty stations in a schedule of daily chores. The day was divided into segments, so that a girl would spend one hour helping in the out-patient clinic, another scrubbing floors in the kitchen, a third preparing food for guests, and a fourth mending sheets and bedding.

At the mission school, girls were prepared for roles as wives and mothers, boys as wage laborers and mission employees; all the while their "spiritual guardians," the nuns and priests, convinced that temporal discipline would instill a sense of responsibility and orderliness, believed that they were encouraging young people to think for themselves and become free of the constraints of custom and tradition (Mispagel in May, Mispagel, and Pfister 1982, 91–92). Local people clearly perceived the mission as a training ground for Westernized gender roles and social habits. Kodi commentary on the value of the Catholic "housekeeping school" (*sekolah rumah tangga*) and "craftshop" (*sekolah tukang*) reflects this:

> We send our daughters to Homba Karipit so they can learn to cook things that only Westerners eat, like bread and cookies. We send our sons so they can see how to build Western furniture—tables, chairs, cupboards, things that never existed in Kodi until they came. But now, in this time of foreign ways [*pata dawa*], we need them. The girls learn to sew dresses and sarungs, and uniforms worn in schools and offices. These skills can bring in money later. Kodi women all learn to weave and tie *ikat* designs into thread. Women on Java and other islands learn to use a sewing machine and to make the national costume of sarung and kebaya, or the skirts and shirts of government bureaucrats. We say that the Catholic school teaches them "foreignness" [*kejawaan*] so they can go other places.

The missionaries, aware of the commercial value of their teachings, commented that "a girl with a sewing machine brings in a bigger brideprice." The investment made by parents who paid tuition for this training was returned to them in water buffalo when their daughters married (Mispagel in May, Mispagel, and Pfister 1982, 91).

The missionaries valued promptness, cleanliness, hourly routines, and schedules as ends in themselves, not only as preconditions for wage-earning employment. Yet although the new "techniques of power" embodied in the regimentation of time, through its segmentation, seriation, synthesis, and totalization, were an attribute of missions and schools in Kodi, as they have been attributes of a great many other disciplinary institutions (Foucault 1977, 139), they were not perceived as confinements and enclosures, but as ways of "opening up" their inhabitants to a wider world of historical forces.

Protestant schoolteachers learned a pedagogical practice that also emphasized timetables, homework, and examinations. Traditional training, by contrast, was through apprenticeship and an initiation. A small boy, for example, might accompany a famous ritual speaker, at first simply carrying the meat but later beginning to assist in sacrifices, to answer his elder's orations with affirmations, and eventually to comment on them and even speak on his own behalf. His fitness for this final stage would be determined by divination. In both government and religious schools, however, a multiple and progressive series of tasks was set, with each stage followed by tests and students constantly supervised to keep them from being distracted from their exercises. Such discipline, according to Foucault (1977), opens up an analytic space that coerces not only bodies but also minds: in learning to obey the new routines of elementary schools, Kodi children also learned to think in the new ways of the churches and offices.

Ideas of discipline and order become ingrained in mundane habits of everyday life; the attention that foreign missionaries dedicated to these more subtle aspects of "education" may constitute their most enduring legacy. While these ideas were cast as part of "development" rather than "evangelization," the two projects were intricately linked, and the first, though avowedly "apolitical," may in fact have had the greater impact on indigenous perceptions and practices. Studies of missionary activity in other parts of Indonesia (Kipp 1990; Bigalke 1984) have noted that in instilling the authoritative imprint of Western capitalist culture, missionaries have often introduced a new worldview but been unable to deliver the world to go with it. Converts, freshly inspired, were frustrated by their inability to maintain the standard they had been taught in school. The newly "rationalized" concepts of time and discipline they had learned could not be easily transferred to distant hamlets where they married and had children.

Recent Reinterpretations

Contact with foreign missionaries and an official, national vision of monotheistic religion has altered both daily routines and intellectual habits on Sumba. In the 1980s, the period of my fieldwork, Kodi debates about what was included within "religion" and what was not included two camps. The first, defenders of the church, put together notes on Kodi language and beliefs, which preserve the coherence and complexity of their own village traditions while comparing them to the principles and events of the Bible. The similarities between Kodi custom and ritual and sacrificial practices described in the Gospels are highlighted. The apostates or exiles from the Christian community, by contrast, have taken a different tack: they record traditional beliefs and practices in the hopes of constructing a parallel system, one that rivals the Bible with alternative explanations of religious problems.

The best-known and most influential document of this antichurch group is a *buku agama marapu kodi,* or "book on the Kodi religion," composed by my teacher Maru Daku and dictated to his schoolteacher son. The author had converted to Christianity in the 1930s after graduating from the first school to open in the region. In 1952, however, he seceded from the church during disputes about the proper burial of the dead. By the 1980s he was a well-known ritual speaker and an authority on traditional custom (Hoskins 1985). Toward the end of my stay he showed me the book he had compiled in response to our discussions of the relations of *marapu* beliefs and Christian dogma. Both its form and its style of argument were shaped by and in opposition to the teachings of the church, which he had learned as a young man. Its originality lay in insights into differences between the two systems and attempts to justify the *marapu* system in counterpoint to the Christian one.

The book begins with a list of the seven classes of spirits that are worshipped—moving from the Creator, on to the first man and woman, the house deity, the clan deity, the spirits of the house and garden, and finally the spirits of the dead. He then noted that "the *marapu* religion has things that are forbidden, just as every religion has its prohibitions." Given the Kodi fondness for the number seven, seven commandments were presented in traditional ritual language, which translated into biblical-like injunctions against stealing, killing, or deceiving one's kinsmen. Obligations to feed the deities and make offerings at certain points of the year were first negatively phrased (highlighting the dangers of presenting the invisible powers with impure food), then positively presented in an outline of each household's calendrical round of sacrifices. In this way moral discipline and temporal order were brought to the forefront, but again in a traditional context.

Sensitive to Christian criticism of the rhetoric of traditional offerings, Maru Daku went on to explain the humility and apparent deception that Kodinese conventionally used in addressing the spirits:

> It is said that the *marapu* religion is a false one, because it is founded on lies contained in the prayers....Even after a large harvest, one must still say that the bag of white rice where the cockatoos play is not full, and the sack of foreign rice where the parrots scamper does not burst at the brim. . . . Even if one has many buffalo and horses, dogs and pigs, one must still ask for more . . . so we always ask for more rice to eat and more water to drink. But this is not greed or deception: it is [done] because in our religion you cannot make yourself appear rich in front of the spirits, you cannot brag or show off in front of them. . . . The *marapu* religion teaches

you to make yourself seem poor to those above, to belittle yourself in their direction and make all that you do appear insignificant.

The contradiction he addresses here has to do only partly with modesty in pleading with the ancestors for fertility and prosperity. It also concerns the crucial difference between the Christian model of personal prayer, with its idiosyncratic expression of desires, and the formalized collective model of traditional prayer. What Dutch ministers interpreted as deception and lying was in fact integrated into traditional religious practice as an etiquette of respect and deference; these strategies defined appropriate attitudes toward the deities and stressed that worldly wealth can never rival the mythological opulence and abundance of the heavenly kingdom.

The book continues by elaborating other Kodi systems of order: a traditional numerology that equates the seven holes in the human body with seven classes of spirits and seven stages of ceremonial accomplishment in the feasting cycle. Social stratification was represented on the model of the human hand, moving from the thumb, which stood for the prominent leader, to the little finger, representing the slave. Rules regulating the performance of ceremonies to shift residence or to call back the souls of those who had died a bad death were included. Local practice was defended as simply "another path" that led in the same direction as that of the Christian church, but one that was known to its followers only through word of mouth (Hoskins 1987c, 156–57).

Finally, he finished with an extended history of the oldest Kodi villages and a genealogy that traced the inhabitants of certain lineage houses back seventeen generations. Obviously modeled on biblical genealogies, this evidence was marshaled to demonstrate the historical depth of Kodi tradition and the fact that links to the time of the ancestral mandate were still intact. "The Christians have their book, but we have our stone ship and our tree altars, whose heritage has been transmitted to us by the language passed down through the generations and the speech sewn up into couplets."

The very eloquence of this plea for understanding and tolerance for *marapu* practice is couched in the terms of universal principles introduced from the outside. As a catalogue of rules and ritual practices, the book is an accurate document that stresses sequences and regimentation. As a dialogue with Christian critics, it presents an apologia in a new vocabulary, an effort to abstract dogmas and principles from a mode of symbolic action whose logic was until then basically implicit. By dictating this text to his son, Maru Daku transformed traditional worship even as he interpreted it, for he believed that only by assimilating *marapu* ritual to the categories of monotheistic religions could its true value be recognized and articulated.

Maru Daku died in 1982, but his work influenced a new generation of Kodi ministers who have also tried to rethink the relations of Kodi custom and Christian belief. In 1984, I attended and taped a synod of ministers and evangelical teachers in Bondo Kodi. Discussion was carried on by three Kodi ministers—Hendrik Mone, Martin Woleka, and Daud Ndara Nduka—who sought to establish a unified church policy on three topics that had been problematic in the past: ritual feasts, marriage, and burial customs. Significantly, the most frequent interpretive strategy was to find a parallelism between Christian theology and the implicit doctrines of local practice, so that an accommodation could be established.

The analysis of worship at traditional altars and feasts provides an illustration of this method of resolution. Pendita Daud, speaking first, noted that in the Old Testament when Jacob dreamed of meeting with God he took a large stone and set it upright as a sign that his land had been given to him by God. He promised God that if He continued to give him blessings and help him along the way, later he would build a house and hold a feast there, to thank the Lord for his blessings. Pendita Daud then explained:

> This is the same sequence that we follow in Kodi feasts, when we start in the gardens, and promise the *marapu* that if they give us prosperity, later we will hold a bigger feast in the ancestral village. Then, if we are allowed to live to continue our efforts, we will drag a gravestone and consecrate it with another feast. In all of these prayers, we may mention the Creator, but we give the requests to our ancestors, since they must serve as messengers. In fact, the Creator is always connected to them, as if by a slender thread. But since the Creator is too far, the Kodi embraces first those who are closer to him—his ancestors. Local customs such as we have here do have a religious content, but it is still obscure. Since it was handed down by oral tradition, the names may have been confused.

It is common for local evangelists to invoke the authority of the Old Testament and its parallels with Kodi ritual practices. The peoples of ancient Israel, indeed, are presented as having had almost exactly the same customs as the Kodi ancestors, with practices like polygamy, interregional warfare, the taking of heads (although the Bible's most famous "head-hunter," Judith, is confusingly female), and the levirate often being cited. The story of the ancestral migration from Sasar to Sumba and the division into different language groups is interpreted as a variant of the Tower of

Babel story, with present generations diverging from a more complete and unified order.

The New Testament was the text first carried into Kodi villages, and it is the only one so far translated into Sumbanese languages. Increasing literacy, however, has made the Old Testament more accessible; as a result, that book is often cited to furnish legitimating links to the ancestral past. Its reports of feasting, sacrifice, and political conflict appear familiar and understandable and are used to justify the continuation of local practices they resemble. "Our ancestors were like King Solomon and his companions, who did not know Jesus but prayed to the Supreme God under their own name for him." With this argument, the fulfillment of obligations to hold a promised feast or to rebuild an ancestral house can be defended even after conversion. Since it provides a Christian context for pagan practices, the Old Testament also reveals their value in maintaining the fabric of collective life and especially the integrity of exchange networks. "Even if we do not listen to the voices of the dead, we must respond to those of the living," some converts explained to account for their participation in feasts. Debts are reckoned not only to the ancestral spirits, but also to living companions who had given shares of meat at earlier feasts and deserved to be repaid.

Pendita Daud defended local custom in remarkably relativistic terms:

> Custom [Ind. *adat*] cannot be considered paganism [Ind. *kapir*]. Culture [Ind. *kebudayaan*] cannot be considered paganism. Neither custom nor culture is the enemy of the church. A better term than *agama kapir* is *agama suku*, the religion of a particular ethnic group. *Marapu* beliefs are the indigenous religion of the Kodi people, but we cannot say that they are all wrong. The gospel came into the world through the culture of Israel. In Sumba, the gospel has to be brought in through local culture, so that custom can help to communicate the gospel message.

What is most remarkable about this passage is the way it takes the "national" Indonesian concepts of "custom" and "culture" and uses them to bring traditional practices in through the back door, so to speak. If only "paganism" is the enemy of the church, and these traditional practices, rather than being really pagan, are in fact simply misapprehended versions of the gospel message, then it is possible for a person to be both a practicing *marapu* worshipper and a good Christian. That would seem to be the syncretistic message of his remarks, though still veiled in the rhetoric of a national vocabulary.

That same year, a *woleko* feast was held in Kaha Deta, Balaghar, at which these principles were put into practice. Sponsored in part by the family of the first Christian minister in the area, it was held in his ancestral village and featured prayers in ritual language and sacrifices. The ritual orators were asked to give a full history of the obligations and promises that formed the background to the feast, but to mention neither the seven layers of heaven and six layers of land that their words would travel past nor any specific upperworld deities. The Creator was named and praised, and the ancestors were acknowledged as honored predecessors, but no message-bearers were invoked.

The innovations of this feast were intensely debated. Some praised the revitalization of Kodi feasting in a "modern" mode; others condemned it as a *woleka tana dawa*, or "feast from a foreign land," which did not remain faithful to any traditional norms. One old priest said it was a *bungkus tanpa nasi* (Ind.), a "leaf bundle without the rice"—that is, although the top and bottom of a spiritual hierarchy were left, there was little filling in between. "If *marapu* are listening, they will refuse to hear this message," he said, "since it doesn't follow the stages [*katadi*] that we know from custom."

Rationalized Paganism: Old Rites in New Times

Debates about the validity of these innovations continue, informed by an awareness of the different temporalities at stake. On the one hand, some people proclaim the entropic view that posits a gradual but irrevocable moving away from origins and ancestral completeness, with the recent wave of conversion just another aspect of this decline. For them, the past represents an ideal that cannot be realized in this world, an actuality lost to subsequent generations. On the other hand, there are those, like Pendita Daud, who employ a "historicist" view of tradition to argue for the continuing relevance of the past to the present. In the following passage, for instance, he interprets the meaning of sacred objects to a audience of Protestant religious teachers:

> When Kodi people pray to stones or trees or sacred objects, they are praying to them as objects that contain a history, that are part of their past. They are used as reminders and intermediaries [Ind. *penyalur lida*] to carry messages to the Creator, who is the ultimate audience of these prayers. The *wudi pa hamulla, watu papendende*

["tree planted, stone erected"] is simply a proof from the past which shows that they, too, called the Lord for assistance.

His remarks were controversial and provoked a response from his superior in rank, Pendita Woleka, that "Jesus Christ is the only intermediary needed by Christians. They do not need rocks or trees or ancestors." Many, however, were convinced that the church should accept that ancestral rites provide a form of indigenous education with regard to culture and history: "Christians can go to them because they should also learn from the past, but their prayers must be addressed only to the Creator."

This appeal did not fall on deaf ears. Although some church leaders insist on a narrower interpretation of the content of "religion," many followers clearly wish to accept Christianity *along with* traditional practices. They want someone to develop an argument for syncretism that makes sense to its real judges—the ambivalent and divided villagers of the region, who do not want to abandon their ancestors yet still seek to move into a new and wider world.

The canons of modesty exemplified by traditional prayers suggest that in the distant past there existed a form of perfection which has gradually been eroded; as a result, contemporary ritual speakers are actively struggling against a loss of knowledge and diminished spiritual powers. Yet even as they suffer this loss, they are at the same time acquiring the means to record these traditions in writing and compile authoritative texts of ritual observance. Because of these new technologies and the influence of notions of "religion" and "belief" introduced by the Indonesian state, any form of Kodi *marapu* worship that survives into future generations will endure in transformation. Already today it is becoming a "rationalized paganism," inscribed in a new temporality and articulated in a new language.

The historical changes described here detail a gradual shift from a focus on ritual action and standards of correctness to one on religious dogma and belief. In this process, an "internal conversion" (Geertz 1973) occurs as religious concepts are gradually lifted "above" or "outside" the concrete realm of ordinary life and integrated into systems whose aim, at least nominally, is a more logical coherence. The multitude of concretely defined but only loosely ordered sacred entities that "involve themselves in an independent, segmental and immediate manner with almost any sort of actual event" (Geertz 1973, 172) are giving way to a more developed and integrated body of religious assertions. The wider problems of meaning— the reasons for suffering and for death—are coming to be addressed on an abstract plane, instead being attacked piecemeal and opportunistically by the search for a particular person or spirit who happens to bear a grudge.

"Belief" is a category of rationalized religions, and conversion is possible only once beliefs have reached a level of conscious articulation (Hoskins 1987c). "Conversion" implies a historicist temporality, for it requires an awareness that a great change is involved and that new forms of worship will substitute for older ones instead of simply supplementing them. Conversion is usually limited to prophetic religions, which are exclusive and require an unqualified commitment. "Adhesion," by contrast, is typical of traditions that more pragmatically seek "to satisfy a number of natural needs, to set a seal on the stages by which a life is marked, and to ensure the proper working of the natural processes and sources of supply on which its continuance depends" (Nock 1933, 8).

Kodi *marapu* worshippers were born into the cult of their ancestors; they did not consciously choose it or have an opportunity to examine its basic tenets. For these reasons, earlier generations are best described as simply "adhering" to a tradition passed down from their forefathers. In the first period of dialogue with the church, many prominent Kodi tried to "adhere" to the prestige and power of the foreign creed without fully "converting." For many years the two systems were seen as complementary modes of ritual action, one attuned to the ancestral villages, the other to the world of education and government service. Conflicts over ritual procedure (the burial of the dead, participation in feasting and sacrifice) led to an awareness of logical inconsistencies and abstract principles implicit in *marapu* ceremonial. The potential for conversion thus emerged only gradually, as part of a dialogue conducted initially in terms of notions of ritual correctness and contrasting practices and only later reformulated using the "religious" vocabulary of doctrine and belief. In the face of the challenges of state pressures and missionary activity, however, the *marapu* tradition must now be chosen or rejected, reinvented or lost.

Can a "rationalized paganism" have a viable existence in the late twentieth century? Perhaps not as a formal religious affiliation, since the politics of New Order "progress" do not tolerate the *marapu* label. But as an element of a syncretic Christian church, led by native ministers who are nevertheless fundamentally sympathetic to the traditions of their ancestors, Kodi ritual practices will, it seems, continue in a somewhat altered form. By breaking down a holistic indigenous world of ceremonies related to the ancestral spirits into the officially defined domains of custom (Ind. *adat*), culture (Ind. *kebudayaan*), art (Ind. *kesenian*), and religion (Ind. *agama*), government officials and church authorities conspired to erase the dangerous "religious" elements of traditional practice while preserving a bit of local color and pageantry. Their tactics, though, have been turned back on them by a new generation of native interpreters, who use these very categories to keep alive a heritage that maintains "the thread going back through the ancestors" as a meaningful time line.

Tradition lives on in the age of "history" (*sejarah*), but only by being reinvented in ways that separate it from stigmatized categories and exploit a national rhetoric of cultural diversity and village democracy. These are the debates to which we turn next.

11

The Past as Ideology

New Heroes, New Histories

The stranger mother speaks with oil in her mouth, the foreign father
has sugar on his tongue; but the bridges remain to be built, and the
rivers remain to be crossed.

> A Kodi commentary on the Golkar
> electoral campaign of 1987

In the last chapter I argued that "religion" emerged as a category of Kodi
life only after important historical changes occurred in the twentieth
century. The same could be said for "history," which in the Indonesian
term *sejarah* is also a relative latecomer to local discourse. The concept
has come, moreover, with a very specific form and intent: in creating
"history," Kodi commentators joined the nationalist quest for an Indonesian past (Reid 1979) and committed themselves to an ideology of progressive, directed time that would take them "out of darkness and into
light" (Anderson 1990).

The "darkness" of the past was, in this vision, recent, coinciding with
the period of colonial domination. Before the shadows of Dutch conquerors
fell across the islands, there was an earlier, glorious past of Indonesian
unity. The concept of historical progression was thus presented as the
recovery of a national destiny, a "return" to the splendor of the precolonial
empires and a realization of indigenous social democracy in a new era.

A great many aspects of modernity came very suddenly to Kodi, tele-
scoping stages of a long historical development into an encounter of just
a few years. The meeting with the Indonesian *sejarah* gave "history" a
very specific ideological content.[1] *Sejarah* in its current sense refers not

---

[1] The Malay word *sejarah* originally had the sense of "family tree" or an oral
tradition handed down through the generations (Bottoms 1965, 180) and is close
in meaning to the term *silsilah*, or "genealogy," tracing a line of descent back
through time. While some critics of Malay sources have characterized them as "a
mixture of truth and legend, fantasy and fact, entertainment and instruction"
(Bottoms 1965, 181), it is perhaps more interesting to note the fact that they were
frankly partisan and *situated* views of the past, offering not a global vision but an
individual or group perspective.

so much to a discipline as to a vision of the past, described by a prominent Indonesian historian as a response to the "insistent demands for a nationalist historiography and for national myths, from which new confidence can be gained and sustenance drawn" (Soedjatmoko 1965, 404). This form of history emerged as an authoritative form of discourse in postindependence Indonesia, one with its own rules and precedents.

Indonesian nationalist history contrasts with earlier genres such as *silsilah* (genealogies), *babad* (court chronicles), or *hikayat* (dynastic accounts). Like Kodi narratives, these written texts were connected to a particular descent line or specific heirloom objects, and they described additions to the past and a variety of instantiations of the traditional order. In the genealogies, metonymic links to the past were defined by descent, whereas in narratives the links were metaphoric, defined by successful precedent (Valeri 1990, 169). Traditional Malay sources include the biographies and autobiographies of important persons, which come somewhat closer to the modern genre of historiography. The particular dynastic standpoint of a royal family, for example, provided a subjective window on the past and transmitted the traditions and values of the ruling class. The life of a usurper, by contrast, showed that events did not follow an unbroken line but could deviate in arresting ways. The progressive, directed "history" of national liberation developed mainly in imitation of Western models, but it was not without some patterning on earlier forms of discourse about the archipelago's past.

History and Heritage

It is a truism in anthropology that societies of any complexity try to *"make* history repeat itself" (Peel 1984, 111), because such repetition serves to legitimate the present. The importance of the "past in the present" has been associated with the lines drawn between "traditional" and "modern" societies, or between hierarchical and egalitarian ones (Bloch 1977). I would offer another set of polarities as offering a different perspective on the past, one pole stressing a continuing "heritage" from the past, with the other emphasizing a rupture between past and present that is "history." In the first view, the past is still alive and used day after day to provide moral examples, to interpret the future, and to invest both the individual human life and the nation with a sense of destiny. In the second, the past is dead, and "history" performs an autopsy on its corpse, gazing with an objective and disinterested eye on the illusions of another era. The exponents of critical history trace its emergence to the collapse of a unified, coherent vision of the past:

> History . . . is not the past. The past is always a created ideology
> with a purpose, designed to control individuals, or motivate socie-
> ties, or inspire classes. Nothing has been so corruptly used as con-
> cepts of the past. The future of history and historians is to cleanse
> the story of mankind from those deceiving visions of a purposeful
> past. The death of the past can only do good so long as history
> flourishes. Above all, one hopes that the past will not rise phoenix-
> like from its own ashes to justify again, as it often has, the subjec-
> tion and exploitation of men and women, to torture them with fears,
> or to stifle them with a sense of their own hopelessness. The past
> has only served the few; perhaps history will serve the multitude.
>
> (Plumb 1969, 17)

While I do not share the view that modern historians can escape the
limitations of time and perspective with which all chroniclers of the past
have had to deal, I preserve this distinction in order to turn it in another
direction: "history," I argue, presents an ideology of cumulative, irreversible change, a process that contrasts strongly with the "heritage" of many
non-Western societies. The two perspectives must first be defined as ideal
types, opposing interpretive stances, so that we can then focus on their
interaction in concepts such as the Indonesian *sejarah*.

"History" and "heritage" offer contrasting views of the relation of past
and present. If the past is seen as "history," it is part of a linear time line,
marked by distinct, nonrepeating events in which individuals emerge as
actors and their exploits are unique occurrences. In this case, the past
refers to a particular and concrete series of actions, which are discontinuous
with the present. "History does not repeat itself," in the strict sense of the
term. If, however, the past is seen as "heritage," it *can* be repeated, though
always in somewhat transformed form because it contains not specific
events but somewhat richer and vaguer potentialities. Instead of a line of
unique occurrences, the past is an array of established sequences, like the
stages of a ritual, which can be instantiated in various forms. Thus, a
headhunting raid may be carried out by many different actors, but they
must follow the proper procedures. Its characteristic ritual forms (songs,
dances, offerings) can even be adapted to other contexts without a total
loss of meaning. The "heritage" of the past allows for a more flexible
synthesis of new senses that are attached to a shared sequence.[2]

[2] After writing this chapter, I came across E. V. Daniel's 1991 article "Three Dispositions Towards the Past: One Sinhalla and Two Tamil," which also deals with
the contrast of "heritage" and "history," associating the former with the Jaffna
Tamils and the latter with the Buddhist Sinhalese. While there are certain differ-

The contrast of the two is most marked in terms of individual action. When people act to realize a historical consciousness, they expect their acts to rearrange the order of things irrevocably. They see themselves as individuals who leave their signature on the past, creating a finished chapter that may be reopened and reread but not rewritten. When people act as members of their wider cultural heritage, they see themselves as taking the place of an ancestor, avenging an inherited "debt of blood" and thus continuing a pattern of reciprocities that is itself timeless. They impersonate an ancestral persona, negating their own individuality and historicity at the same time that they emphasize the importance of their heritage.

If events happen only once, they must emerge as "history." If they can happen many times, with minor variations, then they embody a living tradition that no mere event can alter dramatically. "History" in this sense is largely a product of the discontinuities of Western civilization, and the view of the past that it inspires is every bit as ideological as that of "heritage." Each of these views is, in practice, an emphasis and not a global, deterministic vision. There can be local and regional variations in the degree to which each term holds sway.[3]

The Indonesian notion of *sejarah* was born in the context of revolutionary struggle, which repudiated the colonial past by nostalgically evoking an earlier, precolonial heritage. Visions of the glory of Majapahit, Srivijaya, and Mataram were used to erect the idea of "Indonesia" as a moral community that preceded and yet somehow survived Dutch colonial interventions. The new nation had to be created in the imagination as well as in practice. The bases of unity were laid by asserting that despite the great linguistic and religious differences which divided Indonesian peoples, they shared a common cultural background and the experience of common struggle against colonial domination. While some Indonesian intellectuals favored the internationalism of Islam or Marxism, they were eventually defeated by a "nationalist orthodoxy" which wedded the progressive view

---

ences between our uses of the term, he also articulates a view of heritage as continuous with the past and history as discontinuous, using the Peircean vocabulary of *rhemes* and *dicisigns* to distinguish the two. My interpretation here accords with this view of heritage as a "fill-in-the-blanks" approach to the past, but I do not make the same claims he does for a relation between a "historical religion" (Buddhism) and the genesis of historical consciousness. There can be a number of reasons for discontinuities between past and present, and this chapter suggests some other ones.

[3] In another piece (Hoskins forthcoming[1]), I argue that in East Sumba headhunting is seen as "history" (and may have been seen in this way for over a hundred years), while in West Sumba it is "heritage"; the practice, in other words, served different functions and interests on the two sides of the island.

of "history" to reclamations of a lost past (Reid 1979, 295–98). The need for a radical rupture of the prevailing power structure was justified by arguments for a return to an earlier order. This earlier order was not examined too closely, however, since the specific attributes of the remembered past threatened to dissolve rather than confirm the newly defined unity of Indonesia. Nationalism fed on a view of the past as heritage[4] to legitimate the models it provided for the future.

Nationalism on Sumba

The slow pace at which Indonesian national history developed was due in part to tensions between groups that sought a revival and strengthening of their own heritage and resisted identification with an artificial new polity of Dutch making (Reid 1979, 282). In creating a nationalist movement, Javanese and Sumatran leaders often clashed, and their priorities were markedly different from those of leaders in the more distant, eastern fringes of the archipelago such as Sulawesi or the Moluccas. Sumba, too, already in the colonial period a backwater, remained more a witness than a participant in the formative years of Indonesian nationalism.

The center of the nationalist movement of the Lesser Sunda Islands was the Timorsch Verbond, an organization formed in 1922 under Rotinese and Savunese leadership. After the 1945 declaration of Indonesian independence, it was transformed into the Partai Demokrasi Indonesia, a political party that continues to the present. Support for national unification and independence was unwavering in the region; it continued strong even through the formation of the State of Eastern Indonesia (Negara Indonesia Timor), when Dutch forces temporarily regained control of the Timor archipelago. Chronicled by I. M. Doko, a Savunese leader who oversaw the transfer of civil authority to local officials in Kupang, the seamless progression of the popular will to nationhood was finally realized in the new state of Indonesia (Doko 1982).

Although political consciousness on Sumba was relatively low, the sons of noble families who were sent to school in Timor, Java, and Sulawesi supported the nationalist movement. Japanese forces tried to play on nationalist aspirations when they invaded the island in 1942; the Japanese occupation, however, was a time of brutal deprivations which, if anything, provoked a nostalgia for the colonial period. Nevertheless, when the Japa-

---

[4]Instead of referring to this body of customs as *adat*, the Indonesian term often used to mean a branch of law, I prefer the term *heritage* because it suggests that what is passed on from one generation to another is not only custom or narrative ("oral tradition"), but also objects and the meanings attached to them.

nese left, Sumbanese leaders joined others in calling for immediate independence (Kapita 1977).

The transfer of power from the Dutch colonial officer to the local nobles who held positions in the State of Eastern Indonesia was achieved without a single shot being fired on Sumba. H. R. Horo, the Kodi administrator who headed the Council of Sumbanese Rajas, simply ordered a change of flags in the regency capital of Waingapu. The ease of the changeover on Sumba contrasted sharply with violent and drawn-out conflicts elsewhere. On this isolated island, at any rate, there was a marked disjunction between the rhetoric of armed struggle (Ind. *perjuangan*) that was used generally to describe resistance to foreign domination and the bloodless cession of colonial authority that occurred in 1949.

Perhaps because they perceived that "something was missing" in their experience of the changeover, Sumbanese writers looked to their own past for people who would fit the new category of national hero (Ind. *pahlawan*): "Through the anti-Dutch struggle of the *pahlawan*, each people in the archipelago found a formula to relate its own unique experience of the past with the new nationalist identity" (Reid 1979, 294). Because struggle conspicuously did *not* occur at the time of independence, legitimation for the "Sumbanese spirit of resistance" (Ind. *semangat perlawanan Sumba*) was sought in a more distant time of violence and unrest. Finally, the search came to focus on the Kodi figure of Wona Kaka.

The Headhunter Before History

Wona Kaka was the warrior from the headhunting village of Bongu who led the resistance against the Dutch from 1911 to 1913 (see chapter 4 and the discussion of the urn and staff as competing symbols of governmental rule). Here, we look back at this period through a different lens, that of nationalist historiography. The retrospective glance of many present-day people in Kodi has come to emphasize these early raids on the colonial army as a model and justification for the legitimate use of violence in a struggle for local autonomy. In this way headhunting has been invested with a new ideological content owing to its association with the leader of an anticolonial resistance movement.

Headhunters in contemporary Kodi are described in Indonesian as "heroes" (*pahlawan*), and the tradition of predatory raids on enemy peoples has been reinvented as a tradition of heroic opposition to appropriating native lands. Like many peoples who have felt driven to refashion the past in order to establish precedents for the revolutionary transformation of the present (Hobsbawm 1983), the people of Sumba have raided their own past, creating a new form of "local history" that fits a mold cast in the steaming caldron of the struggle for national independence. Understanding the new meaning given to headhunting requires an excursion back into the period of colonial contact, followed by an analysis of the stages of its reinterpretation in the 1950s through 1980s.

Headhunting came before history for the people of Kodi, in the sense that no explanation or justification of the practice based on past events was summoned. The lowlanders of Kodi, Laura, and Bukambero were bound in an unending cycle of deadly reciprocity that opposed them to the highlanders of Weyewa, Rara, and Ede. Raids would be undertaken because of a message from the unhappy ghost of a former victim, who asked to be avenged. They were an intermittent form of warfare; war parties were not formed unless some misfortune had provoked a divination, revealing the ghost's anger. In certain cases, vengeance was more immediate, and raids were performed to end the mourning period for an important noble (Hoskins 1989a; Djakababa 1988). The cycle of raiding and revenge that bound highlander and lowlander together in a deadly reciprocity was described as resembling the long-burning coals of ironwood and tamarind (*api kyomi, api kyaha*), which can never be extinguished. In contrast, the murderous feuds that to this day occasionally erupt between Kodi clans are described as shorter-term flare-ups, like fires in the elephant grass or undergrowth (*api ngingyo, api kahumbu*). Within the same language or dialect group, feuds can be resolved through negotiation and a payment of blood compensation (*tapo*) in horses, buffalo, and gold. Outside these boundaries, the ancestral spirits demanded a more exacting revenge.

Heads were taken only as the "replacement of throats cut, share of limbs twisted in anger" (*koko ngole helu, kalengga langa mbani*). No new raid could be undertaken without a specific mandate from the ancestors. The grief and passion of the community had to be expressed in signs of spiritual anger: in the language used in divinations before a raid, the skull tree itself was said to "boil with heat," the stone circle surrounding it to "steam with anger" (*nyawako katoda, wyuhuka kalele*). The memory of an unavenged death could cause fevers, fires, and other misfortunes, which would afflict the village until its members agreed to take up arms to seek a replacement for the head taken. The implements set aside for boiling the captured heads to remove the flesh were anthropomorphized into greedy spirits that were also hungry and asked to be fed:

Our throats are not yet quenched	Njana maghana pango a kokoma
Says the ladle that isn't satisfied	Wena a kaco inja magholi
Our bellies are not yet full	Njana mbanu pango a kambuna
Says the pot that isn't content	Wena a kambela inja mbanu

Human skulls stored in the ancestral village of Ndelo commemorate a violent and glorious past. These skulls were unearthed and displayed when the headhunting house was rebuilt. 1980. Photograph by the author.

A divination was held whenever the headhunting implements were found to exhibit this "heat," and diviners used a spear intermediary to question the spirits about the reason for their anger. If a headhunting raid was asked for, a chicken had to be sacrificed to "raise up" (*manu kede*) the warriors for the raid; auguries read in the chicken's entrails predicted the success or failure of the strike.

Headhunting was deliberately ritualized: done only in large war parties, riding horses decorated with fine red cloth and jingling bells, the head-hunter aimed to "dazzle" his opponent and hence unnerve him. The splendor of the hunter of human heads was deliberately contrasted to the simplicity required of the hunter of wild animals, who could wear no finery or gold ornaments and had to move in silence and secrecy through the forest.

The Origins of Local Resistance

Dutch forces received a relatively warm welcome when they came bearing a gold staff of office, which they planned to bestow upon the local leader chosen as raja by a Kodi council of elders. As long as they remained trading partners who recognized local leaders and contributed to the sacred patrimony of Kodi villages, Europeans did not threaten the coherence of local categories. Earlier heroes, after all, had courted the favor of foreign powers, using objects acquired from them to prove their mastery of leadership qualities. But when, contrary to earlier foreign powers, the Dutch tried to control local affairs, they were perceived as enemies rather than sources of power and authority. A new kind of hero was needed to challenge and oppose them, one who would tap a larger regional base and create a new form of resistance.

The first violent clashes occurred after a period of several months in which labor was conscripted to build a bridge across the Kodi River. One day Tila Gheda, the wife of a nobleman from the headhunting village of Bondo Kodi, returned home and showed her husband a Dutch coin she had been given to secure her silence after the Dutch commander made sexual advances on her and a slave attendant. Her husband, swearing revenge, immediately recruited two companions to help him ambush and kill the four soldiers guarding the construction site at the bridge. The heads of the victims were cut off but not taken away; their rifles, however, were seized and taken back to the headhunting cult house, where they were stored in the right front corner (*mata marapu*), home of war trophies and harvest offerings. A messenger was sent to Rato Loghe Kanduyo, the first raja (*toko*), to tell him what had happened.

Dutch forces retaliated before Kodi leaders could assemble. They burned

Tossi, destroying the center of calendrical rituals for the whole region and killing several older inhabitants in the blaze. The urn and other heirlooms, fortunately, were hidden safely in the gardens. The raja called an emergency meeting to respond to the attack, then sent a delegation to Bongu, home of Wona Kaka, to ask him to lead a war party. The warrior leader, already famous for taking Weyewa heads on raids to the highlands, refused their pleas three times. Only when the rifles captured from the Dutch and stored in the headhunting house of Bondo Kodi were brought to him and ceremonially presented did he accept. He knew how to use firearms from experiences with shotguns in a neighboring region; thus he was able to attack the Dutch with their own weapons.

Many of the taboos that traditionally applied to severed human heads were transferred to the guns: they could not be brought into any of the villages associated with *nale* and the promotion of life and had to be stored as ritual objects in headhunting cult houses. The new enemy was called the "foreigner with bound buttocks, stranger with clipped hair, white man with cat eyes, yellow fur on the snout" (*dawa kalambe kere, dimya klippye longge, kaka mata wodo, ryara wulu ngora*), enlarging the older category of a "foreign mother, stranger father" to include the peculiar attributes of white men.

The Dutch commander fled to the other side of the river, where he and his troops sought refuge with the subraja of Bangedo, Rato Tende. The Dutch forces were allowed to stay in the village of Parona Baroro, under the protection of Rato Tende, who seemed to have taken them in as his own fictive kin. Rato Loghe set off with his gold staff of office to negotiate a payment of blood compensation. Since no Dutch heads had been taken in this round, his offer of buffalo and gold was, he thought, a reasonable proposal to restore peaceful relations.

The Dutch, however, understood a ruler's responsibilities differently. They captured and beat Rato Loghe to punish him for the deaths of the soldiers, forcing him to march in a wooden harness for several days to the Dutch fortress in Memboro, where he eventually died. The death of the first Kodi raja turned the whole population against the Dutch. For the next three years numerous raids and large armed battles were mounted against the Dutch forces. Warriors came to join Wona Kaka from all the villages of Kodi Bokol, hiding in small hamlets in the interior where they were fed and housed by the local people. Casualties during those years were much heavier than they had ever been under traditional intermittent headhunting raids. Some Kodinese from Bangedo fought briefly for the Dutch forces (cf. Hoskins 1985) and were killed as traitors, their deaths lamented in dirges that also note their kinship bonds. A famous battlefield was renamed "the place where many people died" (*hamate tou danga*), and almost every clan village set aside a special area outside its gates for those who had died a violent ("hot") death and could not be brought inside the circle of ancestral tombs.

Finally, all the people dispersed through the fertile interior were ordered to move to their ancestral villages along the coast, where they could be kept under better supervision by the Dutch. Abandoned gardens were burned to prevent rebel forces from harvesting the young corn and tubers. Most of the rice harvest was completely lost, the neglected fields becoming choked with weeds. Hardship and hunger soon translated into popular pressure for a negotiated settlement. A Dutch civilian named Theedens who had taken seven Sumbanese wives served as the intermediary, promising personal safety to Wona Kaka and his men if they would surrender.

The truce was negotiated in a ceremony held on the hill facing Bondo Kodi, a place renamed the "cliff where the shields were burned, the incline where the spears were surrendered" (*tanjulla tunu tonda, tawada waro nambu*). The gallantry of Wona Kaka's warriors was praised by a famed orator, Ndengi Wyanda, whose words have been preserved within oral tradition:

They fought at the last *mangata* bush, I say to you	Woloni tanduko mangata we do monaka
But the weapon was no longer sharp	Ta na wuli wyalikya a lakiya
The knife of the small horse	A kioto ana ndara
They made a final try in the elephant grass, I say to you	Rawini eloko kapumbuna we do monaka
But the staff of the sword broke	Ta na mbata walikya a kendana
Like iron that has grown brittle	A bahi wara wutu
Because they looked down into rivers that were empty of shrimp	Torona ba na tingeroka a limbo njaingo kurana
The mouth of the hunting net fell open	Na tawewaka a ghobana pokato kalola
Because they looked up at the betel palm that had no fruit	Torona ba na tangeraka a labba njaingo wuna
The rope of the mousetrap grew slack	A makuna a katedeho marengga

Exhausted by the long struggle, Wona Kaka and his band were finally betrayed by the Dutch. They were not physically harmed, but they received a punishment almost worse than death. They were sent into exile on a great white ship, which came to pick them up in the harbor at Bondo Kodi and carried them off to Java. Wona Kaka himself was never to return. Haghu Ndari, a fellow clansman from Bongu, did eventually come back to Sumba after fifteen years away. But the spirit of armed resistance to the Dutch colonial power was effectively broken.

From Headhunting to Regional Resistance

Several analytical questions emerge from this account: (1) Why were Dutch heads not taken, since the task of waging war was delegated to members of a headhunting clan? (2) How were the events of Wona Kaka's time used to create a sense of regional unity, which emerged only through this resistance movement? And (3) how has local identification of head-hunters and heroes effected the transformation of these events into an anticolonialist "history"? Answering these questions demands further explanation of the historical context in which new forms of opposition took shape.

The Dutch could not be assimilated into the traditional category of enemy, used for the highland people specifically, because of differences in both their technology of warfare and the rules of combat they observed. Raids to take heads from neighboring peoples assumed that both groups were fighting by the same rules, which invariably involved reciprocity: heads were taken only to avenge earlier beheadings, and since the Dutch did not take Kodi heads, there was no reason to take theirs. Yet these categories were not so clear at the time. One man told me his grandfather in Bondo Kodi had cut off the head of a Dutch soldier "out of rage" after his brother was killed, but then shamefacedly left the head beside the body because it could not be properly consecrated. Another informant said the warriors must have held a divination in the skull-tree house after the first killings to ask the ancestors whether or not heads should be taken. He supposed that the ancestral spirits had forbidden them from doing so, saying that "a foreign head could never cool the anger created by the loss of a Sumbanese."

Members of headhunting villages traditionally avenged deaths among their close kin and affines or by specific request. Because Wona Kaka's mother had come from Bondo Kodi, he had a reason to fight on behalf of the men from that village, whom he addressed as his "steps and doorway" (*lete binye*), the source of his own life and home of his mother's brother. But it was not members of his mother's village who asked him to lead a war party; rather, the first Kodi raja had asked him to do so, to avenge the members of Tossi who had died in fires set by the Dutch soldiers.

The legitimacy of the first raja was established by the same events that created Wona Kaka as a regional resistance leader. Messengers who brought news of the ambush to Tossi wanted Rato Loghe to serve as a mediator in resolving a violent dispute, as was often done in the past. But because the Dutch colonial government had created the office of raja as head of a polity, they decided to hold him responsible for the actions of his "subjects." Their retaliatory raid on Tossi thus determined new lines of opposition by punishing a ruler for actions taken without his knowledge. It was not until he had died for them that Kodinese came to regard Rato Loghe as their true representative. Eventually his request for revenge, made through the gift of rifles to Wona Kaka, assumed the grander dimensions of a mandate for organizing a large-scale regional resistance.

The problem of the ritual significance of Wona Kaka's war party, therefore, is more than a macabre curiosity. In a political transformation, the first Kodi raja was posthumously recognized as speaking for the region as a whole. In a second transformation that followed, new rules for warfare were developed that bound all Kodinese in opposing foreign invaders. The delegation of power from Tossi to the headhunting villages that carried out the raids acquired a new sense: without the sanction of the ceremonial center, Wona Kaka's resistance would have fallen into the category of local feuding, and antagonism between Greater Kodi and Bangedo could have been played up to take on the proportions of a civil war. But the Dutch commander *made himself* into the enemy of the whole region by refusing to negotiate with his own appointed ruler. By assuming a regional political unity that did not yet exist, he created a ruler who would suffer for the rebelliousness of his people and a hero who opposed outside invaders from a large popular base.

Wona Kaka's acceptance of the gift of the captured rifles is now interpreted by Kodi commentators as the acceptance of a mandate to lead a regionwide resistance movement. His willingness to fulfill an unprecedented historical role is explained through the magical power of the rifles and the influence of the skull-tree altar. His descendants in Bongu told me, "If he had not already felt the heat of his ancestors within him, he would not have dared to hold the Dutch weapons." They continue to identify him as a headhunter, emphasizing the gory details of earlier raids rather than playing them down, much as others do in regions where headhunting once flourished and has now been suppressed (Rosaldo 1980). The reasons for this emphasis, I suggest, lie at the intersection of Kodi martial traditions, an imported model of the past, and a new kind of nationalist rhetoric.

The Javanese-derived Model of the Past

The first written documentation of Wona Kaka's resistance (besides brief mention in the Dutch administrator's report; Couvreur 1915) comes from the Kodi native administrator of the postcolonial period, H. R. Horo. Horo's account (1952) was written partly to legitimate his own position as a local leader who served the Dutch as a colonial raja, administered the island during the Japanese occupation, and authorized the first raising of the Indonesian flag. He wanted to show his respect for Rato Loghe, his predecessor whose quarrel with the Dutch led to death in prison, and at the same time to endorse the colonial system of choosing local leaders from among prominent elders and elevating their position into that of a hereditary ruler.

Horo's version of Wona Kaka's "life story" presents him as a brave warrior who defended the prerogatives of the first Kodi raja. Instead of emphasizing the oral tradition of the rape accusation that triggered the initial attack on the Dutch soldiers, he lists a series of insults to the authority of the first raja and a contemptuous gesture made by the Dutch lieutenant when Rato Loghe complained of the rigors of forced labor on the bridge. The story becomes more a drama of violations of a sacred ruler than one of territorial invasion. Its narrative organization is like that of military histories of the independence struggle on Java, detailing battles and losses and naming those Kodinese who are known to have died from each village. No mention is made of the fact that Rangga Baki, Horo's own ancestral village, is located in Bangedo and that its members were among those who originally supported the Dutch forces and, indeed, held Rato Loghe captive under one of their lineage houses. More important, no mention is made of the fact that the office of raja did not exist before the colonial period. In fact, the two Tossi rajas (Rato Loghe and Ndera Wulla) are legitimated by traditional narratives that associate their home with the center of calendrical ritual. After both had died without leaving any direct descendants, the Dutch colonial administration chose H. R. Horo as a successor, thus filling the position by appointment instead of hereditary succession.

The Kodi raja signed a "short declaration" of annexation (Du. *korte verklaring*) that recognized his right to represent the people of the region during his own lifetime but did not constitute a continuing claim to rule in future generations. Since there was no Kodi "king" before the colonial period, Horo's references to insults inflicted on the "sacred power of traditional rulers" (Ind. *kesaktian raja-raja*) borrow an idiom of divine kingship that applied to other parts of Indonesia, but not to precolonial West Sumba. Despite its linguistic and ceremonial definition as a domain, Kodi's constitution as an independent polity was as imaginary as those historical fictions that first linked Indonesians into a single national community.

The development of regional identities in relation to a national center involved a continuing process of identifying local heroes and communicating this narrative to higher authorities. Copies of Horo's manuscript were sent to Jakarta for a "cataloguing" of national heroes in government archives. In 1975, the first junior high school built in Kodi was named after Wona Kaka. This recognition prompted the principal of the new school to write his own biography of the hero (Gheda Kaka 1979). In a style spiced with nationalist rhetoric and claims of suffering and injustice at the hands of the Dutch, Gheda Kaka describes Wona Kaka as opposing "350 years of colonial subjugation" of Indonesians in the Netherlands East Indies. In that the colonial presence in Sumba lasted less than three decades, identification with the longer period of colonial control in Java and the Moluccas is, to say the least, somewhat misplaced. The principal's account begins with the struggle, then moves backward and forward in time to provide details. Here is the rather florid opening passage:

> Day after day, week after week, month after month, the blood was falling in great floods on our beloved homeland, from both the bullets of the White armies and the waves of flames that swallowed up the houses and gardens of the local populace, since it was imagined that these could threaten the colonial system of control. The horrifying events and cruelty of the past months had made the members of Wona Kaka's resistance force all the more hot-livered and ready to fight.
>
> (Gheda Kaka 1979, 1)

Using accounts of heroes elsewhere in the archipelago as models, these Sumbanese writers strove to create a local "history" that conformed with other patterns of immortalizing resistance leaders—in which statues of them were erected in public places, universities were named after them, and official honors were posthumously bestowed upon them (Anderson 1978). Wona Kaka is made "Indonesian" by being identified as a "Sumbanese Diponegoro" (Horo 1952)—an identification that serves not only to legitimate a Kodi leader within the national context but also, indirectly, to assimilate Sumbanese models of leadership to Javanese ones.

Diponegoro was a prince of the Jogjakarta royal house who led the Java War of 1825–30, in which a number of aristocrats throughout Central and East Java rebelled against Dutch colonial policies. For centuries before Diponegoro arrived on the scene, ancient Javanese stories had told of a "just king" (ratu adil), the renewer and maintainer of cosmic order, who would fuse Indic notions of successive cosmic periods with the Islamic belief in the coming of the Mahdi. Diponegoro himself had a vision that convinced him he was the divinely appointed future king of Java and would be aided by the spiritual power of the earlier kingdom of Mataram and the Goddess of the South Seas (Ricklefs 1981, 111). His actions revived this myth, and although his revolt failed, his five-year anticolonial struggle prefigured the nationalist movement of the twentieth century. When independence did come over a hundred years later, the memory of Diponegoro was given a new place of importance in awakening the Indonesian people to the struggle for national pride and independence (Kartodirjo 1972; Locher 1978). After independence, a new myth of Diponegoro was born, one not oriented toward a future seen simply as a repetition or partial restoration of the past, but shaped by interactions with the Western world and expectations of autonomous nationhood (Locher 1978, 78).

Sumbanese heard of the rebellious prince through inspirational accounts of Indonesian leaders published after independence and school textbooks that highlighted the history of local resistance to colonialism (Notosusanto et al. 1976). Wona Kaka's resistance and Diponegoro's had numerous parallels: the anger at violations of local authority, the building of a series of "fortresses" throughout the interior to serve as bases for guerrilla activity, and the leader's eventual betrayal by a promise of safety followed by imprisonment and exile.[5]

To praise Wona Kaka's rebellion, both Horo and Gheda Kaka use the format of nationalist narratives that describe Diponegoro's life. The capture of Dutch rifles is compared by Horo to taking possession of a Javanese kris, and the violation of Diponegoro's ancestral lands at Tegalrejo by the construction of a railway is linked by Gheda Kaka to the construction of the bridge at Bondo Kodi. Differences in time and circumstances are collapsed to promote the fiction of a single anticolonial history that was repeated in different places throughout the archipelago.

Sumbanese chroniclers joined in the wider task of creating a new mythical pattern based on the modern notion of the hero. Some early nationalist histories suggested that the twentieth-century Indonesian independence movement in fact revived an ancient polity that had territorial and political viability as far back as the fourteenth-century kingdom of Majapahit (Hadhi 1952; Nichterlein 1974). Others followed the more moderate pol-

---

[5] The choice of Diponegoro as the "model hero" for these Sumbanese accounts (instead of the Ambonese Pattimura or Minang Imam Bonjol) stems only partly from superficial resemblances in events, but also from the prestige of Javanese culture and its early identification as *the* outside power. Although stories of other national heroes eventually found their way into Sumbanese classrooms and government offices, the idea of a "foreign hero" (*tou mbani dawa*) has always had Java as its primary referent because of the long tradition of a mythologized origin from "Java" and the sense of Jakarta as the center of all history.

icy of tracing the beginnings of nationalism to nineteenth-century uprisings and revolutionary organizations (Sitorus 1951; Tirtoprodjo 1961) but still anachronistically described local rebellions as opposing the whole colonial system. One contemporary Indonesian commentator on this process ascribes these retrospective identifications to "the impact of the historical attitude of Indonesian traditional culture" on students and the public: "This influence can be seen in the strong inclination to mythologize, the precipitous inclination to see relationships of moral significance between events that are not necessarily related at all. The popularity of pseudo-Marxist teleology may be indicative of a predisposition rooted in traditional Indonesian culture towards deterministic or eschatological forms of the historical process" (Soedjatmoko 1965, 411). His reference to "traditional culture," however, has little to do with Sumbanese traditions of tribal warfare and headhunting; it refers instead to Javanese prophecies of a world renewer, whose concentration of mystical power would eventually turn around an unjust social order.

This idea of "Indonesian tradition" clearly ignores certain crucial differences in indigenous notions of history, power, and authority. The Javanese polity has been described as centripetal, focusing on a "syncretic and absorptive center" (Anderson 1972, 47) where power is concrete, homogenous, constant in quality, and lacking moral implications (Anderson 1972, 8). Ascetic practices store and concentrate power in an individual for later use, but the rigors of self-denial are directly related to the creation of a "potent self" who will receive the delayed rewards of the sacrifice it has made (Keeler 1987, 45). Although the accumulation of power is stressed more than its exercise, a single ruler can be both a "passive center" and an "active executor" at different moments in a temporal process.

Both asceticism and the mystical concentration of power in a single center are alien to the Sumbanese symbolic world. In sharp contrast to the centralized Javanese polity, in Sumba those who legitimate power do not exercise it. Instead, a division of powers opposes the priests of the "source villages" to the warriors at the periphery (Hoskins 1987c). The right to take up arms had to be ritually sanctioned by the Sea Worm Priests and the first Kodi raja, and the military commander could never be the same person as the priestly authority. The dispersion and delegation of powers from the source village did not weaken its influence; rather, it displayed the power structure's diarchic form. A Java-centric interpretation of the Sumbanese political scene alters the structure of these power relations in an important way, for it galvanizes historical significance into a single "hero" with mystical powers rather than spreading it among different figures. Wona Kaka, namely, was only half of a symbolic polarity that also included Raja Loghe Kanduyo. The headhunter was not a hero who claimed his own spiritual power, but rather the military "master of force" who served the supposedly immobile and constant source of ritual authority.

Thus Diponegoro was in fact a very different figure from Wona Kaka. Written accounts, even by local chroniclers, tend to "Javanize" their portraits of local heroes because of the literary and narrative conventions that they follow. When Jakarta-based historians read such accounts as source materials for the construction of a national history made up of composite local histories, they are dealing with pieces of a jigsaw puzzle that have already been cut to more or less uniform size and dimensions. Center-periphery relations within the new nation-state are structured by a play of mirrors: literate representatives of peripheral cultures in the outer islands (particularly those of relatively small scale) reinterpret their own traditions to fit a given narrative mold, reflecting back a version of historical events acceptable and familiar to the centralized power.

The Conflict of Heritage and History: Local Reimaginings

Reactions to these developments among Wona Kaka's clansmen and descendants have been ambivalent: while they are grateful for the attention he is receiving, they are embittered by what they feel to be distortions of the events, and there is a feeling that he has somehow been taken away from them, both literally and figuratively. In the literal sense, it is believed that because he died in exile in Java, his soul has not been able to return to the ancestral village and is still wandering lost through the skies. It must be called back with a special ceremony to allow him to assume his proper position as an honored ancestor in the village. Wona Kaka's figurative removal derives from the fact that his memory has been invested with an ideological content taken from the nationalist movement. The ritual meaning given to headhunters as a category has been lost, while his role has a defender of regional autonomy has been distorted to fit externally imposed categories.

Wona Kaka's descendants say he fought the Dutch to defend Kodi against outside invaders. His new role as a symbol of anticolonial struggle on a large scale is part of a campaign by the distant Indonesian state (called the "foreign mother, stranger father," as were the Dutch) to bring Sumbanese more fully under the control of national officials. Their awareness of this paradox is indirect, but it underlies current movements to initiate a ritual cycle to "call back" Wona Kaka's soul and reincorporate him in the ancestral community of Bongu.

The impetus for this new ritual cycle comes from pagans in a new situation of religious diversity. In 1980, Christians made up 20 percent of the population, and there was much debate about the place of ancestral observances for Christian converts (Hoskins 1986, 1987a). The cult of Wona Kaka as a "historical figure," an official "hero," played an interesting role in the debates that took place in the 1980s regarding how he should be called back into the local community. Since he was sent into exile before any Kodinese had converted, even Christians agree that he must be called back with pagan ceremonial. But local Christian leaders are uneasy about the implications of official sanction for the ceremony, which would also legitimate implicit claims for local autonomy.

In 1984 and 1985, elders in Bongu expressed their fears and their hope for the impact of the ceremony:

> We cannot pronounce his ritual names now because that would be already calling him. He would feel a twitch when we said his name, and his spirit would awake for no reason. We need a consensus, with the Christians helping us to give him a proper burial. They say the days of headhunting are past and cannot be passed on to our descendants.
>
> Yet the fierceness [mbani] that burns inside us is not only to take heads. It can also focus on new enemies. People are afraid to bring his soul back among us. They say it will make us rise up again to defend insults to our honor. The village will become "hot" again, even without the smoking and burning of the skull tree inside it.

The self-promotion of this passage does not conceal the implicit threat of returning Wona Kaka's soul from exile: once he is again among his descendants, the rebellious spirit of this once-powerful ancestor could infect them anew.[6]

[6] Suggestions that hostility against the central government might find a new focus are related to the dynamics of local party politics. The Indonesian Communist Party (PKI), founded in 1924 and active until 1965, was instrumental in developing a nostalgia rooted in interpretations of former "heroes": "The classless society was presented as a reincarnation of a romanticized Majahpahit, seen as a great egalitarian age before the Dutch had come and, significantly, before Islam. The heroes of PKI were Diponegoro, Kyai Maja and Senet from the Java War. The messianic prophecies of the Ratu Adil (Just King) were also harnessed to PKI appeals" (Ricklefs 1981, 166). Members of Bongu, Wona Kaka's headhunting clan, had been active not in PKI (which hardly reached the western tip of Sumba), but in Sukarno's original party (Partindo) and in the Indonesian Democratic Party

Rivalries between Bongu and Tossi also play on the balance between the obligations of the source—the passive authority of the raja—and the active executer—the headhunting clans. A popular song at the time of my fieldwork was the farewell sung by Rehi Wyona, Wona Kaka's second wife, as she saw her husband standing on the ship that would carry him into exile—an ironic reflection on current transformations concealed in a poignant lament about the loss of a local hero to overseas powers. Biting criticism of the nation-state and local authorities lies under the veil of poetic allusion:

Oh Wona Kaka Kodi—because of them	Wu Wona Kaka Kodi—Oha awa naka
Father of the firm net	A bapa kareco londo
Myangilo of the gold breastplate[7]	Myangilo la maranggga
The children of Tossi of wide renown	Ana tohi lendo ngara
Made you the spear they threw off	Pa nambu tanggu gheghu nggumi
Because of the mother of the heirloom jar	Oha awa naka inya pandalu ndongo
Byaraho the sitting ruler	Byaraho maboto
The children of the golden kapok tree	A ana wei marongo rara
Made you the sword they stabbed with	Pa teko tonggu taba nggumi
Because the yellow forelock burned with shame on father	Oro meri na a hungga rangga rarana a bapana
Because the foreign lime boat was profaned on mother	Oro a kabana a tena kapu dawana a inyana
Yours was the back burned by the sun	Watengoka kadengi diru lodo
Yours was the hair loosened for combat	Landa hangoka longge tembe keho
The spider omen dancing before my eyes	Na tanonokaka nggengge ura mata
The dove striking its chest in sorrow	Na kambakaka rowa taba ngahu

---

(PDI), and thus had been associated with Sukarno's mystical populism and leftist sympathies. Awareness of the wider political context underlies the implied threat of the "resurgence" of the fierceness of this former headhunting clan.

[7] Her ironic invocation of the "praise names" of famous ancestors within Tossi underscores an argument that present-day descendants have not fulfilled their traditional roles. The gold breastplate and the "firm net" that once captured the moon from the heavens both suggest an unmoving authority that would not bend to more recent foreign interlopers. Her invocation of Rato Mangilo and his ancestral mandate to guard the heirlooms of the region suggests that the traditional leaders neglected their obligation to honor Wona Kaka and his descendants.

They come to take you in a rooster
cage

They imprisoned you in a hen's nest

Shipping you in the hull of kapok
wood

Hanging you on the white hero's
horse

Carrying you to the base of the
watery horizon

Traveling to the end of the Milky
Way

Crossing the wide seas

Plunging through the deepest ocean

I let my eyes wander up

To the river's edge where they hang
nets

But I see only migrating birds

Who look down on the ocean's depths

I listen with my ears

To the incline of the muddy valley

But I see only spotted fowl

Below the land of groves

Let them return you with the river

To the land where your blood has
spilled

To the land of the Kodi valley

Let them roll you with the tides

To the stones where your navel cord
fell

To the stones of Kodi villages

To be greeted here by the mother
holding a red bark headcloth

To be greeted here by the father with
a fine man's loincloth

From Tossi of wide renown

From the golden kapok tree

A mai jeke mangu keko nggumi kikya

A mai hodo mangu rambe nggumi
kiya

A woti wunikya la tena mbolo rongo

A hali ngunika la ndara njelo kaka

La woti nggunikya ela kere wei
langgara

La hali nggunikya ela hambali loko
mbaku

Panggarongo loro wu mangadi

Tolekongo a limbu wu mandattu

Panara kongo matanggu wenggu

Yila kahiku lende dala

Dihikya ha limuho malando

Yila tarada limbu loro

Pa tokolongo tilunggu wenggu

Yila tawada punda rere

Dihikya a kahilye nggoko koko

Kawawa tana hembo

A konggolo kalunikya wango loko

Ela tana mbogho ruto mu

Ela tana mbali byapo

A walikyo kalumunikya mbanu nale

Ela watu mbupu lede mu

Ela watu kere napu

Yi dongga a inya na pandedengo rowa
rara

Yi dongga a bapa na hamanggana
hanggi ryundu

Wali tohi lendu ngara

Wali wei marongo rara

The text ridicules foreign notions of heroes, speaking of the white ship of
exile as "hanging him on top of the white hero's horse"—using the conventional name of the heroic protagonists of Kodi epics. The singer reproaches the leaders of Tossi for not acting to return Wona Kaka from his

exile. Once he had finished serving for them, he should have been returned to a hero's welcome—depicted here by gifts of many fine clothes from the great mother-father village. Since none of this was forthcoming, the song implicitly attacks the authority of traditional leaders and jeers at efforts to fashion Wona Kaka as a "hero" without doing anything to help him or his descendants. The song is thus inscribed in a potentially volatile local context where the diarchic division of authority is being debated. Her search for Wona Kaka in the waters and valleys is a conventional expression of loss, but here it takes on an additional edge: she says that the territory no longer appears as Wona Kaka's own land, but as another one, where headhunters are made to serve new masters. The warrior delegated by Tossi to fight the invaders ("the spear they threw off, the sword they stabbed with") has become the "weapon" of new invaders who twist local traditions to fit new ideological ends.

Regency-level government officials spoke favorably of subsidizing traditional rites to recall the soul of this lost hero (much as they subsidize funerals of government officials), but local leaders expressed caution. They were nervous about mixing an ancestral ceremony with national propaganda efforts, especially concerning a rebel whose heritage could ignite political clashes between government authorities and the prime symbol of resistance to outside forces.

The traditional ceremony would require "finding" and "summoning" the soul in a *yaigho* ceremony (Hoskins 1987b), then making more sacrifices so that the stone sarcophagus prepared by his descendants might be safely opened. When a body is irrevocably lost (as in deaths through drowning), some of the person's belongings may be placed in the grave to represent the corpse—most often his betel pouch, accompanied by a weapon, headcloth, and some clothing. None of these has survived for Wona Kaka, but his descendants made two requests of me in hopes of acquiring what they considered acceptable substitutes. The first was to look for his gun, which they thought had been sent back to Holland (where it proved untraceable). The second was to make a special photographic copy of an old plate depicting a group of men in Kodi warrior dress, identified as the rebels who were sent into exile on the "great white ship" that sailed to Java in 1913. Lota Mahemba, a Bongu man who accompanied the Kodi raja to Java in the 1950s, saw the plate hanging in a hotel in Surabaya, with the subjects identified only as "Sumbanese." He obtained the negative, which he brought back to Sumba, but no one there had the equipment to print it. In this instance, the use of a photograph to substitute for a corpse, as is sometimes done in other parts of Indonesia (Siegel 1985), epitomizes the ironies of the situation: if he *is* the one in the picture,

Wona Kaka may have been the very first Kodinese to be photographed, immortalized and frozen into a glass plate image for Western eyes. His physical reality, however, the bones that by rights should repose in the village center, remain missing from his ancestral home. To reassume his proper position among his descendants, an image formed by foreign technology must be introduced into Kodi, ritually processed, and transformed from its alien substance into a local product. Only once the faded photograph has decayed within the traditional stone grave will Wona Kaka have really come home.

The Hero Created by History

The many versions of Wona Kaka's life and deeds that have emerged over the past sixty years allow us to reflect on the meaning of the notion of "hero," the extent to which heroes are seen as the appropriate actors in "history," and the notion that individuals "make history" with an awareness of the consequences of their actions.

As argued in chapters 3 and 4, Kodi origin narratives are often attached to objects and locations rather than to persons. Although they are bound, as the persons are, to these heirlooms by ties of genealogy, the sense of a "Great Man," a single protagonist who plays a decisive role in reshaping the concepts of his time, is missing. People provide links, not ruptures, in Kodi thinking about the past. Thus, a new notion of "history" was required to produce a "hero" fit to carry such a burden on his shoulders. The first generation of people to settle the Kodi region, the ancestors evoked in *marapu* rites, were personalities remembered in narratives, but they were not assigned a decisive role in changing the course of events. While the ancestors were a crucial link to the past and could serve as intermediaries in ritual communication, they were "path breakers" only in the sense that they established precedents, not in the sense that they inspired a new sort of consciousness. What Wona Kaka actually intended to bring about by his actions will remain a mystery, for after he was sent into exile he was never heard from again. But as he sailed away from his homeland his importance as a symbol of other events over which he had no control was only beginning.

The particular meaning that headhunting assumed in "history" (*sejarah*) was the legacy of Wona Kaka's defeat. The warrior leader became the hero of a rhetoric of local autonomy, a symbol not of despotic rule but of collective vigor and the desire to repel foreign invaders. Simultaneously, headhunting came to be seen as a contested tradition, a proving ground for the ideological control of the past. The idiom of enmity remained in ritual commemorations of this earlier era, but the content of these commemorations was now peaceful rivalry, not military confrontation.

A volatile ambiguity remains about what exactly might constitute "external domination." Kodi oral traditions speak of Wona Kaka as fighting against the "heavy hand of the foreign mother, stranger father," which in 1911 referred to the Dutch colonial forces. In the present, the "foreign mother, stranger father" is the national government in Jakarta and its representatives who rule from Java or the provincial capital on Timor. If Wona Kaka was a defender of "village democracy" who opposed subservience to any power from outside the island, his struggle should continue even after Indonesian independence. When he is anachronistically praised for "opposing 350 years of colonial subjugation," a deliberate effort is made to transfer the longer and more brutal history of Java's colonial domination to islands where the Dutch were in control for less than thirty years.

Wona Kaka is praised in local written accounts as the first Kodi person to stand on the stage of history. As the earliest "historical figure" (Ind. *tokoh sejarah*), his rupture with the past brought about a new awareness of the wider global context and the ability of local people to respond to this context. The category of headhunters was decisively historical because it has always been problematic in relations with outside forces. When the Dutch first took over administrative control of the island, they prohibited headhunting, the slave trade, and the raiding of foreign ships. The headhunter thus came to epitomize Kodi's precolonial traditions, nostalgically portrayed in nationalist slogans of a "primitive village democracy."

"History" (*sejarah*) was defined by its having been written down, recorded for an audience, and also by the idea of a tradition of illustrious examples. Wona Kaka was a hero because he could be compared to other heroes, because he instantiated a recognizable type. "History" comprised an accumulation of events, irreversible in the direction of their progress and not repeated at specific intervals. Narratives about the ancestors, by contrast, involved constant repetitions—the same games played and replayed, the same ritual powers transferred from one valley to another.

The Sumbanese focus on Wona Kaka as the first actor in the new heroic mold might appear to suggest that they shared the view of traditional society as "cold," unheated by history, and thus unchanging (Lévi-Strauss 1966). By starting "history" with the colonial encounter, the Sumbanese do not deny earlier transformations of their society; they do, however, assess their significance differently. History, in their usage, is not "about" the society it depicts; it *is* the process of that society's emergent self-consciousness. Before the resistance against the Dutch, there were trade relations with European powers, local feuds and headhunting raids, narratives and ancestors whose chronologies were uncertain. "History" began when regional autonomy was challenged and the Kodinese became part of a larger world of interacting forces. It was not the presence of written documents that made these events "historical," but their consequences—the awareness of cultural identity through loss of autonomy.

In the early years of this century, Mauss ([1920] 1969, 576) noted that the concept of nation had "a negative content before anything else: often a rebellion against foreigners, a hatred of all others, even those who are not oppressors." Indonesian nationalism had its genesis in an awareness of cultural difference and a realization of the asymmetries associated with colonial hegemony (Nawawi 1971). It was also, from the beginning, linked to a heroic tradition and a construction of individual actors that depended on Dutch intervention. Pluvier (1968) has shown that an image of the native as rebel was part of the polemical content of much Dutch colonial writing, and Vlekke (1959, 384) argues that even Sukarno, leader of the Indonesian revolution, was a colonial creation: "Paradoxically, one could say that Mr. Sukarno owes his present high position to the attention given to him by the governor-general De Jonge, for his long terms of imprisonment and internment made him a hero in the eyes of his people."

The history of nationalism is related to the history of individualism, because the nation itself is conceived as an acting subject, a sentient being with certain rights to self-determination and self-rule. In creating themselves as a collective subject, Indonesians stress the deeds of a few extraordinary individuals both as models for others and as imaginative vehicles for the nation's subjectivity. Resink (1986) has noted that the notion of historical subjectivity is more accepted in "Indocentric" accounts of the colonial period, attributing this acceptance to the pluralist and syncretic character of the Indonesian population. It was the aim of the Kodinese "native intellectuals" who wrote the first accounts of Wona Kaka's life to present him as a model for Kodi subjectivity, to create a hero who would embody the values and ideals of his people and would show how these agreed with the national goals of integration into the newly independent state.

The ambiguities that surround the development of a nationalist historiography are evident to Indonesian historians themselves, who may participate rather reluctantly in the process of creating new national myths, from which confidence can be gained and moral sustenance drawn. Soedjatmoko (1965, 405) notes:

> The passage from a scientifically justifiable historical interpretation into a historical myth signifies the social process through which society at large takes possession of this image, digesting it, grossly

simplifying it and thereby suiting it to its own often subconscious purposes. In a period of heightened self-assertion which nationalism constitutes, there is a great intensification and acceleration of this process of socialization of historical images and of this search for a new and significant relationship with the past and even for national self-justification through history. There is an acutely felt need to view history from a particular perspective which derives from an intensified expectation of the future.

Myths such as the one that presented the great Majapahit empire as the forerunner of Indonesian unity have been most influential when linked to a deterministic view that the historical process was guided by natural design: here the nation's uniqueness was stressed alongside notions of a manifest destiny, with traits of the traditional agrarian regional cultures being elevated into immutable virtues.

Modern Indonesian notions of history are influenced by both the nationalist model of heroic resistance and an earlier (largely Javanese) tradition that emphasized mythic precedents for present actions. Messianic expectations that surrounded Diponegoro's rebellion were later partly converted into expectations concerning national independence. Retrospectively, Diponegoro, like Wona Kaka, has been given a place as one of the precursors of the struggle for national liberation. In a similar fashion, small-scale armed resistance in isolated parts of the archipelago has been reinterpreted as expressing a unified anticolonial struggle. More sophisticated local historians acknowledge that "Indonesian nationalism was not produced by the local struggles although it later fed on their memory" (Nawawi 1971, 163). Nevertheless, the new "heroic tradition" uses the legitimating power of the past to link early anti-Dutch resistance to current loyalties to the nation as an imagined community.

If history is defined simply as public knowledge of the past, then its status as an artifact of cultural systems must establish a relationship between the present and the past. The crisis on which Indonesian historians have concentrated in creating their own history was not the making of a society, but rather the confrontation with a colonial power. The part of the past set aside and given a new meaning as history was not a narrative heritage of ancestral journeys and the founding of villages; it was instead the part that contained a clear historical protagonist, a likely candidate for the preestablished type of the "hero."

The headhunter who was asked to use magical new weapons to attack Dutch colonial control was thus assimilated to the "heroes" that most Indonesian schoolchildren read about—guerrilla fighters in the independence struggle. Traditional narratives and songs concerning his exploits were collected and recorded in Indonesian writings as "history." The rebel who opposed Dutch control has thus, ironically, become the tool of a new kind of ideological control: the integration of distant regions into the nation-state through assertions of a shared past.

Although Wona Kaka's resistance has been reinterpreted as a part of nationalist history, his own descendants have been reluctant to embrace this view, preferring to see him as a leader of local warriors who fought against external domination. Their position maintains a view of the past as "heritage": Wona Kaka was fulfilling a traditional role, repeating the acts of vengeance carried out to many times in the past by his ancestors. He did not intend to appear on the stage of "history" by initiating a unique event—an act of anticolonial resistance; he wished only to defend the honor of his own house and region. His descendants may enjoy the glory that his actions have brought to them; even so, they insist that they owe him the ritual duty of a reburial before they can claim to tap the power of that spiritual heritage.

My distinction between a Kodi construction of the past, which I call their "heritage," and the externally introduced ideology of sejarah has many dimensions. The one preserves evidence of the past and procedures for evaluating it that valorize a vanished order; the other encourages an alienation from much of the past but preserves records of certain persons and events who are seen as meaningful to the course of nationalist struggle. The one looks to objects and their locations as the starting points for narrative accounts, while the other prefers biographies of heroic protagonists. The one emphasizes continuities and the legitimating power of the ancestors, while the other seeks out discontinuities and the ruptures that gave birth to a new society.

In the contested interpretation of the Wona Kaka story, "history" and "heritage" compete against each other. The first resorts to official channels for support—naming the local junior high school after him, printing and distributing brief biographies; the second proposes a ritual resolution—a rite to call back his soul from Java and build a grave for him on Sumba. If Wona Kaka is made a fully "historical" figure, it will be necessary to admit that the old age of glory is definitively past. If, however, he remains part of an ancestral heritage that defends the integrity and autonomy of Kodi, his soul can be invoked in traditional ceremonies to provide new energy for a continuing struggle. Although efforts have been made to construct a memorial to Wona Kaka's resistance, the tension between these two interpretations, still unresolved, has blocked a resolution in the ceremonial idiom of either traditional ancestral ceremonies or government commemorations.

12

The Embattled Chronologer
The Politics of the Calendar

Those who count the months now whisper in the shadows
Those who measure the year now move in silence
The knots they tie are left unheeded
The lines they carve are disregarded.

> A Kodi reflection on changes
> in calendrical authority

As should be clear from the preceding chapters, for the Kodinese as for many other peoples, a calendar is not a piece of paper to be hung on the wall but a highly charged arena of interaction—a debating ground, at times even a battleground. The political significance of time reckoning in the area was evident in narrative traditions about the origins of Kodi social institutions, where the priest of the calendar is the symbolic anchor of the whole polity. The politics of time has attracted considerable attention in recent years, for with conversion came the new Christian time unit of the week (the naming and defining attribute of the church), and with nationalism and independence the new historical time unit of the epoch. Both constructs have transformed local notions of time, to the extent that the Kodinese sometimes speak of recent changes as a shift in the temporality of the heavenly bodies themselves. Although units such as the day, season, and year have a local origin, they are now perceived in a wider context; thus it seems that "the sun now sets differently, the moon now rises strangely" (*na pa hekango a pa tama lodo, na pa hekango a hunda wulla*).

Nowhere is the disjunction between traditional and recently introduced modes of reckoning time more evident than in the conflicts over the timing of the *pasola*. While the authority of the Rato Nale to "measure the months and count out the year" is not directly challenged, hardly subtle pressures have been brought to bear to "rationalize" the timing of Kodi calendrical rites to correspond to the Roman calendar. Such pressures stem both from a misunderstanding of the flexibility and negotiability of Kodi time reckoning and from a failure to appreciate the importance of the Kodi calendar in a regional system that includes most of Sumba.

As a result of such pressures, the *nale* festivities and the *pasola* have become out of sync with the ecological rhythms they were supposed to mirror. A highly inauspicious event has become commonplace: the sea worms often do not swarm on the morning of the ritual performances. *Nale* ceremonies, therefore, must frequently be performed without the presence of the *nale* themselves. To understand why this happens, we must first examine the social consequences of this disruption, then the technical problems of primitive calendars involved.

The Politics of Sea Worm Festivities

It was at the height of the rainy season, in the damp, muggy months of the Kodi new year in 1980, that I first went to visit the Rato Nale of Tossi in his ritual confinement. Sitting calmly in the shadows of his veranda, he was pounding betel nut as he watched the sky cloud over for another downpour. For the past month he had remained within the Sea Worm House at the center of the village. He did not join the others who went to work in the gardens and could not touch or eat the newly ripened crop of corn that they brought home. He could not travel by motor vehicle, sing or speak in a loud voice, or even wander outside the stone walls of his own village. He was the highest-ranking ritual specialist in all of Kodi, yet he appeared at that time to be the most afflicted. His "brooding" in that particular year concerned a new series of threats to his authority and to the health and prosperity of the people of the region, which I was not to hear about for some time.

Ra Holo, the "holder of the new year" (*na ketengo a ndoyo*) in Tossi, was a dignified, retiring man of fifty, with a lean face and large, haunted eyes. He had been called to assume the office when he was in his thirties, "just a child" as he described himself, after a period of several years when the office had been vacant. The House of the Sea Worms had been burnt down in the sixties, and none of the proper rites could be performed until it was rebuilt.

His reticence, despite his cordiality and hospitality, sprang in part from a profound ambivalence about his role as guardian of such a sacred tradition. "I was asked by my grandmother to do this," he would say humbly, referring to the divination in which the spirit of Mbiri Kyoni spoke to designate him as the next Rato Nale. "She was a great priestess, a person who knew the secrets of the months and the years, and I am an unworthy successor."

Supposedly the Sea Worm Priest is not just a carrier of important knowledge and mythological narratives; he is also their shaper. Yet unlike

Ra Holo's position as the Rato Nale has become increasingly embattled as government officials take over many of the functions once held by calendrical priests. 1988. Photograph by Laura Whitney.

other chronologers such as the Mayan daykeeper (Tedlock 1982) or Incan calendrical priest, the Rato Nale does not possess a large amount of esoteric knowledge. He has rights to certain narratives that are fairly well known, and in his task of counting he observes the seasons and pays some attention to the stars; but his astronomical competence is scarcely more than that of the average layman, in a society where the names and attributes of constellations are little known or commented on.

The Rato Nale, then, represents less an ideal of knowledge than one of ritual discipline. By his own immobility, he brings unruly forces into control; by his own confinement, he keeps disorder at bay. Ritual action, and in this case inaction as well, are the key to his ceremonial importance. He is, in short, less a sage than a moral exemplar.

In the first year that I attended the festivities referred to as the "Kodi New Year," I was received by Ra Holo in the central ceremonial village of Tossi and followed him as he made offerings to the ancestral spirits. On the morning that the worms were supposed to begin their swarming, though, as I rushed to the coast along with others carrying baskets and small troughs, there was a disappointment: the worms had not arrived. Despite several evenings of ribald singing along the beaches, offerings of betel nut scattered on the tombstones, and all the complications of arranging the *pasola* combat, the deities from the sea did not show up to watch these festivities held in their honor.

"Why has this happened?" I asked the others who ran down to the beach expectantly. "What does it mean?"

Most of them were not particularly distressed. "It means that the big swarming will not come until March," they said. "It isn't a good sign for the year, but the worms are certain to come after the next moon. Their absence now means the harvest will be poor in Kodi this year. The rains have shifted away from us and will fall on Wanokaka instead [where the *pasola* is held in March]. We will have to plant more corn and more tubers to fill the empty bellies of the next months."

The failure of the sea worms to arrive was obviously inauspicious but not catastrophic. It was—as I was soon to learn—an occurrence that was not unexpected in this particular year, for reasons concerning the now-contested area of calendrical authority. The reference to fertility being transferred from the harvest to other domains played on a form of rivalry between Kodi, the acknowledged source of the sea worm ritual and the *pasola* combat, and districts like Wanokaka, Gaura, and Lamboya, which have more recently incorporated the celebration into their ceremonial system.

More mysteriously, the Rato Nale himself had very little to say about the worms' absence. He was not surprised and simply stated, stoically, "This is what we should expect nowadays. There have been so many changes." I tried to get him to interpret the auspiciousness or inauspiciousness of the event, but he would comment no more. The only other thing he said, a bit sourly, was that "Ra Ndengi was right to stay home."

Although I knew that Ra Ndengi was the Rato Nale of Bukubani, his ritual counterpart, and I had been told that he was sick on the day of the *pasola* and would not be attending, I did not immediately link these two comments. It was only later, when others filled me in on some of backstage drama surrounding the events, that I came to see what was going on.

In January of that year, both Ra Holo and Ra Ndengi had been visited by officials from the governor's office in Waikabubak. They announced a new policy: in order to "improve and upgrade" the quality of traditional ceremonies, they would need to be told the dates of the *pasola* ahead of time so that important guests could be notified and "distinguished outsiders" could be brought to witness the spectacle. "The *pasola* has become a symbol of the local culture of Nusa Tenggara Timor," they argued; "it shows our courage, our skills in horsemanship, and our heroic resistance to Dutch colonialism." They revealed that a statue of Sumbanese men on horses and carrying lances had been erected just outside the main airport of the provincial capital of Kupang, and there were new efforts to discover how this "exercise for war," as they called the *pasola*, may have contributed to the regional resistance led by Wona Kaka. Ra Holo, as a man who had received an elementary education and spent some time in government service, understood that this was a form of pressure, and one very hard to resist.

Traditionally, the date for the swarming was not announced until seven days before the event, when the Rato Nale told the people that he had sacrificed a chicken to mark the first day of the seven-day countdown after the full moon. His decision that *this* moon was Nale Bokolo meant that others could begin preparing their chickens and rice for the move to the coast.

Impatient with delays and uncertainties, a former district administrator declared hotly: "I can count the days and nights as well as anyone!" and asserted that all he needed was a calendar telling him when the new moon would appear in February. Other people protested this claim: "You are not the priest who holds on to the year," he was told by a rival. "The Kodi months are not the same as the foreign months, so you cannot know unless you have been watching the stars and the seasons as the priests have."

The Roman month of February was usually, but not always, the month when the *pasola* performance was held. By imposing an external calendrical system on the traditional ceremonial season, the district administrator was trying to establish an exact correspondence that was not, in fact, possible. He knew that the Roman months did not begin with a new moon and so recognized part of the problem; nevertheless, he countered that "we know the worms come in the second month of the year, so why should we wait for the priests to count it out?"

Ra Ndengi withdrew from the conflict and refused to comment on it at all. Ra Holo, called into the district office by the current head of government, confessed to a certain confusion. "I know only what I was taught and the way they told us to count," he said simply. "The Kodi months are not the same as the foreign ones, but if you want to announce the date when you think it will be, we will not fight you. Still, it is dangerous to try to dictate to the *marapu*. Who knows if the sea worms will come?"

Other commentators, more forcefully, said that they thought the government efforts to meddle in the traditional calendar would endanger the health and prosperity of the whole region. Using the veiled language of ritual speech, they whispered to me:

When you start to count the months	Ba na kede a baghe wulla
You swim deep among the white swirling pebbles of the surf	Na pangnani jalo nani a walla watu kaka
When you start to measure the year	Ba na kede ghipo ndoyo
You climb high on the unstable bough of *kamoto* leaves	Na panene jeta nani a tenda rou kamoto
Not even the foreign mother, stranger father	Mono inde diyo a inya dawa, bapa dimya
Can hide where the nets do not catch them	Na laiyo ela pandouna nja pa ghena dala
Or climb where the winds do not blow	Na laiyo ela pandouna nja pa li pyaringi

Their words suggested ominous consequences. And indeed, when the *pasola* was held on the date announced by the government spokesman, no sea worms swarmed off the western beaches. Only after the next moon did they appear, making March 6 the "large swarming" instead of the "leftover one" (*nale wallu*). The harvest that followed, moreover, was a very poor one, the rains were sparse and insufficient, and many young rice plants never filled with golden kernels as they should have. The damage was worst in Mbali Hangali, the home of the former district administrator, but all over the area traditionalists speculated that it was related to efforts to meddle with the traditional calendar.

Ra Holo himself declined to given an opinion on the issue. Instead, on my next visit, he asked me to make a chart of the Kodi months to show to government officials, so if they decided to set the dates again they could do so more accurately. He said it was important to explain something of how the system worked but confessed that he could not fully understand what was involved in "shifting" the months from one year to another. Although he knew well that it was difficult to predict exactly which day the sea worms would swarm, he had no idea that he was grappling with the abstract problem of intercalating the lunar calendar and the solar year.

The Problems in Primitive Calendars

Ra Holo was not alone in his confusion. The study of variation in notions of time and time reckoning has long been vexed with such problems, and it is increasingly difficult in the modern world to find groups whose original, preliterate temporalities have not been clouded or even permanently distorted by comparison with the now ubiquitous Western calendar.

In the earliest description of Sumbanese notions of time, Samuel Roos, the first Dutch official to travel on the island, reported that "there are no names for the days or the weeks. The Sumbanese live, in what concerns the reckoning of time, as in all else, in a continuing state of ignorance." He did record fourteen different names for periods of time within the year, which corresponded roughly to the Malay category of "moons," but noted a high amount of inconsistency in informants' statements: "Among fifty Sumbanese, only one will be encountered who is able to give the names of the periods in the proper order or who can say which is the present month" (Roos 1872, 70).

Inconsistency is not, however, the same thing as ignorance. Many students of non-Western time systems have found people hard to pin down on which lunation it is, and they have often interpreted discrepancies as signs of laziness or lack of care. More recent and sophisticated analyses, however, have revealed that a certain flexibility may be necessary to keep annual cycles adjusted to seasonal variations in variable ecological regions (Aveni 1989; Turton and Ruggles 1978). Temporal knowledge is an attribute of individuals as participants in organized societies, and it varies with the social needs of the group.

Two of the most famous peoples in the ethnographic literature, the Nuer and the Trobrianders, have lunar calendars that are complexly calibrated to conjoin natural and social needs. Evans-Pritchard (1940, 100) tells us that the Nuer conceptualize the named moons in relation to the activities that they perform, and are much less concerned with the lunar cycle than the round of subsistence activities in which it is inscribed: "Nuer do not to any great extent use the names of the months to indicate the time of an event, but generally instead to some outstanding activity in process at the time of its occurrence." Similarly, in Kodi many events are situated in time as before or after the harvest, before or after planting, and to a certain extent people may try to figure out what name to give a month on the basis of these activities. However, the degree to which Kodi month names are fixed varies throughout the annual cycle.

Malinowski (1927, 211) believed that the Trobrianders did not have a calendar in any full sense because he could locate only ten common names for the months of the year (he thought, on the model of the Roman calendar, that there should have been twelve). He noted, however, a fair amount of regional variation in which month was given which name, and this was related to the timing of the *milamala* harvest festival, which—as in Kodi—was supposed to coincide with the swarming of sea worms (also called *milamala* in the Trobriand language). Edmund Leach (1950, 245), relating Malinowski's data to other Pacific societies, provides clues to unravel these differences; he also suggests an underlying pattern that is found, in a different form, in the Kodi calendar as well.

The purpose of any calendar, lunar or otherwise, is to measure the progress of the seasons and make possible the accurate prediction of their arrival. But the concept of the year as a fixed number of days (365.24 for the solar year) is an artificial temporal development associated with an advanced state of astronomical knowledge. Therefore, it is the periodicity of the seasonal cycle that is appreciated first, by all early chronologers, and not the duration between successive periods.

If, as in most primitive calendars, the year is first divided into periods by naming the moons, some mechanism must exist for intercalating the lunar and solar years. Because the lunar month consists, astronomically, of 29.53 days, a lunar year of twelve months would be only 354.36 days long. Each year, as the months were named and passed in succession, there would be a gap of 10.87 days, and after three years the months would have fallen behind by one in relation to the solar cycle. If an extra month is inserted in the lunar year once every three years, the two calendar years will be closely synchronized but not completely congruent. Once every twenty-nine years or so, a further intercalary month would be required. The problem that faces every user of a lunar calendar, therefore, is how to keep the "counting of the moons" in pace with the passage of the seasons—the part of Kodi chronology referred to as the "measuring of the year" (*ghipo a ndoyo*), so that the wet and dry seasons do not slip away from the months named for the activities of planting and harvesting.

Evidence from the Wogeo, Yami, and Trobriand calendars surveyed by Leach (1950) suggests that this is done by adding—in certain years—an additional lunar month. Obviously, some ritual authority is needed to decide when the addition must be made, and some external check is needed to keep the two calendars in synchrony. Materials from many parts of the Pacific suggest that the annual swarming of sea worms is often what provides this external check, with the sequence of ceremonial activities coordinated around this event.

If, as in the Trobriands, the festival of the sea worms is staggered from one district to another, the total number of month names may not add up to thirteen or even twelve, because a group of month names may be counted but not named, or counted only *after* the occurrence of the festival itself. Malinowski had argued that the use of month names by the Trobrianders was not calendrical but simply a haphazard correlation of gardening activities with the sequence of the moons; "gardening seasons," he said, "constitute the real measure of time" (Malinowski 1927, 211). Gregory Forth's meticulous examination of temporal classification in Eastern Sumba likewise does not address the issue of intercalation. He says Rindi *wula* are periods "of varying and indeterminate lengths . . . and do not coincide with the lunar months" (G. Forth 1983, 59), so they cannot be used for intercalation.

Yet even if we grant that the occurrence and naming of a particular moon is reckoned according to natural phenomena and social activities, this does not mean that there is not also a rudimentary calendrical function. The Rato Nale's role in "counting the months and measuring the year," after all, permits measured numerical prediction of coming events and is thus an independent scheme of time reckoning that goes beyond haphazard empiricism. As Leach (1950, 249) says, "if some event in the seasonal cycle is required to occur at some point in a lunar sequence, then a true calendar must exist, and this implies the existence of a correlation." The correlation is perhaps less evident in East Sumba, where the annual appearance of the sea worms is not ritually celebrated, but it is nevertheless indicated in the names of the months.

In addition, inconsistencies in the names reported for moons in Kodi and other districts of Sumba suggest that (1) there is a definite period of "forgetting the moon name," which is where the flexibility and possible intercalation must be found; and (2) the festivities held in Kodi require the prediction of the worm's swarming and thus work a bit differently from the Trobriand example. Thus, I argue that a Kodi lunar calendar does exist and that its functioning was once of great political significance. Reconstructing how it works today involves a delicate and complicated examination of a tradition under fire and a continuing struggle to keep an indigenous temporality alive in the face of new incursions.

Lunar Calendars in a Regional System

Leach proposes that the swarming of the sea worms off the southern edge of the Trobriand island chain each year following the full moon that falls

Table 5. Scheme of the Trobriand Calendar

Kitava	Kuboma	Kiriwina	Vakuta
1			
2 Milamala	1		
3	2 Milamala	1	
4	3	2 Milamala	1
5	4	3	2 Milamala checkpoint
6	5	4	3
7	6	5	4
8	7	6	5
9	8	7	6
10	9	8	7
—	10	9	8
—	—	10	9
1 (same as Vakuta)	—	—	10
2 Milamala	1	—	—
	2 Milamala	1	—
		2 Milamala	1
			2 Milamala checkpoint

Sources: After Leach 1954a and 1950. Reprinted in Aveni 1989, 175.

between October 15 and November 15 (our time) is used to "restart the year" and keep the ten-month lunar calendar in concert with the seasons (table 5). The "sea worm month" of Milamala, he argues, must in fact be considered as a set of four months that are broken down regionally among the different districts of Kitava, Kuboma, Kiriwina, and Vakuta. Only the people of Vakuta are able actually to observe the swarm, so their calendar serves as the checkpoint for the others. Once the swarming occurs, the people of Vakuta call the next full moon "the moon just past *milamala*." In order for the intercalation to work, that is, they must name the moon *retroactively*: the year is "extended" if the worms fail to show up at the appointed time. In practice, then, one year in three has thirteen months, since the *milamala* is duplicated periodically to keep the moon names in sequence with the worms. As Leach (1950, 254) sums it up:

> The whole territory can thus complete a 12-month cycle without any one area bothering to count more than 10 months. So long as each group knows the relative position of its own "calendar" to that of its neighbor, the system is complete. . . . Clearly it is a much

simpler piece of intellectual analysis to know that one celebrates *milamala* one month later than someone else than to bother working out whether the year really contains 12 or 13 months.

Leach's case that the sea worms can be used to restart the year and keep it in sync with the seasons is convincing on a hypothetical level, and it explains the staggering of Milamala in different districts to permit adequate prediction of the festive season's approach. Yet it is not necessarily the only method used by the Trobrianders, or even the predominant one in all districts. One wonders what other social factors are involved when the moon "goes silly," to use the Trobriand term, and the Milamala is extended. Is this inauspicious? Does it confirm or threaten the position of Vakuta relative to the other districts? One commentator compares the event somewhat facetiously to "those of us in northern climes celebrating another December if snow didn't arrive in time for Christmas" (Aveni 1989, 176). In fact, a more complex system would seem to be involved, one that involves potential conflict between Vakuta, the "standard-bearer," and other districts that use alternate methods.

Leo Austen, the resident magistrate whose description of Trobriand calendars forms the basis of Leach's discussion, believed that observations of the stars were the defining feature of Trobriand garden periods. Native astronomy involved a "counting or reckoning" not only of the moon but also of constellations and was centered on a man in the Wawela village of Kiriwina who held the office of "local astronomer." "Garden times" corresponded not to lunations but to named star groups, most notably the Pleiades, Aquila, and Orion's Belt. All of the garden magicians (*towosi*) had some knowledge of the seasonal garden times, which they needed to regulate the phases of work involved in cultivating *taitu* yams. The old man in Wawela, however, was the greatest authority, and his knowledge became the basis of Austen's own standardization of the calendar, since "the native himself often needs leading in the right direction, especially in those years when there are thirteen months (when the moon goes 'silly')" (Austen 1939, 240–41).

In describing and systematizing the Trobriand garden times in terms of European months and dates, Austen effectively destroyed the functions of the traditional astronomer and garden magicians. He assumed the familiar "white man's burden" of "rationalizing" the calendar in the name of progress and increased productivity:

> There were famines in ancient times, but that may have been due to poor tools and late planting (owing to the moon having gone "silly")

but nowadays the yearly harvests should be greater than in the olden days, and the native should have more spare time. It is most important for the European, be he missionary, government official or trader, to understand Trobriand horticulture, for by knowing the important phases of gardening and the times when they should be taking place, he will be able to regulate his contact with the Trobriander so that he will not interfere with most necessary work. Again, the European will be able to watch that the native himself does not waste his time when he should be doing important garden work.

(Austen 1939, 251–52)

As on Sumba, local government assumed the task of ordering people back into their gardens when the rains seemed to be approaching, thus displacing the traditional authorities who had once fulfilled that function.

Austen (1939, 247) notes, however, that astronomical knowledge was unevenly distributed throughout the Trobriands; in particular, he wrote, "the Vakutans have lost most of their star-lore, since it was unnecessary when they could always adjust their calendar correctly by the appearance of the *palolo* annelid [sea worm]." This comment suggests to me that both systems of intercalation—one based on astronomical observation, the other on the sea worm swarming—coexisted but were of greater or lesser importance depending on the region. Leach (1950, 256) acknowledges that his model may have required a "supplementary stellar check" three months later, or a judgment based on the Pleiades, but is unwilling to sacrifice the principle that the different regional calendars depend on one another for verification.

Sumbanese regional calendars show a similar range of similarity and difference. Month names collected in four districts of East Sumba (Kambera, Kapunduk, Umalulu, and Mangili; table 6) and West Sumba (Lauli, Wanokaka, Anakalang, and Lamboya; table 7) all contain references to the swarming of sea worms, which they may use for coordinating annual cycles. Months are named after seasonal activities, and because the onset of rainfall and the blossoming of particular plants vary slightly in time across regions, some deviation is to be expected. All over the island the sea worm swarming is called *nale* or *ngeli*, and it falls in the moons that correspond roughly to February and March. Most calendars name two moons after the sea worms, in Kodi there are three (with the center one marked as the largest swarming), and in Lamboya five. Significantly, the word *nale* itself is sometimes given the Indonesian translation *musim* ("season"); in other words, it can be used as a phase of the solar year and not only to refer to the worms themselves. All of the Sumbanese calendars have a period of prohibitions and ritual silence, called the "bitter months" in the west (*wula padu, piddu,* or *podu*) and the "older months" (*wula tua*) in the east.

The amount of agreement between the calendars is strongest concerning the moons when the sea worms are said to swarm and—in the west—the timing of the bitter sacrifices. In the seven interviews I conducted in different districts,[1] all my informants situated these events at roughly the same period in relation to the Roman calendar. There was much less consistency in the naming of the moons that fall toward the end of the dry season—roughly July, August, and September. One person, speaking about the Lamboya calendar, said that there were no month names for that period (Mitchell 1984). In Wanokaka, this period includes a month that "has no name" (*wula dapangara*); in Anakalang it is a month that "is not counted" (*wula dapa disa*).

Austen (1939, 244) also noted a period of "calendrical amnesia" among his Trobriand informants, which he situated in the period following the first new moon in June and extending until the heliacal rising of the Pleiades. In this "time of confused ideas" it would be possible to intercalate a thirteenth month without much popular awareness of the fact, because very few people know the moon's name at that time.

My field experience revealed a similar pattern in Kodi (table 8). After *wula padu* (the "bitter months"), people were well aware of what lunar month they were in and could give the Kodi name for the moon quickly, especially as the dates of Nale Bokolo approach or are still in the recent past. If asked for the name of the Kodi moon toward the end of the dry season, however, most informants will stop to count the months out on their fingers, consulting others and trying to remember the proper sequence of named moons. Inconsistencies that I recorded in eliciting the sequence of named months all concern the period from June to September, the common pattern being to invert the order of the two month pairs named for flowering plants (Rena Kiyo/Rena Bokolo and Katoto Lalu/ Katoto Bokolo).

It therefore seems reasonable to expect that if there is slippage in the

---

[1] The materials from Lauli, Wanukaka, Lamboya, and Anakalang were collected in 1979 during an initial survey of West Sumba before beginning fieldwork in Kodi. For Wanukaka, Lamboya and Anakalang I have also consulted the work of Western ethnographers (Mitchell 1984; Keane 1990; Geirnaert Martin 1992). The four interviews in Kodi were conducted in 1980, 1981, and 1986. All the calendars of East Sumba were collected by other ethnographers (Roos 1872; Adams 1969; G. Forth 1983; Mitchell 1984). Although I visited East Sumba in 1988 and tried to ask people about such matters in Kapunduk and Pau, no "local authority" was willing to present a version for the record.

Table 6. Regional Calendars of East Sumba

	Kambera	Kapunduk	Umalulu	Mangili
1	Hibu	Habu	Hibu	Habu
2	Mangata	Ngali Kudu or Wai Kamawa	Ngeli Kudu or Wai Kamawa	Ngali Kudu
3	Ngeli Kudu	Ngali Bokulu or Mbuli Ana	Ngeli Bokulu or Mbuli Ana	Ngali Bokulu
4	Ngeli Bokulu	Mangata	Mangata or Pamangu Langu Paraingu	Mangata
5	Paludu	Paludu	Paludu	Paludu
6	Langa Paraingu	Ngura	Ngura	Ngura
7	Wula Tua	Tua Kudu	Tua Kudu	Tua Kudu
8	Kawuluru Kudu	Tua Bokulu	Tua Bokulu	Tua Bokulu
9	Kawuluru Bokulu	Kawuluru Kudu	Kawuluru Kudu or Landa Kawuluru	Kawuluru Kudu
10	Wai Kamawa	Kawuluru Bokuku	Kawuluru Bokulu	Kawuluru Bokulu
11	Ringgi Manu	Ringgi Manu	Ringgi Manu	Ringgi Manu
12	Amu Landa	Tola Kawulu	Tula Kawuru	Tula Kawuru
13	Wandu Bokulu			
14	Wandu Kudu			

Sources: I consulted four sources: Roos's (1872) month names collected in Kambera; Adams's list from Kapunduk in 1969 (Adams fieldnotes); G. Forth's 1975 collection from Umalulu (in Forth 1983); and Mitchell's (1984) notes from Mangili. I have rearranged all of the lists to correspond to the numbered sequences of Roman month names; Roos's list originally began with Kawuluru Kudu, Adams's with Mangata, Forth's with Tula Kawuru, and Mitchell's with Habu.

Notes on month names and their meanings

Hibu/Habu ("nesting") and Mangata ("white flowers") are used in West Sumba as well.

Ngeli and Ngali are variants on the name of the sea worms, whose presence in the sea is apparently observed though not ritually celebrated in East Sumba.

Wai Kamawa refers to a small cephalopod.

Mbuli Ana means to "thrash children" when food supplies are low.

Pamangu Langu Paraingu is a feast of souls ceremony once performed annually.

Paludu is the "time of singing" as one harvests corn and other crops.

Ngura is said to refer to any "young plants" (Forth 1983, 61).

Tua Kudu and Tua Bokolu are the "revered, respected months" after the harvest, considered an inauspicious and dangerous time and marked off as a period of restriction and quiet (similar to the "bitter months" in the west).

Kawuluru is a spiraling wind, and Landa Kawuluru is its crest.

Ringgi Manu is when chickens cover themselves from the cold.

Tula Kawuru means "time of the Pleiades" and refers to the first sighting of this constellation at the beginning of this period.

G. Forth (1983, 64) explains apparent discrepancies in the final months of these calendars by noting that wandu in the Kambera language is a more general term for the dry season and not usually a month name. He also suggests (1983, 61) that "the order in which Roos presents the terms is mostly inaccurate," but the month names do resemble those he found in Umalulu, though "many of the component terms of this classification are no longer widely known or employed in East Sumba."

Table 7. Regional Calendars of West Sumba

	Lauli[a]	Wanukaka[b]	Lamboya[c]	Anakalang[d]
1	Mangata	Hi'u	Mangata	Mengata
2	Nale Lamboya	Nale Laboya	Nale	Laboya
3	Nale Wanokaka	Nale Wanukaka	Nale Gouru	Nyale Bakul
4	Nale Mubbu	Ngura	Nale Moro	Nibu
5	Ngura	Tua	Ro Huli	Mura
6	Boda Rara	Bada Rara	Nale Ngisi	Tua
7	Meting Katiku	Metingo Katiku	Nale Mabu	Bada Rara
8	Menamo	Oting Mahi	Kaba Ro Yayu	Regi Manu
9	Pattina Mesi	Dapangara or Pidu Tou Danga	Kaba Pari Biru	Dapa Disa
10	Podu Lamboya	Pidu Lamboya	Podu Lamboya	Wadu Kei, Wadu Bakul
11	Podu Lolina	Kaba	Padu Patialla	Pidu
12	Koba	Mangata	Kaba	Hibu, Kaba

[a] From Rato Podu, Tarung.
[b] From Kering Hama.
[c] From Y. D. Kole.
[d] From Umbu Anagoga.

Notes on month names and their meanings
Mangata or Mengata refers to the blossoming of a white-flowered shrub.
Nyale Bakul means "great sea worm swarming."
Nale Mubbu means "sea worms that have already dissolved," while Nale Moro means "raw sea worms."
Ngura means "young tubers"; Nibu means "spear blossom."
Mura means "unripe," while "tua" means "ripe."
Ro Huli means "leaves of wild tubers."
Bada Rara or Boda Rara can be translated as "red" or "yellow-orange fields" and refers to the golden color of ripening paddy.
Nale Ngisi means "to bear fruit," and Nale Mabu means "mature or dissolving fruit"; both refer primarily to the rice harvest.
Meting Katiku means "black heads" and refers to the image of many people bending down in the fields to harvest the rice.
Menamo refers to threshing the harvest with the feet (cf. Ind. *menyamun*).
Regi Manu means "covering chickens" to protect them from cold.
Pattina Mesi and Oting Mahi both mean "boiling salt."
The "bitter months" of taboos are variously called Padu, Pidu, and Podu, with Pidu Tou Danga meaning "of many people." Patialla is a region near Lamboya.
Both Koba and Kaba refer to the "bland months" that are free of taboos. In Lamboya, the first stage is "bland tree leaves" (Kaba Ro Yayu) and the second is "bland freshly harvested rice" (Kaba Pari Biru).
Wadu Kei and Wadu Bakul mean "little or great drought."
Hibu, Hi'u, and the Kodi Habu all refer to the "nesting month" for birds.
Dapa Disa means the month that "cannot be counted," and Dapangara means the "month that cannot be named."
See also Mitchell 1984; and Keane 1990, on Wanukaka and Anakalang calendars.

Table 8. Variations in Reports on the Kodi Calendar

	Tossi	Bukubani	Homba Karipit	Balaghar
1	Nale Kiyo	Nale Kiyo	Nale Kiyo	Nale Kiyo
2	Nale Bokolo	Nale Kodi	Nale Bokolo	Nale Bokolo
3	Nale Wallu	Nale Wallu	Nale Wallu	Nale Wallu
4	Bali Mbyoka	Bali Mbyoka	Bali Mbyoka	Bali Mbyoka
5	Rena Kiyo	Rena Kiyo	Katoto Lalu	Rena Kiyo
6	Rena Bokolo	Rena Bokolo	Katoto Bokolo	Rena Bokolo
7	Katoto Lalu	Katoto Lalu	Rena Kiyo	Katoto Walarongo
8	Nduka Katoto	Katoto Bokolo	Rena Bokolo	Katoto Walakare
9	Padu Lamboya	Padu Lamboya	Padu Lamboya	Padu Lamboya
10	Padu Kodi	Padu Kodi	Padu Kodi	Padu Kodi
11	Habu	Habu	Habu	Habu
12	Mangata	Mangata	Mangata	Mangata

I collected the names of the months from four specific "authorities"—Ra Holo, Rato Nale of Tossi; Ra Ndengi, Rato Nale of Bukubani; Tanggu Bola, an elder in Homba Kapirit; and the Rato Nale of Weingyali, Balaghar—as well as asking a wide range of ordinary people about them.

Notes on month names and their meanings

Three stages are noted for the sea worm celebrations: Nale Kiyo (the minor phase or the preparations), Nale Bokolo (the major phase), and Nale Wallu (referring to the residue or leftover sea worms).

Bali Mbyoka refers to the opening up of the rice shaft filled with grain.

Rena Kiyo and Rena Bokolo are the minor and major phases of the harvest and refer to foodstuffs whose fruit is ready to be taken.

Katoto means a blossom, which opens up partly (Katoto Lalu) or all the way (Katoto Bokolu). In Balaghar, it is specifically the flowers of the cottonwood tree (Wala Rongo) and the "buffalo tree" (Walakare). The end of the blooming period is suggested in Nduka Katoto ("enough blooming").

Padu is the "bitter" month of silence and prohibitions.

Habu refers to the period of bird nesting.

Mangata is a flowering white shrub.

References to other regions occur in the naming of Padu Lamboya and in the use of the name Nale Kodi instead of Nale Bokolo for the month in which the sea worms are collected in Kodi.

traditional lunar calendar, it will occur in the period of vagueness and confusion, when people are distracted by the accelerated temporality of the feasting season with its large-scale gatherings.[2] From the time of the rice harvest of April–May until the bitter sacrifices that precede planting, people say that "the moon is watched only for dancing." What this means

[2] Austen's account indicates that many Trobrianders tend to "forget" the month names in the period of greatest ceremonial activity, which falls after the harvest and is now the cricket season. As on Sumba, a prolonged ceremonial season is

is that since singers and orators face dancers across the central plazas of the ancestral villages, if the feast can be coordinated with the full moon, spectators will enjoy it much more. The full moon of the ceremonial period, indeed, is sometimes called "the full moon of dancing" (*wulla taru, nenggo ore*), instead of one of the conventional calendrical names being used. Thus, I side with Austen over Leach in supposing that an intercalary month must come in the period of the "dancing moon" and not at the sea worm swarming, but I agree with Leach that the swarming can work as checkpoint and corrective device. In the end, therefore, I think that both seasonal indicators in the dry season *and* the sea worms are used to keep the lunar calendar synchronized with the solar year.

The evidence concerning Sumbanese "native astronomy" is more difficult to assess. The calendars of West Sumba make no reference to the movement of other celestial bodies, focusing exclusively on social activities (harvesting, singing, ritual silence) and natural phenomena (the blossoming of certain plants, the nesting season for birds, the appearance of animals in the sea).[3] The last month of the East Sumba calendars is called the "time of the Pleiades" (*tula kawuru*; lit., "the prop of the cluster") and falls in late November or early December. G. Forth's (1983) informant in Rindi used this month as the starting point for his list of month names. An Eastern Sumbanese myth about the Pleiades tells of a brother and sister who committed incest and were separated by being banished to opposite ends of the sky. They turned into stars and became associated with the all-knowing and all-powerful deity of the heavens (Kapita 1976a, 166). In one version, their exile was the beginning of the division of the year into a wet and dry season, and hence essential to the genesis of garden crops. They were sent away "so the maize may reach its early stage of growth, and the rice may make its first appearance above the ground." When one of the three children born of this union was killed, furthermore,

---

sometimes blamed for poor harvests: "It has been known for cricket to keep early planting back, for at times a wave of enthusiasm for games passes through the Trobriand villages, and then for several weeks work is held up while matches take place, day after day. Even the women and children get the cricket fever and play matches among themselves. Cricket is a splendid game and should be encouraged as much as possible, but it should be organized so as not to interfere with gardening" (Austen 1939, 52).

[3] Anakalang, the district closest to East Sumba both geographically and culturally, might be a possible exception: Keane (1990, 33) notes that the Anakalang month of Mangata (found in all the other West Sumbanese calendars) is associated with the "seven brother and eight sister stars," which evidence from other parts of Sumba indicates must be a reference to the Pleiades (G. Forth 1983). Although the constellation does not actually specify the month, it was cited by informants when describing the seasonal cycle.

food crops were created from the body (G. Forth 1981, 86–87; Kapita 1976a, 166).

The myth is a variant of one collected in West Sumba, which interprets the constellation as representing the "seven brothers and eight sisters" who migrated to the island together and intermarried. The last sister had no one to marry, so she became the wife of Lord Rat, who cut open her pregnant body to pull her down the hole into his underground home. After four days, her body was transformed into rice (Hoskins 1989b, 434). (See also text #4 in chapter 3, on the origin of bitter and bland months.)

Many other Eastern Indonesian peoples recognize that the Pleiades and Antares are never present in the sky at the same time (Arndt 1951, 1954; Barnes 1974, 117–18), and throughout the Pacific these celestial bodies assume an important place in the mythology of Polynesian peoples, including the Maori, Hawaiians, Marquesans, Tahitians, and Marshall Islanders (Nilsson 1920, 126–27).

In Kodi, the Pleiades are called the "signs of the year" (tanda ndouna), and many people are aware that the heliacal rising of these stars corresponds to the coming of the rains and thus to the period of planting. A few other stars and star clusters are named, but they seem to designate general seasons rather than specific months. Antares, for example, is called the "man in the sky" (tou ela awango); the evening rising of this star marks the start of the feasting period (as in Rindi; see G. Forth 1981, 86).

The presence of Antares and the "morning star" (presumably Venus) is considered necessary to the ritual singing of the dry season (July–October). The end of a long night of yaigho orations is signaled by a verse that explicitly mentions the constellations:

When the new day dawns	Ba na mahewa a helu
When light comes over the land	Ba na mandomo a tana
Along comes the star with a Savunese shield	Emenikya a mandune tonda haghu
Along comes the glowing red star	Emenikya a motoroma rara

Orion is observed and a story is told: In the early hours of the dawn, first three smaller stars become visible, followed by a large red one, which would seem to be Betelgeuse. It is perceived as the procession of a great lord (tou rato pinja) and three companions: his pig (mandune wawi); his slave, Lero Nggata (tou papawende); and his warrior guardian, who carries a Savunese shield (mandune tonda haghu).

Astronomical observation apparently plays a greater role in East Sumba, where the sea worm swarming is not ritually celebrated and in fact rarely observed. G. Forth (1983) suggests that the Pleiades and Antares are used in a binary sense as seasonal indicators, but they are not explicitly pegged to the moons or the lunar-based calendrical system. Kodi materials tend to support this idea, with the addition that a greater reliance on the *nale* has supplanted extensive stargazing.

The idea of "major" and "minor" sea worm swarmings may be something of a fiction, or at least open to conflicting interpretations. Affected by factors such as rainfall, tides, and ocean currents, the exact moment of the swarming of the sea worms is triggered by the waning light of the moon. The tail end of each worm swells and fills with eggs or sperm; then the worm travels to the beaches and buries its head in the sand as the posterior, genital parts break off and swim to a rendezvous at the surface. Each large female cluster of eggs is surrounded by a knot of smaller males, which twist and writhe in a sexual dance. The scientific literature on this marine annelid, a segmented worm of the Eunicid family (*Leodice viridis*), mentions two swarmings (Saunders 1977) but does not explain how the lunar illumination might work differently in neighboring districts. As a *Zeitgeber* that entrains the animal to a lunar periodicity, it is also reported to produce two swarmings on the southern coast of Savu (Fox 1979a, 153).

It is perhaps more accurate, therefore, to say that the swarming occurs in either February or March, with a few of the worms showing up early or late. The Kodinese say they catch "the heads" the first day, then "the bodies" at the main swarming, and only "the tails" on the last day. The conventional wisdom that there are two swarmings, with the most abundant one on the predicted day, allows the Sea Worm Priest's prediction to be considered accurate if it holds true *for a two-month period*.[4] He can use the major swarming to check the intercalation and then, if needed, correct his predictions for the following year.

What happens elsewhere on Sumba if the sea worms fail to show up? Edgar Keller, who did ethnographic research in Lamboya in 1984–86, reports that the big swarming that is supposed to occur there at the time of *pasola* (also "in February," according to official sources) does not happen most years. The explanation he heard was that the priests in the ritual center of Sodan "made a mistake" in the past, and as a result the ancestral spirits sentenced the Lamboyans to perform the rituals of the *nale* month

---

[4]When one swarming of the sea worms occurs in early March, there should be another smaller swarming of "leftover" worms in April, if there are always two annual appearances. When I asked people if they had ever collected *nale* during the following moon (conventionally named Bali Mbyoka), I was told that groups did not go down to the coast in an organized fashion, but sometimes children did find "the tails" of the worms when playing along the beaches in the harvest season.

without the sea worms being present. Even when the festivities do coincide with the swarming, the priests are not allowed to collect the worms or consecrate them in their ancestral homes (Keller, personal comm.; Hoskins 1990a, 58–59). Geirnaert Martin (1992) confirms this account.

I suspect that this "mistake" had to do with the Sumbanese moons being confused with foreign months; that is, the worms were predicted to arrive "in February," instead of during a particular phase of the lunar cycle. Whether any of the traditional calendars on the island can now operate independently of the printed Western calendar, in fact, is very much in doubt.

The 1980 Controversy over the Dates for Nale

Using our knowledge of other lunar calendars, we can now reexamine the events of 1980 to understand why the synchronization of the sea worm swarming and the *nale* festivities did not work in that particular year. Traditionally, the Rato Nale used seasonal indications and rudimentary astronomy to fix the advent of the "bitter months" (*wulla padu*). Once that date was fixed he simply "counted out" and named four other moons (Habu, Mangata, Nale Kiyo, and Nale Bokolo) to determine when the worm swarming would come. Usually this date fell late in February. My records, for example, indicate that sea worms did swarm in some abundance on February 27, 1981, and on February 15, 1982. However, this disjunction between Kodi moons and Roman months has meant that at times the dates predicted by the Rato Nale do not fall in February—as in 1980, when the worms swarmed in greatest abundance on March 10.

Only much later did I realize that the Rato Nale had in fact forecast this date, but no one had listened to him. On October 30, 1979, just a month after my arrival on the island, I went to visit him in Tossi because of rumors that "a ritual" was being performed that day. The ritual, at which we arrived too late to hear the full invocations, turned out to be the "roasting of the bitter chicken" (*tunu manu padu*), which began the four-month ritual silence of the bitter months. On that day, the Rato Nale had put in motion the naming and counting of months: hence, the moon during which the ceremony occurred bore the name Wulla Padu; the following one, which began November 19, was called Wulla Habu; on December 19 came Wulla Mangata; on January 17, Nale Kiyo; and February 16 signaled the first appearance of the Wulla Nale Bokolo. By consulting an astronomical almanac,[5] one can reconstruct the lunar months

[5] I consulted *The Astronomical Almanac* (formerly the *American Ephemeris and Nautical Almanac*) (Washington, D.C.: U.S. Government Printing Office, pub-

as they were named in the traditional system and realize why the Rato Nale had told government officials he was "not yet ready" to announce the date of the *pasola* at the beginning of February. The new moon, which made its first appearance on February 16, did not become full until March 1, and it reached its zenith on March 3; the sea worms swarmed seven nights after that moment, on March 10, 1980. The swarming of the *nale* worms is a particularly appropriate event for this intercalation, because it is pegged both to a lunar phase (the seventh night after a full moon) and a solar season (the height of the rainy season). In contrast, the *padu* sacrifices do not occur at any specified phase of the moon but are determined purely by seasonal markers—and their impact on the "measuring of the year" can be understood only retroactively by checking the lunar phase in which the sacrifice occurs so the significance of naming the new moon for the yearly calendar will be appreciated.

The functioning of the traditional calendar and its mode of intercalation can be further checked by reconstructing the rest of the lunar months for the period 1979–88 (table 9). We know that the sea worms swarmed for the *nale* festivities and *pasola* performances on February 27, 1981 (because I saw them), and on February 15, 1982 (because I asked an informant to send me a letter to confirm the date). We also know that on two recent occasions—in 1984 and again in 1988—the *pasola* was held in February, but the worms did not put in an appearance until March (March 6, 1984, and March 10, 1988). Performing the rituals without the sea worms is considered inauspicious, since the timing and abundance of the sea worm swarming is said to indicate the timing and abundance of the harvest. "If there are many sea worms, then the year [*ndoyo*] will be a good one," people say, using the term *ndoyo* in its original Austronesian sense (Nilsson 1920, 96) to mean "season" or "agricultural produce."

The blame for mounting these rites at an inauspicious time does not belong to the Rato Nale, for my records of the *padu* ceremonies indicate that they were held at the correct time to keep the named moons in sync with the seasons. Rather, the government officials did not heed the priest's predictions but insisted on holding the *nale* festivities "in February," adhering to the Roman calendar. In 1980, namely, the *padu* sacrifices—which I attended—were held on November 5, at the end of a lunar month (October 9–November 8) that was designated Wulla Padu Kodi. This naming of the month could have been determined in either of two ways: (1) the Rato Nale could have observed seasonal indicators and decided that

---

lished annually). Data on lunar months were collected for the period 1979–88 to check the synchronization of *nale* and *padu* ceremonies with the actual phases of the moon and the swarming of the sea worms.

Table 9. A Speculative Model for Sea Worm Intercalation

Known Dates for the Jousting (Pasola) and Sea Worm Swarming (Nale)		Speculative Dates Based on Published Lunar Calendars	
1980	pasola	Feb. 12	
	nale	Mar. 10	
1981	pasola	Feb. 27	
	nale	Feb. 27	
1982	pasola	Feb. 15	
	nale	Feb. 15	
1983			pasola Feb. 7
			nale Feb. 7
1984	pasola	Feb. 9	
	nale	Mar. 6	
1985			pasola Feb. 23
			nale Feb. 23
1986			pasola Feb. 12
			nale Feb. 12
1987			pasola Feb. 6
			nale Feb. 6
1988	pasola	Feb. 13	
	nale	Mar. 10	

Source: For the speculative dates I consulted the *Astronomical Almanac*, 1980–88 (Washington, D.C.: U.S. Government Printing Office); for the period before 1980 it is called the *American Ephemeris and Nautical Almanac*.

If the speculative dates are correct, then after three years a "lag" between the lunar and the solar cycles causes the sea worm swarming to fall in March instead of February. In order to keep his predictions accurate, the Rato Nale would have had to add an intercalary month at *padu* in 1979, 1983, and 1987. The dates that I recorded for the *padu* ceremony in 1979 seem to indicate that he did so, but official pressures to hold the ceremony in February defeated these efforts and have made the intercalation a retrospective "correcting" instead of a use of traditional methods of timekeeping. If the proper relation between *padu* and *nale* were observed, it seems that the swarming could be kept in sync with the Kodi months, but not with the government ones.

the bitter months must come "later" in that particular year, or (2) the Rato Nale could have used the timing of the sea worm swarming in 1980 to determine the moon names *retrospectively*. Since the worms swarmed on March 10, he would consider the moon from February 16 to March 15 as Wulla Nale Bokolo and simply count out eight more moons until the proper time for Wulla Padu.

Either method would have allowed him to predict the next swarming, which occurred in the moon that ran from February 4 to March 5—coming, on schedule, seven nights after the full moon "sat" on February

20. My questions about what method he used to determine this chronology elicited an ambivalent response:

My grandmother Mbiri Nale told me to watch the signs of the year [*tanda ndoyo*]. She repeated these verses about the coming of the bitter months:

When the dust of the dry season swirls	Ba na kambukongo a mara tana
When patches appear in dry grass	Ba na kolokongo a rumba rara
The chickens must be readied for	Tanaka ena a manu
Closing off the cycle of the dry season	Na tondanya la handomo mara tana
Returning to the cycle of the sea worms	Na hambalingo na hawungo wulla nale
For our mother of the sea worms	Tanaka inya nono nale
Who floated off like fibers in the tides	Na lingo na pa tenango kandiyako
For our father of the *ipu* fish	Tanaka bapa ipu mbaha
Who vanished like the coconut leaves	Na lingo naikya pa ledengo kalama
Bringing you back from the floods	A konggolo ghu waingo loko la
Returning from the swarming waves	A waliku ghu mbanu nale la

The signs she said to watch for were the winds of the end of the dry season, which blow the dust in little circles, the closing of *dedap* blossoms [*nduka katota*, also the name of the moon just before Padu Lamboya], and the absence of small fish [*teppe, ighya katapa*] in the ocean. These all show that the rains will not be long in coming.

The interview that I conducted in 1980 did not go further than this, because at the time I did not realize how important the timing of the *padu* sacrifices was to the whole calendar. When I returned to Kodi in 1988, however, and once again saw the *pasola* performed in the absence of the sea worms, I realized that a more complex calculation was necessary to keep the Kodi moons in accord with the solar year, and *nale* with *pasola*. I asked if the task of the Rato Nale involved not only counting the moons but also watching the stars, and in particular if he paid attention to the Pleiades. He responded: "There are some stars that are called the signs of the year [*tanda ndoyo*]. They are seven stars [*mandune pitu*] that appear low in the horizon at dusk at the end of the dry season. This is a sign that we should begin planting soon [*tanda tondo*] because the rains will be here soon. But the bitter sacrifice [*padu*] must be performed before these stars are visible, so the stars do not tell us how to count the moons." On Sumba, the Pleiades are usually not seen until late November, when they rise just after sunset. Ra Holo's response here seems to admit to some use of astronomical observation, but he distinguishes between his own task—which is a specialized ritual duty, that of naming the moons in order to predict the arrival of the sea worms—and the more generalized popular knowledge of the wet and dry seasons.

It might appear, from the speculative model I have presented, that the gaps in the sea worm swarming form an almost exact analogue to the Western calendrical "leap year" and that, therefore, it would be possible to achieve the intercalation simply by inserting an additional month every fourth year. This may in fact have been attempted (as it was in Western history), but such a solution would approximate the relation between solar and lunar years only inexactly. If three months were inserted over the course of eight years (as the dates I have given suggest should be done), the remainder after the solar year (365.24 days) was divided by the lunar synodic month (29.53 days) would be approximately 3/8, or .368. If four months were intercalated over the course of eleven years, the remainder would be about 4/11, or .3636 (Aveni 1989, 113). However, any simple mechanical rule would allow for some slippage, and thus probably for some retrospective correction. In fact, the system only works at all because it is determined to be vague and open to social interpretation (Leach 1954a, 120).

Regional Calendars and the Control of Time

A third possibility could explain how the task of intercalation is managed within this calendar, and in particular why many districts of Sumba that do not celebrate the swarming of the sea worms nevertheless name certain moons after this event. The arrival of the worms could in fact be used as an anchor for a more complex system in which one region "checks" its moon names against those of its neighbors. Leach's analysis suggests that such a system exists in the Trobriands, but he does not provide enough ethnographic data to ascertain how it works.

His hypothesis about regional coordination has been taken considerably further by Frederick Damon (1982, 1990), in a study of calendrical transformations along the northern side of the Kula ring. Looking from the vantage point of Muyuw, Woodlark Island, he concludes (1990, 20) that "New Year" ceremonies are not tied to specific phases of the moon but reflect a spatial progression from east to west, with different regions differentiating themselves with respect to equinoxes and an intervening solstice: "The system's rigor concerns space (and kinds of time), not the amount or sequence of time" (1990, 9). While the Trobrianders are vitally concerned with "catching time reckonings" (Malinowski 1927, 205) and "great arguments take place over the naming of the moon" (Austen 1939, 243), in Muyuw a spatial vocabulary is more important than a temporal one for modeling the culture's main principles and institutions (Damon 1990, 17). Damon's analysis suggests a pattern of cultural differentiation, with one area designated as the "timekeeper" and others focusing on other criteria of order. The local astronomer of Wawela would thus occupy a ritual office quite similar to that of the Rato Nale in Kodi.

Looking at the whole set of Sumbanese regional calendars as a system and considering their interrelationships, we see that relations between districts are related to moon names. It would seem that even in the precolonial period there was communication about the timing of seasonal rites. As in many other "primitive" systems of time reckoning (Nilsson 1920), the names of certain moons are either duplicated or distinguished as "greater" or "lesser" versions of each other (thus the Kodi Nale Kiyo and Nale Bokolo, the Umalulu Tua Kudu and Tua Bokolu). In addition, the moons named for crucial calendrical rites (*nale* and *padu* in the western districts) are staggered over several districts, often occurring one month earlier in one district relative to its neighbor. The calendars in fact refer to each other constantly, naming moons after the ceremonial practices of a neighboring domain.

The names of the moons indicate a coordination not only of natural events (sea worm swarmings) but also of *social* events: the ritual celebrations associated with these swarmings. Kodi, as the source of the sea worm festivities, is indeed the "base of the year" (*kere ndouna*) for the whole island. The importance of coordinating the festivities is suggested by the fact that Wanokaka, Lamboya, and Gaura (the other coastal districts that celebrate *nale*) acknowledge Kodi as the source of the rite.[6]

The complex interrelations between the calendars of the districts of West and East Sumba suggest several conclusions:

1. The different regional calendars could have been used, as Leach suggests, to coordinate a common system for the whole island, loosely

---

[6] Stories told in Wanokaka and Lamboya about the coming of the sea worm festivities to their territories appear to be transformations of the Kodi origin narrative (text #1 in chapter 3): when Lendu brought *nale* from overseas, he was given them as a counterpayment for bridewealth, and they were supposed to accompany the bride; instead she killed herself, so the worms became a substitute for her broken body. In Wanokaka, they say that a local woman eloped with a Kodi man, and her grieving husband went on a long journey to search for her; when he finally found her in Kodi, she refused to return home, and her new husband in Kodi paid a new bridewealth in gold and livestock, to which he added the worms as a "gift of life" to replace the reproductive powers of the woman he was removing (I. Mitchell 1981). In both cases, the worms are transferred to take the place of a woman, as a "female valuable" and an alternative source of fertility and vitality.

based on the *nale* swarming. This coordination would be based on a shared understanding of calendrical principles, rather than on direct communication between the ritual officers concerned. The counterpart of the Rato Nale of Tossi is called the Rato Wulla in Wanokaka and Lamboya, but they have never met and, without a common language, could not communicate even if they did meet. Before the recent paving of roads in the 1980s, each district was several days' travel from the next, across dangerous rivers and rugged mountains. In addition, the districts of Kodi and Gaura once took heads from each other, as did those of Wanokaka and Lamboya. Nevertheless, the calendrical priests in the other districts affirm that the method of "counting the moons and measuring the year" originated in Kodi. It must have been through inland districts (Ende, Rara, Weyewa, and Lauli) that the names of the months spread, and the *nale* swarming was used to coordinate a calendrical system shared, with minor variations, by all people on the island.

2.   The moment of intercalation occurs at the *padu* sacrifice, when a new planting year is begun; this point is thus the real "beginning" of the calendar. Immediately before *padu*, people have only a hazy idea of the Kodi moon and are aware that the "bitter sacrifices" can come early or come late, depending on whether or not the rains seem about to fall. The Rato Nale thus performs the important social function of shutting down all ritual activities so as to concentrate the attention of the population on preparing their fields, and he has the delicate task of coordinating this moment with the seasons and the rains. He may use some astronomical signs but relies primarily on seasonal indicators (dust, plants, the sea) and the moon in which the swarming occurred eight months before.

3.   Within the moon called Nale Bokolo, seven nights are counted from the moment at which the moon reaches its zenith in the sky and prepares its descent. In Kodi, this is called the time when the moon "sits" (*londo a bei wyulla*) in the sky, temporarily immobilized in its fullness. Although the swarming is said to occur seven nights after it sits in Nale Bokolo, it takes place only six nights later in Nale Wallu; this is expressed in the couplet *pitu nale ndoyo, nomo nale wallu,* "seven for the sea worms of the year, six for those that are leftover." The training of the Rato Nale includes instruction in "reading the moon" to determine the moment it reaches its zenith—as opposed simply to its fullest phase. The moon's temporary immobility, hesitating at the edge of transition, is symbolically expressed by the ritually enjoined immobility of the Rato Nale.

4.   Within each domain, the lunar calendar appears as an annual cycle with a defined phase of "looseness" or "slack" before the *padu* sacrifices; as a regional system, however, it has a permutational aspect. Different

domains punctuate different parts of the year by holding their most important calendrical ceremonies in various months. The two different months for *nale* festivities (the first celebrated in Kodi and Lamboya, the second in Wanukaka and Gaura) are only one instance of the rotation of "New Year" rites. In Lauli, the most elaborate ceremonies are held at *padu*, so the "New Year" is said to fall in October–November. In Anakalang, the annual cycle climaxes in the "descent to the priest valley" (*purungu ta kadonga ratu*), which usually falls in April.

Social and cultural differences are marked by varying punctuations of time, which also allow members of neighboring domains to attend calendrical rites in other regions as spectators. Damon's argument that the northern Kula ring calendars are structured as a system of continuities and discontinuities could also be made of the Sumbanese months. Although the swarming of sea worms continues to serve as a temporal checkpoint, at least to a certain extent, on Sumba the cultural significance of calendrical variation clearly lies in its character of ordered diversity. While the people of Kodi are still proud to be the "time masters" (*mori ndoyo*; lit., "the masters of the year") of the island, the political centrality of the traditional calendar is coming under ever greater threat.

Epilogue: Stepping In and Out of Time

The two persons who occupied the office of Rato Nale in Kodi Bokol during the 1980s negotiated their positions quite differently. In 1980, when the idea of government intervention was new and its consequences uncertain, neither one of them would discuss the changes openly. Ra Ndengi indicated disapproval by his absence. His younger associate, Ra Hupu, had to shoulder the mantle of priestly functions for the whole region, but did so reluctantly and with many misgivings. In 1988, when the sea worms once again failed to swarm in February, he was willing to speak a bit more openly.

"It is not my business to tell the government when they should invite their guests," he told me. "But neither should they tell us how to count the moons. The *pasola* of our ancestors was staged to greet the sea worms as they swarmed on our shores from across the sea. If we do it without their presence, we are not keeping our promise to the ancestors. Now that so many people are Christian, however, they may not care."

I asked him if the government edict would affect the timing of the *padu* sacrifices, since these set in motion a cycle of month names that effectively predicts the arrival of the sea worms once Nale Bokolo has begun. "No, we will perform the *padu* sacrifices as we have always done, but say the names of the Kodi moons softly and under our breaths so there will not be an overt conflict. They pay no attention to the names of the moons anyway, since they close off the feasting season themselves with government orders."

He referred rather ruefully to a series of government orders issued in the regency capital that put an early halt to livestock slaughter in order to limit the "wasteful" consumption of animals. Citing regional goals of improving economic conditions, these orders preempted traditional calendrical authorities from beginning the four-month ritual silence by roasting the bitter chicken. Since Kodi had sponsored the largest feasts of recent years (several of them involving over a hundred buffalo), the new restrictions were enforced particularly strictly there. Once again, his words implied, official bureaucracies had acted first, leaving him in the position of simply reacting or of offering a retrospective traditional legitimation to events that had already occurred.

In 1980, a government letter, dated September 2 and signed by the regent and district administrator (*camat*), announced that no feasts would be permitted after September 15, "so that all activities could be oriented toward village development, including the cleaning and preparation of gardens in order to await planting and the coming of the rains." The letter came as no surprise, since an earlier announcement in 1976 had expressed the same sentiment, followed in 1987 by yet another. Periodically, the inflationary spiral of feasting was contained by government restrictions, only to burgeon out again in the intervening years. In particular, the government outlawed "chain feasting" (Ind. *pesta berantai*), or feasts that required a "chain" of participants, each one obliged to contribute because of membership in an ancestral village.

The next month, a small group of villagers gathered to roast the bitter chicken in Tossi, making the government-enforced de facto silence into a de jure compliance with the traditional calendar. The Rato Nale held up a small chicken with these words:

This small chicken here	Hena a manu
With only a shrimp's waist	A kenda kura kiyo
This small chicken here	Hena a manu
No more than a banyan flower	A walla kawango kiyo
Will close off the flute playing	Na riri we kingyoka a li pyoghi
Will prohibit the lute singing	Na leta we kingyoka a li jungga
So we will go to dig the land	Onikya la dari cana
Without overstepping a node	Nja do kingoka pa dowa handalu

So we will go to weed the grass	Onikya la batu rumba
Without trespassing a joint	Nja do kingoka pa pala hawuku

As the ceremony came to an end, a young man standing next to me said,

> In earlier times, if someone needed an extension to finish building his house or constructing a grave, he would come to the Rato Nale with a simple gift, a chicken, a piglet, a length of cloth, and ask for the time needed to complete his task. Now when people want to hold a feast after the *padu* sacrifice, they do not come to us. They go to the district office and are told to pay a fine of 35,000 rupiah [approx. $30] so the government will extend the deadline. We were kinder time masters than the district officer.

Ra Holo had decided to make what he could of a situation in which his authority over the calendar was being increasingly diminished. By choosing not to confront his new rivals directly he kept his dignity, but he could only resign himself to the usurpation of his powers. Ra Ndengi, who was perhaps more offended by government interference, was also less concerned to carry on a tradition that seemed broken and devoid of meaning. He avoided conflict by withdrawing completely, retreating into the safety of old age and infirmity. "My eyes have turned foggy," he told me as he turned his gaze toward mine and showed the pale outlines of cataracts. "I cannot be a spectator at the *pasola*. I cannot see what they are doing to it. Why should I go?"

The master of time, thus, expressed his mastery by making himself into an anachronism. He was above time, he could step out of it, and by leaving it behind he could show himself indifferent to the debate about secular activities. His junior associate, wanting others to understand his priestly functions and respect them, asked for my assistance to explain his task to government officials in "rational" terms. We prepared a list of the names of Kodi moons and a suggestion that the date of the sea worm swarming could vary from one month to another.

But a sacred narrative can be "rationalized" only if it loses its unquestioned, separate status. In a modern world with easy access to printed calendars, many people saw little need for the elaborate knowledge that had been transmitted along a line of hereditary priests to keep the lunar calendar coordinated with the solar cycle of seasons. The arrival of the worms and the renewal of the natural world became less important than a performance staged for important visitors who did not care how to "count the moons and measure the year." It was easier to conclude, as regency officials did, that the sea worm festivities occurred "one week after the full moon in February." Local time, first invented and given shape by ritual practice, ceded its place to an imported tradition of literate records.

Kodi, the domain that prided itself on being the "base of the year" (*kere ndouna*) and the "counter of the months" (*ghipo wulla*) for the whole island, was becoming increasingly aware of its own parochialism. "The numbers of people who listened when we spoke was once very great," Ra Holo complained to me, "but now it is shrinking." Competition with bureaucratic calendars was no longer possible: "They cannot hear our prayers anymore, they hear only the district office's loudspeaker at the market." If local temporality was forced to surrender to a more encompassing national and even international time reckoning, it was not without a protest and a nostalgic sense of loss.

13

Revolutions in Time, Revolutions in Consciousness

The concept of the historical progress of mankind cannot be sundered from the concept of its progression through a homogeneous, empty time. A critique of the concept of such a progression must be the basis of any criticism of the concept of progress itself.

Walter Benjamin, Illuminations

The transformation of a traditional ritual local calendar into a modern, secular, and universal one can properly be called a revolution in time. For much of human history, the calendar has served as the primary instrument of social control, regulating the duration, sequence, rhythm, and tempo of life and coordinating and synchronizing group activities. The legitimacy of the traditional calendar rests on commemoration. It celebrates the past and inscribes the "pathway followed by the ancestors" (*a lara ambu nuhi*) on the annual round of activities. When the calendar remains the most encompassing vision of temporality, the future takes its meaning from the past. Past experience is resurrected and honored as precedent that will provide guidance for future action. As the ritual centrality of the calendar has been displaced and Kodi has entered into a wider global culture, time and temporality have changed dramatically.

Revolutions in time are also revolutions in consciousness. An awareness of the progressive, linear, and cumulative notion of historical time gives a different ideological cast to local notions of the past. Even when efforts are made to preserve tradition, this preservation can no longer be based on simple ideas of continuity but requires a consciousness of possible ruptures and a deliberate decision to maintain "the heritage of the ancestors." The displacement of a ritual calendar that made Kodi the center for the ordering of time caused a shift in temporal perspectives that was to a certain extent irrevocable. It created "history" as an alternative to "heritage" and moved the locus of debate from the various evidences of narratives, objects, and actions to a new form of totalizing vision.

In this final chapter, I pull together the various strands of my argument and show their relevance to wider theoretical issues. My conclusions are of three types: (1) a local-level conclusion, which maps out the particular forms of Kodi temporality as described and analyzed in the chapters of this book; (2) a comparative conclusion, which places Kodi in the wider context of the politics of time within Indonesia and other nations of the developing world; and (3) a theoretical conclusion, which reexamines the relations of totalities and practices from a historicist perspective.

Kodi Temporality

The first problem I address is the difference between a naturalized, immutable concept of "time"—the apparently universal cycle of days, months, and seasons—and a culturally constructed view of the "past," which in Kodi was manifested in the "imported past" of objects and institutions. Looking at ordinary-language time concepts in Kodi, we saw that they are diffuse and form several logical series: one based on celestial bodies, another on domestic routines, a third on genealogy and the succession of generations. Time, born from the moment of human mortality, appears to individuals as many intervals attached to assorted meanings and not part of a grand narrative sequence. While each individual is most directly concerned with "how his or her days are numbered" and his or her own inevitable path through life toward death, this is indeterminate and the anchors of a wider social life must be sought in other, more determinable regularities. The coordination and synchronization of these very different phenomenological notions of time was the task of a ritual actor: the Rato Nale, or "Lord of the Year," custodian of sacred objects that enabled him to construct an overarching cyclical chronology from a diffuse and varied round of annual activities.

The Rato Nale was conceived as a timekeeper, a chronologer, only in the very specific sense that he constructed *synchrony*, the movement of different modalities of time with a coordinated rhythm or as part of a single cycle and a cultural master narrative. The synchronization of social activities depended on a fragile and often diffuse consensus; nonetheless, it is this consensus, expressed through participation in the shared ceremonial system, that constituted Kodi cultural identity. The Rato Nale did not create this synchronized temporal unity by telling stories or explaining the common basis of all the people of Kodi. He did so, and continues to do so, by performing rituals.

The authority of ritual derives from its association with cultural tradition and the power of the past to inform the present. The person who holds the objects also "holds" the stories. Sacred "timepieces" like the trough for the sea worms or the net that once held the moon are connected to the narratives of their acquisition and the regulations concerning their ritual use. This socially constructed time is enacted in ritual performances. By performing the sacrifices of the "bitter" season, the renewing auguries of the sea worm festivities, and the harvest rites before feasting, the Rato Nale creates the "Kodi year."

The rituals of the New Year are texts without authors. In the narratives that trace their origins, a ceremonial welcome is required for the sea worms, and the worms and urn together "choose" the persons who will perform the offerings each year. The content of the rites, what is "said" by their performance, is not attributed to any specific individual. Agency is displaced from persons onto objects and a collective, anterior author, "the founding ancestors," who prescribe the form and procedures to be followed. It is only when the ritual cycle is disrupted, when contingent moments cause a disjuncture in the interlocking cycles, that a new author is needed.

The silence, passivity, and immobility of the Rato Nale was important to his ritual role as the unspeaking priest who kept the whole annual cycle in place. He became almost an object himself, as a representative of what is eternal and unmoving in a shifting world. However, when new forms of political authority and control were introduced under the colonial administration, the single figure of the "master of the year" (*mori ndoyo*) came to be divided in two. The first division was within Tossi, with the active younger house of Rato Pokilo assuming an executive position but still owing ritual deference to the senior, passive "female" house of Rato Mangilo. The second division, which followed the turmoil of the extended resistance struggle at the turn of the century, redefined the "female" house as literally the province of a female priest, and introduced a male counterpart in Bukubani whose ritual role later became preeminent.

The historical shifts caused by the colonial encounter were not the first, nor the last, changes to affect the Kodi ceremonial system. We also saw that the very bases of sharing remain contested in Kodi life. Origin narratives do not trace present institutions back to a single, cosmogonic creation, but to a series of more contingent historical processes. Genealogy, skill in competitive games, and the ability to restore the fertility of the fields—"ritual efficacy"—all interact in establishing the ceremonial hierarchy. Ritual "acts out" these narrative conventions in offerings to the ancestors and in the *pasola* battle, but it does so in ways that highlight social differences and tensions. Rather than simply enforcing conformity to ancestral ways, ritual events provide a reflection on the past that can be critical. They provide an open space within which the relations of objects and persons, events and structures, are constantly renegotiated and adjusted to fit the demands of each new situation.

Exchange plays out temporal relations in a similar kind of open space. A series of exchanges takes the form of a temporal chain, with each exchange creating an obligation that can only be fulfilled in time. Through such temporal chains, cumulative processes are represented and shifts between past and present are reorganized. The particular form of each exchange transaction casts its shadow over the next one. In contemporary Kodi, traditional exchange is regulated by a standard that sees time as determinant of value, but the emerging importance of market relations and wage labor offers a contrasting model by which "time" is reckoned in smaller, monetary units, less closely inscribed on individual biographies. In the not too distant future, the continuity of the temporal chains may well be threatened by this new standard of value. Recent conflicts concerning exchange have focused on the use of time and ritual intervals as a strategic resource, and on the reconstitution of social groups through a rearrangement of the temporal chains of affinity and alliance.

The "New Order" of Suharto's Indonesia has made the externally introduced temporalities of the Christian church and state bureaucracy into realities to be reckoned with on Sumba. Since independence, conversions have dramatically increased, and the power of nationalist ideology has spread to the most distant corners of the archipelago. In Kodi, a new consciousness of the past as "history"—a form of authoritative discourse that is discontinuous with the present—has begun to compete with the earlier perspective, in which the past was seen as a "heritage," a continuous tradition passed down through the generations. Nationalist history situates the real location of the past elsewhere: in Jakarta, on a world stage, in relation to a different heritage.

"History," as experienced by isolated small societies, breaks past and present apart and creates a radical discontinuity between ancestors and their descendants. When the heritage of ancestral precedent is still vital, only those who are able to legitimate their present actions in terms of some past paradigm are respected. When the link between past and present is broken, the past is evoked nostalgically rather than efficaciously, and its power to recreate society disappears. The traditional concept of the past was complex, based on much more than the stereotyped reproduction of earlier events. Innovations appeared and were justified as continuities of a special kind, chosen from an array of alternatives to fit new circumstances.

The idea that time is constitutive of value informs Kodi temporality, making the passage of time into a form of legitimation. The authority of the ancestors and the distant stems, in part, from the perception that their actions have withstood the test of time. If some customary practice has been a part of Kodi society "since ancient times" (*wali la mandei la ma ulu*), this fact in itself is a proof of its validity. If an ancestor brought an exchange valuable into his house and retained possession of it for generations, that continuity legitimates his ownership of the object and its power. If someone has produced many descendants and multiplied the number of people who speak his name in ritual offerings, these new generations are living proof of his importance as founder of the line. Thus, "the past" is not simply inflicted on "the present" to reproduce a static pattern (as is argued in Bloch 1977); rather, it has value *because* of the passage of time and the success demonstrated by longevity.

"The past" is a variable and unstable resource; its connection to calendars and ritual time is equally variable and not always reinforcing (Appadurai 1981). Knowledge of the past is highly valued in many societies precisely because, by revealing that present states are not permanent ones, it supports a consciousness of history and the possibility of change. The play of continuity and discontinuity between past and present can be particularly intense in hierarchical societies, with their complex diversity of temporalizing and detemporalizing narrative genres (Valeri 1990). Hierarchy is necessarily involved in the creation of a notion of "tradition," however contested, since in that process one part of the past is always placed on a higher level than the others.[1]

The amount of the "past in the present" is taken by some as an index of hierarchy, and thus of "systems for hiding the world" and perpetuating social inequalities (Bloch 1977). Yet it is misleading to maintain that the past serves as an instrument of mystification and domination simply because "social theory is expressed in the language of ritual" (Bloch 1977, 288). Rituals provide a system for *knowing* the world as well as for hiding it, in that they constitute an arena for imaginative reconstructions and new totalizations of existing knowledge. In origin narratives, the manip-

---

[1] The content of "tradition" is sometimes taken to be the unassailable, quasi-mythical past, as in Evans-Pritchard (1939, 215): "Beyond the limits of historical time one enters a plane of tradition which merges at one end into history and at the other end into myth." More recent work on the notion of tradition, however, tends to reserve the term for a conscious modeling of former practices—invariant, ritualized, and legitimated through an idea (often false) that the past is being replicated exactly. Eric Hobsbawm (1983, 2) distinguishes an ossified tradition from "custom," which "does not preclude innovation and change up to a point, though evidently the requirement that it must appear compatible or even identical with precedent imposes substantial limitations on it." This sense of "custom" is equivalent to the Indonesian *adat* and to what I have termed the "past which is continuous with the present" in Kodi.

ulation of exchange objects, and annual calendrical rites, the Kodinese reflect on their past and reinterpret it to deal with present problems. Although there is no written historiographic tradition, these traces of the past are critically evaluated as sources of knowledge about the ancestors, and there are clear standards of debate and discussion.

It is now commonplace to assert that no society is truly "without history." If history is defined as simple knowledge of the past, certainly some memory of earlier times is a human universal. What is *not* universal is the perspective taken on the past, the significance that it has in daily life, and the way the past is used to legitimate more encompassing orders.

Kodi presents an illuminating context in which to explore the relations between past and present for three reasons. First, as a society whose ritual system is based on the authority of the ancestors, it shows us that there is no incompatibility between a continuity of ancestral ways and a historicizing perspective on past events. Second, as a society whose social life is dominated by exchange and alliance, it shows that these temporal chains, which are constituted across long and short time spans, are not simply individual "strategies" but more enduring "sequences." Third, as a society now in dialogue with external forces such as the nation-state, the market economy, and the Christian church, it demonstrates an imaginative resilience and an ability to recapture past values with new meanings.

Indonesian Calendars and Chronologies

Although the indigenous calendar of Kodi has provided a focus for this discussion, it is not an anomaly within Indonesia, a nation with an impressive array of systems for reckoning time and preserving knowledge of the past (Ammarell 1988; Casparis 1978). Detailed accounts of the traditional calendars of Kedang (Barnes 1974), Rindi (G. Forth 1983), Tana Ai (Lewis 1988), and Savu (Fox 1979a) have emphasized the place of time-keeping within a wider classificatory order. By contrast, the study of historical narratives on Flores (Howell 1991), Roti (Fox 1979b), and Timor (Traube 1986, 1989) has revealed the great variety of ways in which the past can be constructed even in closely related, neighboring societies.

A significant axis of variation concerns the strategic importance of the symbolic control of time, and thus the position of the timekeeper or calendrical priest. In Kodi, the Rato Nale is the "master of the year" (*mori ndoyo*) and stood traditionally at the top of the ceremonial hierarchy. His authority was connected to the fertility of the soil, the rhythms of nature, and agricultural production. His power was identified as "female," tied to female objects like the urn and located in a female ritual house. In contrast to the Rato Nale stood the Rato Katoda, the warrior leader who hunted heads to enhance the fertility of the region. The equality and sharing emphasized in the calendrical rites of the New Year were related to the most fundamental and unquestionable grounds of social existence, where each person was united to the others by a common humanity. In contrast, the rites of warfare and feasting serve to differentiate persons and establish inequalities, creating "nobles" and "commoners" as well as hierarchy of another sort, based on conquest, redistribution, and debt.

The societies of East Sumba, though they share a ritual calendar related to the arrival of the sea worms, give this regulation of time a very different political significance. Here the priest is no longer an autonomous figure, but subservient to the authority of the noble ruler (*maramba*). In Umalulu (Melolo), the priest (*ratu*) can be killed by the ruler and have a slave substituted in his place (Kapita 1976b). In Kapunduk (Kanatang), his genealogical claim to priority has been usurped by the noble lineage, although he can still regulate the agricultural calendar (Adams 1971a). In Rindi, the nobility have appropriated virtually all the functions of the priests, and calendrical rites are now celebrations of noble privilege (G. Forth 1981).

On the island of Roti, a similar process seems to have displaced the ritual leader known as the "head of the earth," who now has only commoner status (Fox 1979b). On Timor, the Great Lord of Wehali now presides over a miserable little house, emptied of sacred objects, but maintains his traditional authority as the "source" of the island's ritual and political system (Francillon 1980; Traube 1989). The priests of Tana Wai Brama on Flores trace a line of precedence back to the distant past and use origin narratives to legitimate their control of calendrical ceremonies similar to the Kodi rites of "bitter" and "bland" (Lewis 1988).

It would appear that wherever political power was centralized and consolidated under the leadership of a single ruler, the authority of the priest was undermined. Bali, with its famously complicated water temple system, may be a partial exception, since there a commoner priest (the Jero Gde) has been able to claim partial autonomy in the context of regulating irrigation and agricultural processes (Lansing 1991; Valeri 1990). Even so, this autonomy was never such that it could directly challenge the royal ruler. In other areas of Indonesia, calendrical priests like the Batak *datu* once seem to have had greater political power than they do today; now they function mainly as diviners and healers (Steedly 1989). The Toradja priest of the seasons (called the *indo pare*, or "rice mother," expressing his symbolic femininity) has much greater influence in the egalitarian northwest region of Toradja land than in the more hierarchical south (Coville 1989).

Thus we find an incompatibility between the primacy of a ritual calendar and the more complex political systems of kingship and, eventually, nationhood. This incompatibility, moreover, underscores a tension between ideals of local autonomy and indigenous self-determination, on the one hand, and attempts to synchronize diverse social activities, on the other.

J. T. Fraser (1989) has noted that a society's view of the world is, to a great extent, its view of time, whether this time is seen as a directed, unilinear progression, a punctuated series of interlocking cycles, or a constant oscillation between past models and present practice. It is not only in Kodi that timekeeping instruments and notions of chronology were once part of the "imported past." In ninth-century Java, one of the most complex calendars in the world was developed by integrating an indigenous system of nine weekly cycles with the lunar-solar calendar of the Indian year (Casparis 1978, 5). A 3-day cycle of named days intersected with a 5-day market week and a 7-day week labeled with Hindu terms for celestial bodies, culminating in a 210-day calendar "year," in which each day was defined in relation to its position within the nine cycles. The most propitious day for planting and harvesting, getting married, building houses, or burying the dead was calculated by diviners, who read wooden (*tika*) or palm-leaf (*wariga*) calendars that charted the combination of particular days in the weekly cycles (Casparis 1978).

In Bali, that system is still used to set the dates for festivals and religious holidays, and it has been interpreted as providing the basis of a detemporalized, static concept of time (Geertz 1973; Goris 1960). Gregory Bateson (1970, 135) was the first to articulate this calendrical attitude as a specific relation between past and present: "The modern Balinese . . . does not think of the past as a time that was different and out of which the present has sprung by chance. The past provides him with patterns of behavior, and if only he knows the pattern he will not blunder and need not be tongue-tied. . . . The past provides not the cause of the present but the pattern on which the present should be modeled." This idea of the past as exemplary, providing paradigms for present action, is very close to the idea of a continuity between past and present that I have called "heritage." It does not imply a radical departure from Western notions of time and the past, which include both "history" and "heritage" and are so multiple and various that attempts to describe them often founder on the diversity of possible perspectives (Lowenthal 1985).

Geertz's famous essay "Person, Time, and Conduct in Bali," first published in 1966, continued Bateson's lead in adducing the linkages among systems of personal names, status titles, the taxonomic calendar, and the "immobilization of time" into a "motionless present" (Geertz 1973, 404).

Critics have noted that while many Balinese may share this perspective, it is not necessarily that of people in positions of power and authority, such as kings and high priests, who are more interested in the narrative legitimation of the past (Vickers 1990, 169). Geertz's focus on the ceremonial, the aesthetic, and the immediate turned attention away from other contexts of Balinese life (such as healing and black magic) that emphasize the personal, emotional, and historical (Wikan 1989, 1990).

Geertz's essay acknowledges an interplay of historical forms but does not dwell on discords between them, maintaining that court chronicles (*babad*), Shaka chronology, and Hinduistic notions of successive epochs are "of secondary importance in the ordinary course of everyday life" (Geertz 1973, 391). If, however, the idea of the "past as pattern" is maintained as a cultural heritage, it is now being challenged by a new template of historical action associated with national struggle. Geertz wrote that Balinese were becoming acquainted with a more progressive concept of time, which involved "pushing events toward their climaxes rather than away from them" and introduced a new scheme of "original greatness, foreign oppression, extended struggle, sacrifice and self-liberation, and impending modernization" (1973, 410).

In retrospect, this new concept of time can be seen to have much greater importance than Geertz assigned to it in his original essay. Based on fieldwork in the later 1950s, that piece was written just before the bloody slaughters of 1965, which brought home the relevance of a "developing nation state whose center is elsewhere" (1973, 409). In the last years before the most dramatic climax of Indonesian history, time may have appeared immobilized, but after many thousand Balinese were killed in the wake of an alleged coup no one could deny the force of national history and its ability to disrupt even the most carefully calibrated ceremonialism.

Geertz raised an issue in that essay which has informed this whole book: What is the relation of conventional notions of time to the culturally constructed concept of the past? And how have these notions been transformed by historical events? A quarter century later, the methods we use to propose answers may be somewhat different. The present study emphasizes the diversity of perspectives in narratives, the interpretation of objects, and ritual action. The integration of culture that Geertz referred to as an octopus, "a viable if somewhat ungainly entity" (1973, 408), is in the end less important than the existence of dialogue between mutually contradictory and competing points of view.

Traditionalist proponents of cultural continuity, I argue, now consciously ascribe to an idea of "heritage" that opposes the externally introduced form of "history" they have encountered. We need to understand how things were made meaningful in the past, the forms of meaning and coherence that they were given, before we can interpret how they have changed and how that change is significant. A "historical event" does not exist as an abstract, absolute entity. It is a moment selected from a temporal continuum by an act of remembering. The memory of events is preserved in various forms of reflecting on the past, which include telling stories, assigning specific locations to houses, heirlooms, and graves, and performing the rites of the New Year. Each genre of knowledge about the past helps to make sense of events and continuities in its own way. Narrative chronology does not assume the privileged form of historical discourse it has in Western historiography but interacts with other traces of the past.

Totalities and Practices

These questions bring us back to the wider debate about the genesis of historical consciousness and the role of totalities versus practices. Bourdieu (1977, 164) has argued that indigenous calendars perpetuate a "synoptic illusion," which is divorced from the "real, practical time" of everyday experience. They are, he says, part of a totalizing, objectifying system of classification through which "every established order tends to produce . . . the naturalization of its own arbitrariness."

When the social world is so taken for granted that its order appears natural and immutable, then the instruments of knowledge of the social world can indeed said to be "political instruments," with the theory of knowledge becoming a dimension of political theory (Bourdieu 1977, 165). My analysis has established that the calendar is an institution that belongs not only to the perception of time ("the system of knowledge") but also to the indigenous political system ("the system of domination," in Bourdieu's terms). Yet it does not follow from this that indigenous calendars are merely, or even primarily, tools of political domination or that their articulation is part of the "objectivist fallacy" of the anthropologist (Bourdieu 1977, 106).

Bourdieu's critique of earlier studies of the calendar (primarily, it would seem, the work of Evans-Pritchard) is based on what he sees as the disengagement of theory from practice:

> A calendar substitutes a linear, homogeneous, continuous time for practical time, which is made up of incommensurable islands of duration, each with its own rhythm, the time that flies by or drags, depending on what one is *doing*, i.e. on the *functions* conferred by the activity concerned. By distributing *guide-marks* (ceremonies and

tasks) along a continuous line, one turns them into *dividing marks* united in a relation of simple succession, thereby creating *ex nihilo* the question of intervals and correspondences between points which are no longer topologically but metrically equivalent.

The calendar, in his view, is created as a false object of thought, "a totality existing beyond its 'applications' and independently of the needs and interests of its users" (1977, 105–6).

There are two problems with this criticism. First, it ignores the conventional and constructed nature of all perception of time. Second, in trying to dissolve "objectified time" into the play of "needs and interests" in practice, it imposes an ethnocentric folk model of human motivation (the calculating "rational man") on the diversity of social action. I will treat each problem in turn.

Since Kant we have been aware that our notions of time are not imposed by a physical reality but created by an activity of the mind. Temporality is a form of sensibility, in that time is not abstracted from experience but presupposed by it. Durkheim ([1912] 1965, 10) showed long ago that it was not possible even to conceive of time "without the processes by which we divide it, measure it or express it with objective signs." Hubert's classic study of temporal representations begins with the principle that time cannot be studied in the abstract, but only as a system of relations between the points that divide time and the intervals they create (1909, 197). As Leach (1961, 135) points out, "We talk of measuring time, as if it were a concrete thing to be measured, but in fact we *create time* by creating intervals in social life. Until we have done so there is no time to be measured." An all-embracing notion of time that includes both repetitive and irreversible change is, he argues, a religious notion, "one of those categories which we find necessary because we are social animals rather than because of anything empirical in our objective experience of the world" (Leach 1961, 125).

Thus, an important purpose in holding festivals is to order time and provide a way of discussing concepts that cannot be expressed without some social or cultural convention. In an earlier article on the attitude of the Algerian peasant toward time, Bourdieu (1968, 56) acknowledged the necessity of a social structuring of time perceptions: "The Kabyle peasant lives his life at a rhythm determined by the divisions of the ritual calendar which exhibit a whole mythical system." Technical and liturgical acts are integrated in a system he termed a "mythology-in-action" (1968, 57), in which the peasant does violence to the nourishing earth in order to fecundate her and wrest her riches from her.

The disjunction that Bourdieu asserts exists between "practical time" and "ritual time" emerges because the intervals of subjective experience are not equal and uniform and do not correspond to measured time: "The islands of time which are defined by these landmarks are not apprehended as segments of a continuous line, but rather as so many self-enclosed units" (1968, 59). Duration is estimated on the basis of the time it takes to perform a certain task, and space is evaluated by the "experience of activity" (thus, a given location is said to be "a day's walk away").

A problem with this formulation is that it is still based on social conventions, which are needed for people to communicate about time. The week is named on the basis of the time lapse between two markets, and the experience of time is perceived and remembered in terms of collective categories. The diagram of seasonal activities recorded by the anthropologist is said by Bourdieu (1977, 106) to misrepresent the practical reality of the experience of time passing:

> By cumulating information which is not and cannot always be mastered by a single informant . . . the analyst wins the *privilege of totalization*. . . . He thus secures the means of apprehending the logic of the system which a partial or discrete view would miss; but . . . he will overlook the change in status to which he is submitting practice and . . . insist on trying to answer questions which are not and cannot be questions of practice, instead of asking himself whether the essential characteristic of practice is not precisely the fact that it excludes such questions.

The "totalizing privilege" is a particular perspective on social life that is not the exclusive prerogative of the analyst. It can also be exercised by an insightful and reflective member of the society and is, to a certain extent, enjoined on persons in certain important ritual positions, such as that of guardian of the calendar. This is not to say that a high-ranking priest perceives the whole logic of the system, or understands it in the same terms as an outside observer, but only that a form of "totalization" *is* involved in indigenous systems of knowledge.

Calendars form an important part of the cultural heritage passed down from the ancestors in a great many societies, and certainly in Kodi the sequence of ritual performances (*katadi marapu*) constitutes an ordering of time. Bourdieu's criticism of the authority of calendars is not convincing because of abundant evidence that local people articulate calendrical knowledge in their own genres (origin narratives, spatial maps, the ritual functions of objects). The calendar cannot be seen as the result of a simple "connivance between the anthropologist and his informant" (Bourdieu 1977, 219) or an "illusory order." Nonetheless, his argument can bring us to ask another important question: What is the role of different kinds of knowledge in the collective representation of time, and what are the political consequences of the distribution of this knowledge?

For some peoples, temporal concepts are "encyclopedic," in the sense that they describe their knowledge *of* the world and its processes (Sperber 1975). This sense would seem to correspond in some way to Bourdieu's notion of "practical time," since it is rooted in empirical activity but is nevertheless a shared convention. For other peoples, temporal concepts are "symbolic," because they point to other constructions and constitute a model around which much of the culture is explicitly interrelated.[2] In Kodi, the symbolic centrality of the calendar means that time relations—ideas of age, precedence, duration, and temporal location—are used to express political positions and social asymmetries. The fact that temporal knowledge is not uniformly distributed only contributes to its hierarchizing functions, by limiting access to a valued and codified cultural competence.

Yet the very fact that certain privileged persons may "totalize" their knowledge of the calendar means that competing alternative perspectives will inevitably arise. Thus, Bourdieu's attack on the "officializing strategies" of those anthropologists who neglect the diversity of local perspectives is completely justified. The very processes of contesting and debating the significance of temporal intervals in feasts, exchanges, and calendrical rites demonstrate the importance of this form of symbolic knowledge.

The idea that "needs and interests" are revealed in "practical time" is reminiscent of Bloch's theory of an opposition of "ritual" and "practical" time, where practical time provides the language with which to criticize and change the prevailing structure of ritual inequality. Many of the criticisms of Bloch's argument (Bourdillon 1978; Howe 1981; Appadurai 1981; Peel 1984) also apply to Bourdieu's construction, with the caveat that at least Bourdieu does not assume that "practical time" is universal in its forms. However, in proposing that rational, calculating "strategies" *are* universals, Bourdieu commits his own version of economism.

Bourdieu castigates the "economism" of many Marxists and materialists for idealizing precapitalist economies as ruled by "disinterested" con-

---

[2]Sperber (1975, 109) defines symbolic knowledge as "neither about words nor about things, but about the memory of words and things. It is a knowledge about knowledge, a meta-encyclopaedia in the encyclopaedia." Our knowledge of the world is a way of storing information, which is represented by statements and semantic connections between categories. Symbolic knowledge deals with representations that are "in quotes" and shows their interrelations.

cerns for honor or ceremonial redistribution. He argues instead, and rightly, that we must include not only material goods but also honor and prestige within the sphere of sought-after valuables. His insights into the tempo of exchange transactions and the sense in which "time must be invested" and "symbolic capital is always *credit*" (1977, 180, 181) have revitalized the study of exchanges over time, and I have incorporated them in my analysis in the second section of this book.

Yet while I agree that forms of prestige and renown attached to a family may be readily convertible into economic capital, I still find the basis of the notion of "symbolic capital" problematic. Knowledge is not, and cannot be, a commodity in the same way that materials goods are. It can be made "scarce" by rules that limit access to certain types of knowledge, but scarcity is not an *inherent property* of systems of knowledge. Nor, more importantly, is the commodity the best model for valued objects, qualities, or attributes generally. In arguing that time is constitutive of value in Kodi ceremonial exchange, I maintain that sacrificial animals are not commodities but rather expressions of an investment of human life. Time measured along a full life span is not "time converted into money" but a merging of individual biography with its symbolic expression in horns, tusks, or other measures.

The metaphor of calculation cannot be extended indiscriminately into all spheres of life without falling into a tautological utilitarianism which asserts that people are always pursuing their "real" advantage even when they seem to be pursuing "symbolic" goals such as the favor of the ancestors, the fulfillment of kinship obligations, or the splendor or ritual display (Errington 1989). What is "real" to the analyst is ultimately only that which can be converted into economic goods and thus is subject to a minute calculation of advantage.

Western economism is a folk theory that developed in the particular historical context of seventeenth- and eighteenth-century Europe. Albert Hirschman (1977) argues that before the triumph of capitalism, the ideological groundwork for an economistic perspective was laid when "rationality" came to be merged with "calculation." Reason was put in the service of maximizing wealth, and the calculation of advantage became the hallmark of the "rational man." A historicist perspective thus relativizes some of the claims of economism to universal truth by detailing the specific conditions that led to its appearance. Since the time of Malinowski this prototypical Economic Man has been little more than a straw man, an easy target to be attacked when developing contrasts with other forms of economic rationality (Malinowski 1922; Sahlins 1972). It seemed, in fact, that substantivist theorists in the tradition of Polanyi had given this limp stuffed shirt a proper burial some time ago.

The effect of Bourdieu's concept of "symbolic capital" has been to pump new life into the old straw man, who has been resurrected as Calculating Man or the Great Strategizer.[3] Bourdieu's valuable insights into the temporal rhythms of exchange have been obscured by excessive attention to his model of strategic manipulation. The concept of "symbolic capital" homogenizes the differences between gifts and commodities, qualities and quantities, and goods and services. In the vague, generalized sense in which the term is used, we could certainly say that time constitutes an important form of "symbolic capital" among the Kodi people. But to do so would accomplish very little; indeed, the ultimate result would be to cast the mechanisms by which time is given value into the shadows.

"Time" is valued in Kodi in more than purely economic terms. It is not simply "bought" and "sold," "wasted" or "well spent." Time is the line that runs through people's experience of the world, defining its poignant brevity but investing our search for meaning with an urgency and passion that produces vitality in the face of death. On this shared, universal surface of time, the Kodi people have constructed a cultural image of their past as a heritage worthy of preservation. And, in the face of a new, more ephemeral concept of "history," this is what they still strive to do.

The Calculating Man enshrines an individualism of a particularly callous and ruthless kind, for it assumes that the "agents" involved in exchange transactions and political manipulations are atomized individuals out for their own gain. Yet in fact, the "agent" in any given society is not a universal category but a cultural one. One must not assume that the temporal span of a collective strategy can be reduced to the manipulations

---

[3] Bourdieu's concept of *habitus* is an effort to escape the view that all human action is motivated solely by calculation, since some acts are performed out of an unconscious adherence to objective structures, perceived as an unreflective second nature: "the forgetting of history which history itself produces" (1977, 78). Yet because the *habitus* is defined by the absence of imagination and reflection and by an unthinking submission to daily routines, it leaves no space for reconceptualizations, innovations, or new totalizations. The only moving force in Bourdieu's scheme is the calculation of rational advantage; the *habitus* provides the inert mass against which this force moves. The *habitus* is also the site where objective structures impinge on subjective experience, for while it provides "predispositions, tendencies and inclinations" (1977, 241), it can also result in "regulated improvisations" (1977, 78) through which structure is "embodied" in practice. Bourdieu's attempt to capture "the dialectic of the internalization of externality and the externalization of internality" (1977, 72) is laudable, but the concepts he uses to do so seem to resolve into the same dichotomies they seek to oppose.

of individuals; after all, frequently the "transacting parties" are not people but houses, villages, or even larger groups. Notions of personhood vary across cultures and include complex forms of interrelationship extending back through time and often including ancestors as "transactors." The invisible witnesses to a promise or covenant are more likely to "act" to enforce it (by inflicting illness, misfortune, or other sanctions) than the visible witnesses, who are constrained by social norms to wait in silence. In a society like Kodi, some very valuable objects are also invested with agency and become part of the field of action.

While I do not propose to include ancestors and heirloom valuables among the "agents" who "calculate," the fact that they are perceived in this way by the Kodinese means that a theory of social action in Kodi cannot be limited to autonomous individuals. The person as a social actor is suspended in a web of relations that must be taken into account in any analysis of individual motivations and goals. Because these goals concern the general problems of the quality of life, they cannot be reduced to simple calculations of material or "symbolic" advantage.

The past is itself a totalizing vision that transcends the perspectives of individual actors. A view of the past is necessary to the notion of collective identity implied by the idea of "culture," which is rooted in the perception of a common and distinctive point of historical departure. Kodi origin narratives tell us what it is to be Kodinese, providing models of shared action and experience for all members of the society. The existence of an image of the past does not imply that all present actions must be adjusted to fit an ancient prototype; rather, they are understood in relation to a corpus of ideas inherited from the past. When the past is a living heritage, there is a clear preference for incorporating precedents into contemporary action. When it is seen as a more discontinuous history, the passage of time is acknowledged by getting it on record that things used to be different.

The desire to break away from earlier illusions or injustices has motivated some modern historians to declare "the death of the past" (Plumb 1969), in the naive belief that modern historiographic techniques can put an end to mythologizing and misrepresenting what actually happened. I cite this view of "history" not because I find it plausible, but because its claim to a complete separation of past representations from present interests is the logical extreme of a position based on the (largely Western) ideology of a progressive, linear conception of time. In opposing "history" of this type and "heritage," I highlight two extreme visions of the past: one valorizing a total severing of ties between the present time and that of our ancestors, the other valorizing the forging of new linkages wherever possible.

The new Indonesian national history, or *sejarah*, incorporates notions of both history and heritage to mobilize identities within a new communal framework, searching for precedents in diverse regional heritages while insisting on a directed historical trajectory. The glorious past of Majapahit and Mataram is evoked alongside accounts of the sufferings of the colonial period to create a sense among all Indonesians that their fates, in the future as in the past, must hang together. Thus "history" is seen as a series of episodes of anticolonial resistance that occurred, in different places and at different times, all over the archipelago. It transformed many peoples, with different languages and varied cultural traditions, into a single national community, conscious of a shared past and a shared destiny.

The vision of the collective Indonesian past presented by *sejarah* has achieved a remarkable degree of national integration across great geographic, linguistic, and cultural barriers. The occasional notes of disaffection and resistance that are sounded in places like Kodi reflect the resilience of indigenous notions of time that stress continuities with an ancestral tradition, but even these are gradually giving way to the wider vision of a more encompassing historical progression. Local perspectives, however, retain the power to inflect world processes at the level of the imagination. When nationalist historians try to present an image of Indonesia as a moral community, unambiguously bounded and filled with a historical mission, their own ideological practices can be turned around. New forms of "local knowledge" resist domination from the center by formulating their own version of heroic history, proposing alternative versions of the life of a hero like Wona Kaka or the meaning of a category like "custom" (*adat*). The indigenous temporality of the ritual calendar is ceding to the power of printed, "universal" calendars, but at the same time notions of cycles, synchrony, and intersecting trajectories are emerging as important components of what could be called a new national mythology. Most of this new mythology comes from beyond Sumba, as it has for centuries, when the past was imported and reshaped to fit local social and political institutions.

One major concern of this study has been to highlight the internal diversity of notions of time, the past, and the calendar. The time of the ancestors, of the world of exchange, and of present ritual performances is complex and has many interpenetrating levels. As J. T. Fraser (1989, xii) puts it, "What used to be regarded as a uniform flow which embraced equally all structure and processes is revealed as a nested hierarchy of qualitatively different temporalities." These "nested levels," in his formulation, are the seasonal successions of the calendar (the "ecotemporal"), the cumulative time of living bodies (the "biotemporal"), and the more encompassing awareness of finality and the place of the past (the "nootemporal," time that is "known" and not simply experienced).

Each of these "levels" corresponds to a form of Kodi temporality discussed in this book, notably the calendar, the temporal chain of exchange value, and the culturally constructed image of "heritage" or "history." Contrary to Fraser, however, I do not see these temporalities as permanently "nested" and would prefer to describe them as "strands" that can be pulled up into certain contexts but that remain largely invisible in others. As an anthropologist I regard the problem of the hierarchical integration of temporalities as an empirical rather than a theoretical question; that is, I assume that the relationship of different temporalities may vary between cultures and within a single culture over time.

A multistranded temporality permits us to understand the interactions of the representations, uses, and significance of different notions of time without foreclosing the question of which is more encompassing and hierarchically superior. The idea of absolute time is being called into question by a number of other scholars, who have documented the merits of earlier relativistic chronologies (Wilcox 1987) and discussed a diversity of time concepts (Bender and Wellbery 1991).

In Kodi, the ritual superiority of the Rato Nale gave preeminence to a social synchrony modeled on seasonal changes and the cycle of the moon, which provided, at least to some extent, a vision of a wider cultural order. The assessment of exchange value in the measurement of time using animals' bodies complemented calendrical time with a biotemporal measure of cumulative change, which was totalized by a series of origin narratives that constructed the past around a series of contested objects, locations, and ritual offices. The recent privileging of one specific strand— the view of the past as "history," although placed within a wider national "heritage"—can be seen as a highly specific cultural expression that is neither universal nor necessarily desirable. By looking at the "play of time" on a distant island that has been only partly integrated into wider world systems, we bring our own assumptions into sharper relief and come to see them differently.

Playing Back over Time

Recent years have seen a new interest in the study of temporality, partially as a result of the "postmodern turn" and its questioning of the universalist assumptions of time and history (Bender and Wellbery 1991). Many of these studies, however, have unconsciously reproduced an ethnocentric interpretation of the place of time in the modern world, at the expense of other forms of temporality in all their complexity and diversity. Reinhart Koselleck (1985) argues that the late eighteenth and early nineteenth centuries were the historical threshold of a new *temporalization* of experience—a conception of unified and all-pervasive change as occurring in and through time. Time, in his view, is no longer a locational marker but a medium that generates new experiential configurations: the a priori of the modern world.

Has modernism reinvented time, or has it simply provided additional variations on certain familiar themes? As an anthropologist skeptical of the forms of temporal distancing that can lead to the devaluation and dismissal of the conceptual schemes of other peoples, I am not easily convinced. Stephen Jay Gould (1987) notes that metaphors of lineal progression ("time's arrow") and recurrence ("time's cycle") have long been with us, and recent reconceptualizations in physics and geology have tended to make distinctions between these two metaphors relative rather than absolute. While people in our own age may want to conceive of themselves as inhabiting a "new" time, this conception is suspect for its ties to implicit evolutionism, a hidden agenda based on notions of "progress," and the assumption that Walter Benjamin (1969) notes of a homogeneous, empty Time.

The temporalization of experience in a different mode can be discerned in Kodi concrete symbols like the arc of the buffalo's horn, the unmoving authority of the heirloom urn, and the sea worms washing up on the shores in anticipation of the rice harvest. These work as metaphors for the passage of biographical time, the enduring importance of the past, and the recurrent cycle of the seasons. It is unfair to argue that a world in which notions of time are different from our own is *detemporalized*—as if one era could really be said to have "more time" than another.

The particular consciousness of time realized in Western historical writings is, of course, culturally constructed; it is especially evident in the forms of history that assume a collective unity encompassing all individual sequences of events. Whiggish history is, however, not the pinnacle of temporalization but only a peculiar variant on it. Homogeneous Time and its links to progress no doubt owes much to the invention of the clock and the revolutionary effect that its mechanical model of time's passage has had on modern life (Landes 1983, 1990); but the chronological time of printed calendars and the mechanical time of hours and minutes has always coexisted with lived experience, in which other models and perceptions may be more immediately relevant.

Phenomenological studies remind us that although homogeneous Time expresses a notion of progress that has struggled to achieve mastery over other, homelier metaphors of time's passing, its success has been only partial. Local knowledge and individual concerns and motivations continue to affect our perception of time, giving priority to significant ancestors, particularly vivid memories, and the quest for meaningful patterns of life.

In the writings of philosophers, historians, and social thinkers, the problem of time has been looked at through three major lenses: classificatory, with a focus on the "total" system; phenomenological, with a focus on variable "lived experience"; and historical, with a focus on periods and epochs. The argument of this study is that these domains should not be seen as discrete, but as connected. The interpenetrating representations of calendars, human biographies, and historical events draw them together in both social experience and social memory (Connerton 1989).

Ethnographic writing about time has followed a similar tripartite division, with some studies stressing the collective classification of time (Evans-Pritchard 1939, 1940), others its phenomenological aspects (Tedlock 1982), and still others its place in world history (Bloch 1985). A recent critical review of the literature (Munn 1992, 113) notes that this separation of topics has resulted in the "compartmentalization" of calendrical time, biographical time, and historical time. No other study to my knowledge has analyzed the interaction of these three modes in a local context, including the impact of changes associated with "modernization."

By bringing together a large body of ethnographic materials pointed toward questions of time, I have tried—in a modest and incomplete way—to question the validity of the notions of "modern times" that are often bandied about. Kodi temporality is not, in fact, a "premodern" form, located along some ladder of temporal stages that will ultimately culminate in fully "temporalized" consciousness. It provides an alternate temporality, which is expressed metaphorically in stacks of buffalo horns or the eyelashes plucked from exported animals so the herd can be regenerated back at home. The time of individual lives is meted out in comparison to the lives of domestic animals and the pathways of exchange valuables. The time of collective tradition is preserved in "history objects" that remain the inalienable property of a constantly shifting descent group. The time of the calendar and the repetitive cycle is expressed in ritual commemorations of original sacrifices and the playful, festive mood that celebrates life owing to a heightened awareness of its brevity.

Death is a part of our consciousness of time and of our own self-concept. None of us escapes the finality of an end to our own temporal existence; but the example of an alternate temporality can show us other ways to bear this burden and other ways to understand the significant ties that bind both past and present to conceptions of a future life.

Bibliographic References

Adams, Marie Jeanne
    1969   *System and Meaning in East Sumba Textile Design: A Study in Traditional Indonesian Art.* Yale Southeast Asia Studies Cultural Report 16. New Haven: Yale University Press.
    1969–71   Field notes. Typescript.
    1970   "Myths and Self-Image Among the Kapunduku People of Sumba." *Indonesia,* no. 10: 81–106.
    1971a   "History in a Sumba Myth." *Asian Folklore Studies* 30 (2): 133–39.
    1971b   "Work Patterns and Symbolic Structures in a Village Culture, East Sumba." *Southeast Asia* (Carbondale, Ill.) 1: 320–334.
    1974   "Symbols of the Organized Community in East Sumba, Indonesia." *Bijdragen tot de taal-, land- en volkenkunde* 130: 324–47.
    1979   "The Crocodile Couple and the Snake Encounter in the Tellantry of East Sumba, Indonesia." In *The Imagination of Reality: Essays in Southeast Asian Coherence Systems,* ed. A. L. Becker and A. Yengoyan. Norwood, N.J.: Ablex.
    1980   "Structural Aspects of East Sumbanese Art." In *The Flow of Life: Essays on Eastern Indonesia,* ed. J. J. Fox. Cambridge, Mass.: Harvard University Press.
Ammarell, Gene
    1988   "Sky Calendars of the Indo-Malay Archipelago: Regional Diversity and Local Knowledge." *Indonesia,* no. 45: 85–104.
Andaya, Leonard
    1975   "The Nature of Kingship in Bone." In *Pre-Colonial State Systems in Southeast Asia,* ed. A. Reid and L. Castles. Monographs of the Malaysian Branch of the Royal Asiatic Society, no. 6. Kuala Lumpur: Council of the Malaysian Branch of the Royal Asiatic Society of Britain.

1981   The Heritage of Arung Palakka: A History of South Sulawesi (Celebes) in the Seventeenth Century. The Hague: Martinus Nijhoff.

Anderson, Benedict
1972   "The Idea of Power in Javanese Culture." In Culture and Politics in Indonesia, ed. C. Holt, B. Anderson, and J. Siegel. Ithaca: Cornell University Press.
1978   "Cartoons and Monuments: The Evolution of Political Communication Under the New Order." In Political Power and Communications in Indonesia, ed. K. Jackson and L. Pyle. Berkeley and Los Angeles: University of California Press.
1983   Imagined Communities: Reflections on the Origin and Spread of Nationalism. London: Verso.
1990   Language and Power: Exploring Political Cultures in Indonesia. Ithaca: Cornell University Press.

Appadurai, A.
1981   "The Past as a Scarce Resource." Man, n.s., 16: 201–19.
1986   "Introduction: Commodities and the Politics of Value." In The Social Life of Things: Commodities in Cultural Perspective, ed. A. Appadurai. Cambridge: Cambridge University Press.

Arndt, P.
1951   Religion auf Ostflores, Adonara und Solor. Studia Instituti Anthropos, vol. 1. Wien-Modling: Missionsdruckerei St. Gabriel.
1954   Gesellschaftliche Verhältnisse der Ngadha. Studia Instituti Anthropos, vol. 8. Wien-Modling: Missionsdruckerei St. Gabriel.

Atkinson, Jane Monnig
1987   "Religions in Dialogue: The Construction of an Indonesian Minority Religion." In Indonesian Religions in Transition, ed. R. Kipp and S. Rodgers. Tucson: University of Arizona Press.
1989   The Art and Politics of Wana Shamanship. Berkeley and Los Angeles: University of California Press.

Austen, Leo
1939   "The Seasonal Gardening Calendar of Kiriwina, Trobriand Islands." Oceania 10: 30–53.
1950   "A Note on Dr. Leach's 'Primitive Calendars.'" Oceania 20: 333–35.

Aveni, Anthony
1989   Empires of Time: Calendars, Clocks, and Cultures. New York: Basic Books.

Bakhtin, Mikhail
1981   The Dialogic Imagination: Four Essays by M. M. Bakhtin. Austin: University of Texas Press.
1984a   Rabelais and His World. Bloomington: Indiana University Press.
1984b   Speech Genres and Other Late Essays. Austin: University of Texas Press.

Barnes, Robert
1974   Kedang: A Study of the Collective Thought of an Eastern Indonesian People. Oxford: Clarendon Press.

Bateson, Gregory
1970   "An Old Temple and a New Myth." In *Traditional Balinese Cul-
            ture*, ed. J. Belo. New York: Columbia University Press.
Bender, John, and David E. Wellbery, eds.
1991   *Chronotypes: The Construction of Time*. Stanford: Stanford Uni-
            versity Press.
Benjamin, Walter
1969   *Illuminations*. New York: Schocken Books.
Biersack, Aletta, ed.
1991   *Clio in Oceania: Toward an Historical Anthropology*. Washing-
            ton, D.C.: Smithsonian Institution Press.
Bigalke, Terence
1984   "Government and Mission in the Torajan World of Makele-Ran-
            tepao." *Indonesia*, no. 38: 85–112.
Biro Statistik
1986   *Sumba Barat Dalam Angka*. Kabupaten Sumba Barat, Propinsi
            Nusa Tenggara Timur.
Bloch, Maurice
1977   "The Past and the Present in the Present." *Man*, n.s., 12: 278–
            302.
1985   *From Blessing to Violence: History and Ideology in the Circum-
            cision Ritual of the Merina of Madagascar*. Cambridge: Cam-
            bridge University Press.
1989   "Foreword." In *Ritual, History, and Power: Selected Papers in
            Anthropology*. London: Athlone Press.
Bloch, Maurice, and Jonathan Parry
1989   *Money and the Morality of Exchange*. Cambridge: Cambridge
            University Press.
Bock, Carl
1881   *The Headhunters of Borneo*. London: S. Low, Marston, Searle &
            Rivington.
Bohannan, Laura
1952   "A Genealogical Charter." *Africa* 22: 301–15.
Bohannan, Paul
1955   "Some Principles of Exchange and Investment Among the Tiv."
            American Anthropologist 57: 60–69.
1959   "The Impact of Money on an African Subsistence Economy." *Jour-
            nal of Economic History* 19 (4): 491–503.
1967   "Concepts of Time Among the Tiv of Nigeria." In *Myth and
            Cosmos: Readings in Mythology and Symbolism*, ed. J. Middle-
            ton. New York: Natural History Press.
Bottoms, J. C.
1965   "Some Malay Historical Sources: A Bibliographical Note." In *An
            Introduction to Indonesian Historiography*, ed. Soedjatmoko. Ith-
            aca: Cornell University Press.
Bourdieu, Pierre
1968   "The Attitude of the Algerian Peasant Toward Time." In *Mediter-*

ranean Countrymen: Essays on the Social Anthropology of the Mediterranean, ed. J. Pitt-Rivers. Paris: Mouton.

1977   *Outline of a Theory of Practice*. Cambridge: Cambridge University Press.

1990   *The Logic of Practice*. Cambridge: Cambridge University Press.

Bourdillon, M. F. C.

1978   "Knowing the World or Hiding It: A Response to Maurice Bloch." *Man*, n.s., 13: 591–99.

Buhler, Alfred

1951   "Bemerkungen zur Kulturgeschichte Sumba." In *Südseestudien. Gedenkschrift zur Erinnerung an F. Speiser*. Basel: Museum für Völkerkunde.

Casparis, J. G. de

1978   *Indonesian Chronology*. Handbuch der Orientalistik: Indonesia, Malaysia, and the Philippines, 3d sec., pt. 1. Leiden and Cologne: E. J. Brill.

Clifford, James, and George Marcus

1986   *Writing Culture*. Berkeley and Los Angeles: University of California Press.

Cole, Fay-Cooper

1912   *Chinese Pottery in the Philippines*. Field Museum of Natural History, Publication no. 162; Anthropological Series, vol. 12, no. 1. Chicago: Field Museum of Natural History.

Collingwood, R. G.

1946   *The Idea of History*. Oxford: Clarendon Press.

Connerton, Paul

1989   *How Societies Remember*. Cambridge: Cambridge University Press.

Couvreur, A. L.

1915   "Memorie van Overgave." Photocopy of typescript from the Royal Dutch Archives of the Tropical Museum, Amsterdam.

1917   "Aard en wezen der inlandsche zelfbesturne op het eiland Soemba." *Tijdschrift van het binnenlands bestuur* 52: 206–19.

Coville, Elizabeth

1989   "Centripetal Ritual in a Decentered World: Changing Maro Performances in Tana Toradja." In *Changing Rites, Changing Lives*, ed. C. Cunningham and S. Russell. De Kalb: Northern Illinois University Press.

Cuisinier, Jeanne

1956   "Un calendrier de Savu." *Extrait du Journal Asiatique* 111–19.

Damon, Frederick H.

1982   "Calendars and Calendrical Rites on the Northern Side of the Kula Ring." *Oceania* 52 (3): 221–39.

1990   *From Muyuw to the Trobriands: Transformations Along the Northern Side of the Kula Ring*. Tucson: University of Arizona Press.

Daniels, E. Valentine

1991   "Three Dispositions Towards the Past: One Sinhalla and Two Tamil." *Social Analysis* 15: 22–41.

Dening, Greg
    1991   "A Poetic for Histories: Transformations That Present the Past." In *Clio in Oceania: Toward an Historical Anthropology*, ed. A. Biersack. Washington, D.C.: Smithsonian Institution Press.

de Roo van Alderwerelt, J.
    1890   "Eenige mededeelingen over Soemba." *Tijdschrift voor indische taal-, land- en volkenkunde* 33: 565–95.
    1906   "Historische aanteekeningen over Soemba." *Tijdschrift voor indische taal-, land- en volkenkunde* 48: 185–316.

Djakababa, Cornelius Malo
    1988   "The Saga of Yoseph Malo, Raja of Rara and Ede." Typescript.

Doko, I. H.
    1982   *Sejarah Perjuangan Kemerdekaan di Nusa Tenggara Timur*. Kupang: Offset Press.

Downs, R. E.
    1955   "Headhunting in Indonesia." *Bijdragen tot de taal-, land- en volkenkunde* 111: 40–70.

Durkheim, Emile
    [1912] 1965 *The Elementary Forms of the Religious Life*. New York: Free Press.

Eliade, Mircea
    1954   *The Myth of the Eternal Return*. Princeton: Bollingen Foundation, Princeton University Press.

Ellen, Roy
    1986   "Conundrums About Panjandrums: On the Use of Titles in the Relations of Political Subordination in the Moluccas and Along the Papuan Coast." *Indonesia*, no. 41: 46–62.

Errington, Shelley
    1983   "The Place of Regalia in Luwu." In *Centers, Symbols, and Hierarchies: Essays on the Classical States of Southeast Asia*, ed. L. Gesick, Yale Southeast Asian Monographs 26. New Haven: Yale University Press.
    1989   *Meaning and Power in a Southeast Asian Realm*. Princeton: Princeton University Press.

Evans-Pritchard, Edward
    1939   "Nuer Time-Reckoning." *Africa* 12: 189–216.
    1940   *The Nuer*. Oxford: Oxford University Press.
    1961   *Anthropology and History*. Manchester: Manchester University Press.

Fabian, Johannes
    1983   *Time and the Other: How Anthropology Makes Its Object*. New York: Columbia University Press.
    1991   "Of Dogs Alive, Birds Dead, and Time to Tell a Story." In *Chronotypes: The Construction of Time*, ed. J. Bender and D. E. Wellbery. Stanford: Stanford University Press.

Ferguson, James
    1985   "The Bovine Mystique: Power, Property, and Livestock in Rural Lesotho." *Man*, n.s., 20: 647–74.

1988   "Cultural Exchange: New Developments in the Anthropology of Commodities." *Cultural Anthropology* 3: 488–513.

Firth, Raymond
1965   *Primitive Polynesian Economy*. New York: W. W. Norton.

Forth, Christine
1982   "Rindi Oral Narrative: Nine *Ana Lalu* Tales." Ph.D. diss., Oxford University.

Forth, Gregory
1981   *Rindi: An Ethnographic Study of a Traditional Domain in Eastern Sumba*. The Hague: Martinus Nijhoff.
1982   "Time and the Expression of Temporality in Eastern Sumba." *Ethnos* 47: 232–48.
1983   "Time and Temporal Classification in Rindi, Eastern Sumba." *Bijdragen tot de taal-, land- en volkenkunde* 139: 46–80.
1985   "Kambera Temporal Classification: A Note on an Early Reference." *Bijdragen tot de taal-, land- en volkenkunde* 141: 139–42.

Foucault, Michel
1977   *Discipline and Punish: The Birth of the Prison*. Trans. Alan Sheridan. New York: Pantheon Books.
1978   *The History of Sexuality*. Vol. 1: *An Introduction*. New York: Pantheon Books.

Fox, James J.
1971   "A Rotinese Dynastic Genealogy: Structure and Event." In *The Translation of Culture*, ed. T. O. Beidelman. London: Tavistock.
1977   *Harvest of the Palm: Ecological Change in Eastern Indonesia*. Cambridge, Mass.: Harvard University Press.
1979a   "The Ceremonial System of Savu." In *The Imagination of Reality: Essays in Southeast Asian Coherence Systems*, ed. A. L. Becker and A. Yengoyan. Norwood, N.J.: Ablex.
1979b   "'Standing' in Time and Place: The Structure of Rotinese Historical Narratives." In *Perceptions of the Past in Southeast Asia*, ed. A. Reid and D. Marr. Asian Studies Association Publication no. 4. Singapore: Heinemann Educational Books.
1980a   "Introduction." In *The Flow of Life: Essays on Eastern Indonesia*, ed. J. J. Fox. Cambridge, Mass.: Harvard University Press.
1980b   "Models and Metaphors: Comparative Research in Eastern Indonesia." In *The Flow of Life: Essays on Eastern Indonesia*, ed. J. J. Fox. Cambridge, Mass.: Harvard University Press.
1980c   "Obligation and Alliance: State Structure and Moeity Organization in Thie, Roti." In *The Flow of Life: Essays on Eastern Indonesia*, ed. J. J. Fox. Cambridge, Mass.: Harvard University Press.
1980d   *The Flow of Life: Essays on Eastern Indonesia*. Edited by J. J. Fox. Cambridge, Mass.: Harvard University Press.
1987   "Southeast Asia: Insular Traditions." In *The Encyclopedia of Religion*, ed. M. Eliade. New York/London: Macmillan/Collier Macmillan.

Francillon, Gerard
1980   "Incursions upon Wehali: A Modern History of an Ancient Em-

pire." In *The Flow of Life*, ed. James J. Fox. Cambridge, Mass.: Harvard University Press.

Fraser, J. T.
1975   *Of Time, Passion, and Knowledge: Reflections on the Strategy of Existence.* Princeton: Princeton University Press.
1989   *Time and Mind: Interdisciplinary Issues.* Madison, Wis.: International Universities Press.

Geertz, Clifford
1966   *Person, Time, and Conduct in Bali: An Essay in Cultural Analysis.* Yale Southeast Asia Studies Cultural Report 14. New Haven: Yale University Press.
1973   *The Interpretation of Cultures.* New York: Basic Books.
1983   *Local Knowledge.* New York: Basic Books.
1990   "History and Anthropology." *New Literary History* 21 (2): 321–36.

Geirnaert Martin, Danielle
1987   "Hunt Wild Pig and Grow Rice: On Food Exchanges and Values in Laboya, West Sumba (Eastern Indonesia)." In *The Leiden Tradition in Structural Anthropology*, ed. J.P.B. de Josselin de Jong. Leiden: E. J. Brill.
1989   "Textiles of West Sumba: The Lively Renaissance of an Old Tradition." In *To Speak with Cloth*, ed. M. Gittinger. Los Angeles: Fowler Museum of Cultural History.
1992   *The Woven Land of Laboya: Socio-Cosmic Ideas and Values in West Sumba, Eastern Indonesia.* Leiden: Centre of Non-Western Studies.

Gellner, Ernest
1964   *Thought and Change.* London: Weidenfeld & Nicolson.

Gheda Kaka, Gregorius
1979   "Sejarah Wona Kaka." Typescript (used in secondary school instruction at SMA Homba Karpit, Kodi).

Giddens, Anthony
1984   *The Constitution of Society: Outline of the Theory of Structuration.* Berkeley and Los Angeles: University of California Press.

Goody, Jack
1968   "Time: Social Organization." In *The International Encyclopedia of the Social Sciences* 16:30–41. New York: MacMillan/Free Press.

Goris, R.
1960   "Holidays and Holy Days." In *Bali: Life, Thought, and Ritual*, ed. J. L. Swellengrebel. The Hague: Martinus Nijhoff.

Gould, Stephen Jay
1987   *Time's Arrow, Time's Cycle: Myth and Metaphor in the Discovery of Geological Time.* Cambridge, Mass.: Harvard University Press.

Gregory, Christopher A.
1982   *Gifts and Commodities.* New York: Academic Press.

Gronovius, D. J. van den Dungen
1855   "Beschrijving van het eiland Soemba of Sandelhout." *Tijdschrift voor Neerlands Indie* 17 (1): 277–312.

Hadhi, Kartono
1952   Sejarah Pemimpin Indonesia. Jakarta: Balai Pustaka.
Haripranata, H., S.J.
1984   Ceritera Sejarah Gereja Katolik Sumba dan Sumbawa. Ende,
             Flores: Percetakan Offset Arnoldus.
Harris, Marvin
1977   Cows, Pigs, Wars, and Witches. New York: Random House.
Heine-Geldern, Robert
1945   "Prehistoric Research in the Netherlands Indies." In Science and
             Scientists in the Netherlands Indies, ed. P. Honig and F. Verdoorn.
             New York: Foris.
1956   Conceptions of State and Kingship in Southeast Asia. Southeast
             Asia Program Data Paper no. 18. Ithaca: Cornell Southeast Asia
             Program.
Helmi, Rio
1982   "Pulau Sumba antara Mitos dan Realisasi." Mutiara, May 25, 33–
             35.
Hirschman, Albert O.
1977   The Passions and the Interests: The Political Arguments for Cap-
             italism Before Its Triumph. Princeton: Princeton University Press.
Hobsbawm, Eric
1983   "Introduction: Inventing Traditions." In The Invention of Tradi-
             tion, ed. E. Hobsbawm and T. Ranger. Cambridge: Cambridge
             University Press.
Hoekstra, P.
1948   "Paardenteelt op het eiland Soemba." Batavia: John Kappee.
Holquist, Michael
1981   "Introduction." In The Dialogic Imagination: Four Essays by M. M.
             Bakhtin. Austin: University of Texas Press.
1984   "Introduction." In Rabelais and His World, by M. M. Bakhtin.
             Bloomington: Indiana University Press.
Horo, Hermanus Rangga
1952   "Riwayat hidup pahlawan Wona Kaka." Typescript received from
             the author, circulated in West Sumba and sent to Jakarta National
             Archives.
Horton, Robin
1967   "African Traditional Thought and Western Science." Africa 37:
             50–71, 155–87.
Hoskins, Janet
1984   "Spirit Worship and Feasting in Kodi, West Sumba: Paths to Riches
             and Renown." Ph.D. diss., Harvard University.
1985   "A Life History From Both Sides: The Changing Poetics of Per-
             sonal Experience." Journal of Anthropological Research 41 (2):
             147–69.
1986   "So My Name Shall Live: Stone Dragging and Grave-Building in
             Kodi, West Sumba." Bijdragen tot de taal-, land- en volkenkunde
             142: 31–51.
1987a   "The Headhunter as Hero: Local Traditions and Their Reinterpre-
             tation in National History." American Ethnologist 14 (4): 605–22.

1987b   "Complementarity in This World and the Next: Gender and Agency in Kodi Mortuary Ceremonies." In *Dealing With Inequality: Analysing Gender Relations in Melanesia and Beyond*, ed. M. Strathern. Cambridge: Cambridge University Press.

1987c   "Entering the Bitter House: Spirit Worship and Conversion in West Sumba." In *Indonesian Religions in Transition*, ed. S. Rogers and R. Kipp. Tucson: University of Arizona Press.

1988a   "The Drum Is the Shaman, the Spear Guides His Voice." *Social Science and Medicine* (special issue entitled "Healing in Southeast Asia," ed. P. van Esterik and C. Laderman) 27 (2): 819–29.

1988b   "Etiquette in Kodi Spirit Communication: The Lips Told to Speak, the Mouth Told to Pronounce." In *To Speak in Pairs: Essays on the Ritual Languages of Eastern Indonesia*, ed. J. J. Fox. Cambridge: Cambridge University Press.

1988c   "Matriarchy and Diarchy: Indonesian Variations on the Domestication of the Savage Woman." In *Myths of Matriarchy Reconsidered*, ed. D. Gewertz. Sydney: University of Sydney Press.

1988d   "Arts and Cultures of Sumba." In *Islands and Ancestors: Indigenous Styles of Southeast Asia* (catalogue for the Metropolitan Museum of New York), ed. D. Newton and J.-P. Barbier. Munich: Prestel Publications.

1989a   "On Losing and Getting a Head: Warfare, Exchange, and Alliance in a Changing Sumba, 1888–1988." *American Ethnologist* 16 (3): 419–40.

1989b   "Burned Paddy and Lost Souls." *Bijdragen tot de taal-, land- en volkenkunde* (Anthropologica, special issue on eastern Indonesia, ed. C. Barraud and J.D.M. Platenkamp) 145 (4): 430–44.

1989c   "Why Do Ladies Sing the Blues? Indigo, Cloth Production, and Gender Symbolism in Kodi." In *Cloth and Human Experience*, ed. A. Weiner and J. Schneider. Washington, D.C.: Smithsonian Institution Press.

1990a   "Equal and Unequal Contests: Men, Horses, and Gods in Sumba's Pasola." *Cosmos: Journal of the Traditional Cosmology Society* (special issue on contests, ed. A. Duff-Cooper) 4 (1): 29–60.

1990b   "Doubling Descent, Deities, and Personhood: An Exploration of Kodi Gender Categories." In *Power and Difference: Gender in Island Southeast Asia*, ed. J. M. Atkinson and S. Errington. Stanford: Stanford University Press.

1993   "Violence, Sacrifice, and Divination: Giving and Taking Life in Eastern Indonesia." *American Ethnologist* 20 (1): 159–78.

In press   "Gold Given for the Bride: Body Imagery in an Indonesian Exchange System." In *Images of Women in Religious Art*, ed. T. M. Luhrman. Cambridge, Mass.: Harvard University Press.

Forthcoming (1) "The Heritage of Headhunting: Ritual, Ideology, and History on Sumba, 1890–1990." In *Headhunting and the Social Imagination: Ritual Warfare in Southeast Asia*, ed. J. Hoskins.

Forthcoming (2) "Introduction: Headhunting as Practice and as Trope." In *Headhunting and the Social Imagination: Ritual Warfare in Southeast Asia*, ed. J. Hoskins.

In prep. "From Diagnosis to Performance: Ritual Frames and Medical Practice in Kodi, West Sumba." In prep. for *The Performance of Healing*, ed. C. Laderman and M. Roseman.

Howe, Leopold E. A.
1981 "The Social Determination of Knowledge: Maurice Bloch and Balinese Time." *Man*, n.s., 16: 220–34.

Howell, Signe
1989 "Of Persons and Things: Exchange and Valuables Among the Lio of Eastern Indonesia." *Man*, n.s., 24: 419–38.
1991 "Access to the Ancestors: Reconstructions of the Past in Non-Literate Society." In *The Ecology of Choice and Symbol: Essays in Honour of Fredrik Barth*, ed. R. Gronhaug, G. Haaland, and G. Henriksen. Bergen: Alma Mater Förlag.

Hubert, Henri
1909 "Etude sommaire de la représentation du temps dans la religion et la magie." In *Mélanges d'histoire des religions*, ed. H. Hubert and M. Mauss. Paris: Félix Alcan.

Jensen, Adolf E., and Herman Niggemeyer
1939 *Hainuwele: Volkserzahlungen von Molukkeninseln Ceram.* Frankfurt am Main: Vittorio Klostermann.

Jolly, Margaret
1984 "The Anatomy of Pig Love." *Canberra Anthropology* 4 (2): 81–92.

Kapita, Oembu Hina
1976a *Masyarakat Sumba dan Adat-Istiadatnya.* Waingapu: Gereja Kristen Sumba.
1976b *Sumba dalam jangkauan Jaman.* Waingapu: Gereja Kristen Sumba.
1977 *Ludu Humba Pakangutuna (Sajak Nyanyian dari Mangili dan Umalulu).* Waingapu: Gereja Kristen Sumba.
1979 *Lii Ndai: Rukuda da Kabihu dangu la Pahunga Lodu (Sejarah Suku-Suku di Sumba Timur).* Waingapu: Gereja Kristen Sumba.
1982 *Kamus Sumba/Kambera-Indonesia.* Waingapu: Gereja Kristen Sumba.
1983 *Tata Bahasa Sumba Timur dalam Dialek Kambera.* Ende, Flores: Percetakan Offset Arnoldus.
1986 *Pamangu Ndewa/Perjamuan Dewa.* Ende, Flores: Percetakan Offset Arnoldus.
1987 *Lawiti Luluku Humba/Pola Peribahasa Sumba.* Waingapu: Gereja Kristen Sumba.
n.d. "Memboro." Typescript of field notes.

Kartodirjo, Sartoro
1972 "Agrarian Radicalism in Java." In *Culture and Politics in Indonesia*, ed. C. Holt, B. Andseron, and J. Seigel. Ithaca: Cornell University Press.

Keane, Edward Webb
1990 "The Social Life of Representations: Ritual Speech and Exchange in Anakalang (Sumba, Eastern Indonesia)." Ph.D. diss., University of Chicago.

Keeler, Ward
1987   *Javanese Shadow Plays, Javanese Selves*. Princeton: Princeton University Press.

Keller, Edgar
1988   "Fashioned Words of Despair: The Ritual Speech of a Dispossessed in Laboya, West Sumba." Paper prepared for the 7th European Colloquium on Indonesian and Malay Studies, Bern, Switzerland.

Kipp, Rita
1990   *The Early Years of a Dutch Colonial Mission*. Ann Arbor: University of Michigan Press.

Knaap, G. J., ed.
1987   *Memories van overgave van gouverneurs van Ambon in de zeventiende en achttiende eeuw*. The Hague: Martinus Nijhoff.

Koloniale Verslagen
1852–1930   Government documents published by the Netherlands Indies. The Hague.

Kopytoff, Igor
1986   "The Cultural Biography of Things: Commoditization as Process." In *The Social Life of Things: Commodities in Cultural Perspective*. Cambridge: Cambridge University Press.

Koselleck, Reinhart
1985   *Futures Past: On the Semantics of Historical Time*. Trans. Keith Tribe. Cambridge, Mass.: MIT Press.

Kruseman, J. D.
1836   "Beschrijvning van het Sandelhout Eiland" (after the testimony of J. Batiest in 1832). *De Oosterling* 2: 63–86.

Kruyt, Albert C.
1921   "Verslag van eene reis over het eiland Soemba." *Tijdschrift van het Koninklijk Nederlandsch Aardrijkskundig Genootschap* 38: 513–53.

1922   "De Soembaneezen." *Bijdragen tot de taal-, land- en volkenkunde* 78: 466–608.

Kuipers, Joel
1990   *Power in Performance: The Creation of Textual Authority in Weyewa Ritual Speech*. Philadelphia: University of Pennsylvania Press.

Lambooy, P.
1937   "Het begrip 'Marapoe' in den godsdienst van Oost Soemba." *Bijdragen tot de taal-, land- en Volkenkunde* 95: 425–39.

Landes, David S.
1983   *Revolutions in Time: Clocks and the Making of the Modern World*. Cambridge, Mass.: Harvard University Press.

1990   "The Time of Our Lives." *Social Science Information* 29 (4): 693–724.

Lansing, J. Stephen
1991   *Priests and Programmers: Technologies of Power in the Engineered Landscape of Bali*. Princeton: Princeton University Press.

Leach, Edmund R.
    1950   "Primitive Calendars." *Oceania* 20 (4): 245–66.
    1954a   "Primitive Time Reckoning." In *History of Technology*, ed. C. Singer, E. Holmyard, and A. Hall. Oxford: Clarendon Press.
    1954b   *Political Systems of Highland Burma*. Boston: Beacon Press.
    1961   "Two Essays Concerning the Symbolic Representation of Time." In *Rethinking Anthropology*. London: Athlone Press.
Lévi-Strauss, Claude
    1966   *The Savage Mind*. Chicago: Chicago University Press.
    1969a   *The Elementary Structures of Kinship*. Boston: Beacon Press.
    1969b   *The Raw and the Cooked: Introduction to a Science of Mythology*. New York: Harper & Row.
Lewis, E. Douglas
    1988   *People of the Source: The Social and Ceremonial Order of Tana Wai Brama on Flores*. Dordecht and Providence: Foris Publications.
Locher, G. W.
    1978   "Myth in a Changing World." In *Transformation and Tradition*. The Hague: Martinus Nijhoff.
Lowenthal, David
    1985   *The Past is a Foreign Country*. Cambridge: Cambridge University Press.
Luckas, Y.
    n.d.   "Sejarah Gereja Katolik di Sumba dan Sumbawa." Waitabula: Gereja Katolik Sumba. Mimeo.
McKinley, Robert
    1979   "Zaman dan Masa, Eras and Periods: Religious Evolution and the Permanence of Epistemological Ages in Malay Culture." In *The Imagination of Reality: Essays in Southeast Asian Coherence Systems*, ed. A. Becker and A. Yengoyan. Norwood, N.J.: Ablex.
McKinnon, Susan
    1991   *From a Shattered Sun: Hierarchy, Gender, and Alliance in the Tanimbar Islands*. Madison: University of Wisconsin Press.
Malinowski, Bronislaw
    1922   *Argonauts of the Western Pacific*. London: Routledge & Kegan Paul.
    1927   "Lunar and Seasonal Calendars in the Trobriand Islands." *Journal of the Royal Anthropological Institute* 157: 203–15.
    1935   *Coral Gardens and Their Magic*. Bloomington: Indiana University Press.
    1954   *Magic, Science, and Religion*. New York: Doubleday.
Maltz, Daniel
    1968   "Primitive Time Reckoning as a Symbolic System." *Cornell Journal of Social Relations* 3 (1): 85–112.
Marcus, George, and Michael J. Fischer.
    1986   *Anthropology as Cultural Critique*. Chicago: University of Chicago Press.
Mauss, Marcel
    [1925] 1967 *The Gift*. New York: W. W. Norton.

[1920] 1969 *La nation.* In *Oeuvres*, vol. 3. Paris: Editions de Minuit.

May, Hermann-Josef, Felicitas Mispagel, and Franz Pfister
  1982   *Marapu und Karitu: Mission und junge Kirche auf der insel Sumba.* Bonn: Hofbauer Verlag.

Maybury-Lewis, David
  1989   "The Quest for Harmony." In *The Attraction of Opposites: Thought and Society in the Dualistic Mode*, ed. D. Maybury-Lewis and U. Almagor. Ann Arbor: University of Michigan Press.

Mitchell, David
  1982a   "Endemic Gonorrhoea in Sumba." Paper presented to the 4th conference of the Asian Studies Association of Australia, Melbourne.
  1982b   "Folk Medicine in Sumba: A Critical Evaluation." Paper presented at the Annual Indonesian Lecture Series, Monash University, Melbourne.
  1984   "The Wanokakà Calendar: Fieldnotes and Reflections." Paper presented at the Workshop on East Indonesian Ethnography, Australian National University, Canberra.

Mitchell, I. G.
  1981.   "Hierarchy and Balance: A Study of Wanokaka Social Organization." Ph.D. Diss., Monash University, Melbourne.

Munn, Nancy D.
  1992   "The Cultural Anthropology of Time: A Critical Essay." *Annual Review of Anthropology* 21: 93–123.

Nawawi, Mohammed A.
  1971   "Punitive Colonialism: The Dutch and the Indonesian National Integration." *Journal of Southeast Asian Studies* 2 (2): 159–68.

Needham, Rodney
  1957a   "Circulating Connubium in Eastern Sumba." *Bijdragen tot de taal-, land- en volkenkunde* 113: 168–78.
  1957b   "Kodi Fables." *Bijdragen tot de taal-, land- en volkenkunde* 113: 361–79.
  1960   "Jataka, Pancatantra, and Kodi Fables." *Bijdragen tot de taal-, land- en volkenkunde* 116: 232–62.
  1968   "Endeh: Terminology, Alliance, and Analysis." *Bijdragen tot de taal-, land- en volkenkunde* 124: 305–35.
  1970   "Endeh II: Test and Confirmation." *Bijdragen tot de taal-, land- en volkenkunde* 126: 246–58.
  1980   "Principles and Variations in the Structure of Sumbanese Society." In *The Flow of Life: Essays on Eastern Indonesia*, ed. J. J. Fox. Cambridge: Harvard University Press.
  1983   *Sumba and the Slave Trade.* Centre of Southeast Asian Studies, Monash University, Working Paper 31. Melbourne: Monash University.
  1987   *Mamboro: History and Structure in a Domain of Northwestern Sumba.* Oxford: Clarendon Press.

Nichterlein, Sue
  1974   "Historicism and Historiography in Indonesia." *History and Theory* 8 (3): 253–72.

Nilsson, Martin P.
1920   *Primitive Time-Reckoning: A Study in the Origins and First De-*
            velopment of the Art of Counting Time Among the Primitive and
            Early Culture Peoples. Skrifter utgivna av Humanistiska Veten-
            skapsfundet. Lund: Gleerup.
Nock, A. D.
1933   *Conversion: The Old and the New in Religion, from Alexander*
            the Great to Augustine of Hippo. Oxford: Oxford University
            Press.
Nooteboom, C.
1940   *Oost Soemba: een volkenkundige studie.* Verhandelingen van het
            Koninklijk Instituut voor de Taal-, Land- en Volkenkunde van
            Nederlandsch Indie, vol. 3. The Hague: Martinus Nijhoff.
Notosusanto, Nugroho, et al.
1976   *Sejarah Nasional Indonesia untuk SMA.* Jakarta: Balai Pustaka.
O'Connor, Stanley J.
1983   "Art Critics, Connoisseurs, and Collectors in the Southeast Asian
            Rain Forest: A Study in Cross-Cultural Art Theory." *Journal of*
            Southeast Asian Studies 14: 400–408.
Ohnuki-Tierney, Emiko, ed.
1990   *Culture Through Time: Anthropological Approaches.* Stanford:
            Stanford University Press.
Onvlee, Louis
1929   "Palatalisatie in eenige Soembaneesche dialecten." In *Bataviasch*
            Genootschap van Kunsten en Wetenschappen. Weltvreden: Kolff
            & Co.
1938   "Over de weergave van 'heilig' in het Soembaasch." *Tijdschrift*
            voor indische taal-, land- en volkenkunde 78: 124–36.
1973   *Cultuur als antwoord.* Verhandelingen ven het Koninklijk Insti-
            tuut voor Taal-, Land- en Volkenkunde, no. 66. The Hague: Mar-
            tinus Nijhoff.
1977   "The Construction of the Mangili Dam: Notes on the Social Or-
            ganization of Eastern Sumba." In *Structural Anthropology in the*
            Netherlands, ed. P. E. de Josselin de Jong. The Hague: Martinus
            Nijhoff.
1980   "The Significance of Livestock on Sumba." In *The Flow of Life:*
            Essays on Eastern Indonesia, ed. J. J. Fox. Cambridge: Cambridge
            University Press.
Onvlee, L., and Oembu H. Kapita
1932   "Kodi." Transcripts of field notes made on a visit to Kodi, compiled
            by Onvlee and typed by Kapita in 1979; typescript obtained from
            Oembu Hina Kapita.
Ortner, Sherry
1984   "Theory in Anthropology Since the Sixties." *Comparative Studies*
            in Society and History 26: 126–66.
1989   *High Religion: A Cultural and Political History of Sherpa Bud-*
            dhism. Princeton: Princeton University Press.

Parmentier, Richard J.
1985   "Times of the Signs: Modalities of History and Levels of Social
        Structure in Belau." In *Semiotic Mediation*, ed. E. Mertz and R.
        Parmentier. Orlando: Academic Press.
1987   *The Sacred Remains: Myth, History, and Polity in Belau*. Chi-
        cago: University of Chicago Press.
Parry, Jonathan, and Maurice Bloch, eds.
1989   *Money and the Morality of Exchange*. Cambridge: Cambridge
        University Press.
Peel, J.D.Y.
1984   "Making History: The Past in the Ijesha Present." *Man*, n.s., 19:
        111–32.
Pietz, William
1985   "The Problem of the Fetish I." *Res* 1985, no. 9: 5–17.
1987   "The Problem of the Fetish II: The Origin of the Fetish." *Res* 1987,
        no. 3: 23–46.
Plumb, J. H.
1969   *The Death of the Past*. London: Macmillan.
Pluvier, J. M.
1968   "Recent Dutch Contributions to Modern Indonesian History."
        Journal of Southeast Asian History 18: 201–25.
Rappaport, Roy
1968   *Pigs for the Ancestors*. New Haven: Yale University Press.
Reid, Anthony
1979   "The Nationalist Quest for an Indonesian Past." In *Perceptions of
        the Past in Southeast Asia*, ed. A. Reid and D. Marr. Asian Studies
        Association Publication no. 4. Singapore: Heineman Educational
        Books.
1983   *Slavery, Bondage, and Dependency in Southeast Asia*. St. Lucia,
        Australia: Queensland University Press.
1988   *Southeast Asia in the Age of Commerce, 1450–1680*. Vol. 1: *The
        Lands Below the Winds*. New Haven: Yale University Press.
Renard-Clamagirand, Brigitte
1988   "Li'i Marapu: Speech and Ritual Among the Wewewa of West
        Sumba." In *To Speak in Pairs: Essays on the Ritual Languages of
        Eastern Indonesian*, ed. J. J. Fox. Cambridge: Cambridge Univer-
        sity Press.
1989   "Uppu Li'i, Fulfill the Promise: Analysis of a Wewewa Ritual."
        Bijdragen tot de taal-, land- en volkenkunde (Anthropologica,
        special issue on Eastern Indonesia, ed. C. Barraud and J.D.M.
        Platenkamp) 145 (4): 464–77.
Resink, G. I.
1986   *Indonesia's History Between the Myths*. The Hague: Martinus
        Nijhoff.
Ricklefs, M. C.
1981   *A History of Modern Indonesia*. Bloomington: Indiana University
        Press.

Ricoeur, Paul
1988   *Time and Narrative*. Vol. 3. Chicago: University of Chicago Press.
Rodgers, Susan
1981   *Adat, Islam, and Christianity in a Batak Homeland*. Southeast
            Asia Series no. 62. Athens: Ohio University Center for Interna-
            tional Studies.
Roos, Samuel
1872   *Bijdrage tot de kennis vaan taal-, land-, en volk op het eiland
            Soemba*. Verhandelingen van het Bataviasch Genootschap van
            Kunsten en Wetenschappen 36. Batavia.
Rosaldo, Renato
1980   *Ilongot Headhunting*. Stanford: Stanford University Press.
Sahlins, Marshall
1972   *Stone Age Economics*. Chicago: Aldine-Atherton.
1981   *Historical Metaphors and Mythical Realities: Structure in the
            Early History of the Sandwich Islands Kingdom*. Ann Arbor:
            University of Michigan Press.
1985   *Islands of History*. Chicago: University of Chicago Press.
Sanjek, Roger
1991   "The Ethnographic Present." *Man*, n.s., 26: 609–28.
Saunders, D.
1977   *An Introduction to Biological Rhythms*. New York: John Wiley.
Schulte Nordholt, H. G.
1971   *The Political System of the Atoni of Timor*. The Hague: Martinus
            Nijhoff.
Scott, James
1976   *The Moral Economy of the Peasant*. New Haven: Yale University
            Press.
Sherman, D. George
1990   *Rice, Rupees, and Ritual: Economy and Society among the Sa-
            mosir Batak of Sumatra*. Stanford: Stanford University Press.
Siegel, James
1979   *Shadow and Sound: The Historical Thought of a Sumatran Peo-
            ple*. Chicago: University of Chicago Press.
1985   "Images and Odors in Javanese Practices Surrounding Death."
            Indonesia 36: 1–14.
Singarimbun, Masri
1975   *Kinship, Descent, and Alliance Among the Karo Batak*. Berkeley
            and Los Angeles: University of California Press.
Sitorus, L. M.
1951   *Sejarah Pergerakan Kebangsaan Indonesia*. Jakarta: Balai Pustaka.
Soedjatmoko
1965   "The Indonesian Historian and His Time." In *An Introduction to
            Indonesian Historiography*, ed. Soedjatmoko, M. Ali, G. J. Re-
            sink, and G. M. Mahur. Ithaca: Cornell University Press.
Sperber, Dan
1975   *Rethinking Symbolism*. Trans. Alice Morton. Cambridge: Cam-
            bridge University Press.

Steedly, Mary
1989 "Innocence as Authority: Shifting Gender Roles in Karoese Curing Ritual." In *Changing Rites, Changing Lives*, ed. S. Russell and C. Cunningham. De Kalb: Northern Illinois University Press.

Strathern, Andrew
1972 "African Cattle Complexes and Melanesian Pig Complexes." *Oceania* 42: 127–39.

Strathern, Marilyn
1988 *The Gender of the Gift*. Berkeley and Los Angeles: University of California Press.

Tambiah, Stanley J.
1979 *A Performative Approach to Ritual*. London: Proceedings of the Royal British Academy.
1985 *Culture, Thought, and Social Action*. Cambridge, Mass.: Harvard University Press.

Tedlock, Barbara
1982 *Time and the Highland Maya*. Albuquerque: University of New Mexico Press.

Thomas, Nicholas
1989 *Out of Time*. Cambridge: Cambridge University Press.
1991 *Entangled Objects: Material Culture and Colonialism in the Pacific*. Cambridge, Mass.: Harvard University Press.

Thompson, E. P.
1967 "Time, Work-Discipline, and Industrial Capitalism." *Past and Present* 38: 56–97.

Thornton, Robert
1989 "Time Scales and Social Thought." In *Time and Mind: Interdisciplinary Issues*, ed. J. T. Fraser. Madison, Wis.: International Universities Press.

Tirtoprodjo, Susanto
1961 *Sejarah Pergerakan Nasional Indonesia*. Jakarta: Balai Pustaka.

Traube, Elizabeth
1981 "Affines and the Dead." *Bijdragen tot de taal-, land- en volkenkunde* 136: 90–115.
1986 *Cosmology and Social Life: Ritual Exchange Among the Mambai of East Timor*. Chicago: University of Chicago Press.
1989 "Obligations to the Source: Complementarity and Hierarchy in an Eastern Indonesian Society." In *The Attraction of Opposites: Thought and Society in the Dualistic Mode*, ed. D. Maybury-Lewis and U. Almagor. Ann Arbor: University of Michigan Press.

Turner, Terence
1985 "Animal Symbolism, Totemism, and the Structure of Myth." In *Animal Myths and Metaphors in South America*, ed. G. Urton. Salt Lake City: University of Utah Press.

Turner, Victor
1969 *The Ritual Process: Structure and Anti-Structure*. Chicago: Aldine.
1987 *The Anthropology of Performance*. New York: Performing Arts Journal Publications.

Turton, David, and Clive Ruggles
1978   "Agreeing to Disagree: The Measurement of Duration in a South-
            western Ethiopian Community." *Current Anthropology* 19 (3):
            585–600.

Valeri, Valerio
1980   "Notes on the Meaning of Marriage Prestations Among the Huaulu
            of Seram." In *The Flow of Life: Essays on Eastern Indonesia*, ed.
            J. J. Fox. Cambridge, Mass.: Harvard University Press.
1989   "Reciprocal Centers: The Siwa-Lima System in the Central Mo-
            luccas." In *The Attraction of Opposites: Thought and Society in
            the Dualistic Mode*, ed. D. Maybury-Lewis and U. Almagor. Ann
            Arbor: University of Michigan Press.
1990   "Constitutive History: Genealogy and Narrative in the Legiti-
            mation of Hawaiian Kingship." In *Culture Through Time: An-
            thropological Approaches*, ed. E. Ohnuki-Tierney. Stanford:
            Stanford University Press.
1991a   "The Transformation of a Transformation: A Structural Essay on
            an Aspect of Hawaiian History (1809 to 1819)." In *Clio in Oceania:
            Toward an Historical Anthropology*, ed. A. Biersack. Washington,
            D.C.: Smithsonian Institution Press.
1991b   "Afterword." In J. Stephen Lansing, *Priests and Programmers:
            Technologies of Power in the Engineered Landscape of Bali*. Prince-
            ton: Princeton University Press.

Van den End, T.
1987   *Gereformeerde Zending op Sumba, 1859–1972. Een bronnen pub-
            licatie uitage van de Raad voor de Zending der Ned. Herv. Kerk.*
            Alphen aan den Rijn: Aska.

Van Gennep
1960   *The Rites of Passage.* London: Routledge and Kegan Paul.

Van Heekeren, H. R.
1956   *The Urn Cemetery at Melolo, East Sumba (Indonesia).* Jakarta:
            Berita Dinas Purbakala.
1972   *The Stone Age of Indonesia.* 2d ed. The Hague: Martinus Nijhoff.

Van Wouden, F.A.E.
[1935] 1968 *Types of Social Structure in Eastern Indonesia.* The Hague: Mar-
            tinus Nijhoff.
[1956] 1977 "Local Groups and Double Descent in Kodi, West Sumba." In
            Structural Anthropology in the Netherlands, ed. P. E. de Josselin
            de Jong. The Hague: Martinus Nijhoff.

Veeser, H. Aram
1989   *The New Historicism.* New York: Routledge.

Versluys, J.I.N.
1941   "Aanteekeningen omtrent geld en goederenverkeer in West Sumba."
            Koloniale Studien, 433–82.

Vickers, Adrian
1990   "Balinese Texts and Historiography." *History and Theory*, 158–
            78.

Vlekke, B. H.
1959   *Nusantara: A History of Indonesia.* Bandung: Van Hoeve.
Volkman, Toby Alice
1985   *Feasts of Honor: Ritual and Change in the Toraja Highlands.* Urbana: University of Illinois Press.
Webb, R.A.F.
1986   *Palms and the Cross: Socio-economic Development in Nusatenggara.* Townsville, Australia: Centre for Southeast Asian Studies, James Cook University of North Queensland.
Weiner, Annette
1985   "Inalienable Wealth." *American Ethnologist* 12 (2): 210–27.
Whorf, Benjamin L.
1964   "An American Indian Model of the Universe." In *Language, Thought, and Reality,* ed. J. B. Carroll. Cambridge, Mass.: MIT Press.
Wielenga, D. K.
1911–12   "Soemba: reizen op Soemba." *De Macedonier* 15: 303–8, 328–34; 16: 144–50.
1916–18   "De Zending van de Gereformeerde Kerken. Voor zendingstudiekringen. Soemba 1: Historie." *De Macedonier* 20: 137–46, 161–69, 201–14, 225–37, 299–309, 332–39, 353–59; 21: 3–11, 33–43, 77–83, 107–12, 129–36, 170–77, 204–10, 239–46, 269–72, 299–309, 359–67; 22: 16–22, 33–40, 76–80, 110–17, 145–51, 172–78, 235–39, 270–75, 298–305.
Wijngaarden, J. K
1893   "Naar Soemba." *Mededeelingen van wege het Nederlandsch Zendelinggenootschap* 37: 352–76.
Wikan, Unni
1989   "Managing the Heart to Brighten Face and Soul: Emotions in Balinese Morality and Health Care." *American Ethnologist* 16: 294–312.
1990   *Managing Turbulent Hearts: A Balinese Formula for Living.* Chicago: University of Chicago Press.
Wilcox, Donald J.
1987   *The Measure of Times Past: Pre-Newtonian Chronologies and the Rhetoric of Relative Time.* Chicago: University of Chicago Press.
Witkamp, H.
1912   "Een verkenningstocht over het eiland Soemba." *Tijdschrift van het Koninklijk Nederlandsch Aardrijkskundig Genootschap* 29: 744–75; 30: 8–27, 484–505, 619–37.
Zerubavel, Eviatar
1981   *Hidden Rhythms: Schedules and Calendars in Social Life.* Chicago: University of Chicago Press.
1985   *The Seven Day Circle: The History and Meaning of the Week.* New York: Free Press.

Index

Compositor:	Terry Robinson & Co.
Text:	10/13 Aldus
Display:	Aldus
Printer:	Malloy Lithographing, Inc.
Binder:	Malloy Lithographing, Inc.